# The Irish in Manchester c. 1750–1921

Manchester University Press

# The Irish in Manchester
## c. 1750–1921
### Resistance, adaptation and identity

MERVYN BUSTEED

Manchester University Press

Copyright © Mervyn Busteed 2016

The right of Mervyn Busteed to be identified as the author of this work has been asserted by him in accordance with the Copyright, Designs and Patents Act 1988.

Published by Manchester University Press
Altrincham Street, Manchester M1 7JA, UK
www.manchesteruniversitypress.co.uk

*British Library Cataloguing-in-Publication Data is available*

ISBN 978 0 7190 8719 6 *hardback*
ISBN 978 1 5261 3435 6 *paperback*

First published by Manchester University Press in hardback 2016

The publisher has no responsibility for the persistence or accuracy of URLs for any external or third-party internet websites referred to in this book, and does not guarantee that any content on such websites is, or will remain, accurate or appropriate.

Typeset by Koinonia, Manchester

# Contents

| | | *page* |
|---|---|---|
| | List of figures | vi |
| | Acknowledgements | viii |
| | Introduction | 1 |
| 1 | Early connections, 'Little Ireland' and stereotypes | 7 |
| 2 | Famine influx and residential clustering: Angel Meadow | 41 |
| 3 | The Catholic Church | 75 |
| 4 | St Patrick's Day: evolution of a celebration | 118 |
| 5 | Revolution and reform: 1790s to 1850s | 145 |
| 6 | Elections and meetings: 1870–1921 | 172 |
| 7 | Fenians, martyrs and memories | 206 |
| 8 | Decline, revival and rising | 248 |
| | Conclusion | 268 |
| | Index | 274 |

# Figures

Unless otherwise stated illustrations are from the author's private collection.

1. Angel Meadow study area: Irish districts and Catholic places of worship in mid-nineteenth-century Manchester — page 13
2. Little Ireland: land use, early 1840s — 19
3. Dr James Phillips Kay (Kay-Shuttleworth) — 24
4. Angel Meadow: land use, late 1840s — 47
5. Child street hawker (Salford Diocese Archives) — 55
6. Percentage of Irish in Angel Meadow, 1851 — 57
7. Irish presence in Dyche and Simpson streets, Angel Meadow, 1851 — 58
8. Baptisms in Manchester Catholic churches, 1775–1834 (based on Irish Poor Report) — 78
9. St Patrick's church, cemetery, orphanage and school, 1849 (Ordnance Survey Five-Foot Plan, 1850) — 81
10. Perceived dangers to young Catholic people in lodging houses (Salford Diocese Archives) — 101
11. Perceived dangers to young Catholics: innocent Joe and Joe's dubious pal (Salford Diocese Archives) — 102
12. Alderman Daniel McCabe on his election as Manchester's first Catholic Lord Mayor (Salford Diocese Archives) — 181
13. Daniel Boyle, Manchester alderman, Nationalist MP for North Mayo and notable organiser of the Irish vote (Salford Diocese Archives) — 182
14. Rallying the faithful for the 1894 School Board election (Salford Diocese Archives) — 188

15 'Colonel' Thomas J. Kelly, 'Head Centre' of the IRB, rescued from the police van with Timothy Deasy; photograph possibly from the late 1860s (Greater Manchester Police Museum and Archives) 210
16 Details of the 1913 Manchester Martyrs commemoration (Greater Manchester Police Museum and Archives) 227
17 The martyrs respectably and safely groomed and repackaged in 1888 (*Weekly* [later *Catholic*] *Herald*, 23 November 1888) 229
18 The Irish National Foresters organise a procession in 1902 (Greater Manchester Police Museum and Archives) 254
19 Conradh na Gaeilge (Gaelic League) organises a language collection in 1908 (Greater Manchester Police Museum and Archives) 256

# Acknowledgements

Some of the material in Chapter 1 appeared as '"The most horrible spot?": the legend of Manchester's Little Ireland', *Irish Studies Review*, 13 (winter 1995-96), pp.12-20 (www.tandfonline.com); parts of Chapter 2 as 'Irish migrant responses to urban life in early nineteenth century Manchester', *Geographical Journal*, 162:2 (1996), pp. 139-53; parts of Chapter 4 in '"Plentiful libations of whisky, perfervid Irish oratory and some religious sentiment": celebrating St. Patrick's Day in Manchester, 1825-1922', in J. Strachan and A. O'Malley-Younger (eds), *Ireland: revolution and evolution* (Oxford: Peter Lang, 2010), pp.81-99; and parts of Chapter 7 as 'Parading the green: procession as subaltern resistance in Manchester in 1867', *Political Geography*, 24:8 (2005), pp. 903-33; '"Fostered to trouble the next generation": contesting the ownership of the martyrs' commemoration ritual in Manchester 1888-1921', in N. Moore and Y. Whelan (eds), *Heritage, memory and the politics of identity: new perspectives on the cultural landscape* (Aldershot: Ashgate, 2007), pp. 69-82; and 'The Manchester Martyrs: a Victorian melodrama', *History Ireland*, 16:6 (2008), pp. 35-7.

My accumulated debts to people and institutions over the years are so great that I hesitate before trying to pay tribute out of fear that I will omit some of the truly deserving, but I will try to be comprehensive and can only apologise in advance for any omissions.

Three institutions provided financial support. Manchester Geographical Society awarded a number of grants which were used to employ recent Manchester University geography graduates to extract data from census reports and newspapers. A grant was also awarded from the Research Fund of the School of Geography, and Manchester Statistical Society awarded £1,000.

# ACKNOWLEDGEMENTS

Staff in several institutions were most helpful in making their collections available for study. In particular I must thank my fellow members of the Manchester and Lancashire Family History Society. They gave me access to all the material from the 1851 census for Manchester which their members had laboriously extracted from the enumerators' books in the days before such data were available online, and they also provided opportunities to share my findings in a series of talks to the society. I would particularly like to thank Marnie Mason, Margaret Thornton and the late Terry Broadhurst and Peter Dolan. I would also like to thank the staff of the John Rylands Library on Deansgate and on the Manchester University campus, Dr Michael Powell and the staff at Chetham's Library, Manchester, the staff of the Greater Manchester Archives Centre on Marshall Street, Dr Duncan Brody of the Greater Manchester Police Museum, the National Library, Kildare Street, Dublin, the Sidney Jones Library of the University of Liverpool and the Local Studies Department of Liverpool Central Library. I owe two special debts. The first is to the staff of the Local Studies and Archive Departments of Manchester Central Library for their great patience and cheerful helpfulness down the years. The second is to Father David Lannon of St Augustine's Catholic church, All Saints, Manchester, the archivist for Salford diocese, who presides over a priceless resource with great care, patience and cheerfulness.

Certain individuals played a key role in encouraging me to embark on and persist in the study of the Irish in nineteenth-century Manchester. The late Professor Brian Rodgers of Manchester University School of Geography provided early encouragement, as did Emeritus Professor Brian Robson, who first suggested I write a book. Professor Mike Rose pointed me in the direction of the Family History Society. Terry Wyke of Manchester Metropolitan University History Department also prompted me to think of a book-length study. Early research efforts were undertaken with my colleague Dr Rob Hodgson, and we published some of the first results together with Tom Kennedy. Dr Paul Laxton of the Geography Department of Liverpool University provided sage advice in those early stages. Joe Flynn and his comrades in the Manchester Irish Education Group have given me frequent opportunity to share findings and ideas at their fine series of public lectures and conferences through the years, and Michael Forde of the Manchester Irish World Heritage Centre has always been a source of encouragement. I am also indebted to successive generations of geography undergraduates at Manchester University who submitted quite cheerfully to my research findings in lectures and seminars.

Amongst other individuals whom I must thank for their assistance and encouragement are Graham Bowden and Nick Scarle of the Drawing

Office of the School of Geography at Manchester University, who drew the maps and diagrams, Professor John Belchem, Wyn Bromley, Professor Patrick Buckland, Sister Elizabeth Cahill, Gill Callander, Anna Challans, Isobel Chaplin, Danny Claffey, Jo Cooksley, Professor Graham Davis, Eileen Derbyshire, Professor Marianne Elliott, Emeritus Professor Emrys Evans, Ian Gavin, Brian Griffin, Ed Hall, Sean Hutton and my fellow members of the British Association for Irish Studies, Alistair Leithead, Tom Mills, Dr Nicola Morris of Chester University, Maureen Mulholland, Fergus O'Connor, Patrick O'Sullivan, Margot Power, Kate Richardson, Helen Steele, Diane Urquhart, Janet Wallwork and Rev. Dr Nigel Wright. Sadly, Walter Cassin, Roland Griffin, Seamus Morgan, Liam McLaughlin and Professor Frank Neal died before this book was published – in their time all were great sources of encouragement. The anonymous reader made suggestions which have greatly enhanced the final product. I have tried as far as possible to acknowledge all sources and apologise for any omissions. Errors of fact or interpretation are entirely my own. Finally, thanks are due to Fiona Little for copy-editing, Hilary Faulkner for the index and to Emma Brennan, Paul Clarke, Dee Devine and Rebecca Mortimer at Manchester University Press for all their help.

But, above all, thanks to my wife, Helen, who makes everything possible and worthwhile.

Liverpool, June 2015

# Introduction

In recent years studies of the Irish diaspora have flourished, with the growth of work on the Irish in Great Britain particularly notable. Within this body of work there has long been a focus on nineteenth-century Irish movement across the Irish Sea, and some notably fine overviews have been produced.[1] Certain themes have constantly recurred. One is focused on the causes of the outflow from Ireland, often accompanied by analysis of the extent to which Britain was a relatively attractive destination. In both cases emphasis is on economic factors, supplemented by political, socio-cultural and personal considerations. A second theme is the temporal and regional pattern of settlement in Britain, noting how the level of emigration fluctuated with varying economic conditions on both sides of the Irish Sea and how the geography of settlement was influenced on the macro scale by employment opportunities and in detail by the location of cheap accommodation, existing Irish communities and familial links. Within this literature there has been a lively debate on the extent to which the Irish shared residential space with the native population. A third theme has centred on questions of employment, the traditional picture arguing that the successive Irish inflows were overwhelmingly unskilled or semi-skilled working-class and largely remained in these categories. Running alongside and closely related to this narrative, the fourth theme stressed the material poverty of the Irish immigrants, their notably bad housing and living conditions and the varieties of anti-social behaviour which often went in tandem. A fifth preoccupation has been the significance of Roman Catholicism as the faith of the great majority of the immigrants and its centrality not merely to the spiritual life of individual migrants, but in the social, cultural and, indeed, the political life of Irish migrant communities. The sixth body of work took up this latter dimension and focused on the political activities of the Irish in Britain, the extent to which they were expressed through parliamentary or violent means and the relationship to contemporary British political causes and movements. Often linked with these last two themes is a discussion of the reactions of native reactions to the incomers, the relationships which developed between the two and the extent to which the Irish integrated with British society and the degree to which they were and remained a people apart.

This steadily growing volume of work has variously deconstructed, challenged and refined many of the earlier generalisations on Irish migrants in nineteenth-century Britain and has taken the discussion into previously neglected dimensions of the migrant experience. Amongst these are the presence of a middle class and its role in both ecclesiastical and secular organisations, the lapse rate amongst Catholic migrants, the presence of a Protestant element, the life of migrant Irish women, the performance of Irishness in public space and the impact of the Irish on the literary, artistic and broader cultural life of nineteenth-century Britain. Much of this work has been conducted through the prism of regional and local studies, using census material, local newspapers, church records and whatever archival sources and personal papers have survived the ravages of time, neglect, ignorance and the blitz of the Second World War.[2] A good deal has once again focused on the large urban areas where most Irish settled, but there have also been studies of how the Irish fared in smaller urban settlements. These have shown how place is important, that personality and locality can bring about subtle but significant modifications of a general picture and that situations can alter over time.

Given its significance in the history of Britain as the pioneer city of the industrial revolution, it is surprising that until the 1990s there was little academic research on the Manchester Irish.[3] This is particularly puzzling, given that throughout most of the nineteenth century Manchester had the fourth largest Irish population of all the cities of Great Britain. Moreover, it was in Manchester that traditional anti-Irish prejudices were given a renewed lease of life by a pioneering study of working-class living conditions published in 1832 which scapegoated the Irish for many of the problems thrown up by rapid urban industrial development. In addition, it was in Manchester that there occurred a colourful succession of iconic incidents in late 1867 which generated hero figures, popular balladry, an Irish nationalist anthem and an enduring commemoration ritual, all of which resonated throughout Ireland and the diaspora for decades. In addition, the Irish organised for elections to the local school board and the city council, producing public representatives who were to become notably active in civic and broader Irish nationalist affairs.

The present work is an attempt to repair some aspects of this omission. It focuses on the Irish in Manchester during the nineteenth century and the early years of the twentieth. It is not intended as a comprehensive overview of all aspects of Irish life during that period. Rather, it focuses on the place the Irish devised for themselves in the life of the city, with particular reference to the extent to which they preserved their sense of Irish identity whilst making their way in one of the most dynamic world cities of the period. Until the arrival of Jewish refugees from the pogroms of imperial Russia in the late nineteenth century, the Irish, marked out by accent, religion, and politics and, in many cases, language, were the most exotic element in the city's population. This study focuses on the extent to which they retained their Irish identity through communal social solidarity, residential clustering, religious loyalties, communal celebration and political aspiration, whilst adapting the institutions, mores and institutions of the host society for their distinctive purposes. It is probably true that many Irish on arrival in Britain quietly abandoned their distinctive religious practice, language and political outlook and merged with the host population, a trend which alarmed the Catholic Church in particular, provoking recurrent anxieties over 'leakage'. But, as will be shown, significant numbers retained at least some of these features and eventually came to occupy prominent places in the social geography and cultural life of the city.

Identity is a malleable social construction, subject to constant renewal and reinvention. During the period under discussion British national identity underwent some significant shifts in definition. For centuries the French, and to a lesser extent the Spanish, had filled the role of the great foreign Catholic 'other' against which popular English and later British popular nationalism had been defined. Anti-Irish sentiment was if anything even longer lived. It underwent periodic renewal during the nineteenth century as Irish Catholic immigration waxed and waned and the Irish were made scapegoats for many of the social and economic ills generated by the revolutionary changes in economic and social geography which coincided with their arrival. Subsequently, their involvement in distinctive political campaigns for Catholic emancipation, Irish self-government and Catholic education continued to mark them out from the mainstream of British society. The interaction between these sometimes contending forces is a major theme of this book, which looks at the processes working for interaction, inclusion, differentiation and the compromises involved.

The first chapter traces the gradual development of links between Manchester and Ireland, largely through the build-up of commercial connections, but also noting the two-way movement of people across the Irish Sea. It examines the process whereby commercial and seasonal links gradually led to the growth of a substantial resident Irish-born population before the famine influx of the mid- to late 1840s and their concentration in distinct residential districts. It discusses how the relatively small and short-lived 'Little Ireland' area received widespread publicity thanks to the polemics of a conscientious workaholic sanitary reformer who blamed the Irish for many of the ills of industrialisation and thereby helped to give anti-Irish sentiment a new lease of life in nineteenth-century Britain. Chapter 2 switches the focus to Angel Meadow, the much larger and more long-lived Irish neighbourhood on the northern side of the city. It examines the rapid build-up of the resident Irish population of the city in the late 1840s and discusses the spatial distribution of the Irish in the network of streets set back from the main roads of the Angel Meadow study area. It goes on to explain this pattern of residential clustering whilst stressing that there was also constant interaction with city life.

Chapter 3 discusses the significance of the Catholic Church for the migrant Irish. Whilst noting that there was already an English Catholic population, it outlines how the Irish came to dominate this faith community in terms of both numbers and priorities and on occasion troubled the church authorities with their politics. But it also examines how from the earliest times there were concerns amongst the clergy about the external dangers threatening the faithful. These took the form of Protestant prejudice, often stirred up by local preachers such as Rev. Hugh Stowell of Salford or by itinerant lecturers, and Protestant proselytism through the allocation of Catholic orphans and foundlings to non-Catholic homes. Of even greater concern was the danger of 'wastage' of those who neglected their spiritual duties or fell away completely from the faith, seduced by bad company and competing distractions. To guard against such dangers and build up the faithful, a dense network of church-based fraternities, moral improvement and mutual aid organisations was organised. The Salford Diocese Catholic Protection and Rescue Society was one of the most notable guardians of the boundaries of faith and morals, and its journal is a rich source for this study.

Chapter 4 examines the evolution of that most characteristically Irish public festival, namely St Patrick's Day. It discusses how in the 1830s and 1840s it was celebrated at two levels. On the streets it was ill organised and bucolic, often involving drunken fights with locals and members of the Orange Order. In parallel and possibly in reaction to this, there was a regular public dinner which the organisers set out to make as respectable and inclusive as possible, often aiming to raise funds for charitable work amongst the Irish poor and featuring speeches arguing for cooperation and concord amongst Irish people regardless of religious and political outlook. When the celebration re-emerges to public view in the 1870s it was clearly becoming more respectable, being carefully structured on the conventional format of public concerts and meetings and much more Catholic and nationalist in tone, with clergy invariably present, MPs as guest speakers and Irish home rule a constantly recurring theme.

Chapter 5 discusses how Manchester's Irish related to the broader political concerns of the city during the period from the 1790s to the 1850s whilst retaining a keen interest in Irish affairs. It notes the activities of local supporters of the revolutionary United Irishmen in the city in the 1790s but also notes the presence of the Irish amongst those who demonstrated for parliamentary reform and trade union rights at Peterloo in 1819. Daniel O'Connell's campaigns for Catholic emancipation in the 1820s and repeal of the union of Great Britain and Ireland in the early 1840s clearly found support amongst the Manchester Irish. The complicated on-off relationship with Chartism in the city is examined, with particular attention to the fact that the much feared Irish–Chartist alliance in the revolutionary year of 1848 may actually have been a fleeting reality in Manchester.

Chapter 6 examines the role of the Irish in the electoral politics of the city from the 1870s onwards. Following early unsuccessful efforts with independent Irish candidates at local elections, it focuses on the sometimes awkward relationship with the local Liberal party, in which some Irish came to occupy leading roles, its outworking in school board and municipal elections and its rather less significant impact on parliamentary elections. It underlines the fact that by the end of the century there was a small but able group of Irish-born and second-generation Liberal councillors who served both the civic life of the city and the distinctive interests of their Irish Catholic nationalist followers.

Chapter 7 analyses the evolution of the commemoration rituals for the Manchester Martyrs, executed in November 1867, and the quietly intense struggle between moderate and advanced nationalists for ownership of the proceedings, noting that by the early twentieth century it had developed into an inclusive event incorporating representatives of the organisations which had arisen with the Irish cultural revival. It also traces how the events of the 1916 Dublin rising unnerved moderate nationalists in the city until by 1920 the ritual was passing into the control of Sinn Féin and its local support group.

Chapter 8 attempts to trace the hidden history of the Irish Republican Brotherhood (IRB) in Manchester in the years following the incidents of 1867 and notes how the organisation, though not necessarily the outlook it represented, had almost faded away by the 1890s. Thereafter it outlines the gradual revival of a more militant brand of Irish nationalism, the participation of a small group of Manchester people in the rising of 1916 and activities of the Irish Republican Army (IRA) in the city in the years 1919–21, stressing that, whilst sympathy for the struggle steadily grew, actual participation took many forms and outright involvement in military action involved very few. In conclusion, it is made clear that, like so many immigrant groups, the Irish in Manchester were subject to conflicting influences. History, religion, residential clustering, political priorities and celebratory festivals tended to keep them apart, but since they lived in a particularly dynamic British city with a vibrant political and civic culture this meant that whilst they could adapt local institutions and traditions for distinctively Irish purposes, they were simultaneously drawn to share the broader concerns, customs and mores of the city and society as a whole, creating what was in many ways a hybrid identity.

## Notes

1 John Archer Jackson, *The Irish in Britain* (London: Routledge & Kegan Paul, 1963), though dated, is an enduring piece of work raising questions still very relevant to the subject. The most comprehensive overviews since then are, in chronological order, Roger Swift and Sheridan Gilley (eds), *The Irish in the Victorian city* (London: Croom Helm, 1985); *The Irish in Britain 1815–1939* (London: Pinter, 1989); Graham Davis, *The Irish in Britain 1815–1914* (Dublin: Gill & Macmillan, 1991); Roger Swift, *The Irish in Britain 1815–1914* (London: The Historical Association, 1990); Roger Swift, 'The historiography of the Irish in nineteenth century Britain', in P. O'Sullivan (ed.), *The Irish worldwide: history, heritage, identity*, vol. 2: *The Irish in the new communities* (Leicester: Leicester University Press, 1992), pp. 52–81; Don MacRaild, *Irish migrants in modern Britain 1750–1922* (Basingstoke: Macmillan, 1999); Roger Swift, 'Historians and the Irish: recent writings on the Irish in nineteenth century Britain', in D. MacRaild (ed.), *The great famine and beyond: Irish migrants in Britain in the nineteenth and twentieth centuries* (Dublin: Irish Academic Press, 2000), pp. 14–39; Roger Swift, 'Identifying the Irish in Victorian Britain: recent trends in historiography', *Immigrants and Minorities*, 27:2–3 (2009), pp. 178–93.
2 See Roger Swift and Sheridan Gilley (eds), *The Irish in Victorian Britain: the local dimension* (Dublin: Four Courts Press, 1999) for a good selection.
3 J.M. Werly, 'The Irish in Manchester', *Irish Historical Studies*, 18 (1973), pp. 345–58, merely reproduced material from official documents and the work of Friedrich Engels vividly describing poor Irish living and working conditions, with no sustained analysis.

# 1

## Early connections, 'Little Ireland' and stereotypes

This chapter will trace the development of the earliest links between Manchester and Ireland and, noting the growth of military and commercial connections, the build-up of a resident Irish-born population down to 1841. It will then discuss the development of the Irish neighbourhood of 'Little Ireland', the role of Dr James Phillips Kay and other writers in presenting it as the archetypical Irish quarter in Britain and the renewal of historic anti-Irish sentiment in mid-Victorian Britain.

### Early connections

From at least the early sixteenth century there are indications of commercial links between Manchester and Ireland. John Leyland, visiting Liverpool in 1530, remarked, 'Good merchandise at Lypol, and much Irish yarn that Manchester men do by there', though the precise nature of this 'yarn' is not specified.[1] A hundred years later cotton working was firmly established in Manchester, but there were recurring problems with yarn, which was not strong enough to be used as the warp. The solution was to mix cotton with linen yarns, thereby producing a hybrid material known as fustian. In 1641 it was noted that a two-way trade had developed, an observer describing how 'the town of Manchester buys the linen yarn of the Irish in great quantity and weaving it returns the same again to Ireland to sell'.[2] It was noted that 'Where theses Irish merchants haggled over their linen yarn, near Smithy Door, was known as the Patrick Stone'.[3]

Commercial links continued to develop, but the emphasis shifted as fast-growing Manchester became an increasingly significant market for Irish agricultural produce. The eighteenth century saw the growth of an extensive Irish provisions trade, involving the export of butter, cheese, salt beef, pork, fish and ship's biscuit. For some time legislation blocked the import of these Irish products into Britain and Irish producers turned to alternative markets in the British royal and merchant navies, France and the slave plantations in the West Indies. However, the legislative barriers were gradually removed and Manchester drew an increasing amount of its food from Ireland. The ban on Irish live cattle imports was repealed in 1759 and a trade in Irish cattle destined for final fattening and slaughter in Britain grew up. Following the close of the wars with France in 1815 this grew appreciably in volume and altered in nature, thanks to transport developments. The first regular passenger steam service across the Irish Sea began in June 1818 and a regular commercial link was inaugurated in 1824.[4] By the 1840s there were over a hundred crossings per week for passengers and goods. A voyage that previously took a week or even more in adverse winds now on average took fourteen hours, and subsequent competition between steamship companies reduced costs. The cattle trade between Ireland and Liverpool grew rapidly and was soon dominated by animals fattened in Ireland and ready for slaughter on arrival. In the late 1830s Manchester's meat market was dominated by Irish produce, and large numbers of pigs and, to a lesser extent, sheep also made the journey.[5] Development of rail services meant that increasing amounts of Irish butter, bacon, ham, potatoes, cheese and salmon also began to appear in Manchester markets and shops. One commentator observed that for half of the year only Irish produce was available, and dealers in Co. Sligo butter alone had ten shippers in the city.[6] By the 1840s the city's Irish trade had become such a feature that it figured in a broadside ballad:

> The Port of Manchester – A Yarn
> The Union flag is flying,
> By the Company's Wharf, Old Quay,
> And 'Mary' of Dublin lying,
> Unloading her Murphies today
>
> Should your chickens all turn out
> And refuse eggs to lay;
> Why, then- fresh laid ones you may have
> From Dublin every day
>
> You'll have POTATOES, PIGS AND MEAL,
> And butter in such plenty,
> That none but lunatics will steal-
> The New Bailey will be empty [7]

Traffic in people across the Irish Sea was doubtless as long established as trade in goods. As early as 1243 there was such national concern at the numbers of Irish vagrant poor in Britain that legislation authorised their expulsion.⁸ Its subsequent repetition underlines the persistence of the problem. Returns from local authorities and charities indicate their presence in Manchester. The Constables' Accounts for Manchester list a succession of payments to distressed people travelling from and to Ireland. On 2 December 1634 there was a payment of six pence 'to 2 Irish women & a boy yt went to London per pass'.⁹ There was a notable increase in payments in the early 1640s, reflecting the 1641 rising and the subsequent years of instability. In late 1641 the widow Elizabeth Parsiual was paid 2s 6d for the nine Irish who had lodged with her, and on 23 February 1642 ten pence was paid out 'for burying a child & bying a winding sheet came from Ireland'.¹⁰ Subsequently the emphasis shifted back from wartime refugees to people who were simply in want, as in the case of the shilling given on 1 March 1755 to 'Ann Greaves to Ireland child dead'.¹¹ There are also changes in terminology, as with the shilling paid 'To two trampers going to Ireland' on 25 October 1772.¹² Some observers were convinced that such charity did not best serve the interests of the city. When in 1811 local magistrates suggested that indigents should receive three shillings per week, those in charge of disbursements retorted that 'most, even of the Irish, would not expect so much'.¹³ Thomas Armitt, Manchester's visiting Poor Law overseer, giving evidence to the commissioners investigating the state of the Irish poor in Great Britain, argued that local charities drew 'a vast number of Irish and idle vagabonds from all parts'.¹⁴

Manchester's military links with Ireland were long established. There were constant demands on the city for men and supplies, especially in the closing years of the sixteenth century in the campaigns leading up to the final conquest of Ireland.¹⁵ Court Leet records for 1579–80 note: 'paid to the hands of Sr. Edmud Trafford and Mr. Edmud assheton ffor the making of soldiers into Ireland £16'.¹⁶ This was the first of a series of such levies, and another in July 1613, when £3 7s 11d was raised, hints at the burden they imposed: 'The various garrisons in Ireland required constant reinforcement, and special money was collected for that purpose.'¹⁷ Inevitably, there were casualties. In 1598 a local man, Captain William Radcliffe, was killed when campaigning in Ulster, and in August the following year his brother Sir Alexander died when the Earl of Tyrone defeated an English force in the Curlieu Hills of Co. Roscommon. Manchester's efforts were not always appreciated. In 1599 it was reported: 'On raising men to suppress the rebellion in Ireland. The magistracy of Manchester were cautioned not to send any vagabonds or disorderly persons, but young men of good character, who were well skilled in the use of the hand-gun.'[18] Veterans of the Irish wars were frequent recipients of local charity. On 29 March 1618 a shilling was given to 'a poore Souldier who had a pass under the Lo[rd] Deputye of Ireland ... to travaile to york', and on 18 June 1745 the same was given to 'Alex McKie and his wife from Royal Irish Dragoon'.[19]

By the second half of the eighteenth century it is clear that there was a constant flow of army regiments to and from Ireland. On 23 May 1772 a local newspaper noted, 'Major General Mackay reviewed the sixth or Inniskilling Regiment of Dragoons, now quartered in this town, commanded by the Hon. General James Chomondele'; the Constables' Accounts for June note 21s for quartering and on 28 September £5 10s 'for rent of a music room for Inniskilling Dragoons'.[20] Other Irish regiments based in the area included the Irish Fusiliers (87th Regiment), who marched to Mass at St Augustine's Catholic church on St Patrick's Day 1830 'preceded by their band playing "St. Patrick's Day in the Morning"'.[21] The 1851 census recorded several examples of Irish-born soldiers on furlough on census night, such as Corporal Edward Duggan of the 31st regiment at 22 Cable Street. The same source also records the presence of Irish-born 'pensioners' or ex-soldiers, such as Ernest (or James) Cleary of 12 Gould Street, formerly of the 88th regiment, the famous Connaught Rangers, reflecting the fact that discharged soldiers often settled in the garrison towns where their enlistment had expired. But the Irish also served in other regiments, and in the early nineteenth century the majority of recruits to the 47th Foot (Lancashire Regiment) were Irish-born. This reflects the fact that by the mid-Victorian period it has been estimated that 30% of the regular army were Irish-born, with an even higher proportion in the rank of regimental sergeant major and below.[22] Local regiments also served in Ireland, especially during the wars against revolutionary and Napoleonic France. On 21 August 1794, when the Royal Manchester Volunteers (104th regiment) were inspected by General Musgrave, 'Colours were presented to the regiment in St. Anne's Square, after which it marched to Liverpool to embark for Ireland', and in 1801 'the Earl of Wilton's regiment of Lancashire Volunteers returned from Ireland, where they had been doing duty for five years'.[23]

Migrant harvesters were another traditional and transitory element in Manchester's Irish population. From the late eighteenth century onwards increasing numbers of Irish made the journey to Britain to help with the harvest, most coming from the north-western counties of Roscommon, Mayo and Galway.[24] By the mid-nineteenth century there was a well-established pattern of locally recruited groups travelling under acknowledged leaders to Britain, where they worked their way across the country in the summer months, living in outhouses and temporary booths, following the harvests of hay, potatoes, grain crops and hops and scathingly referred to by locals as 'July barbers'.[25] The process was reflected in several ballads:

> Billy O'Rook the Boy
> I greased my brogues and cut my stick
> At the latter end of May, sir
> And off for England I set out
>
> To sail upon the sea, sir
> To reap the hay and corn, sir ... [26]

As for transport, another ballad recorded Pat Molloy declaring how 'I tramped from York to London, with my scythe upon my back'.[27]

The process was vividly described by a migrant Irish harvester interviewed in Manchester in June 1889, when the reporter estimated that his informant was 'fairly typical of the thirty or forty thousand yearly visitors of this class'. The man, aged fifty, came from a village sixty miles from Galway town and close to the River Shannon, where he lived as a tenant on a twelve-acre farm and kept a cow and some pigs, two miles outside his local village. The annual rent was £13, which was paid by the sale of dairy produce, potatoes, the occasional pig and money sent home by his migrant daughter and three sons at Christmas and Easter. Thanks to this and 'with the money from England he managed to live'. The progress of the harvest in England was closely followed in the *Freeman's Journal* newspaper, and the departure of the workers was clearly one of the outstanding events of the year. On the appointed morning sixty had heard Mass at six o'clock and together had travelled the twelve miles to the local railway station, where for five shillings they journeyed to Dublin. There they had a wait of six hours, along with many others. Another five shillings paid for the passage to Britain on a ship so crowded that most slept on deck. 'Arrived in Liverpool the party separated. Some crossed the border into Cheshire, others made for Yorkshire, but the majority took the train to Manchester, which forms a sort of centre.' This individual, like others, had evolved a regular pattern of work and travel. He normally worked for a farmer in Middleton, north-east of Manchester, then proceeded to a farm near Ripon in north Yorkshire; he then worked his way south and eventually back to Ireland.[28] By the 1830s this transitory workforce had become such an integral part of the British farm economy that several authorities were convinced that it was crucial to the national economy. George Cornwell Lewis, responsible for gathering the evidence on the state of the Irish poor in Great Britain, concluded that

The Irish reapers ... have, by supplying the extra hands required at a particular season of the year, conferred a great economical advantage on England ... The large periodical immigrations of the Irish into this country at the harvest season prove an incalculable advantage to our farmers by enabling them to get the harvest both cheaply and speedily cut down. No class of labourers here are much interfered with by such immigrations, whilst they enable the farmer to improve to the utmost every favourable moment for prosecuting the labours of the harvest, a circumstance of vast importance in this variable and uncertain climate.[29]

As late as the 1930s Irish migrant labourers were at work on the harvest in Cheshire.[30]

In the overall scheme of things such an influx at a time when there was a high demand for labour might have been a national economic asset, but Lewis was overlooking the fact that at the local level indigenous labourers bitterly resented the migrant presence and violent conflict sometimes resulted. In late August 1882, at the height of the harvest, there were two examples of what was termed 'the ill-feeling existing between English and Irish labourers'. Drunken English labourers attacked three Irishmen in the Cheshire village of Wetherall, breaking the jaw of one. No action was taken at the subsequent quarter sessions, since the victim had gone to America. However, two Irishmen who had attacked two English labourers in a field near the town of Knutsford were sentenced to nine months of hard labour and another to three.[31] Long before this, however, it had been noticed that some harvesters had settled down to become permanent residents, and by 1851 'agricultural labourer' was appearing as the occupation for Irish-born men and a few women.

## Permanent settlement

There is the first hint of a resident Irish element in Manchester's population in 1592, when, it is recorded, 'Irishmen had begun to settle in the town for in this year, according to the Bishop of Chester's Visitation Book, a number of them were fined for walking in the fields instead of attending service in the parish church'; it is possible that some of the Irish merchants trading in linen yarn mentioned earlier may have taken up residence.[32] Subsequently, there are no specific references to an Irish presence until 1745. However, estimates of Catholic numbers may contain an Irish element, though it is worth bearing in mind that this is a region where an indigenous Catholic population survived the Protestant Reformation. In 1690 only two Catholics were recorded in Manchester, and thirty families in the sixty-square-mile parish in 1700. Itinerant priests

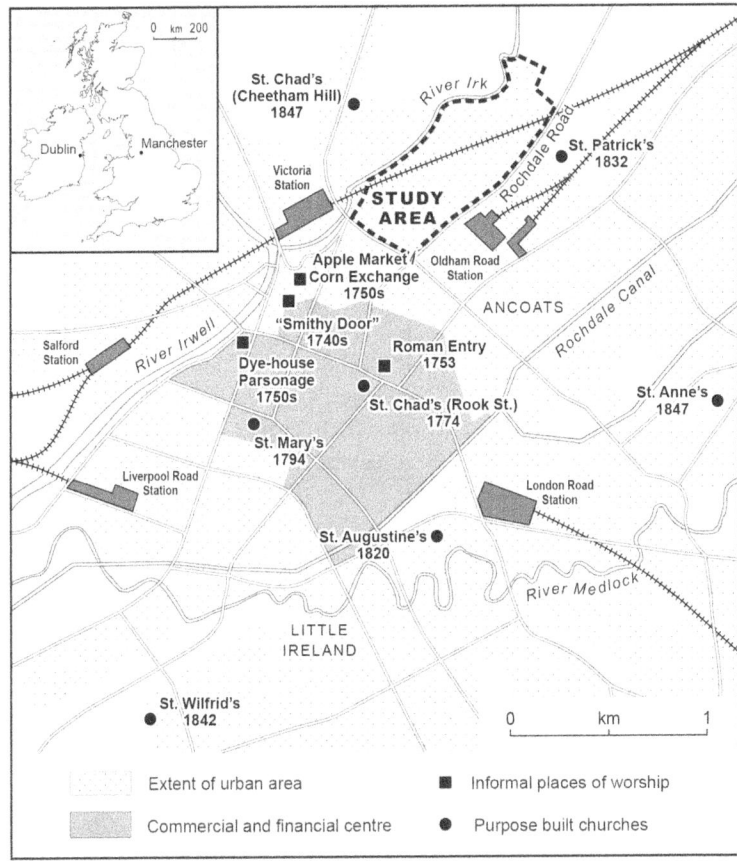

1 Angel Meadow study area: Irish districts and Catholic places of worship in mid-nineteenth-century Manchester

occasionally administered the sacraments, but there was no fixed place of worship until 1741, when small groups began to gather in private houses and vacant buildings. No baptismal register was kept until 1762, and there was no purpose-built church in the city until the construction of St Chad's in 1774 (Figure 1).[33]

It is not until the Jacobite rising of 1745 that there is definite mention of a permanent Irish presence in the city. On his march south to Derby Prince Charles Edward Stuart stayed in Manchester for three days, and during that time about three hundred men joined his army as the Manchester Regiment, the largest single group to rally to the Jacobite cause in England. Of the 163 listed in the final muster, nine were noted as from Ireland and a further two had characteristically Irish surnames.[34] Given that several of these recruits are noted as textile workers, it seems quite likely that current economic distress had led them to enlist in the first army to enter the city. Nevertheless, the episode gained the city the reputation of being a hotbed of Jacobitism and Catholicism, a deeply damaging accusation in those fraught times. Consequently, an anonymous local strove to refute these calumnies by rallying all the evidence to the contrary he could find. Though he had to admit there was a Catholic element amongst the city's population, he explained their presence in strikingly revealing terms: 'God be thanked … it is our peculiar Happiness to have fewer, in Proportion, of the denomination than any other large populous Town in the Kingdom; and those we have are of no Note or Consideration, being chiefly poor Irish, brought to settle here by our Manufacture.'[35] It was a notably revealing statement of migrant motivations and contemporary attitudes.

Reliable statistics on the numbers of Irish in the city were not available until the census of 1841, though there were estimates of varying reliability and motivation. As with many migrant inflows before and since, there was widespread popular and official unease at this influx. Occasional efforts to estimate the Catholic population were provoked by spasms of traditional anti-Catholic sentiment, and may have been exaggerated, as well as containing a native Catholic element. The estimate of two Catholics in the city in 1690 and thirty families in the sixty-square-mile parish in 1700 makes no mention of the Irish.[36] The 1767 Returns of Papists in the Diocese of Chester provide a little more detail, listing 287 Catholics by name, of which twenty-eight had distinctively Irish-sounding surnames. Of the ten men with occupations, six worked in the textile trade.[37] A survey of Lancashire in the late eighteenth century reported, 'above 5000 Irish were settled in Manchester in the year 1787, and I am told that number was afterwards doubled'.[38] An anonymous author writing in 1804 emphasised his disquiet: 'The present number of Catholics in the towns of Manchester and Salford, owing to the excessive influx of strangers, particularly from Ireland, is thought to be from TEN TO FIFTEEN THOUSAND.'[39] The estimates presented to the commissioners gathering evidence for the investigation into the state of the Irish poor in Great Britain when they visited the city in early 1834 varied from 17,000 to 50,000.[40] The most careful and scholarly work on this matter suggests that by 1819 there were 15,000 Catholics in the city, of whom 50% were Irish born, by 1828 there were between 30,000 and 40,000, and by the early 1830s there was a large and well-established Irish community producing a second generation.⁴¹ It is with some relief that one turns to the first generally reliable census, that of 1841, which recorded 30,304 Irish-born residents in Manchester, 12.5% of the city's total population.⁴²

However, all the sources do agree that from the late eighteenth century onwards the Irish population of the city was growing at an increasing rate. This is explicable in terms of relative economic conditions in Ireland and Manchester. In 1785 the patent on Sir Richard Arkwright's cotton-spinning machinery had lapsed, and within the next few years machine spinning of cotton became widespread. This created a production bottleneck, since weaving was not widely mechanised until the 1830s. In the interval, there was high demand for hand-loom weavers, and Manchester merchants sent recruiting agents throughout Britain and Ireland. Peter Ewart, a leading Manchester businessman in the cotton industry, giving his evidence to the commissioners visiting in early 1834, declared, 'About thirty-five years ago there was a great influx of Irish to supply the extraordinary demand which existed at that time for hand-loom weavers; that was the first great immigration of Irish into Manchester.'⁴³ One result was expressed in a piece of doggerel which explained the need for the new St Mary's Catholic church ('the hidden gem'), opened in 1794 in a narrow side street off the city centre:

> the Catholics deemed it quite meet
> To build a chapel in Mulberry Street
> For the trade of the town
> And hands wanted for weaving
> And bread to be found there, poor Irishmen craving,
> Brought an influx of Catholic weavers to town,
> And filled Rook Street chapel to near breaking down⁴⁴

From the early nineteenth century onwards there was a series of economic and demographic developments in Ireland which encouraged more widespread emigration.⁴⁵ Following the end of the French wars in 1815, prices for agricultural goods in Britain, by far Ireland's largest market, gradually shifted to favour less labour-intensive pastoral produce. In the period 1815–25 cereal prices fell by one third.⁴⁶ Moreover, Irish industry began to suffer increasing competition from Great Britain. The Irish parliament had imposed tariffs on a range of imported goods, but one of the terms of the Act of Union of 1801 was the gradual introduction of free trade, which was complete by 1824, ahead of the agreed timetable. The result was particularly damaging for the Irish textile industry. Irish cottons were unable to compete with the Lancashire products in volume, variety, design, colour or price, and the industry began to contract. In late

1829 it was reported that when a relief committee had assisted 433 families of weavers to emigrate from the Liberties district of Dublin, amongst their destinations were 'Manchester … Congleton, Macclesfield and Leeds'.[47] The much smaller woollen and silk industries suffered a similar fate.[48] Penetration of the Irish market was accelerated by steady improvement in steamship links and the Irish road and, later, rail network. Pressures were further increased by the mechanisation and regional concentration of the Irish linen industry. Previously it had been quite widespread throughout Ireland, employing large numbers of part-time rural spinners and weavers, but it now became increasingly mechanised, urbanised and concentrated in the Belfast region, creating a rising level of rural underemployment and unemployment.

Simultaneously, Ireland's population began to grow increasingly rapidly from the late eighteenth century onwards and to bear down increasingly on the resource base: in 1791 it had been approximately 4,800,000, and by 1841 it was 8,100,000.[49] Popular coping strategies varied. One response was to bring more land into cultivation: in the early decades of the nineteenth century increasing areas of marsh and bogland were taken into cultivation, and the upper limits of settlement and cultivated land climbed steadily to unprecedented altitudes. Another option was to utilise land more intensively with particularly productive crops, especially the potato, which became a key element in the rural diet, especially in the counties of the west and south. There was also a trend to switch to the more prolific if tasteless varieties of potato, most notably the 'cup' and the 'lumper'.[50] In addition to these long-term trends, there were also periodic food scarcities. There were fourteen partial or complete failures of the potato harvest between 1816 and 1842, and other crops also fared badly, particularly in 1817–19 (when there was also an outbreak of fever), 1822, 1831 and 1842.[51]

Emigration was another option, and from 1815 onwards increasing numbers left the country. Their departure was facilitated by the advances in transport technology noted earlier. In 1818 the first steam packet, the *Rob Roy*, had linked Belfast to Glasgow, and by the 1820s there were regular passenger services between most of the main Irish Sea ports of Ireland and Britain. Passenger fares in steerage fell as low as three pence for those on the open deck.[52] Migration was now a realistic possibility for all but the very poorest, and it is estimated that between 1815 and 1845 from 800,000 to one million Irish people emigrated to North America and about 500,000 to Great Britain.[53]

Irish migrants travelling to Britain followed routes which were to become well-trodden paths in the nineteenth and twentieth centuries. Those going to Scotland generally came from Ulster and travelled via

Belfast and smaller northern ports to Clydeside. Migrants to south Wales, western England and London were generally from south-western and southern Ireland, travelled via Cork and south-eastern ports and entered Britain via ports on the Bristol Channel.[54] Those travelling to north-western England were mostly from the north-west of Ireland, especially counties Roscommon, Mayo, Sligo, Leitrim and Galway. They travelled via Dublin to Liverpool. This became the main departure point for the rapidly growing numbers from all over Ireland intending to sail to North America. Significant numbers settled in the city itself, until by 1861 it was one of the best-known concentrations of Irish in nineteenth-century Britain.[55] Others fanned out across the country in search of employment. Mr W.G. Grime of Manchester's New Quay Company told the Irish Poor Report commissioners in 1834: 'The Irish who land in Liverpool and come to Manchester, nearly always walk … I have … seen them on the road in parties of from four to twelve persons, including children … I remember once counting seventy Irish in little more than two miles on the Liverpool, near Eccles [close to Manchester], when travelling in a gig.'[56]

Manchester's economic structure offered quite attractive prospects. The city landscape was dominated by the novel sight of multi-storey cotton mills working a shift system, emitting regular flows of workers as shifts changed, brightly lit at night and generating great clouds of steam and smoke from tall chimneys, earning the city the name of 'cottonopolis'. But 'Manchester was never merely a mill town'. Whilst in 1841 over 8,000 men were employed in cotton mills, about 6,000 worked as warehousemen, porters and clerks; 11,427 women were employed in the mills and workshops, but 9,961 worked as domestic servants and 2,251 in dressmaking and millinery.[57] There were also machine manufacturing and repair shops and chemical and dyestuff factories, many originally servicing the cotton industry but later diversifying. The city came to occupy a nodal location in the canal, road and rail networks and became a high-order service centre for much of south Lancashire and north Cheshire; it also developed a significant commercial and financial sector. As with most cities of the time, there was a thriving informal street economy where both adults and young children were to be found hawking rags, fruit, pins, needles, cutlery, kindling and spills for lighting fires and pipes. In times of reasonable prosperity, therefore, there were employment possibilities for all but the very youngest in the family (Figure 5).

By 1841 some Irish were to be found in every part of the city, but there are indications of residential clustering from quite early on. By the late eighteenth century a working-class district had developed on the north-eastern side of the city on the banks of the River Irk (Figure 1), labelled 'New Town' by contemporary cartographers but also known as 'Irish Town' and, more often, 'Angel Meadow'. On 16 August 1819 a large contingent of demonstrators from the town of Middleton, on their way to the great demonstration at St Peter's Fields in support of parliamentary reform and trade union rights, marched along St George's (later Rochdale) Road, which ran along the fringes of the district; the radical leader Samuel Bamford recorded what happened:

> at Newtown we were welcomed with open arms by the poor Irish weavers, who came out in their best drapery, and uttered blessings and words of endearment, many of which were not understood by our rural patriots. Some of them danced, and others stood with clasped hands and tearful eyes, adoring, almost that banner whose colour was their national one, and the emblem of their green island home. We thanked them by the band striking up 'Saint Patrick's Day in the Morning'; they were electrified; and we passed on, leaving these warm hearted suburbans capering and whooping like mad.[58]

Clearly, therefore, by 1841 there was a well-established Irish population in the city and some tendency to residential clustering in certain districts. Of these, Angel Meadow was to develop into the largest and most enduring, but it was another, much smaller and more ephemeral Irish neighbourhood which was to achieve national and international notoriety and to contribute powerfully to the popular image of the Irish urban migrant and the renewal of traditional anti-Irish stereotypes.

## 'Little Ireland'

In the early decades of the nineteenth century Manchester experienced what was probably its most dynamic period of economic and demographic growth. In its expansion the town developed a series of industrial nodes along the rivers and canals which provided transport links, water for steam and convenient sites for waste disposal. One of these agglomerations was situated on the southern side of the city, west of Oxford Street between the Rochdale Canal and a southerly loop of the River Medlock. By 1830 there was a dense concentration of textile mills, foundries, dye works, engineering works, coal and timber yards and three gasworks along the canal and river, and the area was overlooked by at least thirteen tall chimneys discharging effluent into the atmosphere (Figure 2).[59] Physical geography added to the problems. As in many parts of Manchester, the surface geology is river alluvium underlain by boulder clay, which inhibits drainage. Moreover, the Medlock flowed between banks raised above the surrounding streets, and whilst some factory owners had

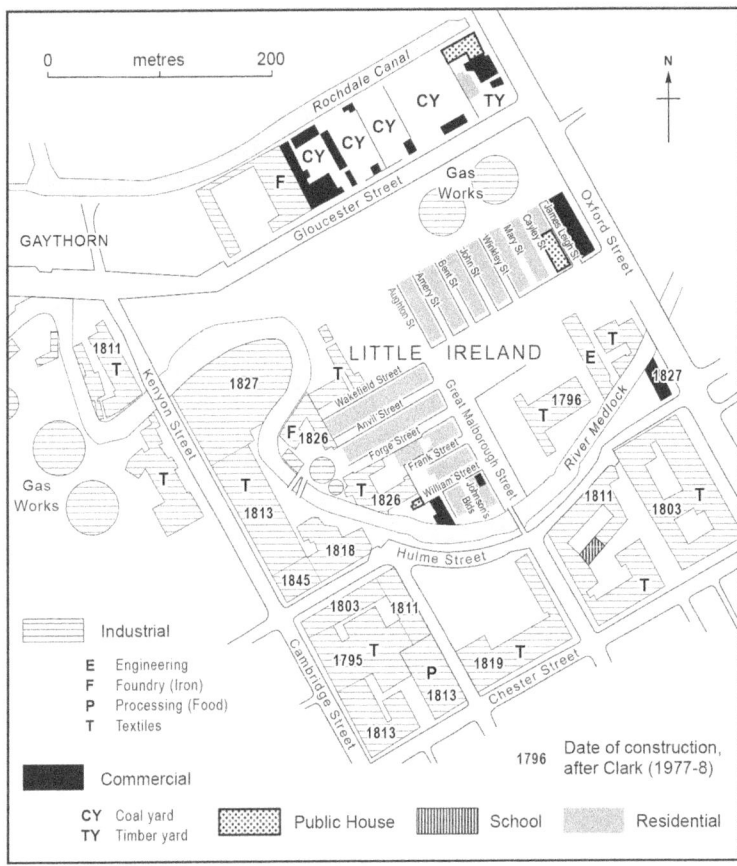

2 Little Ireland: land use, early 1840s

erected river walls and floodgates, these did not extend along the entire length of the river and some areas were subject to flooding, notably in May 1847 when boats had to rescue local inhabitants.[60] The situation was further complicated when earth was excavated to embank Oxford Street and carry it southwards across the Medlock as Oxford Road. Speculative builders quickly took the opportunity to erect small rows of dwelling houses on spare ground around and between the mills and factories. Such a significant number of the newcomers to the area were Irish that the district became known as 'Little Ireland', and the name entered local folklore and official maps.

Given the subsequent wide notoriety of the district, it is important to establish the reality.[61] In the area enclosed by Gloucester Street in the north and the great loop of the River Medlock the 1841 census recorded 1,510 residents on the census night of Sunday 6 June 1841. Of these 963 (63.8%) were born in Ireland and 187 (12.4%) were born elsewhere to two Irish-born parents listed in the census, giving an Irish total of 1,150 (76.2%). There were few Irish living along the main thoroughfares, but there was a high level of concentration in five streets in the interior of the district, whose residents were at least 90% Irish. The concentration was equally marked when individual houses are examined. Of the 177 houses listed in the census with a majority of Irish residents, 166 (93.8%) had another majority Irish house on at least one side, and 1,100 (95.6%) of the Irish lived in houses with an Irish majority.

As will be seen later, this was by no means the largest or the most enduring of Manchester's Irish neighbourhoods. In reality, it had a remarkably short life. By 1849 the Manchester South Junction and Altrincham Railway was opened, and several streets in Little Ireland recorded in the 1841 census were demolished to make way for Oxford Road Station. Cellars used for residential purposes were blocked up as a precaution against the spread of infectious disease. As the area became increasingly valuable to the railway companies as a site for warehousing, residential housing was gradually eliminated. By 1851, therefore, Little Ireland had few inhabitants and as an Irish neighbourhood had ceased to exist. However, its life as a legend was thriving.

## The making of the legend

In 1826 cholera (*vibrio cholerae*), previously confined to Asia, began to spread into eastern and central Europe. Aside from those who had encountered it there, it was totally unknown to European medical practitioners. This, together with the fact that it could break out quite suddenly, diffused rapidly over great distances, died away equally quickly and, when contracted, could run its usually fatal course in speedy and spectacular fashion, provoked popular and official reactions akin to panic. The picture was further complicated by heated controversy within the medical establishment. As contemporary observers monitored the course of events they could detect associations between outbreaks and the built urban environment. It was clear that the areas where the disease was most frequently found were the densely populated working-class districts of the newly developing cities. There were broadly two bodies of thought which strove to explain these associations. The first, known as the 'contagion' theory, argued that all contagious diseases were spread by direct contact between infected persons or with items they had touched. The 'miasmatic' theory, more widely entrenched, argued that infections were caught by exposure to the foul air or miasma given off by decomposing organic matter. Inhalation of such fumes, it was argued, meant the ingestion of elements which then infected victims. The generic term 'fever' was given to such infections, including typhus, typhoid and cholera. The precise processes of infection were not explained, but the striking correlation of disease with potent stench and highly visible urban squalor served to give the argument the status of 'common sense', especially in the minds of the largely middle-class early investigators who entered such districts in the course of their researches in support of urban sanitary reform. The 'miasmatic' argument also benefited from the support of some of the most formidable public health reformers of the early Victorian era, including the long-lived Manchester-born Sir Edwin Chadwick, the equally enduring redoubtable nursing pioneer Florence Nightingale and Dr William Farr, originally a medical statistician and subsequently superintendent of statistics at the general Register Office and overseer of the census reports of 1851, 1861 and 1871.[62]

By June 1831 the cholera pandemic had reached St Petersburg, by early October it was in Hamburg, where riots broke out, and in mid-October an outbreak was confirmed in Sunderland. In that month every local authority in Britain was authorised to set up a Special Board of Health, consisting of local notables, including magistrates, clergy and doctors, with instructions to survey their districts and take precautions against infection. At its meeting of 12 November 1831 the Manchester board received a paper from one of its members with advice to the general public on precautions to be taken against infection. Like many such documents of the time, it consisted of a mix of current medical debate and patronising moral judgement:

> The Cholera Epidemic
> Having made its appearance in this Country, it becomes necessary to take precautions in this town. The means by which it spreads from place to place are not satisfactorily ascertained, but there is reason to think that personal communication with the sick contributes largely to that end. Whilst medical men differ on the above points they are universally agreed that the persons most liable to an attack are, Those who occupy crowded, dirty and ill ventilated dwellings; Those who are ill clothed and fed; Those who are weakened, or disordered by intoxication, or intemperance of any kind; Those who after excessive fatigue are exposed to the night air. The most efficient precautions, therefore, that can be taken against an attack of cholera, or other dangerous disease, will consist in a strict observance of the following maxims. Keep your habitation clean and well aired; Clear away all filth and

rubbish from the ground in front and rear of your house; Procure the most comfortable clothing and the most substantial food in your power; And, in order to do this, Avoid spending your money in procuring the means of intoxication; Abstain altogether from spirits and be temperate in the use of fermented liquors: Be regular in your hours of labour and of rest: Avoid unnecessary communication with the sick.[63]

At this and subsequent meetings the board listed streets considered particularly vulnerable and commissioned sub-committees to inspect them and report back. On 14 December an inspection and report on Little Ireland were authorised. When received on 21 December the report detailed the lack of arrangements for disposal of surface water and waste products, and noted privies

> in a most disgraceful state ... the average number being two [emphasis original] to 250 people ... in many cases the people have no beds and keep each other warm by close stowage on shavings, straw & c.; a change of linen or clothes is an exception.

Whilst they did recommend some measures of 'partial amelioration', the inspectors declared, 'We conceive it will be impossible effectually to remove the evils enumerated ...'. They closed with words destined for endless reproduction: 'In conclusion we are decidedly of opinion that should cholera visit this neighbourhood a more suitable soil and situation for its malignant development cannot be found than that described and commonly known as Little Ireland.[64]

The reality was to prove rather different. There were very few cases of cholera in Little Ireland in the outbreaks of 1832 and 1849.[65] The housing in the district was by no means the worst in the city. Houses in the medieval core and those built in the late eighteenth century were in much worse condition, and in those areas there were few Irish. There are also indications that later reformers working in other parts of the city became impatient with the attention focused on this relatively small area and its declining population. In 1853 a report on the northern neighbourhood known as Gibraltar argued that it was so far gone that 'the only remedy for the evil is to pull it down and clear it away' and added the waspish remark: ' altogether it is very much worse than Little Ireland of such notoriety'.[66] However, these facts did nothing to stop the steady flow of investigators, visitors and writers, who constantly reproduced the concluding words of the 1831 report and added remarks of their own. Over thirty years later, when the area was virtually empty of inhabitants, another report did admit that some houses were 'moderately cleanly' but proceeded to linger on the inadequacies of housing, drainage and waste disposal and could not resist an echo of 1831 with the words: 'If the cholera gets a firm hold in this locality the ravages it will make will be fearful.'[67] But the publicity the area attracted was also deeply intertwined with the unflattering picture it conveyed of the Irish.

The enduring notoriety of the district and by association the Irish in general was in large part due to the vivid writing of one man addressing a local example of a problem which was beginning to preoccupy a significant section of the informed British public. James Phillips Kay was a local doctor born in Rochdale in 1804 into a devout, prosperous Nonconformist family with links to the cotton industry and banking (Figure 3). Educated at a local grammar school, aged fifteen he began work in his uncle's bank, but from quite early on it was obvious that he was outstandingly intelligent, and in November 1824 he entered the Edinburgh University medical school.[68] There he encountered living conditions and an approach to public health which were to influence his outlook for the rest of his life. The university medical school had an international reputation thanks to a succession of distinguished professors. In Kay's time the most notable was W.P. Allison. Though working long before the processes of bacterial infection were understood, Allison, noting the association between living conditions and the likelihood of infection, had developed a methodology unusual amongst his peers. He made a practice of visiting his patients in their homes and kept painstaking records of not only the course of infection, but their living conditions and lifestyle, a model which Kay followed throughout his life.

In Edinburgh both fellow students and staff quickly realised the calibre of the new student from Rochdale. One contemporary noted, 'He became a marked personage in the classrooms, where his earnest never-ending attention to lectures … impressed all … [he] at once threw his whole mental power and inexhaustible energies into these new studies and in his first winter overtook and passed most of his contemporaries.'[69] After his first year Kay spent some time as a pupil at Manchester Royal Infirmary, when he first undertook the study and practical observation of infectious disease, and then, he recalled, 'I spent the autumn in Dublin almost exclusively in practical anatomy. My time and strength were so used up in this pursuit that I had only casual opportunities to observe the condition of the Irish poor.'[70] Shortly after the start of his second year his peers elected him president of their medical society, and in 1826 he was appointed clinical clerk to Allison. Kay subsequently paid tribute to Allison's combination of meticulous record keeping, scrupulous care and indefatigable compassion for patients, describing him as an almost Christlike figure who turned none away regardless of class or condition.

3 Dr James Phillips Kay (Kay-Shuttleworth)

He believed that imbibing Alison's attitudes and methods gave him 'an example never to be forgotten'.⁷¹ Later in 1826, Allison, clearly impressed with his student, appointed him to Edinburgh New Town Dispensary. For the first time Kay came into close regular contact with immigrant Irish who were living in what had once been the town houses of the Scottish aristocracy but had subsequently been turned into 'barracks in the separate rooms of which lodged the poorest and most suffering portion of the urban poor ... in the worst extremities of destitution critical maladies had to be treated in these close and foul room'. He went on to reminisce in revealing terms:

> I have even found the Irishman's pig carried up a suckling, and grown to dimensions which would have rendered its removal almost impossible, occupying with the family a dwelling several stories above the street. The filth of the common stairs was most odious ... it seemed the lees of the population of Scotland and of the immigrant Irish settled in these overcrowded buildings to perish by maladies which no medical skill would often arrest.⁷²

Training and experience in Edinburgh had brought him to adopt an outlook described as that of a 'contingent contagionist', in that he believed that whilst contagion was the most likely source of infection, squalid living conditions and improvident personal habits rendered people more liable to disease. He had also noted an association between Irish immigrants and urban squalor.

But his experiences at Manchester Royal Infirmary and his time as clerk at Edinburgh's Queensferry Hospital during a fever outbreak combined to make him think more widely about the problems of public health. In later life Kay recalled how the never-ending needs of a succession of patients led him to conclude 'how almost useless were the resources of my art to contend with the consequences of formidable social evils. It was something outside scientific skill, or charity, which was needed for the cure of this social disease ... and I gradually began to make myself acquainted with the best works on political and social science.'⁷³ He had begun to travel towards the conclusion that there was an urgent need for radical reform of both individuals and society.

In April 1827 Kay qualified as a physician, and in August he graduated Doctor of Medicine. In December he set up house in Moseley Street in central Manchester, and the following year he applied for the post of physician at Manchester Infirmary, but was unsuccessful. Shortly afterwards he was appointed senior physician at Ancoats and Ardwick Dispensary on the north-eastern side of the city, serving 'a wide district stretching from the Irish town of St. Michael's to Ardwick, and chiefly inhabited by Irish labourers and factory workmen'.[74] It is unsurprising therefore that he was appointed to the Special Board of Health set up in November 1831 and that he quickly became secretary and something of a moving spirit. The board set up a sub-committee consisting of three or four medical practitioners and a druggist for each of Manchester's fourteen police districts, and, on the basis of his Edinburgh training and experience, Kay devised a set of questions for investigation into the housing and living conditions of each area.[75] Cholera finally arrived in June 1832, and Kay and his colleagues laboured amongst the victims until the infection died away in the autumn of that year.

But even before the first cholera outbreak, the combination of his training in Edinburgh and experience in Manchester, together with his reading, led Kay to launch into print, at first anonymously, in April 1832, with *The moral and physical condition of the working classes employed in the cotton manufacture in Manchester*.[76] In order to understand his stance, and in particular the impact of his analysis of the role he assigned the Irish, it is important to understand his world view. Like many of those who sought to improve the living conditions of the fast-growing new working class, he was a devout Christian, deeply imbued with the biblical thought forms and language of his day.[77] Consequently, whilst observation led him to believe strongly that the conditions bearing down upon individuals should be mitigated by government action, he believed equally strongly that the exercise of moral effort by the individuals concerned was essential to bring about improvement: 'Cholera can only be eradicated by raising the physical and moral condition of the community, in such a degree as to remove the predisposition to its reception and propagation, which is created by poverty and immorality.'[78] Kay believed that south-east Lancashire had originally been in an almost Eden-like state, inhabited by people who were 'quaint, honest, and enduring ... full of rare qualities – hardy, broken to toil, full of loyalty to the traditions of family and place – genial, humourous, but coarse'.[79] But, he argued, this relatively innocent state of affairs was destroyed by immigration, the consequences of which provoked him to an eloquent and much-quoted passage:

> Ireland has poured forth the most destitute of her hordes to supply the constantly increasing demand for labour. This immigration has been, in one important respect, a serious evil. The Irish have taught the labouring classes of this country a pernicious lesson ... Debased alike by ignorance and pauperism, they have discovered, with the savage, what is the minimum of the means of life, upon which existence may be prolonged ... and this secret has been taught the labourers of this country by the Irish ...

the contagious example of ignorance and a barbarous disregard of foresight and economy, exhibited by the Irish, spread ... Instructed in the fatal secret on what is barely necessary to life-yielding partly to necessity, and partly to example,– the labouring classes have ceased to entertain a laudable pride in furnishing their houses and in multiplying the decent comforts which minister to happiness. What is superfluous to the mere exigencies of life, is too often expended in the tavern; and for the provision of old age and infirmity, they too frequently trust either to charity, or to the protection of the poor laws...... The contagious example which the Irish have exhibited of barbarous habits and savage want of economy, united with the necessarily debasing consequences of uninterrupted toil, have demoralized the people.'[80]

Declaring that 'In some districts of the town exist evils so remarkable as to require more minute description', he proceeded to exemplify this by reproducing in full the Special Board of Health's report on Little Ireland, stressing that the district was 'chiefly inhabited by the lowest Irish'.[81] Kay did go on to describe other problematic parts of the city and to argue for reform of housing, street layout and formal and moral education, preferably under the aegis of the church, but none of his writings attracted the attention or indeed the infamy of his strictures on the Irish and Little Ireland.[82]

Kay went on to give evidence to the commissioners investigating the Irish poor in Great Britain when they held hearings in Manchester early in 1834. This was in much the same vein as his earlier argument, reinforced by the conviction that the Irish were 'a less civilised race than the natives'.[83] But he now expanded his argument on their malignant influence to make them responsible for the poor quality of housing provided by speculative builders: 'If it had not been for the Irish, there would have been no class of persons whose willingness to put up with so small an amount of convenience, and so large a subtraction from comfort, it would have been prudent to speculate. It would have been next to impossible to find a large body of English, influenced by the debasing example of the Irish, who would have been willing to save money at such a cost of health and comfort.'[84] Subsequently he made it clear that he also blamed immigrants from other parts of Britain, but to the end of his life he remained convinced the Irish played the key role.[85]

The book was so successful that it went into a second edition under Kay's name in November 1832. It has been described as 'the best known of all the literature produced by the cholera epidemic ... a work of sociological genius that was to influence the thinking of an entire generation' and 'one of the cardinal documents of Victorian history'.[86] Its impact was due to style, timing and history. It is undoubtedly well written, combining passionate, urgent conviction, coherent argument, personal observation, plentiful statistics and vivid, if selective, examples. This is hardly surprising since from quite early on contemporaries noted that Kay's works were not merely 'simple narratives of the facts of the case, but coloured and adorned by his imaginative power'.[87] In terms of timing the book struck a chord in addressing contemporary concerns about the nature of British identity and society at a time of extraordinarily rapid change. Kay's book resonated at two levels. Significant elements in British society were unnerved by the ongoing social unrest which had been simmering since 1811, the granting of Catholic emancipation in 1829 – which seemed to question the traditional place of Protestantism as a defining feature of English and British identity – and the outbreak of the mysterious cholera epidemic.[88] Kay's book, arguing for cholera as a metaphor of the infection of the entire body politic by working-class improvidence, fecklessness and immorality thanks to contamination by the Irish and calling for educational, moral and sanitary reform and personal reformation, and warning of the fatal consequences to individuals and society if action were not taken, seemed utterly convincing as diagnosis, warning and prescription, especially to the edgy, insecure emerging middle class.

But this was part of a much broader public debate over what became known as the 'condition of England' question and the role of Manchester as the exemplar of the likely future shape of British society.[89] The transformation of the economic and population geography of the United Kingdom known as the 'industrial revolution' was well under way by the 1830s, bringing in its train unprecedented forms of urbanisation which deeply alarmed contemporary observers. They were alarmed at the sheer numbers of urban centres and their rapid growth rate. Manchester in 1801 had numbered 76,788 people, but by 1841 its population was 242,983, and this was far exceeded in daytime when all the mills and factories were working.[90] The new cities were an alarming assault on the senses, with their spectacularly large mills and factories, some lit at night for shift working, the tall chimneys pouring out smoke and fumes, the daily ebb and flow of working people as shifts changed over, the bustle and noise of pedestrians and the ubiquitous horse-drawn carts, drays and carriages. But it was perhaps the social structure of the new industrial cities which some found most alarming. The largest element in the new population was a working class employed in the steam-driven mills and factories, amongst whom some were recruited locally and many were from distant parts of the United Kingdom. In such circumstances traditional forms of policing and social control were dangerously obsolete.[91] In 1829 Manchester's daytime police force consisted of four beadles, seven assistants and four street keepers, periodically reinforced by about two hundred special constables whose chief qualification was possession of an official truncheon; 'this day police force was supposed to control a turbulent population of more than 150,000 persons, including many thousands of recent immigrants from Ireland'.[92] Moreover, given the scale of the new enterprises and the growing residential segregation made possible by transport technology, traditional informal contacts between employer and worker and the presence of behavioural example by visible role model were no longer possible. For a generation not far removed from the French revolution of 1789 and the Irish risings of 1798 and 1803 and well aware of the French revolution of 1830, the threat seemed all too real. This apprehension seemed to be borne out by ongoing social unrest in Britain and the circulation of radical ideas on parliamentary reform and trade union rights. In Manchester these fears took on reality in the famous 'Peterloo' incident of 16 August 1819. When nervous magistrates ordered local yeomanry and troops to disperse a crowd of thirty thousand demonstrating in support of parliamentary reform and trade union rights, their charge resulted in 18 dead and 636 injured.[93] For conservative commentators this was all too typical of the city's 'unenviable notoriety on account of its rioting propensities' and a warning of things to come.[94]

Kay's vivid writing was therefore a timely diagnosis and prescription for contemporary anxieties and was widely read and avidly discussed. But it drew attention not merely to urban problems in general but to Manchester in particular as the exemplar of what the future held for newly urbanising Britain. One result was a flow of publications analysing Manchester's living and working conditions. Some were reports on the investigative work of local organisations such as the Manchester Statistical Society, formed in 1833, and the Manchester and Salford Sanitary Association, formed in 1852. Others were books by authors who, like Kay, combined concern over both physical and moral welfare.[95] But throughout the 1830s and 1840s 'All roads led to Manchester', and there was a steady stream of visitors to the city, not only from elsewhere in Britain, but also from Germany, Switzerland and France.[96] Almost all had read Kay, and many absorbed his analysis, including the malignant role he assigned to the Irish. Indeed, it has been argued that 'there is no more influential account of the migrant Irish … than Kay's observations on nineteenth century Manchester' and that 'Kay was undoubtedly a key influence in identifying the Irish presence with the evil effects of squalid living conditions. More significantly, Kay's writing became a source book for many subsequent books on the subject'.[97] Moreover, visitors to the city could easily view Little Ireland since it was just a short walk from the city centre and covered such a small area. There they would see everything that Kay's writings and subsequent publicity had prompted them to expect.

Of all the commentators who discussed the new cities and the place of the Irish the most famous is probably Friedrich Engels. His interest in the city arose from the fact that his father was one of the four partners in the cotton firm of Erwen and Engels, in Weaste, Salford. The Engels were a deeply devout Christian family in the Prussian Pietist tradition, emphasising biblical spirituality, personal responsibility, hard work, education and a charitable concern for fellow citizens, all in preparation for the second coming of Christ.[98] By the time he had reached the age of twenty it was clear that Friedrich was highly intelligent, and whilst he inherited some of the work ethic, cultural interests and social concern of the Pietists, he did not share the personal religious faith of his parents. Already by 1839 he had written anonymous articles in local newspapers condemning the working conditions in local mills. It was decided that he should take up residence in Manchester to oversee family interests there and, it was hoped, divert him from his radical politics and friends.

Engels spent two periods in Manchester, from late 1842 to August 1844 and from November 1850 to late September 1870. During that time he led something of a double life. His office was in Deansgate, a major thoroughfare in the commercial heart of the city, and his official home in nearby Great Ducie Street, but it is also clear that from early 1843 he was keeping a second house with his mistress Mary Burns, a second-generation Irish mill worker, and her sister Lizzie. After Mary died in January 1863, Lizzie took on the role until her death in September 1878.[99] During his time in Manchester as corresponding clerk and general assistant there is every indication he was an efficient overseer of the family interests.[100]

On his return to the family home of Barmen in the Rhineland in 1844, Engels began work on *The condition of the working class in England*, which was completed in March 1845 and published later that year in Leipzig. Manchester occupies a central place in the book, and the Irish constantly recur both in the discussion of individual cities and in a section specifically on Irish immigration.[101] In his attitudes Engels was clearly influenced by contemporary prejudices about 'national character' and by Thomas Carlyle's vivid polemic of 1839, accepting his arguments that the Irish had lowered working-class morals, living standards and wages.[102] In describing their living conditions he argues that they have grown up almost without civilisation and with filth, drunkenness, ragged clothing, lacking furniture and sharing their domestic space with animals, usually pigs. He specifically praised Kay's 1832 publication as 'an excellent pamphlet', and described Little Ireland in detail, designating it 'the most horrible spot'.[103] Yet, for all his strictures, he distances himself from Carlyle's assault on the Irish character, describing it as 'exaggerated and one sided', and there are also passages in which he is more generous and understanding of their plight, suggesting that their behaviour, especially their drunken and violent outbursts, might be the desperate reactions of a people struggling to cope with an alien and hostile environment.[104] He argues that the Irish presence deepens the chasm between workers and bourgeoisie, thereby accelerating the revolutionary crisis, and that their open, sentimental and mercurial character leavens the lump of stable coldness in the English outlook. But it appears that Engels's attitudes to the Irish altered as he developed a more sophisticated analysis of the semi-colonial British–Irish relationship, having visited the country with Mary Burns in 1856 and Lizzie in 1869, with Mary doubtless acting as his guide and adviser amongst the Manchester Irish.[105]

The combined result of these writings from Kay and subsequent writers, as they constantly recycled each other's material, was to establish in the popular mind the idea that Irish immigrants in Britain were invariably to be found inhabiting 'Little Irelands', the worst possible quarters of the new cities, living in squalor which they had produced by their own improvidence and fecklessness, lowering the living standards of the native workers by their example and their willingness to work for low wages, congenitally given to drunkenness and violence and threatening the entire structure of society and even the health of the body politic. This crude caricature was used as an instrument of social control, an awful warning of the hellish depths of misery which awaited those of the working class who did not exercise restraint, economy and self-improvement.[106]

But the appeal of such anti-Irish prejudice lay partly in the fact that it was no new thing in English and British cultural history, but was a long-established tradition now renewed in the context of nineteenth-century industrial urban Britain, for whose problems the Irish proved ideal scapegoats. It has been argued that 'Throughout history the most persistent *them* from which English identity differentiated *us* is the Irish' and that 'anti-Irish prejudices constitute one of the longest secular trends in English cultural history'.[107] Like most social constructions, this was a remarkably flexible and multi-dimensional outlook. When Anglo-Irish relations were in a relatively harmonious phase, the Irish were viewed as foolish, emotionally incontinent, especially in their cups, but harmless and good for a laugh. This was expressed in a stream of Irish 'bulls', or jokes, in the newspapers, often with efforts to reproduce an Irish speech pattern and accent. In its account of the May 1847 flooding in Little Ireland, referred to earlier, the *Manchester Courier* could not resist reporting: 'Amidst the danger that was prevalent for a time, some scenes occurred that were not altogether devoid of the comic. We need hardly inform our readers in this poor wretched locality, inhabited almost exclusively by the Irish, there is no scarcity of pigs, and it was not without considerable difficulty and sometimes merriment that some of the grunters were moved to dry land.'[108] In August a *Manchester Guardian* writer, under the appropriate pseudonym Paddiana, reported a conversation with an Irishman who explained that he preferred a lump of hard mouldy bread to stew made from seabirds because 'Faith, I never seen anyone ate them things at all! ... Ogh, I wouldn't take it at all!'[109]

However, when the Anglo-Irish relationship entered fraught periods the less clownish and supposedly more threatening aspects of the allegedly volatile Irish character were highlighted.[110] In Manchester the most vociferous public vehicle for this revival of traditional outlook was the *Manchester Courier*, founded in 1825 in reaction to the steadily mounting campaign to grant Catholic emancipation. But even whilst arguing against a suggestion that Catholic clergy should be paid out of public funds on the grounds that they were a danger to the state, it went on to try and make a significant distinction: 'We do not include under this denomination all members of the Catholic religion indiscriminately; we are speaking merely of the *Irish* Catholics; and whoever will turn to the history of their proceedings during the last rebellion ... will easily convince themselves that there is no crime so black, no cruelty so inhuman, no murder so foul, but has been repeatedly committed under cover of the Roman Catholic faith.'[111] When criticising a petition in support of emancipation in May 1825, the same newspaper dismissed it on the grounds that it was signed by 'the lowest rabble ... [including]... Irish labourers... [and] ... Irish hodmen' and inserted the designation 'a Patlander' in brackets after ten of the first twenty-five signatures, on the clear assumption that this was sufficient to destroy the credibility of the petition.[112]

Allegations of Irish cadging and cunning were common from earliest times, as illustrated by assertions that they were particularly bold and astute in exploiting public and private charity. Mr. Rose, the visiting overseer charged to investigate claims to relief, in his evidence to the commissioners gathering evidence on the state of the Irish poor in early 1834, declared, 'I have no doubt that a great deal of fraud has been practised on the overseers by the Irish ... There is ... more deception about the Irish.'[113] There was also a widespread conviction that the Irish were unduly addicted to drink and illicit distillation, and when they were involved in crimes against the excise their nationality was usually noted.

In January 1848, when Michael Brooks and Michael Garrity were charged with possession of an illicit still, Garrity, in whose house the equipment was found, was described as 'a young Irishman', and was found guilty and sentenced, whilst his companion, his nationality not specified, was discharged.[114] When giving evidence to the commissioners on the state of the Irish poor several of the officials responsible for keeping order in the city declared that whilst illicit distilling was an almost exclusively Irish crime, their overall level of involvement in crime was no greater than Irish numbers in the population.[115]

There was a widespread assumption that the Irish were congenitally and unpredictably violent at both the individual and the group level, and the headline 'An Irish Row' was a regular feature of Manchester newspapers throughout the first half of the nineteenth century. Some reporting focused on violent domestic or neighbour disputes, again with efforts to reproduce Irish accents, and some went to great lengths to emphasise faction fights within the Irish population. In March 1851 there was a report on 'A Raal [sic] Irish Row' in the form of 'a case which convulsed both the magistrates and the parties present at the hearing with laughter'. The charge was 'murtherin and killing against two Irish navigators'. According to the account, 'The entire neighbourhood seemed to be engaged in the melee, fighting with pokers, sticks, and axes, like insensate fiends … it seemed to be concerning the precedence of the rival factions of the McNeills and the Carrolls.'[116] There is good evidence that the common prejudice against the Irish and the districts they inhabited was shared by the authorities charged with the administration of justice in Manchester. When two Irish couples living in Little Ireland appeared in court after a violent neighbour dispute in July 1847, Mr Maud, the magistrate, 'after hearing the prosecution statement, addressed the parties, and said he presumed they were Irish. The prosecutors and prisoners replied in the affirmative – Mr. Maud said the magistrates had come to the determination, where the Irish were concerned, where the Irish quarrelled, and used such weapons as were used in this instance, and exhibited such savage brutality as they invariably did, to send both parties to the sessions, to take their trial. Such savage assaults should have a stop put to them.'[117] The following year, when presiding over a case of alleged stabbing by an Irishman, the same magistrate declared, 'we must have this Irish way of settling differences put a stop to' and sent the case to a higher court where more severe sentences were available.[118] Gradually the conviction grew in some quarters that the Irish were a lower breed of people and possibly not quite sane, as reflected in a report of a faction fight in Killarney in July 1847: 'The screams and yells and savage fury would have done credit to an onslaught of Blackfeet and New Zealanders, while the dancing madness was peculiarly their own.'[119] In the later nineteenth century this would be reflected in the simian features portrayed as characteristically Irish in the cartoons of the day and the pseudo-scientific classification of the Irish as being of a lower level of civilisation than the Anglo-Saxons.[120]

That the Irish were exasperated by such repeated calumnies was revealed by an anonymous Irish correspondent who wrote in December 1848: 'Some time ago, when a crime or outrage was reported, and no clue to the guilty parties obtainable, the customary prefix was "The perpetrators of this base outrage are unknown." This sentence appears to be obsolete now, and the substitute is, "they are supposed to be Irish." This ... ill suits the office of a public journalist, and has a very bad effect.'[121]

## Conclusion

Manchester's earliest links with Ireland were military, commercial and migratory, and with the passage of time all three intensified. By the early nineteenth century Manchester regiments had a long tradition of service in Ireland, Irish regiments were frequently based in the city, and, thanks partly to transport technology, Irish textiles and food were a staple in the city's industry and markets. The spectacular economic take-off of the city proved an increasingly attractive draw for migrants from all parts of Britain, including Ireland. But the accompanying demographic and cultural changes provoked an intense sense of multi-layered crisis within British society. It was the misfortune of the Irish, marked out by religion, accent, politics and, sometimes, language as the most exotic element in Manchester's population until the arrival of east European Jews in the late nineteenth century, to enter Britain in growing numbers as British society was struggling to comprehend and cope with these challenges. It was peculiarly unfortunate that Kay and subsequent writers, who helped make Manchester the epitome of the 'condition of England' question, assigned to the Irish a key role in the painful problems of the new urban industrial age. In so doing they renewed a tradition of 'othering' the Irish as the foil against which the English and later the British had defined themselves, and they established the popular long-lived image of Irish migrants as invariably violent and drunken and dwelling in urban squalor which they themselves had created by their own fecklessness. The arrival of the often fever-ridden impoverished famine refugees in the mid- to late 1840s merely served, in the eyes of some, to confirm this image.

## Notes

1. Peter Aughton, *Liverpool: a people's history* (Lancaster: Carnegie Publishing, 2003), p. 25.
2. Thomas Stevens, *Manchester of yesterday* (Altrincham: Sherratt, 1958), p. 41.
3. William Thompson, *History of Manchester to 1852* (Altrincham: Sherratt, 1967), p. 97.
4. Cormac Ó Gráda, *Ireland: a new economic history 1780–1939* (Oxford: Oxford University Press, 1995), pp. 137–8.
5. Roger Scola, *Feeding the Victorian city: the food supply of Manchester 1770–1870* (Manchester: Manchester University Press, 1992), pp. 45–9.
6. Henry Wilkinson, *Old Hanging Ditch: its trades, its traders and its renaissance* (Manchester: Sherratt & Hughes, 1910), pp. 81–4.
7. *The port of Manchester: a yarn*, Manchester Central Library, Broadside Ballad Collection, Language and Literature Section, f821.04BA1, vol. 1, no. 21.
8. Patrick Fitzpatrick, '"Like crickets to the crevice of a brew house": poor Irish migrants in England, 1560–1640', in P. O'Sullivan (ed.), *The Irish world wide: history, heritage, identity*, vol. 1: *Patterns of migration* (Leicester: Leicester University Press, 1992), pp. 13–35.
9. J.P. Earwaker (ed.), *The Constables' accounts of the Manor of Manchester*, vol. 2: *From the year 1633 to the year 1647 with several important appendices* (Manchester: Cornish, 1892), p. 16.
10. Earwaker (ed.), *Constables' accounts*, vol. 2, pp. 69 and 107.
11. J.P. Earwaker (ed.), *The Constables' accounts of the Manor of Manchester*, vol. 3: *From the year 1643 to the year 1776, with several important appendices* (Manchester: Cornish, 1882), p. 80.
12. Earwaker (ed.), *Constables' accounts*, vol. 3, p. 242.
13. Arthur Redford, *The history of local government in Manchester*, vol. 2: *Borough and city* (London: Longmans Green & Company, 1940), p. 100.
14. *Report on the state of the Irish poor in Great Britain*, House of Commons Parliamentary Papers, 1836, vol. 34: Poor Inquiry, Ireland, Appendix G (henceforth Irish Poor Report), p. xxv.
15. Cyril Falls, *Elizabeth's Irish wars* (London: Constable, 1996).
16. *The Court Leet records of the manor of Manchester*, vol. 1: *From the year 1552 to 1586* (Manchester: Blacklock, 1884), p. 264.
17. Earwaker (ed.), *Constables' accounts*, vol. 2, p. 2.
18. William Axon, *The annals of Manchester: a chronological record from the earliest times to the end of 1885* (Manchester: Heywood, 1898), pp. 43–4.
19. Earwaker (ed.), *Constables' accounts*, vol. 1, p. 42; vol. 3, p. 16.
20. *Manchester Mercury*, 26 May 1772; Earwaker (ed.), *Constables' accounts*, vol. 3, pp. 224, 234.
21. *Manchester Guardian*, 30 March 1830.
22. Harold Hanham, 'Religion and nationality in the mid-Victorian army', in M.R.D. Foot (ed.), *War and society: historical essays in honour and memory of J.R. Western* (London: Elek, 1973), pp. 159–82.

23 John Reilly, *The history of Manchester*, vol.1 (Manchester: Bell, 1861), pp. 281, 284.
24 Ruth A.M. Harris, *The nearest place that wasn't Ireland: early nineteenth century Irish labour migration* (Ames: Iowa State University Press, 1994).
25 C. Bolton, *Salford Diocese and its Catholic past: a survey* (Salford: Catholic Diocese, 1950), p. 174.
26 Manchester Central Library, Broadside Ballad Collection, Language and Literature Section, LF 398.8.S9, vol. 5, no. 407.
27 Manchester Central Library, Broadside Ballad Collection, Language and Literature Section, Q 398.8.S9, vol. 4, no. 510.
28 *Manchester City News*, 22 June 1889.
29 Irish Poor Report, pp. xlvii–xlviii.
30 Mick Burke, *Ancoats lad: the recollections of Mick Burke* (Radcliffe: Richardson, 1985), p. 61. In the 1960s Irish labourers were still being engaged at 'hiring fairs' in the Yorkshire Dales (personal knowledge).
31 *Manchester Guardian*, 19 October 1882.
32 Thompson, *History of Manchester to 1852*, p. 103.
33 John O'Dea, *The story of the old faith in Manchester* (London: Washbourne, 1910), pp. 210–11.
34 A. Livingstone, C.W.H. Aikman and B. Hart (eds), *Muster roll of Prince Edward Stuart's army 1745–6* (Aberdeen: Aberdeen University Press, 1984), pp. 194–9.
35 Anon., *Manchester vindicated: being a compleat collection of the papers lately published in defence of the town in the Chester Courant* (London: Adams, 1749), p. 6.
36 O'Dea, *Story of the old faith*, p. 210.
37 *Returns of Papists 1767 Diocese of Chester, transcribed under the direction of E.S. Worrall*, Catholic Record Society Occasional Paper no. 1 (London: Catholic Record Society, 1980), pp. 88–90.
38 John Holt, *General view of the agriculture of the County of Lancaster with observations on the means of improvement* (London: Nicoll, 1795), p. 213.
39 Anon., *The Manchester guide: a brief historical description of the towns of Manchester and Salford, the public buildings and the charitable and literary institutions* (Manchester: Aston, 1804), p. 123. Capitalisation as in original.
40 Mervyn Busteed and Rob Hodgson, 'Irish migration and settlement in early nineteenth century Manchester, with special reference to the Angel Meadow district in 1851', *Irish Geography*, 27:1 (1994), p. 4.
41 Gerard Connolly, 'Catholicism in Manchester and Salford, 1770–1850: the quest for "Le Chrétien quelconque"' (Ph.D. dissertation, Department of History, University of Manchester, 1980), pp. 137–9, 413.
42 Mervyn Busteed, 'Irish migrant settlement in early nineteenth century Manchester', *Manchester Genealogist*, 32:1 (1996), p. 22.
43 Irish Poor Report, p. 64.
44 F.O. Blundell, *Old Catholic Lancashire* (London: Burns, Oates and Washbourne, 1938), vol. 2, p. 39. Rook Street was the site of the first purpose-built Catholic church in Manchester.

45 Don MacRaild, *Irish migrants in modern Britain 1750-1922* (London: Macmillan, 1999), chap. 1: 'Economy, poverty and emigration'.
46 James Murphy, *Ireland: a social, cultural and literary history, 1791-1891* (Dublin: Four Courts Press, 2003), p. 95.
47 Timothy O'Neill, 'A bad year in the Liberties', in E. Gillespie (ed.), *The Liberties of Dublin: its history, people and future* (Dublin: O'Brien Press, 1977), p. 81.
48 Brenda Collins, 'Proto-industrialisation and pre-famine emigration', *Social History*, 7:2 (1982), pp. 127-46.
49 Mary E. Daly, *The famine in Ireland* (Dundalk: Dundalgan Press, 1986), p. 2.
50 Kevin Whelan, 'The modern landscape', in F.H.A. Aalen, K. Whelan and M. Stout (eds), *Atlas of the Irish rural landscape* (Cork: Cork University Press, 1997), pp. 79-81.
51 Roy Foster, *Modern Ireland 1600-1972* (London: Penguin, 1989), p. 320; Cormac Ó Gráda, *Ireland before and after the famine: explorations in economic history, 1800-1925* (Manchester: Manchester University Press, 1988), p. 73; Ciaran Ó Murchadha, *The great famine: Ireland's agony, 1845-1852* (London: Continuum, 2011), pp. 25-6.
52 Frank Neal, 'Liverpool, the Irish steamship companies and the famine Irish', *Immigrants and Minorities*, 5:1 (1986), pp. 28-61; Roger Swift, *The Irish in Britain 1815-1914: perspectives and sources* (London: Historical Association, 1990), p. 7.
53 David Fitzpatrick, 'Emigration 1801-70', in W.E. Vaughan (ed.), *A new history of Ireland*, vol. 5: *Ireland under the union, I: 1801-70* (Oxford: Oxford University Press, 1989), p. 505; Ó Murchadha, *The great famine*, p. 136.
54 David Fitzpatrick, '"A peculiar tramping people": the Irish in Britain, 1801-70', in Vaughan (ed.), *A new history of Ireland*, vol. 5, pp. 627-31
55 John Belchem, *Irish, Catholic and Scouse: the history of the Liverpool-Irish, 1800-1939* (Liverpool: Liverpool University Press, 2007).
56 Irish Poor Report, p. 72.
57 Alan Kidd, *Manchester* (Keele: Ryburn, 1993), pp. 23-5.
58 Samuel Bamford, *Passages in the life of a radical*, ed. with preface by Tim Hilton, (Oxford: Oxford University Press, 1984), p. 32.
59 S. Clark, 'Chorlton mills and their neighbours', *Industrial Archaeology Review*, 2 (1977-8), pp. 207-9; S. Clark, 'A note on Little Ircland', *Industrial Archaeology*, 14 (1979), pp. 36-40; A. Barry, 'Little Ireland: a study of an Irish community in nineteenth century Manchester' (BA dissertation, Department of History, Manchester Metropolitan University).
60 *Manchester Courier*, 19 May 1847.
61 Mervyn Busteed, '"The most horrible spot"? The legend of Manchester's Little Ireland', *Irish Studies Review*, 13 (Winter 1995-96), pp. 12-20.
62 Edward Higgs, *A clearer sense of the census* (London: HMSO, 1996), pp. 17-19; the bacterium was identified in 1854 by Filippo Pacini, but a full understanding of the processes of infection and diffusion was not arrived at until the work of Robert Koch in 1883.
63 'Proceedings of the Special Board of Health, Manchester', vol. 1, 10 November

1831 – 15 August 1832, Appendix, pp. 5–6, Manchester Central Library, Archives Department (henceforth MCLAD), M/9/36/1; reproduced in A. Kidd and T. Wyke, *The challenge of cholera: proceedings of the Manchester Special Board of Health 1831–33*, Record Society of Lancashire and Cheshire, vol. 145 (Manchester: Record Society of Lancashire and Cheshire, 2010).

64 'Proceedings of the Special Board of Health', pp. 52–3.

65 H. Gaultier, *The origins and progress of the malignant cholera in Manchester* (London: Longman, Rees, Orme, Green & Longman, 1833). Gaultier discussed the first 200 cases in detail, and of these only three were from Little Ireland, including two at one address. J. Leigh and N. Gardiner, *History of the cholera in Manchester in 1849* (London: Simpkin & Marshall, 1849). Of the 814 cases recorded, only five were in Little Ireland.

66 Report of the Manchester and Salford Sanitary Association, Rochdale Road Sub-Committee, 1853, p. 8, MCLAD, M126/2/6/10.

67 Report of the Manchester and Salford Sanitary Association, London Road District Sub-Committee, 3 March 1854, p. 3, MCLAD, M126/2/44.

68 Frank Smith, *The life and work of Sir James Kay-Shuttleworth* (London: Murray, 1923; reprinted Bath: Chivers, 1974).

69 'Notes by Dr. W.C. Henry, M.D., F.R.S., made in 1877 on the Edinburgh, Dublin and Manchester Days of J.P. Kay', p. 1, John Rylands University Library, Deansgate, Manchester, Kay-Shuttleworth Papers, Item 1109.

70 James Phillips Kay-Shuttleworth, *The autobiography*, ed. B.C. Bloomfield, Education Library Bulletin Supplement 7 (London: University of London, Institute of Education, 1964), p. 3. Bloomfield discovered the manuscript, written in 1877, when cataloguing Kay's papers.

71 Kay-Shuttleworth, *The autobiography*, p. 4.

72 Kay-Shuttleworth, *The autobiography*, pp. 3–4.

73 Kay-Shuttleworth, *The autobiography*, p. 5.

74 Kay-Shuttleworth, *The autobiography*, p. 6.

75 R.J.W. Selleck, *James Kay-Shuttleworth: journey of an outsider* (London: Woburn Press, 1994), pp. 64–5.

76 James Phillips Kay, *The moral and physical condition of the working classes employed in the cotton manufacture in Manchester* (London, 1832; 2nd edn 1832); new impression with preface, ed. D.W.H. Chaloner (London: Cass & Co., 1970). All quotations are from the 2nd edition. Kay went on to become a Poor Law Commissioner and the first secretary of the Education Office until suffering breakdown in health and resigning in 1849, when he received a baronetcy. On recovery he went into semi-retirement, but retained a keen interest in education, charitable work and Liberal politics. In 1842 he had married Lady Janet Shuttleworth and changed his name to Kay-Shuttleworth as part of the marriage settlement. He died in 1877.

77 Gerry Kearns and Paul Laxton, 'Ethnic groups as public health hazards: the famine Irish in Liverpool and lazaretto politics', in E. Rodriguez-Ocana (ed.), *The politics of the healthy life: an international perspective* (Sheffield: European Association for the History of Medicine and Health, 2002), pp. 13–40.

78 Kay, *The moral and physical condition*, p. 12.
79 James Phillips Kay, *Four periods of public education as reviewed in 1832, 1839, 1846 and 1862* (Brighton: Harvester Press, 1973), pp 101–2.
80 Kay, *The moral and physical condition*, pp. 21–2, 27.
81 Kay, *The moral and physical condition*, pp. 34–6.
82 MacRaild, *Irish migrants*, p. 157.
83 Irish Poor Report, p. xxxix.
84 Irish Poor Report, p. 57.
85 Kay, *Four periods of public education*, p. 153.
86 Gary Messenger, *Manchester in the Victorian age: the half-known city* (Manchester: Manchester University Press, 1985), p. 88; Selleck, *James Kay-Shuttleworth*, p. 65.
87 'Notes by Dr. W.C. Henry', p. 4.
88 Mary Poovey, 'Curing the "social body" in 1832: James Phillips Kay and the Irish in Manchester', *Gender and History*, 5:2 (1993), pp. 196–211.
89 Don MacRaild, 'Irish immigration and the "condition of England" question: the roots of an historiographical tradition', *Immigrants and Minorities*, 14:1 (1995), pp. 67–85; MacRaild, *Irish migrants in modern Britain*, pp. 156–60.
90 Kidd, *Manchester*, p. 22.
91 Asa Briggs, *Victorian cities* (Harmondsworth: Pelican, 1968), pp. 62–6.
92 Redford, *The history of local government in Manchester*, vol. 1: *Manor and township* (London: Longmans Green & Company, 1939), p. 87.
93 Joyce Marlow, 'The day of Peterloo', *Manchester Region History Review*, 3:1 (1989), pp. 3–7.
94 Benjamin Love, *The handbook of Manchester* (Manchester: Love & Barton, 1842), p. 102.
95 Of these the best-known were probably Peter Gaskell, *The manufacturing population of England: its moral, social and physical conditions* (London: Baldwin & Cradock, 1833); Peter Gaskell, *Artisans and machinery: the moral and physical condition of the manufacturing population considered with reference to mechanical substitutes for human labour* (London: Parker, 1836); Rev. Richard Parkinson, *On the present condition of the labouring poor in Manchester, with hints for improving it* (London: Simpkin Marshall, 1841); Joseph Adshead, *Distress in Manchester (tabular and otherwise) of the state of the labouring classes in 1840–42* (London: Henry Hooper, 1842).
96 Briggs, *Victorian cities*, p. 96; L.D. Bradshaw, *Visitors to Manchester* (Radcliffe: Richardson, 1987).
97 P. O'Sullivan, 'Introduction', in P. O'Sullivan (ed.), *The Irish world wide: history, heritage, identity*, vol. 2: *The Irish in the new communities* (Leicester: Leicester University Press, 1992), p. 3; Graham Davis, *The Irish in Britain 1815–1914* (Dublin: Gill & Macmillan, 1991), p. 57.
98 Christopher Clark, *Iron kingdom: the rise and downfall of Prussia 1600–1947* (London: Penguin, 2007), pp. 124–30; Diarmaid MacCullough, *A history of Christianity: the first three thousand years* (London: Penguin, 2010), pp. 139–40.

99 Roy Whitfield, *Friedrich Engels in Manchester: the search for a shadow* (Salford: Working Class Movement Library, 1988).
100 Tristram Hunt, *The frock-coated communist: the revolutionary life of Friedrich Engels* (London: Allen Lane, 2009).
101 Friedrich Engels, *The condition of the working class in England*, trans. F. Wischnewetzky, foreword by V. Kiernan (London: Penguin, 1987), pp. 123–6; the first English-language edition appeared in the USA in 1886 and in the United Kingdom in 1892.
102 Steven Marcus, *Engels, Manchester and the working class* (New York: Norton, 1985), pp. 102–12.
103 Engels, *The condition of the working class*, pp. 109, 98.
104 Engels, The *condition of the working class*, pp. 124–5.
105 Hunt, *The frock-coated communist*, p. 123.
106 Busteed, 'The most horrible spot', pp. 18–19.
107 Patrick O'Sullivan, 'Further reply to Taylor's "The meaning of the north: the displacement of identity: on being Irish"', *Political Geography*, 13:6 (1994), p. 271; L.P. Curtis, jr, *Anglo-Saxons and Celts: a study of anti-Irish prejudice in Victorian Britain* (Bridgeport, Conn.: University of Bridgeport, 1986), p. 27.
108 *Manchester Courier*, 12 May 1847.
109 *Manchester Guardian*, 18 August 1847.
110 David Hayton, 'From barbarism to burlesque: English images of the Irish character', *Irish Economic and Social History*, 15 (1988), pp. 5–31.
111 *Manchester Courier*, 9 April 1825. Italics original.
112 *Manchester Courier*, 21 May 1825.
113 Irish Poor Report, p. 50.
114 *Manchester Courier*, 12 January 1848.
115 Irish Poor Report, pp. 75–8.
116 *Manchester Courier*, 29 March 1851.
117 *Manchester Guardian*, 21 July 1847.
118 *Manchester Courier*, 28 July 1848.
119 *Manchester Guardian*, 17 July 1847.
120 Roy Douglas, Liam Harte and Jim O'Hara, *Drawing conclusions: a cartoon history of Anglo-Irish relations* (Belfast: Blackstaff Press, 1998); Michael de Nie, *The eternal Paddy: Irish identity and the British press* (Madison, Wis.: University of Wisconsin Press, 2004).
121 *Manchester Guardian*, 29 December 1848.

# 2

## Famine influx and residential clustering: Angel Meadow

By the early 1840s, therefore, Manchester, like most British cities, had a significant Irish population concentrated in distinct neighbourhoods. But from 1845 to the early 1850s there was a rapid growth of Irish numbers in the city as refugees from the famine sought relief. They reinforced the existing Irish districts, especially Angel Meadow on the north side of the city, and provoked a mix of alarm and concern amongst the authorities, the existing population and the Catholic Church.

### The famine

Between 1750 and 1845 the population of Ireland grew from approximately 2,600,000 to 8,500,000, or by 225% in nearly a century, possibly the fastest rate of growth in Europe in the second half of the eighteenth century, but less exceptional thereafter.[1] Explanations have been frequently debated, but it seems that the causes were a mix of relatively cheap housing, fuel and food, especially the potato, which came to occupy a highly significant place in the Irish diet, though there is some doubt as to whether it was the cause or result of population growth.[2] The result was that by the mid-1840s, it is estimated, one third of the tillage area of Ireland was under potatoes, supplying 90% of the calorific intake of three eighths of the population in twenty-six counties.[3] There had been severe food shortages in Ireland in the first half of the eighteenth century, outright famine in 1739–41 and poor harvests and occasional outbreaks of infectious disease in the period between 1815 and the early 1840s, but the events of 1845–52 were unprecedented in severity and duration.[4]

The cause of the famine was the fungus *phythophthora infestans*, commonly referred to as 'blight'. It had first appeared in North America in 1843 and may have originated in South America, from where it was exported in guano, or bird droppings, a popular fertiliser of the period. The fungus spreads most rapidly in hot, humid weather, when it is carried in mist and wind. Settling on the above-ground growth of potato leaves in the form of black spots, the infection travels down into the tubers, which rapidly decompose into a sticky black substance giving off a highly offensive stench. It can survive in dormant form in partially infected potatoes, which, when planted as seed potatoes, develop the full infection in the following year's crop, thereby prolonging and spreading the disease. An entire field of potatoes can be destroyed in a few hours.[5]

By early 1845 the infection had appeared in Germany, the Netherlands and Belgium, and in summer it reached the Isle of Wight. Its diffusion was monitored with growing nervousness by informed observers, and on 20 August Dr David Moore, curator of the botanical gardens at Glasnevin in north Dublin, recorded its first appearance in Ireland.[6] At first there was some optimism that it would not spread any further, but by November it was clear that at least one third of the entire national crop was destroyed, thanks in part to an exceptionally wet summer.[7] A smaller crop was expected in 1846 because of the destruction of so much seed potato, and by early August it was clear that over 90% of what had been planted had been destroyed.[8] The result was that very little seed potato was available for planting and the 1847 crop was extremely small, though ironically there was very little blight that year and the average yield per acre was high.[9] The first six months saw particularly harrowing distress, and by mid-year over three million people were dependent on various forms of official and private relief. In Irish folklore this went down as 'Black '47'.[10] In 1848 there was an increase in acreage planted, and it was estimated that yields were about two thirds of normal.[11] The following year the harvest was generally considered good, except in western counties, where blight returned with some severity. In 1850 both blight and distress were clearly in retreat and in 1851 were largely confined to parts of the far west. By early 1852 it was clear that the famine was over.[12]

The impact on the Irish population was catastrophic. Compared with a total of about 8,500,000 in the mid-1840s, the census recorded a population of 6,552,385 in 1851. There has been some debate over the exact level of 'excess mortality' caused by the famine, with estimates varying from just over 1,400,000 to about 1,500,000 between 1845 and 1851.[13] Up to two thirds of deaths may have been caused by disease rather than simple starvation.[14] The most significant killers were typhus and relapsing fever, dysentery and the accompanying diarrhoea. There were also many deaths from measles, scurvy, scarlatina and tuberculosis, and there were outbreaks of smallpox and cholera. Since large numbers of people were moving around the country in search of food or relief works, crowding into workhouses or travelling with the intention to emigrate, infection spread rapidly.[15]

## The famine Irish in Manchester

Emigration was one response to the famine, and it has been estimated that during the period 1845–55 about 2,100,000 people left Ireland. The great majority headed for North America and about 200,000 arrived in Britain, where they put the existing institutions under massive strain and provoked a variety of reactions from locals, especially in Liverpool, Glasgow and Manchester.[16] There were already indications of a growing number of distressed Irish in Manchester by January 1847, when the possibility of opening a soup kitchen was raised at a public meeting. This was subsequently launched by the Manchester Society of Friends, and the German community offered to hold a concert to raise funds to relieve Irish distress.[17] But not everyone was so welcoming. At a meeting of the Poor Law Guardians a Mr Ross reported that he had found 'in the streets of Manchester an immense number of Irish standing at the corners of streets begging … They were not to allow them to starve, and they were encouraging mendicancy by allowing them to stand in the streets. If they but gave them one meal per day, and allowed them to leave the town, they would be relieving the town, and the starving families also.' But his colleague Mr Rickards was to prove far less sympathetic to the Irish at this and subsequent meetings. He was convinced that greater good would be done if the poor were more self-reliant. As for the Irish, he warned against any acts of generosity since they were 'a most improvident people … we should be having them in droves.' But even the *Courier* was moved by the extreme distress of the famine refugees and editorialised on 'the wretched families to be met with at every street corner are painfully numerous. It is harrowing to the feelings to mark the suffering children … because their parents have no place to shelter them, until they go and beg the means of procuring the scantiest and coarsest food.'[18]

When arrangements for relief finally got under way, there was some surprise that at first there were fewer Irish coming forward than expected. Some suggested they were deterred by the requirement that certain forms of relief were linked to labour, whilst others suggested that Irish men were too proud to apply for charity. It was also noted that many refused soup on Ash Wednesday because of religious observance and took only bread.[19] But before long compassion fatigue set in. By late 1847 there were recurring suggestions that the Irish were no longer worth helping because they practised a combination of rebelliousness, cunning and indolence: 'They cry out for bread, and yet can find money or means to procure powder, shot and firearms.' The contrast was made between 'the patience and fortitude with which the English artizans are just now bearing the pangs of hunger and privation ... [they] suffer without a murmur ... the voice of complaint is scarcely ever heard.' It was claimed that whilst the English beggar asked for help 'in the spirit of mild resignation and solicitude' the Irish equivalent 'forces himself in the path of the passer-by, he is blatant with poetic woes, and gives a high colouring to even the slightest misfortune; moreover he lies unscrupulously and with a loud voice'.[20]

The suggestion that the Irish were holding back from relief works was now replaced by increasingly frequent claims that they were defrauding both private and public charity. It was alleged that Irish families were deliberately heading towards towns where they could place their children in factory jobs and move on, leaving them to be assisted by relief works in time of distress.[21] The growing cost of such relief measures also became a cause of resentment, since the burden was borne by taxes levied on local property, though it has been suggested that this has been exaggerated and that extensive relief measures would have been necessary in any case since this was a time of widespread hardship.[22]

A further cause of anti-Irish feeling was the increased incidence of disease which arrived with the Irish, reinforcing the strictures of Kay and associates discussed earlier.[23] By mid-February thirty-three cases of typhus were recorded in the strongly Irish Angel Meadow district on the north side of the city, and by late May a medical officer was reporting to a meeting of the Poor Law Guardians that south Lancashire and north Cheshire as a whole were suffering from 'the introduction by Irish migrants of malignant Typhus fever, scarlet fever, small-pox and measles'.[24] By now the term 'famine fever' was in use for any feverish infection amongst working-class people, clearly implying that the Irish were responsible for its introduction, though at least one observer was careful to point out that it was the famine refugees rather than the long-term residents who were to blame.[25] By mid-year two emergency hospitals had been opened on the north side of the city to cope with 'the rapid spread of the infection in St. George's or Rochdale Road, and other localities inhabited chiefly by the poor Irish' and there were plans for a third.[26] To meet the emergency the city had been divided into five districts, each with an inspector who visited the homes of those who had applied for relief in order to assess the validity of their claims and also to report any in need of medical assistance. In such cases a cart was sent to carry them to hospital. However, it was clear that these arrangements were under severe strain and in some cases were ignored. In one instance an Irish woman who had arrived from Ireland ten weeks earlier had left the fever hospital (where her husband still lay) with her three children, could find no shelter and was found wandering by the local inspector, who supplied her with food.[27] Some lodging house owners simply carried sick people into the street and left them there in the expectation that passing inspectors would arrange for their removal. In late June it was reported that two men and a woman who had arrived from Ireland three months earlier were found lying in a street in Little Ireland in an advanced state of destitution and illness. It appeared that 'when they were found to have the fever, they had been turned out of some lodging house ... and being unable to walk and having no shelter, they had lain down in despair.' Later that day a further five people were found lying on the ground in the same street, 'all sick with fever and enfeebled both by disease and want of food'. The inspector who found them arranged for a cart to take them to the workhouse.[28]

Irish attitudes towards authority were also blamed for the spread of disease. The Egans were an Irish family of seven who shared a cellar in the Ancoats district on the north side of the city with another family of eight. Two of the Egan children had died in the cellar before the family was removed to hospital, and it was alleged that the delay in seeking help was due to 'the reluctance of the Irish to enter the workhouse or the fever hospitals, and the spread of the fever consequent upon their remaining in their confined dwellings, particularly after one member of the family had fallen sick of the disease'.[29] By September 1847 it was reported that the various fevers were abating, but as early as October there was public speculation that the cholera pandemic then raging could soon reach Britain.[30] It was therefore no great surprise that when the first Manchester case was reported in June 1849 it was in an Irish family of six who had arrived in the city twelve days earlier with the intention of obtaining harvest work. They were found sharing a cellar in Angel Meadow with five other Irish families, giving a total of twenty-six inhabitants, and it was reported that when his wife fell ill the husband had been afraid to contact the authorities, fearing that the couple would be sent back to Ireland.[31]

By late 1851 both the Irish influx and the various infections had died away, but in October that year John Harrop, clerk to the Poor Law Guardians, produced a review of the period 1846–51, during which, he claimed, whilst the relief given to native English claimants had risen by less than

7%, that provided for the Irish had increased by over 300%. For one observer this was proof that a change in the law in 1846 which had lowered the residence qualification for relief had been disastrous because it had the result of 'floating an enormous shoal of paupers hither, to quarter themselves on our local poor rates for life … it has secured to thousands of able-bodied Irish paupers a settlement for life in our manufacturing towns – a permanent maintenance out of the rates.' The editorial writer noted 'the notorious unscrupulousness of the Irish poor as to the sanctity of an oath' and alleged, 'hard swearing will always be in greater favour with the Irish pauper in England than hard work'. The writer ended by arguing that the change in the law meant that local ratepayers not only had to bear the burden of greater expense in normal times from local claimants 'but are still further pressed upon by this Celtic incubus'.[32] As already noted, recent research has challenged such assertions, but their significance lies in the fact that even amongst the most well-informed element in the community this was a firmly fixed conviction. The experience of the years 1845–51 had in many ways given new life to traditional anti-Irish sentiment and helps explain the geography of Irish settlement within the city.

## Angel Meadow

By the time of the census of 30 March 1851 there were 52,504 people in the city who had been born in Ireland, or 16.6% of the total population, and to this should be added second and subsequent generations of families born in Ireland.[33] There were some Irish in every part of the city, but the great majority followed the traditional pattern of Irish migrants in concentrating in the poorer working-class districts. However, within these districts there was a marked tendency for the Irish to be residentially segregated from their fellow workers, and certain neighbourhoods were widely known for their strongly Irish nature. As mentioned earlier, by the early 1850s Little Ireland had been largely emptied of its residential population, but from the early days of the century other parts of Manchester had also become known for housing large numbers of Irish. Of these the largest and most enduring was on the north side of the city in an area widely known as 'Angel Meadow' but also, significantly, as 'Irish Town'. For study purposes Angel Meadow will be defined as the area bounded by the River Irk, Miller Street, Rochdale (previously St George's) Road and Vauxhall Street (Figure 1).

Down to the mid-1740s this area had been quite rural, and the first traces of residential development created a small number of quite

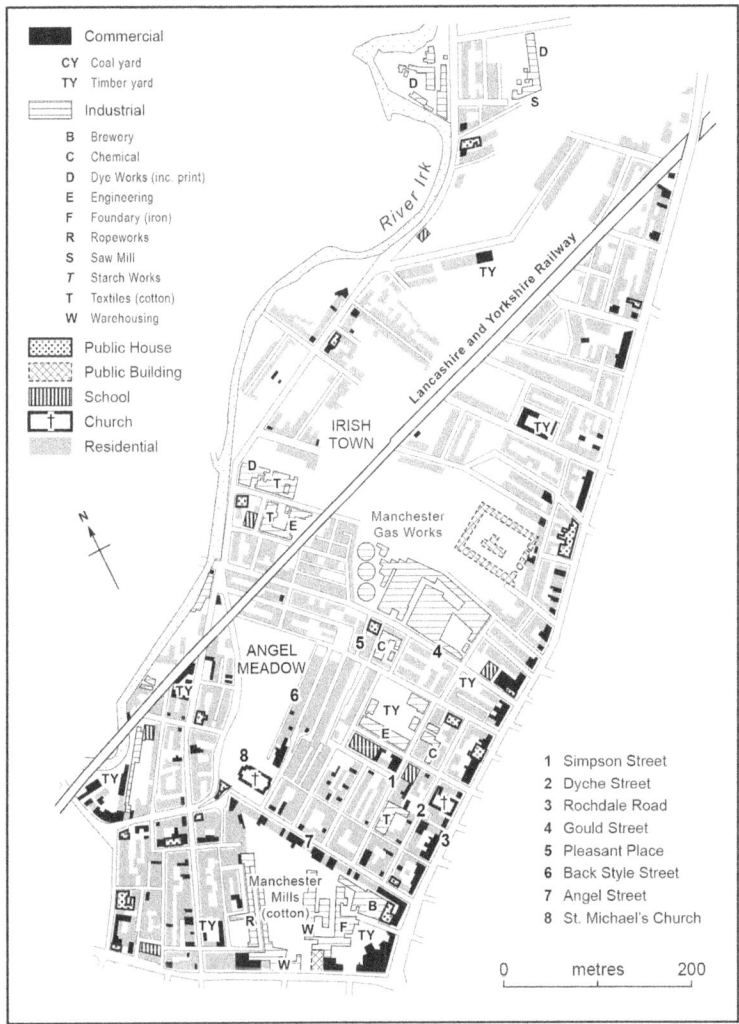

4 Angel Meadow: land use, late 1840s

fashionable streets. By the early 1760s there were Georgian style houses with well-laid-out gardens and orchards along Angel Street and Miller Street on the south-eastern fringe of the area; in 1788 St Michael's Anglican church was opened and quickly became a 'carriage church' patronised by the wealthy. However, developments were under way which transformed the entire district. In 1781–82 Manchester's first steam-powered cotton mill was built by the leading entrepreneur Richard Arkwright at the junction of Angel Street and Rochdale Road on the extreme southern end of the area, and in 1787 vacant land just north of the church was purchased by the Overseers to the Poor for burial of the indigent; Laurent's map of 1795 hints at industrial development at the far northern end.[34] Given that the early mills needed large quantities of water, the banks of the Irk were an optimal location, and by the 1830s the south of Angel Meadow had been totally transformed into one of the most densely inhabited and industrialised parts of the growing city. In 1844 the final major development took place when the Manchester and Leeds (later Lancashire and Yorkshire) railway line was built across the north-western side of the area (Figure 4).[35]

From quite early on the area acquired a reputation for poor housing and living conditions. Some problems were due to physical geography. The underlying geology is a mix of Old Red Sandstone, Permo-Triassic and Carboniferous material, with a heavy overburden of Pleistocene boulder clay, sands, gravels and alluvium. These inhibit drainage and from the outset created problems for the disposal of household and industrial waste, which lay on the surface and quickly putrefied. A further problem was created by the fact that there was a fall of about twenty metres from Rochdale Road to the river Irk, leading to a gravity flow of liquid down streets parallel to the slope which accumulated at the bottom of the gradient. Inspection of the area was the responsibility of the Rochdale Road Visiting Committee of the Sanitary Association, which in a report of April 1853 declared that a principal problem for the district was the presence of large pools of standing water. In one case in a space between two houses this had resulted in 'a huge hole filled with animal matter, which serves as a sort of public privy'.[36] Additional problems were created by the dumping of household and industrial waste in the Irk, which periodically flooded, carrying the effluent into streets and houses. The pattern of industrial development generated a great deal of noxious material. Along the banks of the river and on the nearby slopes were breweries, chemical works, dye works and starch works as well as mills, foundries, warehouses, timber yards, sawmills, a ropeworks and the Manchester gasworks.

In the absence for a long period of any area-wide integrated system for disposal of household and industrial waste, the result was that the Irk became notorious as an open drain. Kay in 1832 described it as a receptacle for 'excrementious matters ... and filth of the most pernicious character',[37] and just over a decade later Engels, standing on a nearby bridge, described it as a narrow, coal-black, foul-smelling stream, full of debris and refuse … In dry weather, a long string of the most disgusting blackish-green slime pools are left standing … from the depths of which bubbles of miasmatic gas constantly arise and give forth unendurable stench even on the bridge forty or fifty feet above … The stream itself is checked every few paces by high weirs, behind which slime and refuse accumulate and rot in thick masses.[38]

The intention behind much of the housing in Angel Meadow, constructed by speculative builders on the areas left vacant between the mills, factories and foundries, was summed up by one Manchester observer: 'The grand point of view of such builders was to obtain the largest possible amount of interest in their outlay, consequently houses were run up in the very slightest manner, without sewerage, yards or even what you would call a road to them.'[39] Subsequent cartographic study and recent archaeological excavation have refined this image. The worst housing in the city was to be found in the medieval core around the cathedral. Towards the end of the eighteenth century there was a good deal of construction for hand-loom weavers working at home, and excavation has revealed that some such structures may have been built in Charter Street, Angel Meadow. Each of the houses consisted of two ground floor rooms and two above, often with long windows to provide light for the weavers. There were also two roomed cellars, some with independent access. Whilst this was clearly rather basic accommodation, the subsequent rapid growth of population and the consequent building boom seem to have led to a steady decline in housing quality. By 1831 much of the rest of Angel Meadow and nearby Ancoats had been filled in with small two-up two-down houses with shallow foundations only two or three bricks deep, often with back access, if any, only via a narrow lane and doors leading into a back yard. Others were built in the style of small courts around a central open space.[40] Some had cellars which landlords rented out for accommodation. During this period the trend to multi-family occupation by groups of families and lodgers became common. Provision of toilets, water supply and sewage relief was utterly inadequate for the numbers involved, and ill health and contagious disease were endemic.

A steady succession of investigators visited Angel Meadow from the 1840s onwards, each observer almost striving to outdo their predecessors in the horrors they uncovered to the point where their comments bordered on the voyeuristic. In 1840 Dr R.B. Howard declared that despite some recent improvements, many streets in Angel Meadow were still 'in an extremely wet, filthy and disgraceful state' and described one as being marked out by 'a large collection of dirt, manure, &c., being the accumulation from a pigsty, and the drainage from a neighbouring filthy street'.

He went on to suggest that Angel Meadow and Ancoats, taken together, were 'by far the worst quarters of the town' in terms of the quality of the streets and houses and the poverty of the residents.[41] Another commentator writing in 1844 noted how 'This district is situated on a thick bed of strong brick clay, and it is impossible any water can be conducted off by absorption ... all the streets were unpaved and unsewered'.[42] Engels was therefore following a well-trodden path when he toured the area and wrote at length on the layout and physical condition of the housing, sketching plans to illustrate his argument on the ways in which the alignment of streets and lanes totally blocked out ventilation and fresh air from entire blocks of houses. Of the district in general he wrote:

> Here all the features of a city are lost. Single rows of houses or groups of streets stand ... like little villages on the naked, not even grass-grown clay soil; the houses, or rather cottages, are in bad order, never repaired, filthy, with damp, unclean, cellar dwellings; the lanes are neither paved nor supplied with sewers, but harbour numerous colonies of swine penned in small sites or yards ... The mud in the streets is so deep that there is never a chance, except in the driest weather, of walking without sinking ankle-deep in every step.[43]

In 1849 the *Morning Post*, prompted by the outbreak of cholera then working through the industrial cities of Britain, commissioned a series of articles on the condition of the urban poor by the journalist Angus Reach. His reports on Manchester and the surrounding towns were published in October and November, when he described Angel Meadow as 'The lowest, most filthy, most unhealthy, and most wicked locality in Manchester'.[44]

The foundation of the Manchester and Salford Sanitary Association in 1852 brought some order and regularity to the surveys of the district, but, given that their prime function was the systematic collection of evidence to bolster the argument for sanitary reform, there was still a tendency to emphasise distress rather than progress. In 1853 the acting secretary explicitly stated, 'My object has been to visit the worst parts of the city, those inhabited by the poorer classes, and to ascertain what are the great evils which there exist; and I have altogether omitted to make mention of those localities which are occupied by the better classes, and which are in a fair and satisfactory condition.'[45] The Rochdale Road committee constantly reported on poor drainage, broken flags and steps, putrid sheets of standing water and occasionally the stench and health hazard from the keeping of pigs or donkeys in private houses.[46] But it was the inadequate provision of toilets and the state of the few which were available which provoked the most frequent and horrified condemnation. In one case the committee drew attention to the fact that in Flag Row '4 houses have no petty [privy] at all. It is well that a rail road is at hand, where the people say they have recourse in their extremity.'[47] Cellars were also a recurring concern. Originally intended for storage purposes, they were rented out to the poorer migrants who crowded into the fast growing city, and this habit became strongly entrenched. Since they were poorly ventilated, overcrowded and ill drained, they were notable sources of infection in the successive outbreaks of infectious disease. In May 1847 a doctor reminded the Poor Law Guardians that in Angel Meadow, 'From the peculiarity of the district, fever and other epidemics are rendered more fatal than in most others; the poor, dwelling in narrow streets and damp cellars, where scarcely a breeze of fresh air visits them, and being so densely crowded, it cannot be a matter of surprise that the ravages of death are so fearful', and he went on to describe one cellar he had visited which housed twenty-seven people, including the body of a child who had recently died.[48] The Rochdale Road committee regularly viewed such places, noting in one visit to a property in Ludgate Street that a fourteen-foot-square cellar containing four beds had 'no ventilation, the heat quite oppressive' and that for nine cellars in Tebbutt Street there was '1 privy, which is in a most dreadful condition, no door, cannot be used, it is in a state of great filth'.[49]

Blame was attributed to various people and institutions. As the committee noted in one visit to Flag Alley, 'the tenants curse the landlord as the cause of the nuisances by which they are surrounded', and it was reported that one landlord of houses in Back Simpson Street had boasted that his overcrowded, damp and dirt properties had not cost him 'one penny in 30 years'.[50] The committee occasionally suggested that the local council was failing in their duty, citing an example where it had been informed of problems but 'the authorities take no notice of these nuisances, notwithstanding that they are repeatedly applied to for the removal of night soil'.[51] But far more often blame was attributed to the bad habits and general fecklessness of the residents themselves. This had certainly been a point made by Kay in his writings of 1832, where he argued in particular that the bad habits exhibited by the Irish and their willingness to live in the cheapest housing and spend their money on alcohol had provided an all-too-attractive role model for the native working classes. Subsequent commentators did not hesitate to follow this line of argument, including his strictures on the Irish. Consequently the reports of the Rochdale Road committee are notable for the frequent tendency to give detailed accounts of squalor interspersed with throwaway remarks stating that local residents were often largely to blame and frequent asides noting the presence of the Irish. All this implied that the Irish were by nature largely responsible for the conditions in which they lived. Problems in Nicholas Street were blamed on tenants, who were described as 'very poor, ignorant and unclean'; those in nearby Back Simpson Street were put down to the fact that 'Habits of the tenants very dirty and indifferent.' Overall, it was stated, 'The dwellings generally in a very dirty state, the inhabitants of the lowest order, principally Irish.'[52] In an effort to change these habits the Sanitary Association arranged public lectures, as in March 1854, when it was emphasised that 'The WORKING CLASSES are earnestly invited to attend.'

In time national and local legislation imposed basic requirements in terms of the dimensions and layout of rooms, access to water and provision of privies, and sewer systems were laid. A bylaw of 1844 declared that each new house should have a privy with a door, and the Police Act of the same year authorised the demolition of houses without independent back access and banned future construction of such houses. In 1866 they were declared unfit for occupation. The local council and police were empowered to fumigate, whitewash and if necessary seal up cellar dwellings, and in 1853 they were declared illegal.[53] The Sanitary Association was keen to ensure that regulations were applied, as in March 1854 when a committee noted that in Edmund's Court 'twelve cottages are now in course of construction, the bedrooms of which are directly over the privies, contrary to the Sanitary Act, neither are the privies as numerous as the Act requires'.[54] But even this committee was moved to admit, however grudgingly, that by early 1854 'In a general way, there is great improvement with respect to paving, sewering & a good supply of water', though it could not resist the rider 'Exceptions made'.[55]

Perhaps the features of Angel Meadow which drew the most long-lasting concern were the proliferation of cheap lodging houses of varying size and quality and the density of occupation in cellars. Successive investigators visited such places and shuddered in horrified fascination. Some dwelt at length on the undoubtedly deplorable physical conditions they encountered. In December 1847, when a Mr Dunn proposed 'Sanitary Reform' at the Young Men's Society on the occasion of the fourteenth anniversary of the Scotch Church in St Peter's Square, he described in detail a nocturnal visit to Angel Meadow in the company of a doctor from the Royal Infirmary and two police officers. At the outset he warned his hearers that he would 'lay aside all false delicacy and consider that he was treating on a disease and addressing them as physicians'; he went on to share his experience of 'what might be fitly termed a plague spot, where festering disease accumulates and wickedness and misery increase, spreading contagion far and wide'. He described how in a garret he found 'the air being so foul and fetid that it made the throat sore to breathe', whilst in a cellar twelve feet square he found ten or eleven people: 'As to furniture, there was none, and they slept upon shavings, and the bedclothes consisted of rags and the clothes they wore upon their backs.'[56]

Throughout the rest of the century the lodging houses of Angel Meadow attracted attention. In a series on 'The slums' in February 1870 the *Manchester Guardian* returned on two occasions to the district and made a point of visiting a selection of homes and lodging houses, the reporter noting, 'Our readers must pardon us if our language becomes somewhat strong, the savour of the place and our indignation alike are so strong.'[57] The following year the newspaper returned to the area in a series on how the census was conducted in the slums, focusing in particular on the smaller streets and courts off Angel Street and St Michael's Square and again noting the number and condition of the lodging houses, though also observing that cellar dwellings, whilst not quite eliminated, were fast disappearing.[58] Even at the end of the century, when much national and local legislation attempted to regulate housing and street layout, a Rev. Mercer reported on both the persistent overall poverty and the bad living conditions and noted the presence of a total of 257 lodging houses, providing over 2,500 beds, many of which would have been multiply occupied in shifts at a charge varying from three pence to one shilling. An interview with a resident noted that the chief problems were overcrowding, filth and the criminality of the clientele.[59] Six years later there were still concerns about the housing in the district, but when the local alderman Daniel McCabe and the local MP Charles Schwann led a delegation to the council the relevant committee could report some progress in the demolition or closure of the worst housing, but rather less in the provision of replacement accommodation.[60]

## Societal threats

Underlying the concern for the living conditions and health of the inhabitants of such districts was a multi-layered fear of total societal breakdown, verging at times on moral panic. Kay in his 1832 writings argued that, unless reform was undertaken in areas such as Angel Meadow, there was

> a turbulent population, which, rendered reckless by dissipation and want, misled by the secret intrigues and excited by the inflammatory harangues of demagogues, has frequently committed daring assaults on the liberty of the more peaceful portions of the working classes, and the most frightful

devastations on the property of their masters ... Their misery, vice and prejudice will prove volcanic elements, by whose explosive violence the structure of society may be destroyed.[61]

Many investigators were shocked at the moral dangers flowing from the mixing of the ages and genders in the overcrowded accommodation. The reporter who visited Angel Meadow in early 1870 wrote with certainty, 'That decency and morality can be maintained amongst promiscuous bedfellows is beyond hope.'[62] The presence of individuals known to the police as thieves was seen as a bad influence on the young, but a more persistent concern was the sex trade. Mr Dunn reserved his greatest sense of shocked incredulity for a situation where a mother lived off the daughter's earnings as a sex worker. Visiting at 1.30 a.m., he found: 'the daughter had just returned home, and it appeared that the mother regularly sits up for her return, and her tea ready for her, with as much care as if she were a good mother, waiting the return of her child from an honest and hard day's work. Indeed, it was evident she had no other feeling than this about her horrid and unnatural livelihood.'[63] Fifty years later the same phenomenon concerned Rev. Mercer, who discussed what he described as 'immorality ... a most painful subject ... the women of the slums are more degraded than the men ... And the class of fallen girls and women is very large and aggressive.' Of the 133 houses in Angel Street and Charter Street, he calculated that only twenty-nine were not involved in prostitution. He went on: 'So recognised are the women of this class as an integral part of the community, that from childhood their mode of life is looked upon as simply one trade the more, one more way of getting a living ... until the remedies are found and applied, think of the flood of virulent poison, of syphilitic disease, which is being distilled into the veins of poor humanity.'[64]

For some the immediate personal danger was more a more pressing issue. Recalling early efforts to provide education in Angel Meadow, one charity worker reminisced:

> Like a huge rabbit warren, it was threaded by a number of narrow and dark passages and streets, which gave every facility for the wrong-doer, who in this district had become much in evidence, to waylay a victim and escape, easily evading capture. The result was that ... Angel Meadow [was] the haunt of the low, the idle and the vicious. It was not safe for respectably dressed persons to pass through the streets alone, even at midday, and many who as a result of either ignorance or bravado, attempted to do so, paid the penalty by being waylaid, or otherwise assaulted or robbed. Bad as it was in the daytime, it was ten times worse by night, when many who dared not be seen in broad daylight would venture forth in search of victims.[65]

Many commentators were convinced that the problem was the lack of religious belief and observance. This was certainly true of Kay, the devout Christian, who argued that 'with pure religion and undefiled, flourish frugality, forethought and industry ... with unfeigned regret, we are therefore constrained to add, that the standard is exceedingly debased, and that religious observances are neglected amongst the operative population of Manchester.' As a solution he pointed to the work of various Christian charities in Boston and London but noted their absence from Angel Meadow and surrounding districts.[66] Several of the Sanitary Association visitors clearly shared this outlook. When they saw the condition of the old burial ground behind St Michael's church they remarked that 'it affords a scene of constant gambling & fighting, particularly on the Lord's day, & also is a convenient place for people throwing down their nuisance, refuse & c ... & it is most desirable that some immediate steps should be taken to remove what is so evidently most detrimental to the health, as well as the morals, of the people.'[67] In one visit investigators

5  Child street hawker

drew attention to what they clearly believed was a telling contrast. The situation in one house was described thus 'One room ... 5 inmates, all very clean go to St. Thomas's church, 2 children attend the Sunday School. English. 2nd room very close & sickly smell ... altogether very dirty.'[68] In 1870 when another visitor went into Angel Meadow on a Sunday morning he contrasted what was happening in churches with what he found: 'The generality of the men who live in this quarter are not greatly given to religious exercises and, as the public houses are not opened, and the museums and botanical gardens are closed by the government, they have little else to do on a Sunday morning but lie in bed.'[69]

One of the features which both alarmed and fascinated observers was the lively street life of the district. In addition to the well-patronised pubs and run-down shops, the area was notable for the constant bustle and movement of a great variety of people through the streets.[70] Some were on the way to and from local factories and mills, but others were part of the informal social life and economy of the street. Some were beggars, others confidence tricksters and pickpockets or members of the 'scuttling gangs, organized bodies of thieves and low characters of every type [who] held their headquarters there'.[71] Some were simply local people passing time of day with neighbours, doubtless seeking relief from the crowded and unpleasant conditions indoors. Others were hawkers, some of them very young children, supplementing the family income by selling fruit, boot and shoe laces or goods such as matches, tapers, kindling, spills and cutlery made at home (Figure 5). There were also itinerant street entertainers, conjurors and musicians playing barrel organs and fiddles, whilst the tradition of the wandering ballad singers, performing and selling their wares, persisted into the late nineteenth century. In early 1870 a reporter in a house in Angel Meadow encountered 'a vagrant blind singer, who says he gets his living in the streets by singing "a few patriotic songs in the ould Irish style"'.[72]

## Irish residential segregation

This latter reference highlights one of the defining features of Angel Meadow, namely the fact that it was the largest and most long-lasting of all the Irish districts in Manchester. As noted earlier, by 1819 a strong Irish presence was notable. Bancks' map of 1831 records an 'Irish Row' at the extreme northern end of the district, suggesting that its character was sufficiently well established to have passed into local nomenclature.[73] In November 1847 a medical officer referred to it as 'what may not inaptly be termed the "Irish ghetto"'.[74] Visitors almost invariably commented on

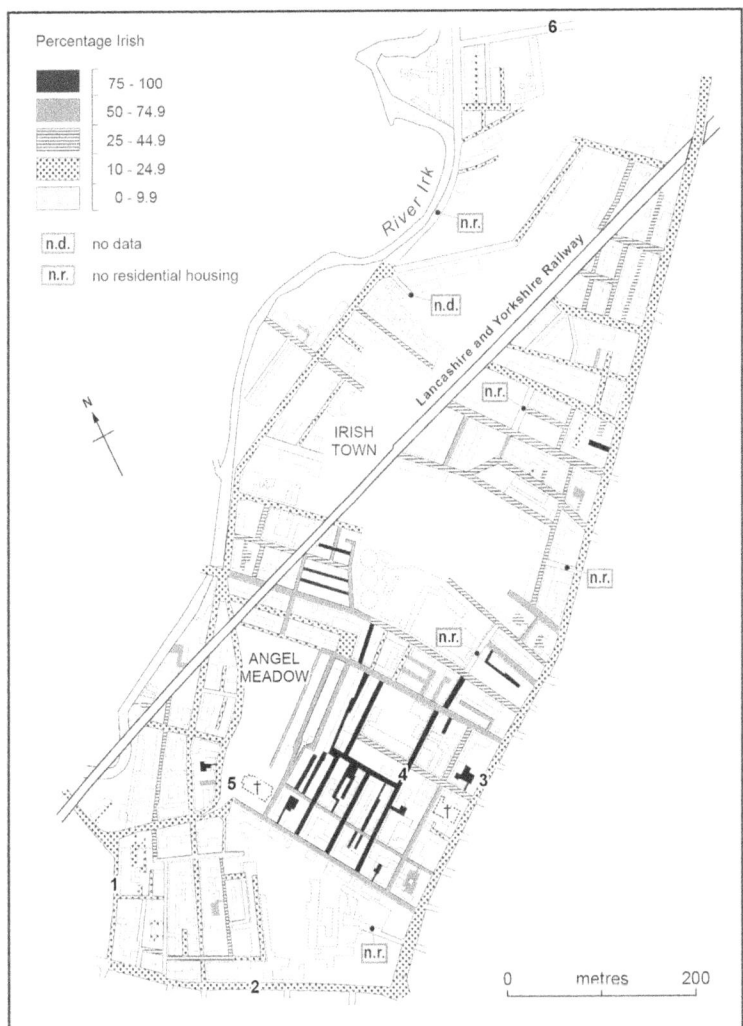

6  Percentage of Irish in Angel Meadow, 1851

the presence of Irish residents, and by association the link between Irish and squalor, already made in reference to Little Ireland, was well on its way to becoming part of the stereotype of Irish migrants in urban Britain.

The extent and pattern of the Irish presence in the district are illustrated by analysis of the enumerators' returns for the 1851 census, taking as the dimensions of the district those noted earlier (Figure 1).[75] On

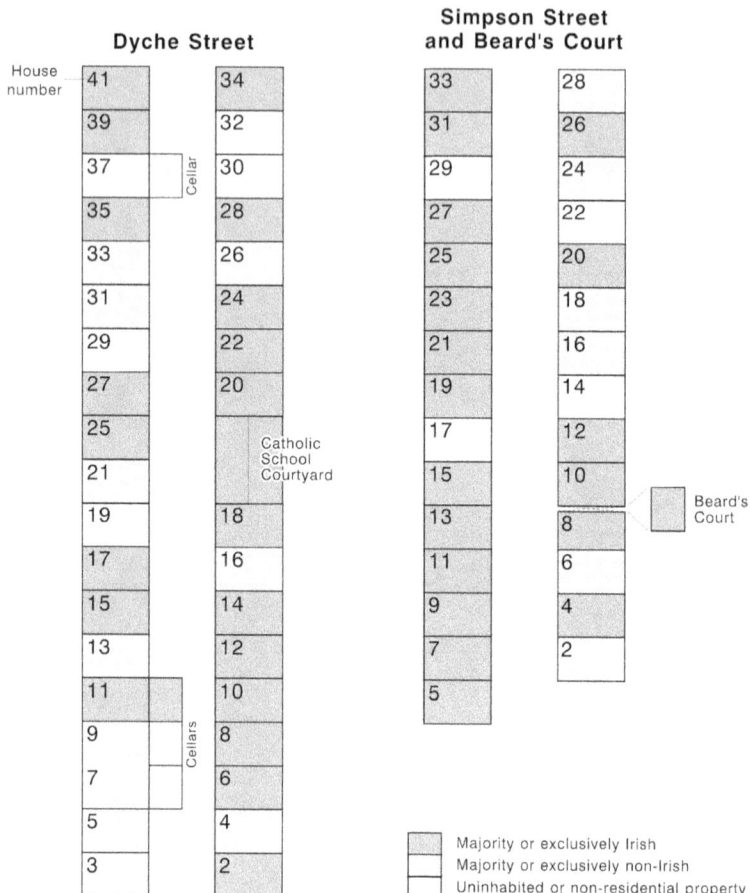

7 Irish presence in Dyche and Simpson streets, Angel Meadow, 1851

census night, 30 March 1851, this area was found to have 18,347 residents, of whom 6,775 (36.9%) were born in Ireland and a further 1,273 born elsewhere to two Irish-born parents who could be traced in the census, giving a total of 8,048 (43.9%) of the population as Irish by this definition. At the outset, therefore, this acts as a useful counter to the easy assumption that the area was uniformly Irish. But mapping those streets which had an Irish majority in their population revealed a pattern of marked residential segregation: fifty-six of the streets in Angel Meadow had an Irish majority, and 5,840 (72.6%) of the Irish lived in such streets. Moreover, the streets which were most strongly Irish, with more than 75% of their residents Irish, were concentrated in a dense network in the south-east of the district, well back from the main roads and streets in a dense interconnecting network of smaller streets and courts (Figure 6).[76] Conversely, in the south-western and north-western parts of the district, there were notably few Irish.[77]

If the scale is altered and individual streets with an Irish majority are examined, there are indications that the Irish tended to concentrate on particular sides or parts of streets. In Simpson Street in the heart of the most intensely Irish area, there were 235 residents in 1851, 75.3% of whom were Irish, and there were twenty-seven inhabited houses; of these houses twenty had an Irish majority, seventeen had an Irish house on at least one side, and fourteen were on the same side of the street (Figure 7). One particularly sensitive measure of social interaction is the selection of marriage partners. In Angel Meadow there were 2,064 married Irish people recorded, of whom 1,842 (89.2%) had married another Irish person. Even if allowance is made for the fact that some would have married before leaving Ireland, it still implies that a large number of the migrant Irish looked for partners amongst their fellow Irish. Clearly at this point in mid-century a significant number of the Angel Meadow Irish were clustering in specific neighbourhoods, residing separately from other people of very similar socio-economic status, and there are strong indications this was also happening in other parts of the city.[78]

The explanation for this pattern of residential segregation lies in a combination of economic resources, the Manchester context and Irish social solidarity. In terms of personal economic resources there were always some quite prosperous people amongst the Manchester Irish, and there are indications they increased in number as time went on, but nonetheless the great majority were relatively poor, especially those who came as famine refugees in the second half of the 1840s.[79] It is scarcely surprising therefore that large numbers were living in the poorer working-class districts of the city in low-quality accommodation. But whilst the Irish shared the general poor housing, living conditions and poverty of the native working class in such districts, they clearly had a tendency to residential clustering with fellow Irish. This can be interpreted as a defensive reaction to the culture shock they suffered when they encountered what must have seemed a remarkably alien physical and sometimes actively hostile cultural environment in Manchester.

The Irish migrants who arrived in Manchester were an overwhelmingly rural people with skills and customs derived from mixed peasant farming. The great majority were strongly Catholic in religion, mostly from the relatively remote north-western counties of Leitrim, Roscommon, Mayo and Galway and largely Irish-speaking.[80] By contrast they were faced with making their way in what for a time was probably the most dynamic urban industrial centre in the world, with an English-speaking and strongly Nonconformist Protestant tradition. One Catholic commentator declared that 'this Catholic population [of Angel Meadow] are the children of Irish parents, who have been driven over here in their poverty, and have come from the simple peasant life on the hill sides and green pastures of their native country'.[81] It is hardly surprising therefore that in reaction to this bleak landscape they fell back on those traditions of social solidarity based on familial linkages, locality and communal cooperation which marked life in peasant rural Ireland. From the outset local observers remarked on the readiness with which those Irish already established in the city took in new arrivals. In his evidence to the commissioners compiling the Irish Poor Report, Peter Ewart, a Manchester cotton entrepreneur, noted how 'Many [Irish] ...come over in order to live on their friends and relations till they can get employment. The Irish are very kind and hospitable to each other and assist one another very much in sickness and distress.'[82] Another Manchester businessman, James Aspinall Turner, noted: 'On account of the number of Irish in Manchester they feel almost as if they were coming to an Irish town, and they show here their national character of hospitality; though they have little to give, they give what they have. They will take in a family of fresh immigrants, though they have only one room, and lie on straw themselves.'[83] Information linkages based on family, friends, locality and institutions have always been highly significant in prompting and encouraging migration, and this process of chain migration was certainly at work in the Manchester situation.[84] The Manchester silk mill owner James Taylor admitted that when he was having trouble with his workers he sent to Ireland for replacements: 'The whole family comes, father, mother and children ... The communications are generally made through the friends of the parties in my employ. I have no agent in Ireland.'[85] Other witnesses remarked, 'Those Irish who are established here send to their friends in Ireland and invite them over, telling them they will do better here than there ... once established, they bring more over, by conveying information to their friends when they see a chance of their finding employment. We always find the future importation of colonists [sic] ... depends principally upon the description of the first colonists.'[86]

This process was certainly at work during 1847, the height of the famine influx, when the search was not so much for employment as for a greater chance of simple survival. In January 1847 it was reported that 'a poor

Irishman who had been here some time, living in a cellar, had his son, son's wife, and four children come over from Ireland and place themselves upon the old man, and the result was that he died; for there was but one bed; the woman fell ill; he gave up the bed to her, lying upon the damp floor and he caught cold and died in a few days.'[87] As already noted the influx grew as the situation in Ireland became more desperate. In late March 1847 it was reported at one of the soup kitchens that amongst their applicants was a widow from Castlerea, Co. Roscommon, with six small children who had left her three-acre holding when threatened with eviction and was given twenty-five shillings to leave voluntarily. She had travelled to Manchester because she had a sister in Little Ireland but arrived to find her dependent upon the local soup kitchen. Since she was a newcomer, strictly speaking she had no right to relief, but at the sight of the children 'with their large sunken eyes, and thin wasted faces … with their little knees bare of clothing, and as bare of flesh … [they] were supplied with soup and bread at the kitchen, and they ate most voraciously'.[88] There are also occasional indications that groups from particular parts of Ireland settled in the same neighbourhood of Manchester and took in lodgers from their home district. The 1851 census reveals that in no. 72 Pump Street there lived the Cavanagh family, the parents born in Co. Kildare, the daughter in Manchester and the two lodgers also from Kildare. In no. 78 all five of the McCann family were born in Kildare, and in no 82 all four of the Waters family plus their nephew were also born in Kildare.[89] In 1849 the reporter Angus Reach noted that the dozen or so people he had encountered in an Angel Meadow cellar were all from Westport, Co. Mayo.[90]

Poverty, readiness to accommodate fellow migrants and the large numbers arriving over a short period in the mid- to late 1840s led to a notable tradition of multiple occupation of living space. In 1844 J.G. Kohl noticed that some Irish 'have voluntarily given up their dwellings in order to live cheaper, by sharing that of another family'.[91] This phenomenon was certainly to be found in Angel Meadow, where one reporter noted, 'it is not uncommon to find 20 or 30 persons living in one house, where there is not accommodation for one-third of that number'.[92] Thus in Angel Meadow the density of occupation was 8.7 persons per house in houses where there was an Irish majority and 6.4 per house where the majority was non-Irish.[93] One result of this high density of occupation has been the tendency to argue that the Irish had a notable tendency to concentrate in cellars. This was certainly the conviction of commentators from Kay onwards, and Reach was clearly of the same opinion when, having visited Angel Meadow and looked at some of the worst housing, he declared,

'There were few or no Irish in the houses we had just visited. They live in more wretched places still – the cellars.'[94] However, analysis of the census returns revealed that there were seventy-nine cellar dwellings in Angel Meadow, of which only twenty-six had a majority of Irish, one was equally divided and fifty-two had a non-Irish majority; of the total of 436 people in the cellars 190 or 43.6% were Irish and 56.4% non-Irish. In other words the level of Irish occupation of cellars in the area was little different from their overall presence in the district as a whole (44.1%). The only significant contrast came in the density of occupation – there were 7.3 Irish per cellar as against 4.7 in the cellars with a non-Irish majority. This finding is borne out by other work in the region, which also found that the assumption of Irish domination of cellars was something of a myth.[95]

One of the great benefits of residential clustering was the ease with which fellow residents could be rallied against real or perceived threats.[96] A French visitor noted that Irish crowds of one or two thousand could appear 'in the twinkling of an eye'.[97] Commentators frequently commented that any attempt to carry out official business in Irish districts provoked a remarkably quick group response. Joseph Sadler Thomas, deputy constable of Manchester, in his evidence to the Irish Poor Report commissioners, informed them:

> In Angel Meadow, or Little Ireland, if a legal execution of any kind is to be made, either for rent, for debt, or for taxes, the officer who serves the process almost always applied to me for assistance to protect him; and, in affording that protection, my officers are often maltreated by brickbats and other missiles. The same remark applies to the execution of a magistrate's warrant ... The Irish are very easily hurried into violence, even by a single one of their countrymen, and at a moment's notice: five minutes will bring together a thousand people at any time.[98]

As already noted, it was widely asserted that the Irish were responsible for most of the distillation in the city, though this too has been questioned.[99] Efforts by excise officers to arrest those operating the stills and confiscate their equipment provoked equally strong local resistance. When an individual was arrested he would utter 'a loud Irish cry ... fighting and struggling, in order to gain time till his friends collect for a rescue'.[100] Efforts to seize the equipment provoked even greater reaction: 'When we go to take a still, we are forced to go armed. They often make resistance, collect mobs of hundreds, almost thousands of persons ... the inhabitants of the neighbourhood instantly collecting round the place'.[101]

The Irish could also rally when institutions central to community life and identity were believed to be under threat. At the end of June 1852 anti-Catholic riots in nearby Stockport had resulted in the death of one person, injury to fifty-one others and the ransacking of the local Catholic church.[102] As 12 July, the day for traditional Protestant Orange Order processions, drew near, tension rose in the Irish districts of the region, including the Hulme district south-west of Little Ireland, where a small Irish population had settled, served by St Wilfrid's church. On 14 July a pub fight spilled over into the street, but fears of sectarian assault had reached such a height that rumour quickly spread that an invasion was under way. The reaction was instantaneous:

> In less than five minutes (the information having been carried by numerous messengers into all the little streets on either side ...) several hundred of Irishmen were seen hurrying in all directions, armed with pokers, stones, hammers & c; and the cry was raised that the Protestants were about to set fire to St. Wilfrid's Catholic church ... The Irish believing or affecting to believe this absurd rumour, rushed along ... in a body and swept the streets of their passengers ... by the time the armed crowd of Irishmen got to the neighbourhood of the chapel, the street in front of it was crowded by a dense mass of people ... At the time the excitement was at its height the priest [Rev. Toole] came out into the street from the vestry ... and addressed the assembled crowd, assuring them there was no cause for the disturbance, and entreating them to go home ... It was repeatedly stated by parties in the street that the chapel has been watched regularly every evening for the last 7 or 8 days by from 50–60 men, in consequence of a rumour, for which we understand there is not the slightest foundation, that the chapel was to be set alight by an Orange mob.[103]

## Moral improvement

The writings of Kay and subsequent observers, the successive epidemics of infectious disease and the work of the sanitary reformers provoked a growing body of national and local legislation to regulate the quality and density of housing, the provision of toilets and water, the disposal of domestic and industrial waste and the number and quality of lodging houses. But commentators were convinced that a key means of tackling what they saw as the equally significant moral squalor were organisations with an edifying agenda of spiritual and moral uplift.

When Rev. Mercer conducted his overview of Angel Meadow in 1897 he had not mentioned any signs of physical improvement, but had concentrated on the moral dangers and suggested that 'One department of preventive work has been much neglected in Angel Meadow, I mean that of clubs and recreative work. Dwellers in slums crave for excitement, and excitement they will have ... There should be clubs for all ages and for both sexes, with billiard tables, games, papers, dancing and all innocent forms of entertainment.' He then proceeded to contradict himself to some extent by noting the presence of local schools and organisations formed by the churches, including the Catholics, and he welcomed the recent launch of the University Settlement.[104]

In actual fact, institutions devoted to raising the moral tone of Angel Meadow had made their appearance since at least the 1820s, when groups of evangelical Christians began distributing Bibles and food and holding meetings. By 1850 they had opened a school in Nelson Street with modest aims of 'a little education, and work was found for those who applied for them'.[105] A Sunday evening meeting was launched in nearby Ormond Street in 1852 with the intention of setting up another school; this was opened in Sharp Street in March 1854 and became part of the Ragged School movement. This had grown out of scattered local efforts to offer instruction in literacy and mathematics to children in the poorest areas of Britain's growing cities. In 1844 the Ragged School Union had been founded, and by 1861 Manchester had seventeen such schools organised into its own union. Subsequently the curriculum expanded to include history and geography for the brighter youngsters; meals were provided and treats organised in summer and at Christmas.[106] The evangelical Protestant tenor of these efforts was reinforced by a religious revival movement in late 1859 and early 1860 and by the visits to the city of the American evangelists C.G. Finney and D.L. Moody, which inspired further evangelistic and social work amongst the working class of such districts.[107]

It was partly in reaction to such evangelistic Protestant activities that the Catholic Church had launched its work in the area. Of the many dangers in the district, one Catholic commentator observed, 'That necessary evil, mixed marriages, is seen in all its worst forms.'[108] Another noted that 'Angel Meadow is honeycombed with proselytism, Ragged schools, Board schools, refuges, soupers, tract distributors, good Samaritans, and "goody bodies" of all kinds poach and proselytise, and drive their unholy bargains.'[109] Elderly Catholics recalled that there had been a church school in the district in the early 1830s run by a one-armed Peninsular War veteran in rooms over a strong-smelling tallow chandler's factory. Fees were graded according to the number of subjects taken by the pupil – these included 'etiquette, or the art of Politeness' for the highest payers. The school was considered 'large, respectable and efficient'.[110]

As with all Catholic schools, religion occupied a central part of the curriculum. In addition to weekday school instruction, the pupils were marshalled on Sundays for procession to morning Mass; there was also an afternoon meeting from two to four o'clock for cathechising by the parish priest of nearby St Patrick's, with prizes for the most distinguished scholar, and an evening gathering.[111] In 1864 St William's church and school were opened in Simpson Street, largely through the efforts of the energetic Canon Sheehan; it was suggested that its presence in the very heart of the district meant it had a strong appeal, but that 'This is peculiarly so with the good Irish hearts round about St. William's.'[112] Subsequently a network of clubs for children and teenagers grew up. The Catholic Working Lads' Club, founded in 1878, had as its primary objective

> the spiritual regeneration and improvement of its members, regeneration in supplying that Catholic tone and spirit which is often lost by contact with non-Catholic influences, and improvement of those not so far contaminated ... no single member of it is ignorant of the fact that attendance at his Sunday Mass ... and his General Communion twice a year are the two chief factors in the general working of the club.[113]

By May 1893 there were 270 young men registered at the club between the ages of twelve and twenty-three. They were marshalled by a group of thirty who divided the district between them, each with a list of addresses which they visited to ensure attendance at weekly Mass. Secular activities at the club included reading in the library, billiards, gymnastics, bagatelle, boxing and soccer. Entertainment on Wednesdays featured 'the magic lantern, boxing ... contests, nigger minstrel and scratch concerts', and each autumn there was a pleasure trip into the countryside and a tea party.[114] In March 1894 during a visit to Angel Meadow, Bishop Bilsborrow was informed that the girls of the Guild of St Agnes would like a club of their own.[115] This was duly launched the following month at St William's with a procession to premises in Nicholas Street, consisting of 'a cottage with a few rooms' where they had facilities to 'sing, sew, knit, read, tell tales, dance and enjoy themselves'.[116] In July it was reported that they had a trip to Blackpool, the writer commenting that they had seen their membership increase and that 'it is a most edifying sight to see them go to Holy Communion on the first Sunday of each month at St. William's'.[117]

Supporters were convinced that, in addition to the spiritual benefits, the clubs had contributed much to the general uplift of moral tone and behaviour in the district. One observer described a local lads' club as 'one of the great institutions of the locality' and, after describing how the district, once notorious for gangs, thieving and prostitution, had seen much improvement in recent years, went on, 'and if the activity and vigilance of our guardians of the public peace is responsible for much of its suppression, it may safely be said the foundation and carrying on of "Working Lads' Clubs" has done as much'.[118] Others agreed, arguing that 'the face of things in the Meadow has completely changed. Scuttling is unknown, and where a disposition to rowdyism is seen, it may safely be said that few, if any, belonging to the clubs are among the lads engaged in it'.[119] Activity based at St William's church and school was regarded by some as a particular boost to temperance. In a tribute to Fr Thompson, who had been based there since 1894, it was declared, 'we believe that considerably less drunkenness is prevalent in this district than ever was formerly the case – in fact, the whole tone of the neighbourhood has been raised to a much higher sense of respectability and morality during your labours amongst us, and you have done much to regenerate this downtrodden district, and, thank God, you have succeeded, for most certainly the improvement is perceptible'.[120]

## Conclusion

The growth of a cluster of Irish-dominated streets in this part of Manchester became in time a significant self-perpetuating feature of the social geography of the city. However, some features of the traditional picture of Angel Meadow and its Irish inhabitants merit careful attention. First, whilst there was a heavy Irish presence in the district, the area was not exclusively Irish – by the definition of Irish used here there was a non-Irish majority, even if a small one, in Angel Meadow. Moreover, though residential segregation in the area was quite marked, there were very few exclusively Irish or non-Irish streets. In Angel Meadow only three streets, containing a total of nine houses, were totally Irish, and only six streets, with twenty-six houses, were exclusively non-Irish. It is also worth noting that whilst the Irish nature of Angel Meadow endured into the twentieth century, the Irish were not fixed within the district. Of a sample of 230 Irish recorded as living in Angel Meadow in the 1851 census, only six were found to be at the same address or next door in 1861.[121] The Irish were a mobile population in pursuit of employment in Manchester and elsewhere. Moreover, it must always be remembered that the great majority of the economically active Irish had to make a daily journey to work which would take many of them into other parts of the city. Such districts were an integral part of the social and economic geography of the city.

Some of the stereotyped ideas about the Irish and urban housing, such as the assertion that they were unduly concentrated in cellars, have already been dealt with. It is also worth noting that though poor-quality housing characterised many parts of Angel Meadow, there were variations in quality within the district. Since, as already noted, the streets sloped from east to west down to the banks of the Irk, the worst conditions were to be found at the bottom of such streets and next to the river, where surface water and waste accumulated. It is also worth noting that few Irish lived in these parts of Angel Meadow and that the poor living conditions overall were a common problem of residents regardless of their birthplace.[122] It is also noteworthy that there were perfectly respectable, clean, well-kept Irish lodging houses in the district, such as the establishment noted by a reporter in April 1871 which had been kept by an Irishman for forty years and had as one of its residents a lodger of twenty-seven years, just as there was a respectable element in the Irish population as a whole.[123] Finally, it is important to note that not all Irish migrants to Manchester lived in the sort of circumstances found in Angel Meadow: there was a middle-class element, some people migrating directly from Ireland as the next step in their career path in business or the professions, others becoming upwardly mobile.

Nonetheless, with all these qualifications, a significant section of the Irish migrant population in Manchester did live in the sort of overwhelmingly working-class district just discussed, and Angel Meadow was the largest and most long-lasting Irish quarter in the city. The mere presence of this distinctively Irish neighbourhood attracted other Irish seeking the comfort and reassurance of 'living amongst one's kind'.[124] An additional factor attracting Irish migrants to the district and holding them there was the presence of the Catholic Church and the steady build-up of parish-based organisations. These helped fix and perpetuate the nature of the district, no matter how unattractive some of its physical aspects and its reputation. Even that considerable element of the Irish migrant inflow who lapsed or were lax in religious observance must have felt drawn in by the familiarity and sociability of such activities in an otherwise totally alien and often physically and culturally threatening environment.

## Notes

1 Cormac Ó Gráda, *Ireland: a new economic history 1780–1939* (Oxford: Oxford University Press, 1995), p. 6; James S. Donnelly, jr, *The great Irish potato famine* (Stroud: Sutton Publishing, 2001), p. 4.
2 Kevin Whelan, 'The modern landscape', in F.H.A. Aalen, K. Whelan and M. Stout (eds), *Atlas of the Irish rural landscape* (Cork: Cork University Press, 1997), p. 88; Mary E. Daly, *The famine in Ireland* (Dundalk: Dundalgan Press, 1986), p. 8.

3 David Dickson, 'The potato and Irish diet before the great famine', in C. Ó Gráda (ed.), *Famine 150: commemorative essays* (Dublin: Teagasc, 1997), p. 19; Ciaran Ó Murchadha, *The great famine: Ireland's agony* (London: Continuum, 2011), p. 7.
4 David Dickson, 'The other great Irish famine', in C. Poirteir (ed.), *The great Irish famine* (Cork: Mercier Press, 1995), pp. 50–9.
5 Daly, *The famine in Ireland*, p. 53; Christine Kinealy, *This great calamity: the Irish famine 1845–52* (Dublin: Gill & Macmillan, 1994), p. 33.
6 Ó Murchadha, *The great famine*, p. 28.
7 Margaret Crawford, 'Food and famine', in Poirteir (ed.), *The great Irish famine*, p. 61.
8 Ó Murchadha, *The great famine*, p. 48.
9 Daly, *The famine in Ireland*, p. 55.
10 For overviews of the various forms of relief, their underlying philosophy and effectiveness, see Daly, *The famine in Ireland*, pp. 67–98; Cormac Ó Gráda, *Black '47 and beyond: the great Irish famine* (Princeton: Princeton University Press, 1999), chap. 2; Kinealy, *This great calamity*, chap. 5; Ó Murchada, *The great famine*, chap. 4.
11 Crawford, 'Food and famine', p. 61.
12 Ó Murchadha, *The great Irish famine*, pp. 172–8.
13 Donnelly, *The great Irish potato famine*, p. 171.
14 Ó Murchadha, *The great famine*, p. 93.
15 For overviews of the relative impact of starvation and disease during the famine, see William P. McArthur, 'Medical history of the famine', in R.D. Edwards and T.D. Williams (eds), *The great famine: studies in Irish history, 1845–52* (Dublin: Lilliput Press,1994), pp. 263–315; Daly, *The famine in Ireland*, pp. 102–3; Laurence M. Geary, 'Famine fever and the bloody flux', in Poirteir (ed.), *The great Irish famine*, pp. 74–85; Laurence M. Geary, 'What people died of during the famine', in Ó Gráda (ed.), *Famine 150*, pp. 95–112; Ó Gráda, *Black '47*, chap. 3; Donnelly, *The great Irish potato famine*, pp. 173–6; Ó Murchadha, *The great famine*, pp. 89–95.
16 Donnelly, *The great Irish potato famine*, p. 178; Frank Neal, *Black '47: Britain and the famine Irish* (Basingstoke: Macmillan, 1998).
17 *Manchester Guardian*, 6 and 13 January 1847.
18 *Manchester Courier*, 16 January 1847.
19 *Manchester Guardian*, 23 January 1847; *Manchester Courier*, 20 February 1847; *Manchester Guardian*, 14 April 1847.
20 *Manchester Courier*, 3 November 1847.
21 *Manchester Guardian*, 3 March 1847.
22 Neal, *Black '47*, chap. 9; H.M. Boot, 'Unemployment and poor relief in Manchester, 1845–50', *Social History*, 15:2 (1990), pp. 217–28.
23 Margaret Crawford, 'Migrant maladies: unseen lethal baggage', in E.M. Crawford (ed.), *The hungry stream: essays on famine and emigration* (Belfast: Institute of Irish Studies, 1995), pp. 137–50.
24 *Manchester Guardian*, 13 February 1847, *Manchester Courier*, 22 May 1847.

25 *Manchester Guardian*, 5 June 1847.
26 *Manchester Courier*, 12 May 1857. This was the main road through Angel Meadow district.
27 *Manchester Guardian*, 30 June 1847.
28 *Manchester Guardian*, 26 June 1847.
29 *Manchester Guardian*, 11 September 1847. To establish a right to poor relief an applicant had to have the legal status of 'settlement', acquired by birth or five years continuous residence. Anyone lacking this status could be removed to the parish in which they had such rights. On these grounds Irish famine refugees did not qualify for settlement, and fear of removal might well have deterred them from making any form of contact with authority. See Frank Neal, 'The English Poor Law, the Irish migrant and the laws of settlement and removal, 1819–1879', in D.G. Boyce and R. Swift (eds), *Problems and perspectives in Irish history since 1800: essays in honour of Patrick Buckland* (Dublin: Four Courts Press, 2004), pp. 95–116.
30 *Manchester Courier*, 13 October 1847.
31 *Manchester Courier*, 27 June 1849.
32 *Manchester Guardian*, 25 October 1851.
33 A study of a small part of the Angel Meadow district of Manchester in 1851, which defined the Irish as those born in Ireland plus those born to two Irish parents traceable in the census, suggested that the figure for Irish-born should be increased by 17.3% to arrive at a truer picture. See Mervyn Busteed, Rob Hodgson and Tom Kennedy, 'The myth and reality of Irish migrants in mid-nineteenth century Manchester: a preliminary study', in P. O'Sullivan (ed.), *The Irish world wide: history, heritage, identity*, vol. 2: *The Irish in the new communities* (Leicester: Leicester University Press, 1992), p. 37. The above definition is used here. Hugh Heinrick, *A survey of the Irish in England (1872)*, ed. A. O'Day (London: Hambledon Press, 1990), pp. 124–5, suggested that the true total of the Irish in Britain could be obtained by simply doubling the census total of Irish-born. For another approach which comes close to endorsing this, see William J. Lowe, *The Irish in mid-Victorian Lancashire: the making of a working class community* (New York: Peter Lang, 1989), pp. 48–50, 72–3.
34 Michael Nevell, *Manchester: the hidden history* (Stroud: History Press, 2008), pp. 80–6; Mike Williams and D.A. Farne, *Cotton mills in Greater Manchester* (Preston: Carnegie Publishing, 1992), pp. 50–1. C. Laurent, *A topographical map of Manchester and Salford with the adjacent parts ... an exact reproduction of the plan of 1795* (Crewe: Historical Society, 1991). St Michael's church, long disused, was demolished in 1936.
35 B.R. Davies, *Plan of Manchester and Salford with their environs etc.*, in E. Baines, *History of the County Palatinate and Duchy of Lancaster* (Manchester, 1836).
36 Manchester and Salford Sanitary Association, Report of the Rochdale Road Visiting Committee, 1 April 1853, p. 4, Manchester Central Library, Archives Department (henceforth MCLAD), M126/2/6/4.
37 James Phillips Kay, *The moral and physical condition of the working classes*

employed in the cotton manufacture in Manchester (London, 1832; 2nd edn 1832), p. 38.

38 Friedrich Engels, *The condition of the working class in England* (Leipzig, 1845); reprinted with foreword by V. Kiernan (London: Penguin, 1987), p. 89.

39 *Manchester Courier*, 1 January 1847.

40 Nevell, *Manchester*, pp. 146–59; Jacqueline Roberts, *Working class housing in nineteenth century Manchester: the example of John Street, Irktown* (Manchester: Richardson, 1979).

41 'Local reports on the sanitary condition of the labouring population in consequence of an inquiry directed to be made by the Poor Law Commission', 1840, pp. 313–14, MCLAD, P1173.

42 *A letter to Alexander Kay Esquire by Dr. John Leigh*. (Manchester: Abel Hayward, 1845), pp. 26, 19.

43 Engels, *The condition of the working class*, p. 93.

44 Angus Reach, *Manchester and the textile districts in 1849*, ed. C. Aspin (Helmshore: Helmshore Local History Society, 1972), p. 53.

45 A.T.H. Watters, *Report of the sanitary condition of certain parts of Manchester* (Manchester: Sowler, 1853), p. 4.

46 Rochdale Road Visiting Committee, no date, probably 1853 or 1854, MCLAD, M126/2/6/9.

47 Rochdale Road Visiting Committee, no date, probably 1853 or 1854, p. 9, MCLAD, M126/2/6/10.

48 *Manchester Guardian*, 15 May 1847.

49 Rochdale Road Visiting Committee, undated, but probably late March or early April 1854, pp. 3, 9, MCLAD, M126/2/10. Parts of the area were excavated in September 2005 by the television programme *Time Team*: see Nevell, *Manchester*, pp. 82–5; the excavation by Oxford Archaeology North in 2009 and 2012 covered a much larger area. L.S. Lowry painted parts of the area on several occasions, most notably in his *View of the Nation* (1936).

50 Rochdale Road Visiting Committee, undated, but probably late March or early April 1854, p. 2, MCLAD, M126/2/6/10.

51 Rochdale Road Visiting Committee, 1 April 1853, p. 1, MCLAD, M126/2/6/4.

52 Rochdale Road Visiting Committee, undated, but probably late March or early April 1854, p. 3, MCLAD, M126/2/6/10.

53 Nevell, *Manchester*, p. 161.

54 Rochdale Road Visiting Committee, undated, but probably late March or early April 1854, p. 1, MCLAD, M126/2/6/10.

55 Rochdale Road Visiting Committee, 16 March 1854, p. 4, MCLAD, M126/2/6/7.

56 *Manchester Courier*, 1 December 1847.

57 *Manchester Guardian*, 23 February 1870.

58 *Manchester Guardian*, 6 April 1871.

59 Rev. J.E. Mercer, 'The conditions of life in Angel Meadow', *Transactions of the Manchester Statistical Society: Session 1896-7*, pp. 165–70.

60 *Manchester Guardian*, 14 March 1903. Starting in the 1930s, Manchester Corporation gradually cleared the area of the greater part of its residential

population, and by the 1960s it was largely given over to car parks and a variety of small manufacturing concerns. Subsequently rejuvenation was launched by a consortium of the Groundwork Trust, Manchester Corporation and the North Manchester Regeneration Trust, and since 2004 a voluntary group, the Friends of Angel Meadow, have been working to restore the southern end of the area as a park (*The Guardian*, 26 April 2005). In 2014 the Cooperative Society opened its new headquarters on the south-eastern edge of the district.

61 Kay, *The moral and physical condition*, pp. 42, 112.
62 *Manchester Guardian*, 16 February 1870.
63 *Manchester Courier*, 1 December 1847.
64 Mercer, 'The conditions of life in Angel Meadow', pp. 172–3.
65 Charles Noar, 'Charter Street Ragged School', July 1915, pp. 2–3, MCLAD, M226.
66 Kay, *The moral and physical condition*, pp. 63–7.
67 Rochdale Road Visiting Committee, 16 March 1854, p. 1, MCLAD, M126/2/6/7.
68 Rochdale Road Visiting Committee, undated, but probably late March or early April 1854, p. 10, MCLAD, M126/2/6/10.
69 *Manchester Guardian*, 23 February 1870.
70 Of the reminiscences of life in Angel Meadow, one of the most useful is Mary Burtenshawe, *Sunrise to sunset: an autobiography* (Manchester: Printwise, 1991).
71 Mercer, 'The conditions of life in Angel Meadow', pp. 175–6; James W. Thompson, 'Glimpses of Angel Meadow: iii', *The Harvest*, 6:68 (1893), p. 192; Andrew Davies, *Gangs of Manchester* (Preston: Milo Books, 2009).
72 *Manchester Guardian*, 16 February 1870; for analysis of these street ballads and their significance for the local Irish see Mervyn Busteed, 'Songs in a strange land – ambiguities of identity amongst Irish migrants in mid-Victorian Manchester', *Political Geography*, 17: 6(1998), pp. 627–65; Mervyn Busteed, '"I shall never return to Hibernia's bowers": Irish migrant identities in early Victorian Manchester', *North West Geographer*, 2 (2000), pp. 15–29; Mervyn Busteed, 'Identities in transition: Irish migrant outlooks in mid-Victorian Manchester', in Boyce and Swift (eds), *Problems and perspectives*, pp. 80–94.
73 *Bancks and Company's plan of Manchester and Salford with their environs etc 1831.* (Manchester, 1832),
74 *Manchester Guardian*, 6 November 1847.
75 For discussion of this invaluable, if flawed, source see W.A. Armstrong, 'The census enumerators' books: a commentary', in R. Lawton (ed.), *The census and social structure* (London: Frank Cass, 1978), pp. 28–77, and Edward Higgs, *A clearer sense of the census* (London: HMSO, 1996). Before this material was so freely available on the internet, Manchester and Lancashire Family History Society very kindly gave me access to its transcribed copies. For its project to retrieve the parts of the census damaged by the blitz of the Second World War, see R. Hulley, '1851 unfilmed census', *Manchester Genealogist*, 31:3 (1995), pp. 189–91; 32:4 (1996), pp. 250–1; and 33:4 (1997), pp. 244–6.
76 Mervyn Busteed and Rob Hodgson, 'Angel Meadow: a study of the geography of Irish settlement in mid-nineteenth century Manchester', *Manchester Geog-*

rapher, 14 (1993), pp. 3-26; Mervyn Busteed and Rob Hodgson, 'Irish migration and settlement in early nineteenth century Manchester, with special reference to the Angel Meadow district in 1851', *Irish Geography*, 27:1 (1994), pp. 1-13.

77 Mervyn Busteed and Rob Hodgson, 'Irish migrant responses to urban life in early nineteenth century Manchester', *Geographical Journal*, 162:2 (1996), pp. 139-53.

78 For exploration of the geography of Irish settlement in nearby Ancoats see Mervyn Busteed, 'Little islands of Erin: Irish settlement and identity in mid-nineteenth century Manchester', *Immigrants and Minorities*, 18:2-3 (1999), pp. 94-127, and Mervyn Busteed, *Patterns of Irishness in nineteenth century Manchester* (Manchester: Manchester Statistical Society, 2001).

79 Neil Smith and Mervyn Busteed, 'A diasporic elite – the emergence of an Irish middle class in nineteenth century Manchester', in C. O'Neill (ed.), *Irish elites in the nineteenth century* (Dublin: Four Courts Press, 2013), pp. 197-208; Lawrence McBride, *The Reynolds letters: an Irish emigrant family in late Victorian Manchester* (Cork: Cork University Press, 1999).

80 Given their religion and generally pro-union politics, Irish Protestant migrants generally merged easily into the mainstream of British society and have proved extremely difficult to isolate for study purposes.

81 Anon., 'Angel Meadow, Manchester: opening of the Girls' Club', *The Harvest*, 7:79 (1894), p. 188.

82 *Report on the state of the Irish poor in Great Britain*, House of Commons Parliamentary Papers, 1836, vol. 34: Poor Inquiry, Ireland, Appendix G (henceforth Irish Poor Report), p. 64.

83 Irish Poor Report, p. 66.

84 Enda Delaney and Don MacRaild (eds), *Irish migration, networks and ethnic identities since 1750* (London: Routledge, 2007).

85 Irish Poor Report, p. 68.

86 Irish Poor Report, pp. 72, 80.

87 *Manchester Guardian*, 6 January 1847.

88 *Manchester Guardian*, 7 March and 4 April 1847.

89 Strictly speaking, until 1901 it was not required that enumerators should enter the county of birth for people born in Ireland, but occasionally, as here, zeal would lead them to do so.

90 Reach, *Manchester*, p. 56.

91 Johann Kohl, *England and Wales* (1844; reprinted London: Cass, 1968), p. 76.

92 *Manchester Guardian*, 6 February 1847.

93 But note that a section of the Irish population was highly mobile, moving around the country in search of employment, especially in summer and harvest time, with the result that they made greater use of cheap lodging houses.

94 Reach, *Manchester*, p. 55.

95 Sandra Hayton, 'Cellar dwellings and cellar dwellers', *Journal of Regional and Local Studies*, 12 (1992), pp. 68-70.

96 Frederick Boal, 'The urban residential sub-community: a conflict interpretation', *Area*, 4 (1972), pp. 164-8.

97 Leon Faucher, *Manchester in 1844: its present condition and future prospects* (1844; reprinted London: Cass & Co., 1969), p. 28.
98 Irish Poor Report, p. 75.
99 Mary Turner, 'Drink and illicit distillation in nineteenth century Manchester', *Manchester Region History Review*, 4:1 (1990), pp. 11–16.
100 *Manchester Guardian*, 2 January 1830; Irish Poor Report, p. 77.
101 Irish Poor Report, p. 76.
102 Pauline Millward, 'The Stockport riots of 1852: a study of anti-Catholic and anti-Irish sentiment', in R. Swift and S. Gilley (eds), *The Irish in the Victorian city* (London: Croom Helm, 1985), pp. 207–25.
103 *Manchester Guardian*, 14 July 1852.
104 Mercer, 'The conditions of life in Angel Meadow', p. 171.
105 Noar, 'Charter Street Ragged School', MCLAD, M226.
106 Kathleen Heasman, *Evangelicals in action: an appraisal of their social work in the Victorian era* (London: Geoffrey Bles, 1962). The work of the Ragged School Union has been described as probably 'The most successful of the agencies established by the evangelicals in their effort to convert the urban poor.' Ian Bradley, *The call to seriousness: the evangelical impact on the Victorians* (Oxford: 2006), p. 43.
107 Edwin Orr, *The second evangelical awakening in Britain* (London: Marshall, Morgan & Scott, 1949), chaps 7 & 10; James Stanhope-Brown, *Angels from the Meadow* (Manchester: Revell & George, 1991); David Bebbington, *Evangelicalism in modern Britain: a history from the 1730s to the 1980s* (London: Unwin Hyman, 1989).
108 Anon., 'Glimpses of Angel Meadow: ii', *The Harvest*, 6:67 (1893), p. 164. Unless otherwise indicated, articles in *The Harvest* are anonymous.
109 'Angel Meadow, Manchester: opening of the Girls' Club', p. 188; 'soupers' was the term used to describe evangelical Protestant charities which offered food to people during the Irish famine on condition that they converted to Protestantism.
110 Monsignor McKenna, 'Recollections of Catholicity in Manchester', *The Harvest*, 10:13 (1897), p. 35.
111 Mgr McKenna, 'Recollections of Catholicity in Manchester', pp. 35–6.
112 J.T., 'Glimpses of Angel Meadow', *The Harvest*, 6:66 (1893), p. 40.
113 'Glimpses of Angel Meadow: ii', p. 164.
114 'Glimpses of Angel Meadow: ii', pp. 163–4; Thompson, 'Glimpses of Angel Meadow: iii', pp. 192–4.
115 Joseph Crilly, 'The bishop in Angel Meadow: Angel Meadow Lads' Club', *The Harvest*, 8:78 (1894), pp. 166–7.
116 'Angel Meadow, Manchester: opening of the Girls' Club', p. 188.
117 'Girls' Club, Nicholas Street', *The Harvest*, 7:82 (1894), p. 279.
118 'Glimpses of Angel Meadow: ii', *The Harvest*, p. 164.
119 Thompson, 'Glimpses of Angel Meadow: iii', p. 194. 'Scuttling' was the practice of young lads making a living by thieving, sometimes with violence.
120 'St. William's, Angel Meadow, Manchester', *The Harvest*, 10:123 (1897), p. 289.

121 Busteed, *Patterns of Irishness*, p. 13.
122 Mervyn Busteed, 'Irish migrant settlement in early nineteenth century Manchester', *Manchester Genealogist*, 32:1 (1996), p. 9.
123 *Manchester Guardian*, 6 April 1871; 'Angel Meadow, Manchester: opening of the Girls' Club', p. 188.
124 Catherine Hurst, *Religion, politics and violence in nineteenth century Belfast: the Pound and Sandy Row* (Dublin: Four Courts Press, 2002), p. 14.

# 3

## The Catholic Church

It is generally agreed that the Catholic Church played a highly significant role in almost every dimension of the life of Irish migrants in nineteenth-century Britain.[1] Nonetheless, two caveats should be borne in mind. First, whilst a good deal of attention will be focused on the social, cultural and political impact of the church, its prime self-defined function was spiritual, namely to preach its version of the Christian message and provide the faithful with opportunities for worship, spiritual solace, instruction and guidance.[2] Second, whilst the great majority of Irish migrants were Catholic, there was a Protestant element, varying in strength, which was especially notable in Clydeside and Merseyside but also represented in Manchester.

This chapter will trace the impact of the Irish on the Catholic population of Manchester and its internal dynamics, the reactions of local Protestants, the gradual build-up of church institutions and its shifting concerns, and discuss the extent to which the church remained Irish in outlook and preoccupations.

### The Catholic Church and the Irish in Manchester to 1845

North-west England was the only region in Britain where there came about a combination of a significant population of native Catholics and a large influx of Irish,[3] which explains why Lancashire was the only county eventually organised into two Catholic dioceses.[4] Following the sixteenth-century Reformation and the establishment of the Church of England, Catholics in Britain were for some time a tiny suspect community, reduced to small groups living quietly in remote rural areas under the protection of the few surviving recusant gentry families.⁵ One such region was Lancashire, where the faithful were served by itinerant priests occasionally administering the sacraments in the privacy of family chapels. Manchester had a history as a centre of Puritanism, taking the parliamentary side in the English Civil Wars of 1641–45, with only two Catholics recorded within its boundaries in 1690.⁶ The locally significant Catholic family were the de Traffords, who, before moving to London on the eve of the First World War, were part of the local gentry elite.⁷ Local Catholics long regarded them with deference and respect. In 1912 a local Catholic publication recalled the marriage of Sir Humphrey, then head of the family, to Lady Annette Talbot in 1855,⁸ and went on to mark the coming of age of the heir apparent in 1913.⁹ In 1908 one elderly Catholic, doubtless relating an anecdote which had long circulated in the community, recalled how Catholics had travelled some distance to hear Mass at the family home of Trafford Hall, south of Manchester:

> and those who had come a few miles were refreshed after Mass with a 'horn' of ale, and bread and cheese, to strengthen them for their homeward journey. This thoughtful kindness and hospitality of the de Traffords was much appreciated by the poor Catholics, and will always redound to their honour and credit. The de Traffords did a great deal in days gone by to keep Catholicity alive in this part of Lancashire.¹⁰

In these circumstances it is hardly surprising that lay people had to take a leading role in Catholic life.

From the mid-eighteenth century onwards economic and social change disrupted this pattern as industrial development drew increasing numbers of people, including Catholics, into the growing urban centres.¹¹ In 1700 thirteen Catholic families had been noted in the city and the surrounding sixty square miles,¹² and an estimate in 1744 suggested seventeen individuals,¹³ but thereafter there was a steady if modest growth, with 287 listed in 1767¹⁴ and an estimate of 1,400 by 1787.¹⁵ Until 1774 Catholic worship in the city had been conducted unobtrusively by peripatetic clergy in private houses or disused buildings, including a former dye house. Later a building north of High Street was adapted to function as both chapel and dwelling house, the facade deliberately designed to look like a private residence. Nonetheless, its covert usage became public knowledge, and the street has been named 'Roman Street' ever since.

The first purpose-built church was St Chad's, which was opened in Rook Street, tucked in behind the city centre, in June 1774, its frontage of plain brick again in the style of a private house. By 1793 it was estimated that there were five thousand Catholics in Manchester;[16] this led to the construction of St Mary's church ('the hidden gem') in Mulberry Street, again just off the city centre, the first purpose-built Catholic place of worship in the city in modern times with an unapologetically ecclesiastical facade. The reason for this development was summed up in the piece of popular doggerel mentioned earlier (Chapter 1). The unashamedly elaborate nature of the building plus the fact that it incorporated a presbytery indicates the relative prosperity of these skilled migrant weavers together with the gradually growing confidence of the Catholic population. The interior explicitly acknowledged the significance of the Irish element in the expanding congregation by the presence of St Patrick holding a shamrock among the statues above the high altar.

The Irish element attracted by the growing economic opportunities discussed in Chapter 2 grew steadily from the early 1780s onwards (Figure 8) and, as has been noted, by 1841 there were 30,304 Irish-born people in the city, or 12.5% of the total population.[18] Clearly, there was a significant Irish population in the city well before the famine influx of the later 1840s, already producing a second generation. Indeed, in his evidence to the Irish Poor Report commissioners in 1834, Rev. Parker estimated that 50% of the Irish in the city had been born in Britain.[19]

The accelerating arrival of this new element had a profound impact on the internal dynamics of the pre-existing Catholic community. It has been argued that by 1800 the native English Catholic Church was growing steadily in strength and confidence and that a gradual transfer of influence and leadership was under way from the long-established recusant gentry families to the steadily growing numbers of clergy.[20] This smooth evolutionary course was now severely disrupted by a rapidly growing influx of Catholics from a very different background. The Irish were different in history, in cultural traditions, in politics, sometimes in language and frequently in wealth and social class. It has been estimated that by 1820 the Irish were the majority amongst Manchester Catholics,[21] and their numbers continued to grow until by the early 1830s it was estimated that they were between two thirds and 90% of the total in the city.[22] They entirely transformed the ethos and outlook of Manchester Catholicism as English Catholics and their concerns were increasingly marginalised,[23] and at times relations between the two were strained and awkward. One English Catholic who attended St Chad's noted how Irish rowdiness sorely tried the patience of the local priest Fr Broomhead.[24] The English were generally at the upper end of the social and economic spectrum, and though the two shared a common faith, they had a strong tendency

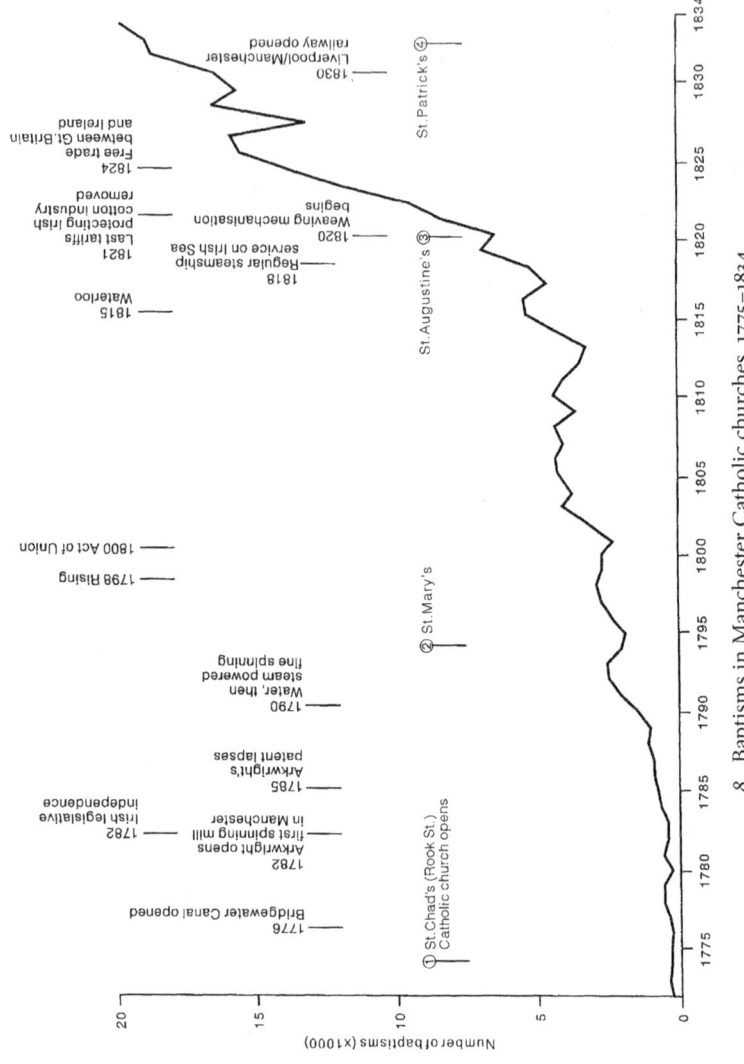

8  Baptisms in Manchester Catholic churches, 1775–1834

to congregate at different local churches. Those of English background tended to worship at St Augustine's, Granby Row, on the south-east side of the city, whilst the Irish were notable at St Mary's, St Patrick's and, on the south-west side, St Wilfrid's (Figure 1).[25]

However, it should not be assumed that the Irish at this stage were uniformly working-class and relatively poor. It is clear that they were producing a second generation and some notable middle-class lay people capable of rising to prominent leadership positions, not only within the Catholic population but on the wider civic stage. One such was Daniel Lee, born in Salford in 1798 to Irish parents and educated at Sedeley Park, Wolverhampton, one of the leading Catholic colleges of the day. Entering the Manchester textile trade, he rapidly became recognised as one of the city's leading salesmen. In 1826 he became a partner in the calico printing firm of Wright and Lee, which in 1852 became Daniel Lee and Co., with two warehouses in Manchester.[26] By this time he was one of the leading businessmen in the commercial life of Manchester, widely respected for ability and integrity. Throughout his life he was a devout and active Catholic – one observer noted, 'all the churches and schools of that denomination in this district have, at various times, received substantial proofs of his devotion'.[27] In 1852 the Vatican made him a Knight of St Gregory in recognition of his charitable work.

Alongside his business and religious activities, Lee was politically active, with a strong interest in Irish affairs. He married a Dublin woman, holidayed regularly in Ireland and made gifts to Irish colleges. He was a keen supporter of Daniel O'Connell's campaigns for Catholic emancipation and repeal of the union and was also active in local affairs. He vigorously supported Manchester's successful campaign for borough status and in 1838 became one of its first magistrates. From 1844 to 1848 he served as Liberal councillor for Trinity ward, Salford, a considerable achievement at a time when anti-Catholic sentiment was far from dead. But as the question of religious education rose up the agenda his outlook altered, and he personified some of the pressures which bore down on Catholics of Irish background. He became an increasingly vigorous advocate of church schools: in 1865 he became chair of the Manchester Catholic Registration Society, formed to locate and organise Catholic voters, and by now he was a supporter of the Conservative Party, believing it to be more sympathetic than the Liberal Party to the Catholic view on church schools. In 1867 the Conservative Prime Minister Lord Derby appointed him a Lancashire magistrate. He died in 1877.

The appearance of individuals such as Lee exemplifies the existence of a materially successful and prosperous element in the Catholic Irish population of Manchester before the arrival of the famine influx in the later 1840s, but there are other indications of wealthy individuals. As early as 1793 John Casey, an Irish-born linen merchant, left £840 in his will as the capital for what became known as the Casey Charity. Until it ceased to function in the late 1840s, this fund was at the disposal of local Catholic clergy to distribute to needy individuals.[28] In 1821 Patrick Lavery, an Irish-born silk merchant whose premises had been in no. 2 Angel Street, died leaving £2,000 to establish a school for girls and a convent of the Presentation Order.[29] The steady growth in the number of churches, presbyteries, parochial halls and schools is also indicative of wealth. In 1838 St Patrick's boys' school opened, and in 1840 St Bridget's orphanage, both of them in Livesey Street (Figure 9); St Augustine's church, Granby Row, consecrated in 1820, was believed to have cost £10,000, and St Patrick's £9,000, enormous sums for the period.[30] Doubtless 'the pennies of the poor' helped, but a great deal of the outlay came from prosperous individuals such as Daniel Lee. Of one newly planned church it was recorded, 'The subscriptions ... were commenced by working men. They, of course, were unable to raise the requisite sum, and, seeing their good intentions, Mr. Lee stepped in to their aid, and handed over ... a very large sum of money. Indeed, it may be said that the church was in great measure built by him.'[31]

The gradual build-up of clerical numbers meant that to an increasing degree leadership roles passed from lay people to clergy. Clearly their primary role was spiritual, involving the conduct of worship, the administration of the sacraments and pastoral work amongst their rapidly growing congregations. On 6 November 1806 Fr Broomhead of St Mary's recorded how, following a course of public instruction, 'we have not had a moment to spare ... our sick ... are now calling us daily 3 or 4 times.'[32] These ministrations to the sick took their toll, since clergy often had to venture into the homes of the dying to administer the last rites, and during epidemics of infectious disease the result could be fatal. Casualties included Frs John Ashurst of St Augustine's (1824), Henry Gillow (St Mary's, 1837) and John Laytham and John Parsons (both St Chad's, 1838), all typhus victims.[33] One account of a priest's walk through Angel Meadow conveys the deference and respect in which clergy were held. It recorded the frequent greeting 'Good morning, Father' and noted, 'There is evidently a pleasure in seeing the priest as he passes by with a cheery word and friendly nod'; when the priest called at a house there was a cosy and heart-tugging scene: 'Neighbours came flocking in, children flock round the doorway, the very cat on the hearth wakes up and makes for the visitor and gives him a friendly rub.' When he reminded everyone of

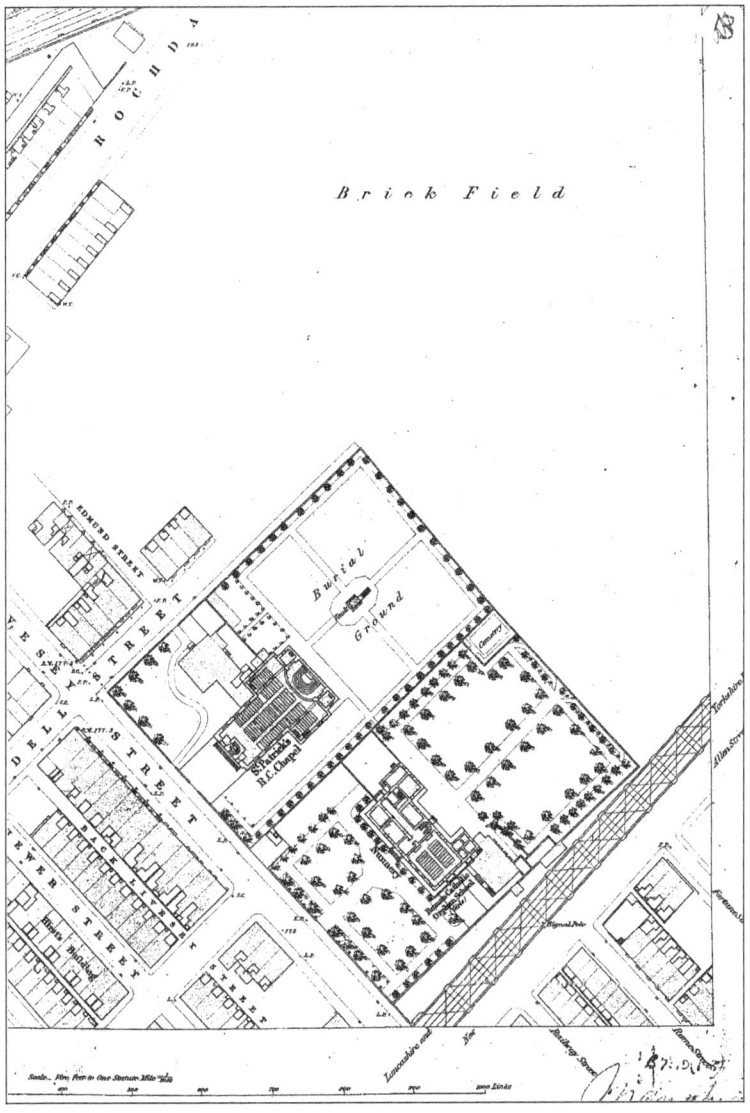

9 St Patrick's church, cemetery, orphanage and school, 1849

forthcoming events and commented on recent poor attendance at Mass, 'such remarks are expected, not resented'.[34]

Many clergy took on additional roles as intermediaries and brokers between their congregations and wider society. When the parliamentary commissioners investigating the state of the Irish poor came to Manchester early in 1834, three Catholic clergy submitted written evidence[35] and two made verbal presentations.[36] Fr Daniel Hearne, the redoubtable Waterford-born first rector of St Patrick's, Livesey Street, whose parish included Angel Meadow, was often called upon to plead on behalf of parishioners who had fallen foul of the authorities. When seventeen people, all of whom the *Manchester Guardian* claimed were Irish Catholics, were in court following a clash with members of the local Orange Order on 12 July 1834, Fr Hearne appeared in court to give character references, arguing that 'very great provocation had been given by persons coming in the procession, and also carrying arms'.[37] Clergy also used their influence to forestall public outbreaks. On the death of Fr Gillow of St Mary's, it was recorded how he 'exercised … a magical spell over the ruder and wilder spirits of the Manchester Catholic world'.[38] On one occasion it was recorded that, encountering a large crowd watching an informal boxing match taking place on the Rochdale Road, the main road through his parish, Fr Hearne 'sprang into the crowd, wielding a mahogany stick, which he let fall upon the shoulders of all indiscriminately. A thunderbolt could not have cleared the street quicker or more completely … Notwithstanding this rough method of reproving the members of his flock, he was greatly beloved; by the poor he was almost worshipped.'[39]

Fr Hearne's concerns went beyond the purely parochial and immediate. He had no qualms about working with clergy of other denominations on public issues which affected his congregation, including Rev. William Gadsby of the ultra-Calvinist Particular Baptist chapel on Rochdale Road. [40] Hearne was a keen advocate of all measures which he believed would relieve the distress of working people. Consequently, he supported repeal of the Corn Laws as likely to lower the price of bread and argued for a shorter working day. In September 1841 he spoke at a public meeting called to discuss the distress of hand-loom weavers suffering from the mechanisation of their trade. He quoted the case of twenty-six families in Old Mount Street, Angel Meadow, who during the previous week had been totally without food.[41] In 1842 when Dr Lyon Playfair visited Manchester during his investigation into the health of towns, Hearne was a member of a committee of local notables set up to collate and present evidence.[42] He was also keenly aware of Irish issues, supported O'Connell's campaigns for repeal of the union and was actively involved in the work of local branches of the repeal movement. In March 1842, as one of the main speakers at a St Patrick's Day dinner aiming to launch a society for the welfare of destitute Irish migrant children, he welcomed the fact that there were guests from all Irish creeds and political parties and spoke strongly in favour of the current temperance campaigns in Ireland being waged by Fr Theobald Mathew.[43] This was a clear illustration that Hearne was under no illusions that alcohol was a serious aggravating factor in the distress of his parishioners. In July that year he invited Fr Mathew to visit Manchester for the dedication of a new organ and a series of services at St Patrick's. At a meeting in the Free Trade Hall attended by the mayor and clergy of several denominations there was much emphasis on temperance as a non-sectarian and non-political cause.[44] During the visit it was estimated that a pledge of abstinence from alcohol was administered in English and Irish to about seventeen thousand people.[45] A later observer believed that at a time when Catholics 'were only gradually coming to the front in public affairs … the position which Father Hearne took up, commanded the respect of all classes, and destroyed a good deal of the prejudice in the public mind against the church and against the priests'.[46]

But Hearne's high public profile was causing concern to church authorities, and it was also clear that he was not easy to work with; relations with one of his curates had reached such a pitch that their dispute had been aired in public during a church service.[47] At Easter services in 1843 Hearne announced his imminent departure, provoking cries of dismay from the congregation and a turnout of thousands for his final appearance on Whit Sunday.[48] He was replaced by Fr Roskill of St Augustine's, but feelings ran high at St Patrick's, and something of a pamphlet war ensued, including a contribution by 'An Irishman', alleging anti-Irish prejudice and political bias.[49] In June 1846 Hearne returned to Manchester for a valedictory meeting at the Free Trade Hall, which was attended by about 3,500 people. There were frequent references not only to Hearne's work for temperance and the distressed, but to his Irish nationality and repeal politics. One address was from 'the repealers of Manchester and Salford to the Rev. Daniel Hearne … They could not but feel deeply the loss of so ardent and devoted an Irishman, of so exemplary and pious a clergyman; being satisfied that the enemies of Ireland and repeal could not obtain a greater triumph than in the removal of the Rev. Daniel Hearne from the town of Manchester.' Hearne responded by reviewing his work for temperance and relief of distress and restated his Irishness and his support for repeal, but urged obedience and submission to the church.[50] Clearly therefore the arrival of such large numbers of Irish even before the famine of the mid- to late 1840s had generated considerable strains within the Catholic population of the district, but it had also given new life to one of the most long-lived strands in English and British popular nationalism, namely anti-Catholicism.

## Anti-Catholicism in Manchester

It has been claimed that of all the groups who arrived in Britain in the nineteenth century few were less welcome than the Irish.[51] In terms of popular prejudice they suffered from double jeopardy. Not only did they experience anti-Irish sentiment, but since the great majority were Roman Catholics, they suffered from the anti-Catholicism which was an integral feature of historic English and later British popular nationalism. In mid-1898 a seventy-year-old recalled the insults suffered by Catholic religious on the streets of Manchester:

> our clergy dared not be seen going about the streets … [nuns] had a very uncomfortable time of it … they have almost had to run the gauntlet through a mass of rabble, armed with clods and missiles to throw as they passed along. I remember that we young fellows attending the Sunday school at St. John's had to complain to the police authorities, and they took no notice of us, so we were compelled to form a body guard for them … some ruffians broke into their convent and robbed them whilst they were at Mass … When I see how [they] can move about now-a days … and how they are respected, I often say to myself 'what changes for the better.'[52]

Anti-Catholic sentiment has been described as 'probably the most ubiquitous, most eclectic and most adaptable ideology in the post-Reformation history of the British Isles'.[53] Like all social constructions, it has proved capable of almost infinite flexibility in relation to time and locality, but there are certain recurring themes. On the negative side, Catholicism was held up as the summation of all that Protestant Britain escaped from at the sixteenth-century Reformation. Moreover these views were found at all levels of society. Amongst the more educated, Catholicism was seen as a demeaning superstition fit only for the credulous and 'inimical to the proper conduct of civil affairs and prosperity alike'.[54] At the popular level, where in some regions the sentiment retained a vulgar vitality well into the early twentieth century, anti-Catholicism was much more visceral. From this perspective Catholic clergy were viewed as tyrannical, exploitative and, in the privacy of the confessional, intrusive and morbidly inquisitive. As the traditional religious orders were gradually restored, some more extreme Protestants alleged sexual impropriety by clergy, especially in convents, and a steady flow of semi-pornographic literature developed, claiming to describe the goings-on. Campaigns were mounted demanding government inspection of convents. Catholic lay people were regarded as gullible, superstitious, clerically dominated and untrustworthy. On the political front, Catholics were regarded as potentially traitorous, subservient to the conspiratorial designs of the Vatican, dedicated to the overthrow of Britain's Protestant constitution and sympathetic to her historic Catholic European enemies.

Closely interwoven with these sentiments was a flattering xenophobic narrative which viewed English and later British history in almost apocryphal terms as the 'story' of a sturdy Protestant people contending successfully against mighty Catholic foes, internal and external. In this account Protestants were the polar opposite of the great Catholic 'other' in that they were independent-minded, materially prosperous and in enjoyment of full religious and political freedom.[55] From the persecutions and burnings authorised by Queen Mary Tudor in the 1550s through the successive wars against Spain, France and Austria and the eighteenth-century Jacobite risings, the threat of the Catholic 'other' proved an invaluable patriotic rallying cry for mobilisation of people and resources. These sentiments were constantly refreshed and expressed through regular festivals and religious services recalling significant events and personalities, accompanied by pageants, re-enactments, processions and celebratory consumption of food and drink. The growing variety of cheap mass-produced publications such as almanacs, street ballads, pamphlets and later newspapers further diffused this flattering fable. In 1563 John Foxe's *Book of Martyrs*, with its stories of gallant Protestants martyred by 'Bloody Mary' and its gruesome woodcuts of torture and death, first appeared and became an instant bestseller; it was soon to be found in almost every Protestant household, no matter how humble, and has never been out of print.[56]

By the late eighteenth century there are indications that some of the atavistic force was ebbing from anti-Catholicism. The fading of the Catholic Stuart challenge, the fact that Catholics were a tiny harmless minority and the spread of enlightenment values led to the first Relief Act of June 1780. It has also been suggested that the burgeoning evangelical revival diverted much Protestant fervour into the campaigns for slavery abolition and moral uplift.[57] But this development was checked by a revival of anti-Catholic sentiment which was to make it one of the dominant sentiments in early nineteenth-century British life. One reason was the growing diversity of the British religious landscape, which some conservative elements saw as a growing threat to the essentially Anglican nature of the British constitution. One element in this anxiety was the extraordinary growth of Nonconformity in terms of both numbers and vitality, 'one of the most remarkable features of British social history'.[58] In part this was due to the evangelical movement of the late eighteenth and early nineteenth centuries, which not only influenced the Nonconformists but penetrated the Anglican Church, thereby broadening its range of internal opinion.[59] But there was also a shift of emphasis within the evangelical movement which made it more eschatological and implicitly more anti-Catholic. Some preachers seized on the more apocalyptic passages in the book of Revelation, with its vivid portrayal of global conflicts, identifying the Catholic Church as a force of destructive satanic evil and interpreting the conflicts as prophecy of the turbulent times of the late eighteenth and early nineteenth centuries. Much of the detail passed over the heads of the general public, but the colourful melodrama of these scenarios fired some sections of the popular imagination, and from the 1820s onwards 'a more dogmatic, millennial nationalist Protestantism came increasingly to the surface'.[60] One result was a more urgent edge to public disputation with and evangelism amongst Catholics, expressed in a constellation of multi-denominational Protestant organisations, especially in the 1820s and 1840s, and fervent talk of a 'second reformation.'

Developments within the Catholic Church in Britain also stimulated Protestant concern. The steady acceleration in the growth of Catholic numbers from the late eighteenth century has already been noted, and by 1840 it was estimated that there were 550,000 Catholics in Britain.[61] Possibly even more striking was their impact on the landscape, with the growing numbers of churches, presbyteries, parochial halls, schools and convents. Moreover, as time passed the churches in particular became statements of growing wealth and confidence, no longer modest chapels tucked away in side streets, but now substantial buildings in prominent sites with soaring steeples making a striking impact on the urban scene. As remarked earlier, clergy and members of orders were increasingly visible on the streets, along with parishioners and children when they paraded in their best clothes in class groups with banners. In Manchester the first Catholic schools procession took place in 1834; a contingent took part in the 1838 coronation celebrations, and in 1844 thirteen schools and six thousand pupils under the banner of St Patrick paraded to St John's church in Salford.[62] Gaining in confidence, Catholics then organised an annual Whit Friday Walk, a tradition which persisted into the twentieth century.[63]

Some Protestant observers were even more alarmed by what they considered 'the enemy within', namely the growing 'Tractarian' or 'Anglo-Catholic' movement in the state church. This originated amongst a group of young Anglican clergy in Oxford in the 1830s and 1840s, the most notable of whom were John Henry Newman, Henry Manning and John

Keble. Their intention was to recapture elements of that Catholicity which they considered the Church of England had lost at the Reformation.[64] Their use of rich vestments and incense and their restoration of Confession, Stations of the Cross and Mass scandalised many: 'Disgust at these illegal practices was almost universal.'[65] For much of the general public all this remained an arcane clerical preoccupation, but to some commentators the fears of ultra-Protestants seemed to have some substance, confirming a general impression that 'The religious stability of the British Isles, and its dependent cultural identities, seemed to be in imminent danger of fracturing into different pieces.'[66]

On the broader political front there was a series of public issues which roused traditional Protestant fears and feelings. One of the most contentious was Catholic emancipation. At the passing of the 1801 Act of Union between Britain and Ireland, Prime Minister Pitt and Castlereagh, the Irish Secretary, had originally intended that emancipation would follow, and although no concrete pledges had been given during negotiations with the Irish hierarchy, this was generally understood.[67] However, in the light of strenuous opposition from elements in the Cabinet, the Tory Party and not least King George III himself, Pitt resigned in February 1801 and resumed office in May 1804, pledging not to raise the issue again. Whilst conservative Protestant elements in Britain and Ireland were delighted, in Catholic Ireland there was a strong sense of betrayal and bitter grievance.[68] For the next thirty years there were periodic efforts to put emancipation through parliament, but the movement in favour did not get seriously under way until Daniel O'Connell founded the Catholic Association in April 1823 and set about the mass mobilisation of the Irish Catholic peasantry in a series of rallies, culminating in his strictly illegal election as MP for Co. Clare in July 1828. A Catholic Relief Act finally passed the following year, but the experience left an almost universally bitter aftertaste. For Irish Catholics it was merely justice too long delayed and achieved only by extra-parliamentary action and in the face of sometimes bitter opposition in which both their religion and their identity as Irish people had been frequently vilified. It was to prove a formative experience in the alienation of Irish Catholics from the British state and the crystallisation of Irish national sentiment.[69] For conservative Protestants it was the thin end of a wedge driven into the Protestant constitution. During the campaign anti-Catholic feeling had been expressed in lurid speeches, pamphlets and mass petitions, whilst in parliament 'the fury of the ultras was the outstanding characteristic of the debates'.[70]

To many of this outlook the Irish Anglican Church seemed to be under particular threat. In reality its situation as the established church in a country where only 12% were adherents[71] was inherently unstable, and successive Whig and Liberal governments sought to tackle the more obvious anomalies until the Gladstone administration finally passed an act of disestablishment in 1869. The Irish Church Temporalities Act of 1833 reduced the number of bishoprics, pruned the income of the remainder and taxed some church incomes. One chronic grievance was the payment of tithes by all to support a church to which only a small minority belonged, and agitation against this led to a long-running 'tithe war' until the Tithe Rent Charge Act of 1838 abolished arrears, reduced payments and merged them with rent.[72] Catholics and many Nonconformists welcomed the changes, but for some in Britain it seemed like further Protestant retreat and Catholic advance. As further evidence they pointed to the increasingly generous treatment of the Catholic seminary of Maynooth in Co. Kildare by governments of all persuasions. In 1845 Sir Robert Peel's Tory government proposed a one-off payment of £30,000 towards repairs and thereafter an annual grant of £26,000. The bill finally passed in June 1845, but provoked one of the most vehement outbursts of anti-Catholic feeling in the nineteenth century, with public meetings, sermons, pamphlets and 8,922 petitions against, and opened a deep divide in the Tory Party.[73]

By far the greatest furore came with the restoration of the Catholic hierarchy of England and Wales in 1850, against which 'the popular upheaval was immense and sustained'.[74] In the early nineteenth century oversight of the Catholic Church in Britain was exercised by the Sacred Congregation of Propaganda. The country was organised into four regions or vicarates, each under a vicar apostolic of episcopal rank. In response to growing numbers the vicarates were increased to eight in 1840, and for the same reason a complete hierarchy was restored in September 1850, with twelve sees under the authority of the newly created office of Cardinal Archbishop of Westminster. This, together with a notably tactless and triumphalist public declaration by the newly installed Cardinal Wiseman, provoked an extraordinary paroxysm of popular Protestant anger.[75] There followed a blizzard of public meetings, publications and petitions against the 'papal aggression'. The Prime Minister, Lord John Russell, fought the 1852 general election on the issue, and legislation was passed restricting the use of territorial titles and right of public procession by the Catholic Church.

Feelings in Manchester generally followed the course of events in Ireland and Britain but with some distinctive local nuances. It has already been noted how in 1746 the presence of some Irish had provoked prejudiced contempt for both their religion and their lowly status. The city was the scene of the first riot between Irish Catholics and Protestants in Great

Britain, in July 1807. A local newspaper recorded how 'Monday last a body of Orange-men, as they are termed, paraded in their sashes and favours to hear divine service, being the anniversary of the Battle of the Boyne; when, on their return, a very serious and alarming affray took place between them and a body of the Greens, as they are called ... The conflict was desperate; several were wounded on each side.' The report went on to praise the exertions of the town constables and local militia in dealing with the conflict and to deplore the incident – 'Let us hear no more of such disgraceful outrages – at which savages and Hottentots would blush' – but went on in terms which implied that such processions were not new: 'The parading with sashes has very properly been suppressed by this town for a few years back: and [we] regret that it was revived on this occasion.'[76] The following week the same publication condemned another manifestation and appealed to higher sentiments:

> Sorry we are to observe another practice, which cannot be suppressed (or punished where detected) with too much promptitude; we mean the writing of 'No Popery' upon the walls & c. with chalk ... The drums and fifes of recruiting parties are also suffered to play party tunes (such as croppies lie down) thro' our streets ... Britons, let this inimitable truth be indelibly recorded on your hearts whatever your faith or opinions may be, never forget that ye are BROTHERS.[77]

Local Catholics felt moved to issue a public statement the following month because

> The society, denominated the Orange Association, having thought it necessary to publish a sort of political creed ... evidently intended to convey, by implication, a reflection upon the Irish Catholics of this populous town and its neighbourhood: we ... think it our duty, in the name of Irish Catholics, so far to defend ourselves ... Too long oppressed as we have been, we ask only to be permitted to enjoy our religious opinions and our modes of worship free from molestation or restraint ... as loyal, and, we trust, useful subjects of a free country, we hope to be permitted to pursue our daily and laborious avocations in peace.[78]

The exclusively Protestant Orange Order or 'Association' referred to had diffused from its original foundation at Loughall in Co. Armagh on 21 September 1795, spreading rapidly through Ireland and attracting not only local people but some soldiers of British regiments stationed in Ireland who were attracted by its Protestant loyalist outlook. Each lodge was organised on the basis of a warrant and pledged to support the Protestant monarchy and later the political union of Ireland and Britain. King William III, who had defeated the Catholic James II at the battle of the Boyne on 12 July 1690, was their hero, his family colour of orange their distinctive badge and 12 July the occasion of annual parades. The first lodge in England was formed in 1798 when the Lancashire Militia returned with warrant no. 220. Lodges then began to appear in the textile towns of the north-west, recruiting not only from ex-soldiers but from Protestant Irish immigrants, especially those in the weaving trade.[79] In 1803 came the first public procession with a parade in Oldham on 12 July,[80] and in 1807 at a meeting in Manchester the lodges in Lancashire were organised into the first County Grand Lodge in England.[81] Of all the constellation of Protestant and anti-Catholic organisations which were to appear in the region during the nineteenth century, this is the most enduring. By 1811 there were twenty-three lodges in and around the city, and there are scattered indications of meetings, often in public houses, until at least the 1830s. But there are also signs of official unease – when a lodge requested permission to participate in the procession celebrating the coronation of George IV in 1821 it was refused,[82] though lodges did participate elsewhere in the region.[83]

As the successive parliamentary efforts to pass Catholic emancipation were brought forward, local organisations in favour and against began to appear. In October 1824 the Manchester and Salford Catholic Association was set up to campaign for 'the restoration of our constitutional rights, on such terms only as guarantee the integrity of our holy religion, and the independence of our pious and zealous pastors'. It was dominated by middle-class English Catholics; it was noted that 'amongst the speakers were a number of the most respectable Catholic inhabitants of the town and neighbourhood', but the meeting also took care to make it clear 'That the thanks of this meeting are due, and are hereby given, to the Irish Catholic Association, for their extraordinary and successful efforts to promote the common cause'.[84] Such growing Catholic assertiveness provoked opponents of emancipation to respond, and on 1 January 1825 they launched the *Manchester Courier*, which made its stance clear from the outset, the proprietors describing themselves as 'advocates of Church and State ... friends of the social order ... [and] the political character and principles of William Pitt ... to whose glorious system of government England is indebted for so large a portion of its present happiness & prosperity'. O'Connell was demonised as 'the noisy zealot', and attitudes to Catholic emancipation were firmly stated:

> A provincial newspaper may be expected to indulge as sparingly as possible in religious controversy – but the politics of the Roman Catholics are now so inseparably connected with their religious sentiments, and their language

and conduct towards those who differ from them in points of doctrine so extravagantly arrogant and intolerant, that it becomes a moral duty in every public writer whose religious sentiments are consonant with our own, to avow himself the champion of the Protestant Church of England, and to lend his aid towards exposing the fallacies and debating the monstrous impositions of its Popish assailants.

A rumour that the Irish Catholic Association was planning a local newspaper provoked the pledge 'Should this threat ever be carried into effect, opposition to the Roman Catholics and their claims will form one of the leading objects of the *Manchester Courier*.'[85] No such newspaper appeared, but this in no way inhibited the *Courier*'s sense of mission, and it took every opportunity to denigrate the tactics of emancipation supporters. Having organised a petition against emancipation it noted with angry indignation how some people had tried to have it declared void 'some advocates of Popery had the meanness to attach the names of *females*'.[86] At one point it was argued that opposition was not aimed at 'all members of the Catholic religion indiscriminately, we are speaking merely of the *Irish* Catholics',[87] but that qualification was rarely observed. When the final Emancipation Bill was making its way through parliament in 1829, it was described as 'the reward of turbulence; a premium upon sedition; a bounty upon rebellion',[88] and when the Act was finally passed in April, it was predicted that it would 'enable the subjects of a foreign power to be the legislators and the ministers of Great Britain … to … elevate Popery and degrade Protestantism'.[89] There may well have been some apprehension as 12 July approached, but in fact the *Courier* reported that the parade by 'a numerous and respectable body of the members of the Loyal Orange Order Association of Manchester' passed off peacefully.[90]

The next five years saw a different picture. In July 1830 there were attacks on three taverns where Orange lodges were meeting for a celebratory meal and their flags were flying, the *Guardian* noting with some relief that though such conflicts were regular occurrences at that time of year 'fortunately, these displays are not very frequent in this town'.[91] The following year was quiet. There were low-level sectarian scuffles in Angel Meadow in February 1832 when a group of Protestants were 'upbraided by their neighbours, who are Catholics, with being "bloody heretics and Orangemen"'.[92] The Orange processions of that year proceeded peacefully,[93] and the same was true of 1833. However, the following two years were very different. In 1834 the conflict, spread over three days, involved incidents surrounding an Orange procession to St George's church in Hulme and subsequently around public houses in streets in Angel Meadow, order being restored by deployment of police, special constables and a detachment of dragoons.[94] That feelings lingered over the summer is borne out by the sectarian overtones of a fight a few days later when 'a party of drunken Irish Catholics' encountered someone they suspected of being an Orangeman and 'determined to make him their first victim'.[95] The following year the outbreak was more limited in both duration and the area involved, which the *Courier* attributed to the fact that 'the Orangemen of Manchester, out of respect for the authorities and with a strong desire to preserve the peace of this great commercial town, suppressed every symbol which could be construed into a ground of provocation', but nonetheless 'some slight outrages occurred' as the lodges returned from a church service on Sunday,[96] there were scuffles the following evening and on the Tuesday at a public house which displayed a portrait of King William III. [97]

This was to be the last large-scale outbreak of communal conflict in the city for almost fifty years.[98] In part this reflected the fact that Catholic emancipation had been passed into law, but it was also a reflection of the hard times encountered by the Orange Order. The recurring conflict which accompanied their processions on both sides of the Irish Sea and wild rumours that the Order was involved in plans for a coup in which its Grand Master, the Duke of Cumberland, would attempt to replace Princess Victoria as successor to King William IV led to the setting up of a parliamentary select committee which issued a notably unfavourable report in 1835. As a result, the Order in Ireland dissolved itself in that year, and the English Order followed suit in 1836.[99] There was also a split in Orange ranks which was not healed until 1876. The Party Processions Act, passed in 1832, renewed in 1850 and 1860 and not repealed until 1872, also severely restricted open-air activities. These developments brought the Order to a low ebb in Britain for several decades, though there are indications that small-scale private events were still held in July. When the Order did re-emerge in Manchester in the late 1860s its demonstrations were still lively and boisterous, but they were more structured and disciplined, links with local Conservative associations had developed, and though the strident anti-Catholicism persisted, Irish political affairs became more central as home rule began to rise up the political agenda.

But if this institutional expression of anti-Catholic sentiment was faltering, until 1865 the cause had a powerful local spokesman in Rev. Hugh Stowell of Christ Church, Salford. Born in the Isle of Man in 1799, educated at St Edmund Hall, Oxford, and ordained in 1823, he arrived in Salford as a curate in 1825 and by 1831 was rector of Christ Church, Salford, a church specially built for him by his supporters. His popularity was derived from a combination of personal qualities and a particularly robust combination of anti-Catholic evangelical Protestantism, Tory politics and social concern. In personal terms he had a commanding presence, a vivid, fervent preaching style in an era when such gifts were widely appreciated and formidable energy.[100] The core of his conviction was that the Protestant institutions and values of the British state were under internal threat from the Anglo-Catholic party, whom he dubbed 'the most insidious agents of the Jesuits',[101] and externally from the growing strength of Protestant dissent and above all from Roman Catholicism. Legislative interference with the Church of Ireland was, he believed, a sign of things to come in Great Britain. His solution was an energetic reassertion of what he believed to be the original Reformation principles of the Church of England, together with an equally vigorous assault on the teachings and activities of the Roman Catholic Church. He held office in many of the various ultra-Protestant organisations which emerged in this period, including the Salford Operatives' Protestant Association and the Manchester Protestant Tradesmen's and Operatives' Association. In 1840 he was involved in a libel case which attracted national attention. Stowell claimed that Fr Hearne had imposed a particularly cruel penance on a parishioner; the jury found for Hearne and imposed damages of forty shillings,[102] but on appeal the judgment was set aside.[103]

Aware of the radical changes in social and economic geography which were challenging the position of the established church in the new industrial towns, Stowell argued for an ambitious programme of building churches and parochial schools, and opposed the concept of non-denominational schools supported from public funds. He repeatedly claimed, 'I never took the remotest part in party politics ... I don't care whether we have a Whig, Tory or Radical representative',[104] but in reality his traditionalist ultra-Protestant outlook led him to give consistent support to Conservative candidates at general elections in both Salford and Manchester.[105] To his supporters, mostly prosperous evangelical lay Anglicans in late middle age,[106] he was 'the faithful and devoted champion of our national Protestantism'.[107] When he died in 1865 he had a funeral 'of almost civic splendour':[108] the route to the cemetery was lined with large crowds, flags flew at half-mast and many shops closed,[109] and the eulogy was delivered by Canon Hugh McNeil, doyen of Protestant campaigners in the north west, who paid tribute to him for 'holding aloft the unfurled banner of the Protestant Reformation and the liberties of England'.[110] Catholics remembered him as 'One of the most eloquent and most bitter caluminators of the Church'.[111]

But for some time there had been indications that sectarian feeling in the city was ebbing. As early as 1852 there had been complaints at a meeting of the Manchester Protestant Operatives' Association that attendance at meetings was dropping and funds were short,[112] and in 1855 the colourful anti-Catholic lecturer 'Father' Gavazzi remarked on the thin attendance at his meetings.[113] Towards the end of his life even Stowell campaigned less on Catholicism and more on social and welfare issues. Meetings on issues such as Anglo-Catholic 'ritualism' still took place – when the Manchester Diocesan Church Association met in early 1868 it pledged to oppose 'the ritualistic observances that were creeping into the Church and assimilating her doctrines to those of the Church of Rome'[114] – but such gatherings lacked the fiery intemperance of earlier days. The proposal to disestablish the Church of Ireland provoked a flurry of meetings both for[115] and against,[116] but a town meeting refused to pronounce on the question.[117] Manchester did experience a visit from William Murphy, one of a dying breed of itinerant anti-Catholic lecturers. Like others in the trade, he claimed to have been converted from Catholicism to evangelical Protestantism and made a career lecturing against aspects of Catholic doctrine. Little public notice was taken of him until the overheated context of the 'Fenian scare' of the late 1860s generated a more edgy atmosphere, especially in places where there was a concentration of Irish Catholic immigrants. Murphy made a practice of speaking in such areas. The Manchester Martyrs drama of September and November 1867 and the Fenian bombing of Clerkenwell prison in December that year further stoked public anger, and Murphy continued his travels into 1868, focusing particularly on north-western towns with a notable Catholic Irish population. His itinerary was marked by outbreaks of riot and unrest, especially in Ashton-under-Lyne in May, when Irish Catholic inhabitants of the local Little Ireland district, adorned with green ribbons and armed with 'sticks, staves, scythe blades, sickles, pistols and stones', clashed with local Protestants decked in 'orange ribbons and rosettes' and armed with 'pieces of broken furniture such as chair and table legs … and throwing stones'.[118] The local Catholic church was damaged, police and the 6th Enniskillen Dragoons were deployed, and some rioters went on to Stalybridge, where there was a further outbreak; there was unrest in Bury.[119] Later that month, even though Murphy had not visited, there was an outbreak in Oldham which was attributed to 'a bad feeling engendered by Murphyism and a hatred of Fenianism', and there were reports that local Orangemen had been making pike heads.[120] It is hardly surprising therefore that when it was announced that he would speak in Manchester in an assembly room in the same street as St Wilfrid's Catholic church, excited and noisy crowds gathered in anticipation. Murphy was arrested and left the city without lecturing. Though he continued his activities for another four years, his audiences waned as the anti-Fenian panic ebbed, and his appearances were increasingly restricted to smaller towns and venues. His career finally came to an end in March 1872 when he died, partly as a result of a severe beating inflicted by local Catholic miners during a lecture series in Whitehaven.[121] His passing in many ways marked the ebb of a long and noisy tradition of sectarian public disputation, a form of street theatre which was to linger for a time in Merseyside and Clydeside and above all in Belfast, but never again found a large-scale public audience in the rest of the British state.

By the early twentieth century the situation of Catholics had changed to the point where in 1902 Dan McCabe, one of Manchester's leading Catholic laymen, an enormously popular Liberal councillor and a leading spokesman for Irish interests, could express the belief that 'Catholics received fair play in the city at the present time' (Figure 12).[122] McCabe was second-generation Irish, a member of St Patrick's church, a regular speaker at St Patrick's Day and Manchester Martyrs commemoration events and a strong advocate of Irish home rule. But his obvious competence and affability had made him universally popular, and in 1913 he was to become the city's first Catholic Lord Mayor and to receive the rare accolade of being asked to serve a second term. Even the *Manchester Courier* noted 'his real aptitude for public affairs … With a popularity that is not confined to party, he takes office inspired by an impetus of public good feeling which few men immersed in the vitriolic maelstrom of politics can ever enjoy.'[123] Ironically, his elevation provoked a manifestation of official anti-Catholic sentiment. It was the tradition for the newly elected Lord Mayor to attend a civic service at the city's cathedral, but McCabe instead attended Mass at Holy Name Catholic church. He was rebuked by the cathedral's Dean Weldon as a disappointing example of 'the spirit of religious exclusiveness', a remark which was condemned by Bishop Casartelli of Salford amongst others.[124] In 1919, when Alderman Tom Fox was elected the first Labour Lord Mayor, Casartelli unreservedly declared, 'For the second time in six years they had a Catholic chief magistrate, of whom they were proud. Catholics now had equal rights, privileges and opportunities as other citizens.'[125] But such confidence about their place in the life of the city had emerged only after the Catholic Church had successfully absorbed the Irish influx of the 1840s and faced other challenges to the faith.

## Catholic associationalism

There has been some discussion in the literature about the level of church attendance among the migrant Irish in nineteenth-century Britain. To some extent this is an offshoot of a wider debate about the level of attendance in Ireland itself during the same period. It is generally accepted that by the end of the nineteenth century the great majority of Irish Catholics were remarkably regular in their public devotions, creating a level of attendance that stood in sharp contrast to Protestant Britain and the rest of Europe and persisted well into the late twentieth century.[126] However, it has been argued that in the early decades of the nineteenth century the picture was rather different. For Catholics the Mass is the central act of worship, and participation a key obligation. It has been estimated that in pre-famine Ireland average attendance was around 40%,[127] with considerable regional variations. These variations may have been due to scarcity of clergy and church buildings in areas of rapid population change, but it has also been suggested that they may have been due to regional contrasts in cultural tradition. It is argued that the highest rates of regular attendance were to be found in those areas with the highest rates of English speaking and modernised commercial life.[128] In the more remote Irish-speaking regions, it is argued, a different tradition of religious observance remained strong, with the custom being occasional attendance at the sacraments, but with Mass, marriage and baptism sometimes celebrated in private homes by peripatetic clergy,[129] and orthodox Catholic teachings surviving in places alongside traditional folk beliefs and practices. Already by mid-century reforms were under way which, by the early twentieth century, would see at least one church in every parish, resident clergy, the growth of regular attendance and the development of a network of confraternities and sodalities, a process of reorganisation and rationalisation which some have dubbed a 'devotional revolution'.[130]

In the very different context of urban industrial Britain it has been estimated that up to 50% of baptised Irish Catholic migrants did not attend Mass.[131] Some may have taken advantage of escape from the social controls of parish and family to the anonymity of urban Britain to cease a practice they no longer believed in. It is equally possible that the low levels of attendance in the early decades of the century were due to the fact that many migrants originated from regions where the traditionally irregular customs discussed above still held. This may well have been true of Manchester, where so many Irish came from the north-western counties of Ireland. It has been suggested that in the late eighteenth century attendance was just over 50%.[132] In late 1806 Fr Broomhead wrote to a colleague that following a recent series of public talks he had been examining converts and first communicants, noting 'many from Ireland of this class from 30 to 40 years old', and early the following year another series of talks yielded first communicants of whom he again remarked, 'many from Ireland from 20 to 40 years old'.[133] By the end of the 1820s it was estimated that the figure for non-practising and potentially lapsing amongst Irish migrants could have been approximately 70%.[134] It is hardly surprising that over the next few decades the church invested heavily not only in personnel and plant, but in a supportive network of organisations and associations.

The influx of Catholic Irish famine refugees in the second half of the 1840s clearly placed massive strain on church resources in Manchester, but by 1908 some forty-one places of Catholic worship had been opened in the previous hundred years, together with associated presbyteries, parochial halls and schools, and several convents, monasteries and charitable homes had also been opened.[135] But alongside the infrastructure and clerical personnel, a dense network of Catholic organisations and associations also developed. These were in fact a Catholic variant of one of the most characteristic features of nineteenth-century British society, namely the tendency for people to organise themselves into groups for a wide variety of shared purposes. Amongst Manchester Catholics they appeared from the early nineteenth century, some proving quite ephemeral, but others enduring. They had a variety of purposes, some being devoted to cultivation of the spiritual life, others to the encouragement of sporting, cultural or intellectual pursuits, some to encouraging seemly behaviour, others to providing insurance against illness and funeral expenses; and doubtless in all cases there was a social dimension.[136] But it has also been argued that they were designed to protect the faithful from the threats presented by the ideas circulating in the non-Catholic world. It is argued that this strong Catholic 'associational culture' developed, particularly from the late nineteenth century onwards,[137] to meet the multiple threat presented by mass education, increasing literacy, the burgeoning popular press, mass participation in sport, popular culture and entertainment and the development of liberalism and socialism within the growing labour movement.[138]

From the 1830s onwards there was a steady growth in guilds and confraternities designed to strengthen the spiritual life of believers – by 1847 there were at least ten in the city and surrounding area.[139] Members of the Christian Doctrine Confraternity were lay people who, on two nights each week, conducted instruction in prayer and catechism in their homes with a group of about six children aged eight and over, whilst the parish priest heard their Confession each Monday. In the 1830s St Mary's church had a flourishing class in juvenile instruction consisting of 150 boys, who wore a uniform of black serge gown with two flowing wings, a black cap and a blue ribbon from which there hung a Maltese cross. The 300 girls at a convent school branch wore brown Spanish-style mantles with black bonnets. All paraded regularly in full regalia, doubtless forming part of the attraction when such public demonstrations were a normal part of the urban cultural landscape.[140] As the church school network developed, the need for such organisations for children faded, but this in turn led to the formation of organisations for past pupils, the most notable of which was the St Patrick's Old Boys' Association founded in 1901 with Dan McCabe as first president. Confraternities and sodalities for adults also flourished, and by the early twentieth century there were local branches of the Brotherhood of St Peter, the Confraternity of the Holy Face of Jesus and the Knights of the Blessed Sacrament, whose first meeting in England took place at Holy Name church in July 1916.[141]

Groups dedicated to leisure pursuits took some time to establish themselves. A Manchester Catholic Literary Society had been established in 1842 but quickly faded. In the second half of the century however, as the Catholic population grew and consolidated, such organisations multiplied. Several groups were formed for those with theatrical and musical interests, including the Catholic Stage Guild, the Lancashire Catholic Players' Society and the Catholic Philharmonic Society, which gave a public concert in the Free Trade Hall in December 1912.[142] There was even a Catholic Esperanto Society. Others catered for sports enthusiasts, such as the Catholic Football League for Manchester and District, the Manchester and District Catholic Cricket Club and the Manchester and District Catholic Amateur Orme Billiard League. Groups also appeared at parish level, including St Wilfrid's Cycling Club. For the more erudite there was the Catholic Lecture Association. Several organisations mobilised women to assist the poor and needy, such as the Catholic Womens' League (motto: 'Charity, Work, Loyalty') and the Ladies of Charity of St Vincent de Paul. The Catholic Needlework Guild, founded in 1887, had 216 members in twenty-one branches by late 1899. Its purpose was 'to provide useful articles for Clothing for the Poor, and to offer the girls and women of all classes the means of exercising charity'. Members undertook to donate at least two articles of clothing each year.[143]

As already noted, clergy such as Fr Hearne recognised that alcohol was a serious problem amongst their parishioners, and in 1838 a Catholic Total Abstinence Society had been formed. Its members met for tea parties, music and socialising and, like many such organisations at that time, regularly paraded in public, with bands, flags and banners, wearing rosettes and medals presented by Fr Mathew.[144] In March 1844 it was suggested that his visit had helped reduce the customary drunkenness associated with St Patrick's Day celebrations,[145] but the problem clearly persisted, because by the mid-1870s there was a well-established Salford Diocese Temperance Crusade, complete with band and uniforms. This became a regular feature of St Patrick's Day gatherings in the Free Trade Hall, where in 1879 they 'walked into the hall playing various national airs'. Clerical speakers at these celebrations repeatedly returned to the need for disciplined temperance amongst the faithful. In that year Bishop Vaughan suggested that they might be backsliding and in need of

> whipping up … He wished them to take to heart this great question of temperance, and he hoped that the police and authorities during the next two or three days would not be able to record any serious cases of drunkenness against Irishmen (applause) … He had made up his mind to institute some special inquiries to ascertain from the authorities how St. Patrick's Day had been passed in this city.[146]

Three years later Canon Kershaw, past president of the crusade, returned to the topic, reminding his audience that one reason for the event was 'to testify to the principles of the Crusade', and at the same meeting Bishop Vaughan jovially 'expressed the hope that, as might have happened in years gone by, none of his Irish flock would run into excess that evening and get into trouble'.[147] The remark was greeted with laughter, but the point had been made. Other organisations with the aim of encouraging sober citizenship in the widest sense included the Catholic Boys' Brigade, the Catholic Young Men's Society and the Catholic Boy Scouts, whose first Manchester troop was founded in 1908. In the early 1840s there had been a number of groups which were essentially defensive reactions to aggressive Protestant evangelism, such as the Salford Catholic Tract Society and the United Order of Catholic Brethren,[148] but as time passed the emphasis shifted to a more confident assertion of the Catholic outlook, as in the case of the Catholic Lecture Association and the Catholic Truth Society, founded in Salford in 1885 and destined to become an international organisation.

That characteristic group of nineteenth-century Britain, the mutual benefit society, was a recurring feature throughout the period. As early as 1819 there was a St Augustine's School Sick Society;[149] the Manchester and Salford Catholic Benefit Society appeared in 1825, and by the 1840s there was a Sick and Burial Club in almost every parish, usually with the priest as overseer,[150] guaranteeing a decent funeral and some support in times of sickness and distress. In 1875 legislation finally brought order and stability to this rapidly growing movement when a national register of friendly societies was set up together with full-time staff to regulate and monitor their activities.[151] Mutual-aid groups multiplied rapidly but also amalgamated and in some cases grew into significant regional and national financial institutions. In Ireland one of the most popular was the Irish National Foresters, whose motto 'Unity, Nationality, Benevolence' summed up its combination of self-help, mutuality and Irish nationalism. Founded in 1877, the organisation spread rapidly in Ireland and amongst the Irish in Britain, and, though it was not under the aegis of the Catholic Church, the overlap in membership was almost complete. In keeping with the nationalist ethos, branches took the names of Irish heroes. The first Manchester branch, the 'Robert Emmet', opened in 1878 and was soon followed by the 'Brothers Shears', 'Parnell' and 'Martyrs'. The secretary of the 'Robert Emmet' was Daniel Boyle, who became one of Manchester's leading Irish personalitie (Figure 13). Born in Fermanagh in 1859, he arrived in the city in 1877, took a post with the Midland Railway Company and quickly became a leading organiser for the Foresters and notably active in both Manchester and Irish nationalist politics. As the Foresters flourished, branches were grouped into districts. Boyle became secretary of the Manchester District, compiled the society's rule book in 1883, served as Grand High Chief Ranger in 1890 and 1893 and presided over three national conventions held in Manchester.[152] By 1900 the Manchester District had 812 members in twenty-three branches, numbers that were generally considered a tribute to Boyle's energy and widely acknowledged administrative abilities;[153] juvenile branches were formed, and regular church parades were held with bands and banners (Figure 13).

But of all the Catholic organisations formed in Manchester in the later nineteenth century, perhaps the most revealing was the Salford Diocese Catholic Protection and Rescue Society, formed in 1886, with a monthly journal, *The Harvest*, launched in October 1887. On 6 February 1883 Bishop Vaughan, concerned with what became widely referred to in the church as 'leakage',[154] set up a ten-man board of inquiry composed of both clergy and lay people to try and discover the extent to which Catholic children in the diocese were being lost to the faith through parental neglect, proselytism and the operation of such public institutions as the workhouse system. They concluded that significant numbers of the abandoned children living on the streets were from Catholic backgrounds, that they had no idea of the exact numbers involved or the extent of parental neglect and that the workings of the courts, prisons and workhouses (despite what was described as 'the considerate and fair treatment of the Guardians') meant many were lost to the faith. The priests of the diocese were contacted, and at a meeting in May 1886 it was concluded on the basis of this survey that at that time 10,456 Catholic children were at risk and that 'the worst enemies of many of those poor children were their own natural parents'.[155] Bishop Vaughan set up the society to protect children from cruel and irreligious parents and to ensure that Catholic children going through public institutions were enabled to practise their religion and on discharge were allocated to Catholic families or church-owned homes.[156] The society was run by an executive committee of four, chaired by the bishop and was supported by twenty-one district committees which publicised its work and raised funds. Subsequently, three homes were set up, an officer was appointed to attend court proceedings and take note of cases involving Catholic children, and churches were asked to organise annual Rescue Society and St Joseph's penny collections.[157]

Tacitly acknowledging that the Irish were the core of his flock, on 17 March 1887 Bishop Vaughan addressed the St Patrick's Day celebrations in the Free Trade Hall and announced to applause that 'it had been determined to put the great work of [the society] under the special care of St Patrick'. Anticipating outside objections, he was careful to make it clear that the aim was not prosletyism but provision for homeless Catholic children, arguing that this would provide a public service by clearing the streets of a potentially criminal element. He then indulged in some flattery, declaring that 'he had never doubted the character of Manchester men … [they] had a strong common sense and a deep sense of justice', and stressed that the leading local newspapers had endorsed the argu-

*10* Perceived dangers to young Catholic people in lodging houses

ment that Catholic children should be placed in Catholic homes. Turning to the work of the society, he reported that over the past five months between forty and fifty children had been 'saved from Protestantism'.[158]

The aim of *The Harvest* was to publicise the work and help raise funds, but it gradually evolved into something like a diocesan newsletter, and as such it opens a window into the changing nature and preoccupations of the Catholic population and the place of the Irish. For the first few years the emphasis was on the material, moral and spiritual threats to Catholic children in spaces and places previously beyond the reach of the church. To illustrate the dangers, several supporters conducted what amounted to field excursions into some of the most run-down areas of the city and published their findings. The language used in describing the visit to the Ancoats district is reminiscent of a military operation or an expedition into a dangerous foreign country: 'We sallied forth to reconnoitre Ancoats by night … We struck into the heart of the country … We slackened rein … We assayed a view of the denizens.'[159] In material terms the explorers found plenty to shock, especially during anonymous stays in places offering temporary accommodation, such as the casual wards of the workhouse and cheap lodging houses, where, aside from physical squalor and constant drinking, they found that 'there is any amount of cursing, and fighting and stealing' and men and older boys instructed the younger boys in confidence tricks and theft (Figure 10).[160]

11 Perceived dangers to young Catholics: innocent Joe and Joe's dubious pal

Of particular concern was the 'free and easy', the public house licensed for singing and dancing as well as alcohol, of which there were 512 in Manchester in 1892.[161] 'They are much frequented by our youth. They enjoy much popularity with both sexes. They are the cause of much sin and unlimited evil.' This particular expedition was accompanied by suitably vivid illustrations of the types of character encountered (Figure 11).[162] In supporting the society it was argued, 'we are saving a young life, full of promise, we are robbing the vast criminal class of an intended victim and we are saving from perdition a soul'.[163] But the danger from drunken, violent, negligent parents was also noted. At one house in Ancoats visitors found 'The father was drinking in a local snug; the mother – gaunt, dirty and sloppy … jugs on the table betrayed previous potations. As for the children, we say nothing; but … there was only one way of cleaning the house – burn it.'[164]

The administrative practices of public institutions were a central concern. Much effort went into publishing detailed instructions on how crucial it was that the religious persuasion of Catholic children should be registered on entry; otherwise they could be given over to the care of Protestant chaplains, which would expose them to 'daily possibility of proselytism'.[165] Further problems arose on discharge, with the danger that young Catholics would be allocated to Protestant households, where they might be tempted by meat on Fridays, boys might be lured from Confession by Saturday sport, and girls were in danger of a fate left to the imagination, especially if for any reason employers discharged them without a reference: 'what wonder that the whispers of doubtful companions are listened to and they take a course which allures only to destroy'.[166] One solution was for Catholics to be elected as Poor Law Guardians so they could monitor registration and placement procedures at the workhouse. Catholic candidates usually allied with local Liberals, and from the late 1880s could usually take four seats on the fifteen-member Manchester board, electing its first female member, Mrs Rose Hyland.[167] Both Bishop Vaughan and his successor Bishop Bilsborrow regularly sent letters to be read out by parish priests, listing Catholic candidates in each union of the diocese and encouraging the faithful to ensure 'the necessary votes required for the return of a Catholic Guardian'.[168] An exchange at a meeting of the Manchester board in July 1902 illustrated a Catholic representative doing his duty. By this time it was the custom for Catholic children to be placed in a Rescue Society home until placements in a Catholic household were available, but one guardian moved that they be retained at the workhouse, upon which Dan McCabe charged that the proposal had 'a sting of bigotry in it … petty, persecuting' and the suggestion was voted down.[169]

Many charitable institutions working amongst distressed children in this period adopted the solution of emigration, in the hope that this would give them the chance of a new start and a better life. For the Rescue Society there was the additional advantage that the children would be placed in Catholic homes. From its earliest days the society sent children to the strongly Catholic province of Quebec, and there were regular reports on the journey and the progress of the migrants. The first party of thirteen sailed from Liverpool on 21 June 1888.[170] A total of 134 children were sent the following year,[171] and Fr Rossall, who accompanied the children, was in no doubt about the value of the programme: 'Everything I saw … confirmed my first impression that it was exceedingly beneficial to the souls and bodies of these poor orphans and deserted children to emigrate them to Catholic Canada.'[172]

The changing contents of *The Harvest* over the years suggest that by the early twentieth century the Manchester Catholic population was evolving into a much more settled, confident community. Three months before his spat with his fellow guardian, McCabe had attended a Rescue Society reunion where he expressed the opinion that 'if they lost control of their children the fault was their own'.[173] But one feature which remained constant was the concern with Irish matters, though not explicitly political issues.

## Irish as well as Catholic?

The Catholic Church in Manchester, as in the rest of Britain, remained strongly Irish not only in numbers but in the preoccupations of its adherents, and this at times created tensions not only with English Catholics, but between the clerical leadership and lay people. Elsewhere in the Irish diaspora, clerics of Irish background quickly ascended to the episcopate, but this was a notably slow process in Britain, and for some time there was also a reluctance to employ Irish-born parish priests, even in areas where the Irish presence was dominant.[174] In Manchester, successive bishops recognised the significance of the Irish and on occasion went out of their way to associate themselves with the community, but they could be equally quick to indicate displeasure. In March 1875, when Bishop Vaughan appeared at the St Patrick's Day celebrations in the Free Trade Hall, he made a point of underlining the need to continue support for the Diocesan Temperance Crusade. He then told his audience 'to considerable enthusiasm' that the sprig of shamrock he was wearing had been plucked on the Hill of Tara in Co. Meath and sent by a friend, and that he was wearing it because 'though an Englishman by birth, he was an

Irishman at heart'.[175] When he took the chair at the same event four years later he remarked that 'he was very pleased very early that morning when he heard the carillons in the Town Hall tower playing the national airs of Ireland (applause) ... He looked upon that, small indication though it may be, as an evidence of the goodwill and kindly feeling which existed in Manchester towards the Irish, that great portion of the population and of the Catholic flock.' Once again he underlined the temperance cause.[176] It was also highly significant that he had announced the launch of the Protection and Rescue Society at the St Patrick's Day celebrations of 1887 and placed the work under the care of St Patrick. But there was an indication of the unease that Irish political activities could create amongst the hierarchy when the Foresters in their green sashes joined the procession to Mass in memory of the Manchester Martyrs in November 1889. On arrival outside St Patrick's church they were informed that the bishop would not permit them to wear their regalia in the church precincts in case it upset other worshippers.[177] The sashes were removed but were replaced on leaving the church, and at the subsequent public meeting it was clear that the order had provoked resentment amongst members at not being able to wear their colours 'in their own church'. The chairman of the meeting exonerated the parish clergyman – 'a true and devoted Irish priest' – and the bishop, blaming 'wire pullers behind the scenes', and praised fellow members for their 'example of prudence and manly self-restraint'.[178]

Vaughan's successor as Bishop of Salford, John Bilsborrow (1892–1903), displayed the same mix of awareness and wariness. When he visited the Catholic Lads' Club in Angel Meadow in January 1894 one of the boys read an address in which he stressed how in their Catholic hearts – 'we ought to say Irish Catholic hearts ...' – they were incomparably loyal, and how 'we glory and boast in being Irish Catholic young men'. The bishop took up the theme and applauded them '[in] being true and faithful to their religion as Irish Catholics'.[179] Late in 1898, however, he faced a major problem. Fr McCarthy, a curate at St James' church, Pendleton, blessed the foundation stone of a monument commemorating the Manchester Martyrs at a ceremony in the city's Moston cemetery attended by James Stephens, founder of the IRB.[180] There followed a series of fiery speeches by the ardently nationalist Maud Gonne amongst others at a public meeting later that evening.[181] Fr McCarthy already had form as a strong Irish nationalist, and in February 1899 the bishop dismissed him, provoking vehement reaction from local Irish Catholics, who were convinced that the motivation was anti-Irish bias. There was already discontent in the district at the alleged domination of local parishes by non-Irish clergy, and in particular the German Fr Saffenreuter of St James' had provoked the ire of the local Irish.[182] In response to McCarthy's dismissal the committee responsible for the martyrs' monument organised a demonstration for Sunday 12 February. Up to six thousand people gathered for the procession and open-air meeting, bands playing 'God save Ireland', 'The wearing of the green' and 'Killarney' and people wearing green handkerchiefs, items of green clothing and ivy leaves. It soon became clear that a deep-seated grievance had surfaced. Leaflets encouraging attendance had carried appeals to the Irishmen of Salford and Manchester to assemble in support of 'another Irish priest sacrificed on the altar of English hate and animosity'.[183] The procession loudly cheered Fr McCarthy and was followed by a public meeting at which a resolution was passed demanding the reinstatement of Fr McCarthy and stating that 'The Irish people were the Catholic Church in Pendleton; and they demanded that a man of their race and nationality should represent them in the Church and minister to their spiritual requirements.'[184]

Bishop Louis Charles Casartelli (Bishop of Salford 1903–25) never seemed to develop any rapport with the Irish. A scholarly product of Manchester's Italian community, he was a man of refined intellectual and cultural tastes who lacked the common touch but was totally at ease amongst the social and cultural elite of the city. He clearly enjoyed the silver jubilee lecture of the Manchester Geographical Society on 5 November 1909, describing the lecturer, the Irish-born Lieutenant Ernest Shackleton, as 'a modest speaker, with Irish wit', and found the dinner the following evening at the Midland Hotel with 280 guests, when he sat beside Shackleton, to be 'a brilliant gathering'.[185] He never appeared at the St Patrick's Day celebrations, but followed high political affairs with a sense of detachment, noting national events such as the royal assent to the Irish Home Rule bill on 18 September 1914 'An historical day … D.G.'[186] However, any development at the national or local level which directly impinged on church interests drew his immediate attention.

The Fr McCarthy case illustrated the fact that at the level of parochial clergy there could at times be more empathy with the Irish than existed at the episcopal level. Clergy were always represented at St Patrick's Day celebrations – six were amongst the platform party in 1897– sometimes with a priest chairing the proceedings, at others times as a main speaker. It is also true that not all foreign priests were out of sympathy with the Irish. The Belgian-born Dean Mussely of St Patrick's generally demonstrated a lively sympathy with his overwhelmingly Irish flock. In 1896, whilst celebrating Mass for the Manchester Martyrs, he told the congregation how he regretted 'the unfortunate severity' of the sentences imposed upon the martyrs and went on to say, 'poor unfortunate Ireland has suffered, and that bitterly, for the faith …. she along with Poland and Armenia, was a martyr nation … the lovely emerald of the west'.[187] At the subsequent public meeting the principal speaker was Fr Cusack, also of St Patrick's, who at that time was president of the Michael Davitt branch of the Irish National League. In 1899, when the public meeting following the Mass for the Manchester Martyrs was held in the parochial hall, Dan McCabe thanked the dean for giving it free of charge and, it was reported, went on:

> This was not the first good act of the Dean towards the Irish people. This was an Irish parish bearing the name of St. Patrick's. In the church they met annually to celebrate the anniversary of the Manchester Martyrs and they never had greater kindness shown to them than by Dean Mussely (Applause). It was he who first procured the green flag with the golden harp, which was on the platform that night, and which floated on the flagpole outside the church every St. Patrick's day and every recurring anniversary of the Manchester Martyrs … Dean Mussely … said he was most happy to be present. It showed they were in touch with one another. He would like to take some of them over to Belgium and show them what Ireland would look like ten years after it had secured Home Rule (Cheers) … If the people had the same chance as the people of Belgium there would be a great transformation (Cheers). He hoped the twentieth century would be quite a young baby of a century when Home Rule would be granted Ireland.[188]

Whilst the contents of *The Harvest* made almost no direct references to Irish political issues, there was frequent reference to current Irish church life and religious traditions and their significance for the universal church. As the progress of the children being taken to Quebec was tracked, there were constant references to Ireland, the Irish diaspora and the usefulness of the network of Irish contacts in smoothing the emigration process. The account of Fr Rosall's first trip recalled the stop-off at Moville '[in] dear old Catholic Ireland', and on landing in Quebec he recalled how 'already I hear in a jolly tone a hearty Irish welcome … from more than one "from the old country"'.[189] The path was further eased by the fact that both the Quebec governor and his deputy were 'good old Irish Catholics' who made the arrangements for the next visit.[190]

St Patrick's Day featured regularly in the magazine in various forms, including doggerel poetry, reminiscences of past celebrations, accounts of the blessing of the shamrock and advertisements for 'Mr. James Foy's Real Irish Night', which ran for a number of years from 1908.[191] There were also weightier items stressing the historic significance of Patrick, as in March 1890: 'There will be little necessity to remind our readers that the 17th of this month … is the feast of St. Patrick, Apostle of Ireland. Most of us have no need of calendar for it. We carry the date in our hearts.' The writer then proceeded to set the Patrician appeal in a wider context: 'while the Church, as a true Mother, enters into all that the heart of the Irish race feels on St. Patrick's day, she calls upon the whole Christendom to join and rejoice with us all the world over, for a Saint for one is a solace for all, and the glory of one part of the Church is a joy to the whole'.[192] In a subsequent article there was a potted biography of the saint and an account of how his ministry triggered the distinctive Celtic monastic tradition and its diffusion into northern Britain and Europe, but the writer carefully abstained from 'a recital of the wrongs, the tyranny, and the persecutions of seven hundred years'.[193] Other items featured Irish prayers, stories of enduring faith under pressure (including penal days in Ireland), tales of Irish saints, accounts of the work of Irish nuns and missionaries and of Irish devotion to the rosary, and biographies of contemporary Irish churchmen. On occasion religiosity, nostalgia and sentimentality came together, as in 'To my mother in Ireland: for my first Mass' by a member of the Jesuit Order.[194]

Accounts of visits to Ireland were a regular feature. Pilgrimages were traced in detail. Following the claims of the Marian apparitions at Knock, Co. Mayo, in 1879, the home county of a considerable number of the Irish in the city, a pilgrimage from Manchester took place as early as 1880.[195] Other visits occurred to ecclesiastical sites such as Ardfert, Lismore and Glendalough, and were written up in travelogues, exhibiting great pride in the achievements of early Irish Celtic Christianity.[196] Some narratives recounted holidays in Ireland, but even here there were occasional asides such as 'how deep seated is the faith in God's providence implanted in the Irish breast'.[197] There was also considerable interest in the material welfare of Ireland, with articles on Irish housing, emigration and education, and in 1901 it was noted, 'There is at present a wide spread revival of the study of Irish.'[198] The campaign for a Catholic university in Ireland was regularly reported, together with the support meeting in Manchester in January 1899.[199] The poor harvests which brought widespread distress to parts of Connemara in the late 1890s were reported in a series of articles, and in March 1899 the West of Ireland Association was formed in Manchester with the aim of encouraging Irish economic activity.[200] Subsequent exhibitions and sales of Irish goods in the city were advertised and commended.[201] Local firms clearly recognised the enduring pull of the Irish brand for this Catholic community, since many of their advertisements in *The Harvest* stressed Irish links. Mr James Doherty of Smithfield market declared that he had 'Irish Bacon and Hams arriving daily';[202] John McLaughlin advertised 'Real Irish Tweeds' and in case someone missed the point embellished his advert with 'Support Home Industry' superimposed upon a shamrock.[203] An agency for supplying servants announced it could supply 'Irish girls just over, well trained, and with first class reference,'[204] and Miss Cull from Co. Down advertised that in 'Rostrevor near the sea' she provided 'Comfortable Apartments with Good Cooking and Attendance'.[205]

But from the early twentieth century Irish items decreased sharply in numbers, possibly because a series of issues arose in Britain which directly impacted upon the Catholic Church. There was a growing concern about the impact of the burgeoning labour movement and the associated philosophies of socialism and communism, but above all the issue of religious education came to the fore with contrasting proposals from a series of Conservative and Liberal governments, and the pages of *The Harvest* became increasingly preoccupied with their possible impact on Catholic schools. Events such as the split in the Irish Parliamentary Party (or Irish party) in 1891 and reconciliation in 1900, the Home Rule Bills of 1893 and 1912 and the 1916 rising were passed over. By the latter date the world war had overwhelmed all other concerns.

## Conclusion

The growing influx of Irish into the Manchester region from the late eighteenth century had a profound effect on the local Catholic Church. Until the early nineteenth century, it is clear that Manchester Catholicism was dominated by indigenous English, many of recusant descent, who had been attracted by the economic opportunities of the rapidly growing town. The earlier sites where occasional worship had been conducted by travelling priests were gradually replaced by modest, discreetly sited, purpose-built churches and resident clergy. Some relatively prosperous middle-class lay persons, including some of Irish background, had emerged who helped finance these changes. From 1815 onwards, however, the situation was transformed as Irish numbers rapidly increased, and by the late 1820s they dominated the Catholic population its leadership and its preoccupations. This process was massively reinforced by the influx of the mid- to late 1840s. These developments placed severe strain on church resources, bringing into the region large numbers of Catholics who were notably different in cultural and historical background and pattern of religious practice. English Catholics found Irish cultural traditions and political preoccupations deeply alien. As for the native Protestant population, their reactions were at times verbally and physically violent, particularly as the Catholic Church grew in numbers, confidence and political assertiveness, and they detected a threat to the historic British constitution.

From quite early on various church-based organisations had appeared amongst the Catholic population, and these multiplied as the century progressed. Some were Catholic versions of the Victorian mania for mutual self-help, whilst others were intended to provide for those who were sick or poor or had fallen on hard times. Some focused on doctrinal instruction, others on devotional practice and still others on leisure activities, but all were intended to protect the faithful from outside threat. One of the most notable and best-documented, the Protection and Rescue Society, originally focused on guarding the Catholic faith of children believed to be in danger from a range of threats that were detailed in its journal, but the changing tone and broadening range of contents of its key publication provide a window into a faith community still sensitive to its special interests, but increasingly confident of its place in the wider civic arena and still strongly aware of its Irish roots and linkages. The Irish influx had clearly placed a great strain on the local Catholic Church, transforming its nature and its relationship with the Protestant host society, but in some ways the Catholic Church in Manchester and Britain as a whole came to rely on the local and national political weight of the Irish to articulate and defend church interests every bit as much as many Irish depended on the church as the basis of their spiritual, social and cultural lives. Clearly there were times when Irish interests and church concerns came into collision, especially over specifically Irish political interests, but there was also anxiety when the Irish relaxed and came together to celebrate 17 March.

## Notes

1 Don MacRaild, *Irish migrants in modern Britain, 1750–1922* (Basingstoke: Macmillan, 1999), chap. 3: 'Spiritual and social bonds: the culture of Roman Catholicism'; Graham Davis, *The Irish in Britain 1815–1914* (Dublin: Gill & Macmillan, 1991), chap. 4: 'Catholics and Protestants'.
2 Sheridan Gilley, 'Roman Catholicism and the Irish in England', in D. MacRaild (ed.), *The great famine and beyond: Irish migrants in Britain in the nineteenth and twentieth centuries* (Dublin: Irish Academic Press, 2000), pp. 147–8.
3 Mervyn Busteed and Rob Hodgson, 'Irish migrant responses to urban life in early nineteenth century Manchester', *Geographical Journal*, 162:2 (1996), p. 140.
4 Peter Doyle, *Mitres and missions in Lancashire: the Roman Catholic Diocese of Liverpool 1850–2000* (Liverpool: Bluecoat Press, 2005), pp. 52–4.
5 J.A. Hilton, *Catholic Lancashire: from Reformation to revival 1559–1991* (Chichester: Philimore, 1994), pp. 1–60.

6 John O'Dea, *The story of the old faith in Manchester* (London: Washbourne, 1910), p. 210.
7 Steven Fielding, *Class and ethnicity: Irish Catholics in England 1880-1939* (Buckingham: Open University Press, 1993), p. 39.
8 Anon., 'A Catholic marriage in 1855', *The Harvest* 23:272 (1910), pp. 124-5. Unless otherwise indicated, articles in this journal are anonymous.
9 'Humphrey the third', *The Harvest*, 26:311 (1913), p. 198.
10 'How the faith came back to Salford, after 800 years', *The Harvest*, 21:250 (1908), p. 147.
11 J. Bossy, *The English Catholic community 1570-1850* (London: Darton, Longman & Todd, 1975), pp. 297-79; Doyle, *Mitres and missions*, pp. 25-6.
12 O'Dea, *Story of the old faith*, p. 210.
13 F.O. Blundell, *Old Catholic Lancashire* (London: Burns, Oates & Washbourne, 1938), p. 34.
14 *Returns of Papists 1767 Diocese of Chester, transcribed under the direction of E.S. Worrall*, Catholic Record Society Occasional Paper no. 1 (London: Catholic Record Society, 1980), p. 90.
15 Gerard Connolly, 'Catholicism in Manchester and Salford, 1770-1850: the quest for "Le Chrétien quelconque"' (Ph.D. dissertation, Department of History, University of Manchester, 1980), p. 134.
16 Connolly, 'Catholicism in Manchester and Salford', p. 135 for 1819 and 1828.
17 Denis Clinch, *Manchester's hidden gem* (Manchester: Jackson, 1993), p. 33.
18 Mervyn Busteed, 'Irish migrant settlement in early nineteenth century Manchester', *Manchester Genealogist*, 32:1 (1996), p. 22.
19 *Report on the state of the Irish poor in Great Britain*, House of Commons Parliamentary Papers, 1836, vol. 34: Poor Inquiry, Ireland, Appendix G (henceforth Irish Poor Report), p. 42.
20 Sheridan Gilley, 'English Catholic attitudes to Irish Catholics', *Immigrants and Minorities*, 27:2-3 (2009), p. 227.
21 Connolly, 'Catholicism in Manchester and Salford', p. 149.
22 Irish Poor Report, pp. 61, 43.
23 Connolly, 'Catholicism in Manchester and Salford', p. 422.
24 Shirley Monkhouse, 'Thomas Eadsworth 1787-1868, part 1: how an Old English Catholic learned to love the Irish!', *Manchester Genealogist*, 48:2 (2012), pp. 174-5. Fr Broomhead was also instrumental in the founding of St Mary's church in Mulberry Street.
25 Connolly, 'Catholicism in Manchester and Salford', p. 149.
26 *Salford Weekly News*, 24 March 1877.
27 *Salford Chronicle*, 24 March 1877.
28 *Casey's Charity: a list of those receiving benefit from funds left 'for the poor Catholics of Manchester' 1794-1847*, transcribed from account books held by Catholic Family History Society (Manchester: Manchester & Lancashire Family History Society, 2004).
29 *Souvenir of the 150th anniversary of the arrival of the Presentation Sisters in*

*England* (1986), p. 18. The school and convent were opened in 1836, next to St Patrick's church, Livesey Street.
30 T.J. Slugg, *Reminiscences of Manchester fifty years ago* (Manchester: Cornish, 1881), p. 190.
31 *Salford Weekly News*, 24 March 1877.
32 Charles Bolton, *Salford Diocese and its Catholic past* (Salford: Salford Diocese, 1950), p. 91.
33 Bolton, *Salford Diocese and its Catholic past*, pp. 123–5.
34 'Glimpses of Angel Meadow: ii', *The Harvest*, 6:67 (1893), pp. 162–3.
35 Irish Poor Report, pp. 42–3; they were Fr Parker of St Chad's, Fr Gillow of St Augustine's and Fr Hearne of St Patrick's.
36 Irish Poor Report, pp. 61–2; Fr Crook of St Augustine's and Fr Hearne.
37 *Manchester Guardian*, 19 July 1834.
38 Blundell, *Old Catholic Lancashire*, p. 41.
39 T. Swindells, 'Rochdale Road, part 7: a Roman Catholic chapel and a notable priest', in *Manchester streets and Manchester men*, 5th series (Manchester: Morten, 1908), pp. 176–7.
40 T. Swindells, 'Rochdale Road, part 5: Rev. W. Gadsby and his chapel', in *Manchester streets and Manchester men*, pp. 160–7; B.A. Ramsbottom, *William Gadsby* (London: Gospel Standards Trust, 2003).
41 *Manchester Guardian*, 4 September 1841.
42 *Manchester Guardian*, 13 September 1843.
43 *Manchester Guardian*, 23 March 1842.
44 *Manchester Courier*, 22 July 1842.
45 *Manchester Guardian*, 22 July 1842.
46 Mgr McKenna, 'Recollections of Catholicity in Manchester (3)', *The Harvest*, 10:115 (1897), p. 76.
47 Connolly, 'Catholicism in Manchester and Salford', pp. 394–413.
48 Mgr McKenna, 'Recollections of Catholicity in Manchester (6)', *The Harvest*, 10:119 (1897), pp. 171–5.
49 Mgr McKenna, 'Recollections of Catholicity in Manchester (7)', *The Harvest*, 10:121 (1897), p. 219.
50 *Manchester Guardian*, 17 June 1846.
51 Robert Winder, *Bloody foreigners: the story of immigration to Britain* (London: Abacus, 2005), p. 194.
52 'Reminiscences of Catholicity in Manchester in the early part of this century', *The Harvest*, 11:129 (1898), pp. 141–2.
53 David Hempton, *Religion and political culture in Britain and Ireland: from the Glorious Revolution to the decline of empire* (Cambridge: Cambridge University Press, 1996), p. 45.
54 Edward Norman, *Anti-Catholicism in Victorian England* (London: Allen & Unwin, 1968), p. 18.
55 Linda Colley, *Britons: forging the nation 1707–1837* (London: Pimlico, 1994), pp. 11–54.

56 Marianne Elliott, *When God took sides: religion and identity in Ireland – unfinished history* (Oxford: Oxford University Press, 2009), pp. 63–4.
57 John Wolffe, *The Protestant crusade in Great Britain 1829–1860* (Oxford: Oxford University Press, 1991), pp. 13–15.
58 Hempton, *Religion and political culture*, p. 152.
59 Ian Bradley, *The call to seriousness: the evangelical impact on the Victorians* (Oxford: Lion, 2006).
60 John Wolffe, *The Protestant crusade*, p. 30. This was particularly true in Ireland and especially in Ulster: David Hempton and Myrtle Hill, *Evangelical Protestantism in Ulster society 1740–1890* (London: Routledge, 1992).
61 Wolffe, *The Protestant crusade*, p. 16.
62 J.V. Wells, 'History of the Catholic procession', in *The authorised official programme of the Catholic Whit-Friday procession* (Manchester: Heywood, 1911), pp. 11,17, Salford Diocese Archives.
63 Steven Fielding, 'The Catholic Whit Walk in Manchester and Salford, 1890–1939', *Manchester Region History Review*, 1:1 (1987), pp. 3–10.
64 Diarmaid MacCulloch, *A history of Christianity: the first three thousand years* (London: Penguin, 2010), pp. 840–2.
65 Norman, *Anti-Catholicism in England*, p. 155.
66 Hempton, *Religion and political culture*, p. 155.
67 Thomas Bartlett, *Ireland: a history* (Cambridge: Cambridge University Press, 2010), p. 234; John Bew, *Castlereagh: enlightenment, war and tyranny* (London: Quercus, 2011), p. 128; William Hague, *William Pitt the younger* (London: BCA, 2004), p. 454.
68 Paul Bew, *Ireland: the politics of enmity* (Oxford: Oxford University Press, 2007), pp. 76–7.
69 Brian Girvin, *From union to union: nationalism, democracy and religion in Ireland – Act of Union to E.U.* (Dublin: Gill & Macmillan, 2002), pp. 1–11.
70 Douglas Hurd, *Robert Peel: a biography* (London: Phoenix, 2008), p. 126.
71 Elliott, *When God took sides*, pp. 104–6.
72 Alvin Jackson, *Ireland 1798–1998* (Oxford: Blackwell, 1999), pp. 41–2.
73 Norman, *Anti-Catholicism in England*, pp. 23–51.
74 Norman, *Anti-Catholicism in England*, p. 52.
75 W. Ralls, 'The Papal aggression of 1850: a study in Victorian anti-Catholicism', in Gerald Parsons (ed.), *Religion in Victorian Britain*, vol. 4: *Interpretations* (Manchester: Manchester University Press, 1995), pp. 115–34.
76 *Cowdroy's Manchester Gazette and Weekly Advertiser*, 18 July 1807.
77 *Cowdroy's Manchester Gazette*, 25 July 1807. Capitalisation as in original.
78 *Cowdroy's Manchester Gazette*, 15 August 1807.
79 Frank Neal, 'Manchester origins of the English Orange Order', *Manchester Region History Review*, 4:2 (1990), p. 16.
80 Kevin Haddick-Flynn, *Orangeism: the making of a tradition* (Dublin: Wolfhound Press, 1999), pp. 204–5.
81 Neal, 'Manchester origins', pp. 12–14.
82 *Manchester Guardian*, 7 July 1821.

83 Neal, 'Manchester origins', p. 18.
84 *Manchester Guardian*, 6 November 1824.
85 *Manchester Courier*, 1 January 1825.
86 *Manchester Courier*, 24 January 1825. Italics original.
87 *Manchester Courier*, 9 April 1825.
88 *Manchester Courier*, 11 April 1829.
89 *Manchester Courier*, 18 April 1829.
90 *Manchester Courier*, 18 July 1829.
91 *Manchester Guardian*, 17 July 1830.
92 *Manchester Guardian*, 3 February 1832.
93 *Manchester Courier*, 21 July 1832.
94 *Manchester Guardian*, 19 July 1834; *Manchester Courier*, 19 July 1834, characteristically headlined 'Orange Procession – Serious Outrages by Roman Catholics'; *Manchester Courier*, 26 July 1834; *Manchester Courier*, 2 August 1834: '… the Orangemen were assailed without the slightest provocation'; *Manchester Courier*, 13 September 1834.
95 *Manchester Courier*, 26 July 1834.
96 *Manchester Courier*, 18 July 1835.
97 *Manchester Guardian*, 18 July 1835.
98 Doubtless there were small-scale scuffles in which sectarian feelings and alcohol played a part, but there was no large-scale riot until a remarkable outbreak in the Ancoats district of the city in July 1888: *Manchester Guardian*, 9 July 1888; *Manchester Courier*, 9 July 1888; *Manchester Evening News*, 9 December 1888.
99 Haddick-Flynn, *Orangeism*, pp. 266–71.
100 R.L. Greenall, *The making of Victorian Salford* (Lancaster: Carnegie Publishing, 2000), chap. 4: 'Protestant watchman: Canon Hugh Stowell and the church in Salford', pp. 84–107; D.G. Paz, *Popular anti-Catholicism in mid-Victorian Britain* (Stanford, Calif.: Stanford University Press, 1992), pp. 115–16.
101 *Manchester Guardian*, 24 December 1852.
102 *Liverpool Courier*, 2 September 1840.
103 *Liverpool Courier*, 1 December 1841.
104 C. Bullock, *Hugh Stowell: a life and its lessons* (London: Home Words Publishing, 1881), pp. 48–9.
105 Paz, *Popular anti-Catholicism*, pp. 204–13.
106 Paz, *Popular anti-Catholicism*, pp. 283–9.
107 Bullock, *Hugh Stowell*, p. 42.
108 Greenall, *The making of Victorian Salford*, chap. 4, 'Protestant watchman', p. 107.
109 *Manchester Guardian*, 14 October 1865.
110 Bullock, *Hugh Stowell*, p. 54.
111 Msg McKenna, 'Recollections of Catholicity in Manchester (8)', *The Harvest*, 10:122 (1897), p. 242.
112 *Manchester Guardian*, 26 June 1852.
113 *Manchester Guardian*, 23 August 1855.

114 *Manchester Guardian*, 18 January 1868.
115 *Manchester Guardian*, 1 April 1868.
116 *Manchester Guardian*, 31 January 1868.
117 *Manchester Guardian*, 10 February 1868.
118 *Manchester Courier*, 13 and 15 May 1868.
119 *Manchester Courier*, 14 May 1868.
120 *Manchester Courier*, 25 May 1868.
121 Don MacRaild, *Culture, conflict and migration; the Irish in Victorian Cumberland* (Liverpool: Liverpool University Press, 1998), pp. 180–3; Don MacRaild, *Faith, fraternity and fighting: the Orange Order and Irish migrants in northern England c.1850–1920* (Liverpool: Liverpool University Press, 2005), pp. 187–92.
122 'Salford Protection and Rescue Society: reunion in Manchester', *The Harvest*, 15:176 (1902), p. 101.
123 *Manchester Courier*, 10 November 1913.
124 *Manchester Guardian*, 18 November and 3 December 1913.
125 *Manchester Guardian*, 24 November 1919.
126 Tom Inglis, *Moral monopoly: the Catholic Church in modern Irish society* (Dublin: Gill & Macmillan, 1987).
127 Sean Connolly, *Priests and people in pre-famine Ireland, 1740–1845* (Dublin: Gill & Macmillan, 1982; reprinted Dublin: Four Courts Press, 2001), p. 103.
128 David Miller, 'Irish Catholicism and the great famine', *Journal of Social History*, 9:1 (1975–76), pp. 81–98.
129 Connolly, *Priests and people*, pp. 103–9.
130 Emmet Larkin, 'The devotional revolution in Ireland', *American Historical Review*, 77 (1972), pp. 625–52.
131 G. Connolly, 'Irish and Catholic: myth or reality?', in R. Swift and S. Gilley (eds), *The Irish in the Victorian city* (London: Croom Helm, 1985), p. 232; *Manchester Guardian*, 10 February 1868.
132 Connolly, 'Catholicism in Manchester and Salford', p. 134.
133 Bolton, *Salford Diocese and its Catholic past*, p. 91.
134 Connolly, 'Catholicism in Manchester and Salford', p. 420.
135 O'Dea, *Story of the old faith*, pp. 212–29.
136 W.J. Lowe, 'The Lancashire Irish and the Catholic Church, 1846–77: the social dimension', *Irish Historical Studies*, 20 (1976–77), pp. 129–55; William J. Lowe, *The Irish in mid-Victorian Lancashire: the making of a working class community* (New York: Peter Lang, 1989), pp. 109–44.
137 Sheridan Gilley, 'Catholic faith in the Irish slums', in H.J. Dyos and M. Wolff (eds), *The Victorian city: images and realities*, vol. 2 (London: Routledge & Kegan Paul, 1973), pp. 837–53.
138 H. McLeod, 'Building the Catholic ghetto: Catholic organisations', in W.J. Sheils and D. Wood (eds), *Voluntary religion* (Oxford: Basil Blackwell, 1986), pp. 411–44.
139 Connolly, 'Catholicism in Manchester and Salford', p. 275.
140 Msg McKenna, 'Recollections of Catholicity in Manchester: 4', *The Harvest*, 10:116 (1897), pp. 105–7.

141 'Grand rally: the Knights of the Blessed Sacrament', *The Harvest*, 29:348 (1916), p. 159.
142 'The Catholic Philharmonic Society', *The Harvest*, 25:302 (1912), p. 291.
143 Catholic Needlework Guild, folder 1: 18b/3, Salford Diocese Archives.
144 McKenna, 'Recollections of Catholicity in Manchester: 4', (1897), pp. 105–7.
145 *Manchester Guardian*, 20 March 1844.
146 *Manchester Courier*, 18 March 1879.
147 *Manchester Guardian*, 18 March 1882.
148 Connolly, 'Catholicism in Manchester and Salford', pp. 187, 268.
149 Connolly, 'Catholicism in Manchester and Salford', p. 18.
150 Connolly, 'Catholicism in Manchester and Salford', p. 273.
151 P.H.J.H. Gosden, *Self-help: voluntary associations in the nineteenth century* (London: Batsford, 1973).
152 *Catholic Herald*, 3 August 1900.
153 'Mr. Councillor Daniel Boyle', *Manchester Faces and Places*, 8:7 (May 1897), pp. 112–16.
154 Wilfrid Hampson, 'Leakage', *The Harvest*, 21:244 (1908), pp. 11–12.
155 Austin Oates, 'The Salford Catholic Protection and Rescue Society: its Silver Jubilee: some reasons for its celebration and commemoration', *The Harvest*, 24:284 (1911), pp. 125–8.
156 'The Catholic Protection and Rescue Society', *The Harvest*, 1:1 (1887), pp. 19–21.
157 'Coming of age of the Rescue Society', *The Harvest*, 20:236 (1907), pp. 123–4.
158 *Manchester Guardian*, 18 March 1887.
159 Don Abondio, 'A ramble by night through Ancoats', *The Harvest*, 1:7 (1888), p. 171.
160 Austin Oates, 'A night in a common lodging house', *The Harvest*, 2:13 (1888), pp. 12–16.
161 Patrick Joyce, *The rule of freedom: liberalism and the modern city* (London: Verso, 2003), p. 206; this gives a very different view of the significance of the 'free and easy'.
162 Austin Oates, 'Saturday night in "the free and easies"', *The Harvest*, 1:2 (November 1887), p. 40.
163 Oates, 'A night in a common lodging house', p. 16.
164 Abondio, 'A ramble', p. 171.
165 'Workhouses and workhouse schools: dangers to faith', *The Harvest*, 1:12 (1888), p. 287.
166 'Workhouses and workhouse schools: dangers to faith', *The Harvest*, 2:17 (1889), p. 108.
167 'Mrs. Rose Hyland', *The Harvest*, 24:285 (1911), pp. 133–4.
168 'Ad Clerum', 23 March 1898, Acta of Bishop Bilsborrow, 1897–98, Salford Diocese Archives.
169 'Guardian McCabe versus Guardian Johnson', *The Harvest*, 15:179 (1902), p. 173.
170 'Emigration: Fr. Rossall's Canadian experiences, no. 1', *The Harvest*, 2:15 (1888), pp. 52–6.
171 'The Salford Catholic Protection and Rescue Society: emigration and our

September party: a chat with our readers', *The Harvest*, 2:24 (1889), p. 271.
172 'Emigration: no. 4', *The Harvest*, 2:18 (March 1889), p. 145.
173 'Salford Protection and Rescue Society: reunion in Manchester', p. 101.
174 Gilley, 'Roman Catholicism and the Irish', pp. 149, 163.
175 *Manchester Examiner*, 18 March 1875.
176 *Manchester Courier*, 18 March 1879.
177 *Manchester Evening News*, 25 November 1889.
178 *Weekly Herald*, 29 November 1889.
179 'The bishop in Angel Meadow: Angel Meadow Lads' Club', *The Harvest*, 8:78 (1894), p. 166.
180 *Manchester Evening Chronicle*, 28 November 1898. See Chapter 7 for IRB.
181 *Manchester Courier*, 28 November 1898.
182 Greenall, *The making of Victorian Salford*, chap. 10: 'Catholics: Father Saffenreuter and the Pendleton Irish', pp. 212–26. Saffenreuter was subsequently moved on following allegations, almost certainly fabricated, of improper behaviour with girls at the workhouse.
183 *Salford Reporter*, 18 February 1899.
184 *Manchester Courier*, 13 February 1899. McCarthy was moved to a parish in the USA. In 1902 he apologised for any adverse comments he had made about the bishop.
185 Bishop Casartelli Diaries, Salford Diocese Archives, Box F 162.
186 Presumably the Latin abbreviation of 'Deo gratia' – 'thanks be to God'.
187 *Catholic Herald*, 27 November 1896.
188 *Catholic Herald*, 1 December 1899.
189 Rob. Rossall, 'Emigration: Father Rossall's Canadian experiences', *The Harvest*, 2:16 (1889), p. 75.
190 Rob. Rossall, 'Emigration: no. 4', *The Harvest*, 2:18 (1889), p. 144.
191 'Mr. James Foy's real Irish night', *The Harvest*, 21:246 (1908), p. 64.
192 'St. Patrick's Day', *The Harvest*, 3:30 (1890), p. 144.
193 'Our indebtedness to St. Patrick and his isle', *The Harvest*, 15:174 (1902), p. 53.
194 Rev. T.J. Shealy, 'To my mother in Ireland: for my first Mass', *The Harvest*, 11:132 (1898), pp. 211–12.
195 O'Dea, *The story of the old faith*, p. 224.
196 'Catholic pilgrimage from England to Ireland', *The Harvest*, 7:83 (1894), pp. 293–6.
197 J. Slater, 'Faith in God's providence', *The Harvest*, 30:361 (1917), pp. 172–3.
198 'Languages in the British Isles', *The Harvest*, 14:163 (1901), p. 78.
199 'A Catholic university for Ireland' *The Harvest*, 12:137 (1899), p. 27.dd.
200 'The West of Ireland Association', *The Harvest*, 12:138 (1899), p. 41.
201 'The Irish Industries Exhibition', *The Harvest*, 14:171 (1901), p. 297; 'The Irish Industries Exhibition in Manchester', *The Harvest*, 15:172 (1902), p. 2.
202 *The Harvest*, 11:132 (1898), p. 231. Capitals in original.
203 *The Harvest*, 15:174 (1902), p. 72.
204 *The Harvest*, 11:132 (1898), p. 204.
205 *The Harvest*, 20:39 (1907), p. 168.

# 4

# St Patrick's Day: evolution of a celebration

As the nineteenth century wore on and the allied concepts of nationalism and the nation state diffused across Europe, amongst the features which emerged were the notion of the national day and the national saint. Both were closely bound into the historical narrative which each nation devised. The date might recall a significant foundational event such as a victory over a foreign foe or the adoption of a constitution, whilst the saint was often claimed to be the original evangelist who won the people to a national religion and subsequently oversaw its fate, especially in times of trial. In the case of Ireland, not only does St Patrick perform the role of patron saint, but the date claimed for his death, 17 March, also provides the Irish with their national day, celebrated in religious services and secular festivity, with the two sometimes in tension.[1] In reality, the narrative of Patrick was as much of a social construction as any other feature of nations and nationalism, and the scanty details of his life and ministry have been extensively worked over by both churchmen and nationally minded historians with specific agendas in mind.

The public celebration of 17 March amongst the Irish in nineteenth-century Manchester followed a distinct trajectory from well-lubricated inclusive gatherings, often with a charitable focus, to increasingly respectable and carefully structured events with a notably Catholic and nationalist flavour performed before multiple audiences.

## Patrick and his day

Christianity was probably introduced into Ireland from Roman Britain during the late fourth century, and by 431 there were sufficient Christians there for Palladius of the church in Gaul to be consecrated by Pope Celestine and 'sent to the Irish believing in Christ as their first bishop'.[2] Patrick is believed to have arrived shortly afterwards, and despite the evidence of the earlier Christian communities and evangelists and the fact that his ministry seems to have been focused on the north of the island, by the seventh century there already traces of narratives pointing to him as the apostle of Ireland.[3] Two centuries later this had been elaborated into all-encompassing accounts in both Latin and Irish hailing him as the originator of the Christian faith in Ireland with a ministry of preaching, miracles and church founding which took him to every corner of the island. His burial place is unknown, but in the ninth century the alleged date of his death on 17 March was adopted as his feast day, involving not only the enjoyment of good food but the preaching of a lengthy sermon, a duality which was to persist.[4] By 1607 the date was noted in the Irish legal calendar as a saint's day; in 1631 Pope Urban VIII recognised it as a feast day, and in 1687 Innocent XI further underlined its significance.[5] By then the day was celebrated by all groups throughout Ireland as both a religious festival and an occasion for secular celebration and symbols such as the shamrock, which the saint was said to have used to illustrate the doctrine of the Trinity, crosses and green ribbons were widely worn.[6] Following the final collapse of the old Gaelic order in the early 1690s, in 1695 the restored Williamite parliament issued a revised calendar of religious holidays which reflected the teachings of the established Irish Anglican Church. It listed twenty-nine such days, but St Patrick's Day was not included. For the next ninety years there was no official recognition of the festival, but by this time it had become deeply embedded in popular practice, especially amongst the Catholic population since their church had given it official recognition. With the passage of time the government recognised its popularity, and St Patrick, with a sprig of shamrock, appeared on coinage in the 1760s. During the latter half of the eighteenth century the Anglican-dominated Irish parliament increasingly asserted its rights against London, and St Patrick was increasingly adopted as a symbol of this new-found awareness in contrast to St George of England. In 1783 King George III instituted the new Order of St Patrick, and the first knights were invested the following year at a ceremony in Dublin Castle, followed by a banquet and dancing. This developed into an annual event. Irish Protestant officers serving abroad with the British army took the custom with them. The first record of St Patrick's Day celebrations in Boston, Massachusetts, is of a dinner organised in 1737 by an officers' club entitled 'The Charitable Society of Boston', and the first parade took place in New York in 1766.[7]

By the early nineteenth century shifts in the Irish political context made St Patrick's day a somewhat ambiguous occasion for Protestants. The passage of the Act of Union in 1801 had created a united political British kingdom but at the popular level Catholics continued to celebrate 17 March in church services and in lively celebrations. Amongst lower-class Protestants the launch of the Orange Order in 1795 and its rapid spread had led to increasing emphasis on dates such as 4 November, the birthday of their hero King William III, and, especially, 12 July, the anniversary of his victory over the Catholic forces of King James II at the Boyne in 1690, which established the Protestant ascendancy in Ireland. Both had previously been occasions for polite dinners, but by the early nineteenth century 12 July in particular had become an occasion for popular Protestant celebrations which took the form of not only church services and dinners but public processions with fife and drum bands and orange sashes, often culminating in clashes with Catholics, which sometimes resulted in injuries and deaths. In this increasingly polarised context the Irish government looked on such events with increasing distaste. It gradually withdrew from any official link with Williamite celebrations, tried to curb their more extreme manifestations and increasingly attempted to present St Patrick's Day as an alternative inclusive festival free of sectarian and political overtones. The traditional investiture and dinner at Dublin Castle on 17 March had continued, but to reinforce its significance in 1829 the viceroy launched the custom of appearing at what was termed 'Trooping the Castle Guard'.[8] In 1866 an observer described the ceremony: army units mustered on the esplanade outside the Royal [now Collins] Barracks, bands played 'a selection of Irish national airs', and then the procession marched along the quays on the north side of the River Liffey, crossed to the south side and proceeded to the yard of Dublin Castle, where at noon the viceroy appeared on the balcony, wearing 'the ribbon and badge of the order of St. Patrick and a bunch of shamrock on the left breast ... the other members of the Vice-regal party were similarly decorated'.[9]

This effort to present the saint as a unifying, uncontentious figure had only limited success because of the increasing polarity of Irish political alignments. Later in the century the Church of Ireland would make an unconvincing effort to present itself as directly descended from the church originally founded by St Patrick,[10] but this merely led to disputation with Catholics who claimed him for their tradition. Presbyterians were never much taken with the notion of patron saints since their reformed tradition strongly condemned the intercessory ministry allocated to them by Catholics, and in any case the Scottish roots of the denomination allocated a founding role to St Andrew. The strengthening of the evangelical element in all the Protestant denominations following the revivals of 1859 led to further downgrading of the notion of the special role of saints. The result was that as the nineteenth century wore on St Patrick became increasingly associated with Catholicism and an icon of Irish nationalism. This was a trend with roots in the early decades of the century, when the Ribbonmen, a rural Catholic defence group largely formed in reaction to the rise of the Orange Order, began the practice of public parading on St Patrick's Day sporting the shamrock and green colours[11] and thereby confirming the link between the saint, the Catholic population and their political aspirations. Subsequently, as the Catholic population grew in confidence, organisations such as the National Brotherhood of St Patrick, the Ancient Order of Hibernians and the Irish National Foresters marked 17 March with church services, dinners and processions, thereby cementing its role in Protestant and unionist eyes as a specifically Catholic and nationalist occasion. Amongst the Irish overseas the link became equally strong.

## Convivial and inclusive: 1825 to mid-1860s

It is possible to detect shifts of emphasis in Manchester's St Patrick's Day celebrations, with a notable change in format and emphasis after the late 1860s, but the enduring double focus of the celebrations was summed up by a speaker who in March 1890 declared, 'The object of the meeting was twofold. In the first place they wished to do honour to the memory of the patron saint of Ireland, he who introduced Christianity into their country ... The second object of their gathering was to testify their enduring faith in the cause of Irish nationality.'[12] The first report of a St Patrick's Day celebration in the city dates from 1825, and down to the late 1860s it is clear that the event was celebrated at two levels. Amongst the elite there were dinners in local hotels attended by leading members of the Irish population, regardless of religion or politics, often with a charitable aim in view. In 1825 it was reported that a dinner was 'celebrated ... by a considerable number of gentlemen, natives of or friends to the sister isle. The dinner and wines were furnished in ... best style, and a variety of loyal and patriotic toasts were drunk.' This was followed by speeches, of which it was reported, 'we are happy to say that they were marked by good feeling, and by that cheering expectation of better days in Ireland, which present prospects seem to warrant us indulging.'[13] The same emphasis on inclusiveness and harmony was discernible seventeen years later at a gathering in another local hotel. The prosperous Catholic layman Daniel Lee presided, a glee club sang, 'the dinner and wines were of the most recherché description, and served in ... best style', and the possibility of establishing a St Patrick's Orphan Society was discussed, since 'In Manchester, where there were so many Irishmen, and particularly of the lower classes, such an institution was especially needed.' Interestingly, Lee thought it necessary to say that 'As the meeting was purely convivial, he sincerely hoped that neither politics nor religion would be introduced'; this remark was followed by the toast to 'The Queen' ('drunk with much enthusiasm') and the singing of the national anthem. Later toasts included 'Prosperity to Ireland', 'The Land we live in' and 'The Town of Manchester'. Other speakers went to some pains to emphasise the importance of unity amongst the people of Ireland, and Fr Hearne attributed recent outrages in Ireland to intemperance;[14] it was reported that 'The proceedings ... were of the most harmonious character throughout'.[15]

These recurring efforts to stress unity and goodwill reveal a nervous awareness that the day could reveal the underlying tensions within Ireland and the Irish in the city. Running parallel with these self-consciously polite and inclusive occasions were celebrations which were much more boisterous and at times overtly nationalist. In 1830 an incident occurred which revealed both popular attitudes and the stresses which lay just under the surface in the Irish population. One source opened its report with 'Wednesday last, being St. Patrick's Day, was celebrated by the sons of Erin with their usual indications of tumultuous joy. Unfortunately, mirth and mischief are inseparable ingredients in the Irish character; and if there were any room for doubt on the subject, the anniversary furnished one or two additional proofs and confirmations of the fact.'[16] Another reported, 'Wednesday last, being the anniversary day of the patron saint of the Emerald Isle, did not pass over in this town without some of the disturbances common to the day.' This incident was triggered after the 87th regiment (Irish Fusiliers) had marched across the bridge from Salford to Mass at St Patrick's church 'preceded by the band playing "*St. Patrick's Day in the Morning*", and accompanied by great numbers of their countrymen wearing the shamrock in their hats'. The regiment returned to barracks without any trouble, but when the accompanying crowd were making their way back into Manchester they found that the gatekeeper had closed the bridge toll gate and was demanding that they each paid the halfpenny fee. The crowd forced their way through and took out their anger on the keeper and the windows of his lodge. Police were summoned, and a man seized, 'but he set up a cry peculiar to the Irish, which brought the whole body to his assistance, and the officers were immediately knocked down, kicked, beaten and their prisoner rescued'.[17]

Later in the day 'a number of drunken brawls occurred in various parts of the town, particularly in the districts inhabited by the wild Irish; but we are happy to report that no very serious consequences resulted'.[18]

Despite this qualification, it became the custom to seek out reports on Irish misbehaviour on 17 March, sometimes with humour, often with indignation. In 1832 it was noted that the Irish celebrated with 'a procession through the principal streets, with flags, banners, & c., most of the persons in the procession wearing green scarves, and bearing the shamrock in their hats'. It was noted that although extra police were at hand in the event of a clash with Orangemen, there was no trouble, but 'A great many of the Irish saint's disciples, however, indulged themselves in such deep potations of the "cratur", that they were to be seen in a state of beastly drunkenness in the streets' and on appearing in court were sent on their way 'after admonitions not to show their devotion to his saintship in like manner again'.[19] By 1838 the Orange lodges had dissolved themselves and it was reported that a local nationalist group planned to parade on 17 March with orange flags draped in black 'to celebrate the triumph they have lately obtained over the loyal Orangemen'. This was avoided, but nonetheless

> A procession took place, with bands of music, flags, banners, & c., the members of the society being decorated with green sashes and favours. To the credit of the members of the suppressed Orange institution, not the slightest notice was taken of the procession by them; and finding no opponents to fight with, the Ribbonmen [sic] were under the necessity either of going peaceably home, or of getting up a row amongst themselves. Like true Irishmen they chose the latter alternative, and about six o'clock in the evening, Mason street and the neighbourhood presented a scene of riot and confusion of a most serious nature … about half a dozen of the principals in the row were taken into custody.[20]

By 1842 some were expressing the hope that Fr Mathew's temperance efforts were responsible for reports that the numbers of Irish in court for drunkenness on 17 March were half of previous totals,[21] and two years later the *Courier* was noting that things were generally peaceful. Even then it tried to have things both ways, reminding readers of what it regarded as normal Irish behaviour and at the same time managing to turn the lack of conflict to Irish disadvantage:

> Yesterday (the 17th) was St. Patrick's Day, and we may add, a day heretofore looked upon by the police with fear and trembling, devoted as it is generally by the lower order of Irish, to hard drinking and the most riotous exhibitions … fortunately for the peace of the borough, or that portion of it comprised in the districts known as 'Little Ireland', and St. George's road … the day

passed over without the slightest outbreak or manifestation excepting perhaps a procession composed of some ninety or a hundred ragged individuals calling themselves 'The Hibernian Society', and whose appearance would have shamed even the redoubtable Sir John Falstaff himself.

Noting that the procession dispersed without any problems, the report continued, 'Whilst we rejoice at the effect, we must deplore the cause of this unusually quiet day, attributable primarily to the strike now unhappily subsisting amongst those engaged in the building trade, owing to which the Irish, who are largely engaged in it, are deprived of the necessary funds, and are consequently prevented from displaying that regard for his Saintship, which, under happier circumstances, would have been their pride and delight.'[22]

Late the following year, with famine distress at its height, the state of Ireland was so disturbed that one observer concluded: 'we cannot overlook the facts which prove ... that those people are, as yet, wholly unfit for the institutions suited to an orderly and peaceable community ... Trial by jury is, no doubt, well adapted to the habits and ideas of thinking of the people of England, but we have been satisfied, for twenty years past, that the Irish are no more fit for its exercise than the Caffres, or the natives of New Zealand.'[23] Fear of these disturbed conditions spreading to the city led to widespread apprehension as St Patrick's Day 1848 approached. Daniel O'Connell's Repeal Association founded in 1840 to campaign for restoration of the Dublin parliament abolished in 1801, had split, the more militant element had launched the Confederate Clubs, and by early March the rising tide of revolutionary fervour in Europe had seen disturbances across the continent and the overthrow of the monarchy in France. In Britain there was a last surge of Chartist reformism, and the great fear was of an alliance of militant Irish and Chartists at a joint meeting in the city's Free Trade Hall on 17 March, with the result that 'the authorities of this city felt no inconsiderable degree of uneasiness in the present excited state of the public mind'. In the event the combination of extensive preparations by the authorities, Catholic Church disapproval and appeals from speakers at the meeting defused the situation. The result was that

> never within the recollection 'of the oldest inhabitant' has so quiet a St. Patrick's Day been known in Manchester ... we are enabled to state positively that there was less drunkenness and disposition to riot than we have ever before known. In this particular day it has always been a sore and grievous trial to poor, excitable Paddy, to refrain from his 'dhrop of whiskey' ... The proceedings of yesterday, however ... prove that even the Irish [sic] may be brought to reason, although as we are aware there are many who look on the idea as chimerical.[24]

As for the meeting itself, 'the numerous assemblage (as exhorted by several of the speakers) retired quietly to their homes'.[25]

Subsequently there are no traces of public celebrations of 17 March until the early 1860s, but newspapers continued to express relief and surprise when the event passed quietly. In 1850 it was noted that the day 'passed over in Manchester in a more than usually quiet and orderly manner. Very few fights, and those only of a trifling nature, took place in any of the Irish quarters of the town … during the day and night there were not more than three or four Irishmen in custody in the different police stations.'[26] Two years later it was reported, 'St. Patrick's Day passed off in Manchester without any of the disturbances or breaches of the peace, by which it has frequently been distinguished. The interference of the police was not required more than on other days, and the number of prisoners brought up at the Borough Court, on Thursday morning was not unusually large.'[27]

Private celebration of the day no doubt continued during these years, but it is not until early in the next decade that traces of public events reappear. These were under the aegis of the National Brotherhood of St Patrick, formed in Dublin on 17 March 1861 and dedicated to Irish freedom and the celebration of all things Irish with a particular emphasis on the national day. It spread widely in Ireland, and it has been estimated there were probably between twenty and thirty thousand members in Britain in the period 1861–62.[28] The first branch in Britain was opened as 'The Irishman's Reading and News Room' in Manchester on 17 March 1861, and five more existed by September, when a Central Council was set up to coordinate activities. Manchester was the most active centre outside London, with branches organising public meetings, lectures and discussion groups and holding St Patrick's Day banquets and tea parties at which all the traditional iconography of Irishness was on display and speakers dwelt on Irish rights and achievements. However, by late 1863 the organisation had been heavily infiltrated by the revolutionary IRB and was fading under opposition from the Catholic Church and eventually from the Fenian leadership, who were wary of the diversion of energies.[29] With its demise, celebrations seem to have reverted to the purely private and traditional fears of rowdiness returned, but now leavened with anxiety about Fenian intentions. Accordingly in 1866:

> Special preparations were made by the military and police authorities in Manchester for the maintenance of order on St. Patrick's Day. The soldiers at the cavalry and infantry barracks [were] arranged that in case of necessity they could readily be placed under arms to render assistance in preserving the peace. During the Saturday night reserves of men were on duty at the respective police stations, and at the Town Hall the detective

department was kept open all night and a strong reserve of officers was kept on duty. Fortunately the tranquillity of the city was in no wise disturbed; we believe that not a single street disturbance was reported at any of the police stations, and St. Patrick's Day was never passed more quietly in Manchester than on Saturday.[30]

This led some to conclude, 'there is reasonable hope to infer that Fenianism is at a discount amongst the dwellers in Manchester. There has been some talk of priestly advice against intemperance. If it be true, the lovers of good order lie under an additional obligation to the Roman Catholic clergy, whose services had been conspicuously useful in the present insane outbreak of pseudo-patriotism.'[31] The following year, which was to see the Manchester Martyrs incidents reverberate around the world, a tiny piece in one newspaper confined itself to noting the quietness of the day and offering a possible explanation: 'There were no indications of disturbance in this city yesterday. Indeed the districts occupied by the Irish were more than usually peaceful. A sharp north east wind prevailed throughout the day, and it was particularly cold at night.'[32]

## Respectable and Catholic

In the years which immediately followed the events of 1867 there are no indications of public celebrations of St Patrick's Day, possibly because the local Irish felt it wise to keep a low profile, though doubtless there were plenty of informal small-group celebrations in public houses and private homes, with the emphasis on the sheer enjoyment of food, drink and entertainment and the company of like-minded people. Once public events did emerge in the mid-1870s they went through a number of changes in structure and emphasis.[33] Throughout the period Catholic churches celebrated 17 March with Masses, sermons on the life and work of Patrick and the blessing of the shamrock. Moreover, there was always a sense of social inclusion to the celebrations. Mr James Foy's 'Real Irish Night' concerts in the Free Trade Hall became something of an institution, and the atmosphere was well captured by one observer in 1908:

> There was, too, an Irish warmth and homeliness about the whole that was no mistaking. All ranks were represented. There were frockcoats and coats with a hod-mark on the shoulder well defined; there were trousers with stately creases and trousers with strings tied round them beneath the knees; and the number of the men with their calling still about them showed how universal is the appeal of this yearly event ... Miss May Farrell and Miss McBride sang in English and Gaelic – a good deal of which latter seemed to be understood.[34]

On the public stage events became steadily more structured, elaborate and decorous, an evolution which the Catholic Church warmly endorsed since it dovetailed with its policy of presenting Catholics as sober, upright citizens worthy of equal treatment within the United Kingdom. By the mid-1880s the structure of the public celebrations had settled into a pattern. On the weekend closest to 17 March there was a meal at a local hotel, attended by the great and the good of the Irish population. Local politicians, clergy and businessmen figured prominently, together with invited guests. The meal itself was variously referred to as 'dinner' or, more frequently, a 'banquet', and was clearly a considerable advance on the 'tea and toast' sneeringly noted by one source in 1877.[35] In 1889, 'After the various courses on the menu had been expended', diners proceeded to a now customary range of toasts and speeches.[36] As time passed the range of celebrants gradually widened to include representatives from the growing number of Catholic and Irish nationalist organisations. The Salford Diocese Temperance Crusade had always been strongly represented, and by the early twentieth century the Irish National Foresters were in regular attendance, often in their regalia of green jackets and white trousers 'and carrying bright halberds'.[37] From 1904 onwards the newly founded Gaelic League took the opportunity for a collection in support of language revival.[38] In 1913 the Ancient Order of Hibernians was represented and its Lancashire board also organised a St Patrick's Day reception and ball. The Foresters also revived the tradition of processions on 17 March, but these now took the form of well-regulated and disciplined church parades with full regalia.[39] In 1914 it was reported, 'Contingents representing the twenty-six divisions in Manchester assembled … at 9.30 o'clock, and headed by the Pipers and Brass Band from St. Joseph's, Longsight, marched to the church, a number of banners being carried by the different contingents.'[40]

Music has always been an integral part of St Patrick's Day celebrations.[41] As already noted, in 1879 the local authorities had marked the day when the bells of the town hall tower played Irish tunes, which were welcomed by Bishop Vaughan as a gesture of goodwill towards the Irish and Catholic population.[42] The diocesan temperance band was a regular feature in the late 1870s and early 1880s, and it became the custom to have entertainment at the banquet and then to proceed to a combined public concert and meeting at the Free Trade Hall. There the musical entertainment comprised both vocalists and instrumental items, but always these were 'national songs … [and] …national music',[43] such as 'Though the last glimpse of Erin', 'Killarney' and 'The minstrel boy'. Patriotic airs such as 'The memory of the dead' and 'The wearing of the green' also figured, but in 1890 it was noted that it remained for the Droylsden Band to raise the feeling of the people to the highest point, and this they did at the close of the entertainment with the magical tones of 'God Save Ireland', which was immediately taken up by the people in every portion of the building. Rising to their feet en masse, with heads uncovered and their faces glowing with enthusiasm, they repeated in one swelling chorus the noble anthem first breathed forth by the three devoted and undaunted Irishmen more than twenty years ago in the same city, but with such different circumstances and such different surroundings.[44]

It was therefore particularly significant when in 1920 the dinner organised by the Irish Self-Determination League of Great Britain (ISDL) chose instead to conclude with the IRA anthem 'A soldier's song'.[45] Perhaps the liminal appeal of such music was best summed up by Joseph Nolan, MP for Galway North, who, presiding over the event in 1890, remarked, 'the great charm of the concert consisted in the fact that the airs carried the audience back in fancy to the dear old land they loved so well'.[46]

Many of the features of these events were modelled on the conventional form of the public meetings and concerts which were such a feature of life in Victorian and Edwardian Britain. They had acquired an air of respectability, which was emphasised by the people who occupied the places of honour on the platform at the concert and meeting. In addition to clergy and local and national political leaders, family parties were a feature. In 1889 amongst those in the platform party were the Ruddin, Boyle, Purcell, Rowland and McLally families and three McDermott sisters.[47] Prominent Irish businessmen were also present on occasion, such as Peter Reynolds and his three sisters, from a Leitrim family who had made their money in a chain of dyeing and cleaning shops and were on the platform in 1889.[48] Also present were the Melia family, Edward in 1892 and Daniel in 1894, who had set up a national chain of grocery shops.[49] In many ways such people were being literally and metaphorically lifted up as exemplars of Irish Catholic middle-class respectability. As if to emphasise how the Irish and their aspirations had become mainstream, prominent local Liberals were often guests, notably C.P. Scott, the renowned *Manchester Guardian* editor and erstwhile Liberal parliamentary candidate. By 1903, largely as result of an energetic campaign by the Gaelic League, 17 March had been made an official bank holiday in Ireland, a rare piece of legislation unanimously supported by both nationalist and unionist MPs.

These were English forms and formats adapted for Irish purposes. The Irishness was driven home not only by the date and the music but by the persistent display of Irish symbolism. From the earliest, the shamrock and the colour green were on display, and organisations such as the Temperance Crusade and Band wore distinctive costume; in 1875 'The

"Hundred Guards" of the Crusade were on duty in uniform' at the Free Trade Hall when Bishop Vaughan made such great show of wearing the shamrock,[50] and in later years the Foresters and the Ancient Order of Hibernians, a strongly nationalist benefit society formed in 1836, regularly appeared in costume with sashes and banners. In 1903 there was a particularly vivid display. Not only were the Foresters present in regalia and with halberds, but several enthusiasts were dressed 'in Robert Emmet costume' in honour of the patriot hanged in a Dublin prison 100 years before, and also on the platform was 'Miss McNamara, dressed in an Irish costume representing "Erin"'.[51] There was a particularly strong showing of shamrock, even by non-Irish, in 1900, after Queen Victoria had given permission for Irish regiments of the British army to wear it on 17 March in honour of their gallantry in the Boer War then raging. Even the traditionally hostile *Manchester Courier* exulted, declaring, 'The wearing of the green was general', though it could not resist suggesting that 'it was, at the same time, perfectly evident that that a great deal of it was not the real stuff'. It also noted that 'on most of the public buildings the British and Irish flags were flying' and that by order of the Lord Mayor the Irish flag was displayed from the corner turrets of the Manchester Town Hall'.[52] But more discerning observers noted that this flag 'was in fact an English modification – the Irish harp and the Union Jack set upon a green ground' and that at a local Irish club the Irish were flying 'the Irish flag pure and simple – the Irish harp upon a green ground'.[53] Two years later this benevolent glow had faded and it was noticed that 'outside the circle of Irishmen in Manchester the saint's day was ignored and the little plant was left unsold'.[54] In 1906 a procession of children walked to St Patrick's church, 'where they were provided with tea, and were afterwards entertained by members of the Gaelic League', and Fr Brennan from Killarney preached in Irish at St Wilfrid's church.[55]

At the formal public level the Catholic Church was always well represented, in the presence of clergy as platform guests, in an active role as speakers and in the focus on matters of church concern. As already noted, for many years temperance was a recurring theme, doubtless with an eye to curbing drunkenness and rowdiness and presenting a respectable front to the non-Catholic and non-Irish public. In 1875 when Bishop Vaughan attended the Free Trade Hall wearing shamrock he spoke about 'the widespread and deep practical effects … produced upon the Catholics of that country by the great temperance movement which covers the United States'.[56] In 1877 he was absent, but Canon Cantwell was present, and the bishop took care to send a message of apology in which he expressed regret at not being able to meet up with the main speaker, Mitchell

Henry, the Manchester-born Home Rule MP for Galway County who was of Ulster Protestant background. Vaughan indicated his approval by describing him as 'my friend ... who has so completely consecrated his life to the service of Ireland'.[57] On occasion clergy chaired the gatherings, as Fr Williams did in 1879[58] and Fr Byrne in 1880,[59] and they were frequently amongst the main speakers, with four – including Bishop Vaughan – addressing the gatherings in 1882[60] and 1884.[61] Possibly the bishop's most notable contribution came in 1887, when he announced the launch of the Rescue Society.[62] Protestant clergy occasionally made an appearance, including the Unitarian Rev. R. McWilliam Lyttle in 1889,[63] but in contrast with earlier gatherings there were no efforts to emphasise the inclusive nature of the event.

## Political and pan-nationalist

As time went on there were subtle shifts in the priority given to Catholic personnel and church concerns. The temperance theme gradually faded, possibly because the gathering was becoming increasingly middle-class and respectable. No bishop after Vaughan appeared at the banquet, the concert or the public meeting, and there was a growing emphasis on political matters. This is not to say that the church was unrepresented. Clergy continued to be a notable presence as prominent guests – no fewer than nineteen were present at the banquet in 1889 and six at the concert and public meeting.[64] There were still clerical speakers at this meeting, some of whom appeared quite comfortable talking about overtly political issues. In 1895 Fr Lynch was the main speaker and took as his theme the need to heal the divisions then splintering the Irish nationalist movement, and Canon DeSplenter proposed the toast 'The Irish Parliamentary'.[65] Another traditional toast was 'the clergy', the response to which was often given by a cleric. If temperance had faded as an issue, it was replaced by the need for church-based education, a topic featuring increasingly in public debate from the 1870s onwards and taken up by both clerical and lay speakers. It was Bishop Vaughan's theme in 1884 when he stressed the need to respect Catholic parents' desire for church-based education.[66] On other occasions there were appeals to support local causes such as the orphanage at St Patrick's[67] and the industrial school at St Joseph's church.[68] But the education issue had much wider implications than the purely local and could at times cause friction between Catholic Church and Irish interests, since the Irish reliance on the Liberals as the party most likely to legislate for home rule was linking them to a party disposed to secular education, a tension explicitly recognised in 1904, when both Canon

Lynch and the Irish parliamentary leader John Redmond acknowledged the problem at the public meeting and strove to square the circle.[69]

There are also occasional indications of unease at the manner in which 17 March had been politicised. Certainly the *Courier* was quick to deplore the trend it detected in 1877:

> There is no reason …why the festival of the national saint should not be worthily celebrated, especially by Irishmen whose absence from their native land renders it all the more desirable to keep alive a spirit of patriotism. It would appear, however, that what ought to be an occasion when political differences are laid aside, and when Irishmen of all creeds and parties should unite in expressing love for their fatherland, has become for the most part, simply a day in which the crude and impracticable doctrines of home rule may be preached … it is a misfortune that the national anniversary should be prostituted by thus being turned to the base uses of a group of restless political schemers. It entirely destroys the spirit of geniality which ought to reign supreme on such an occasion.[70]

A few years later Canon Kershaw was applauded when he stated that 'Nationality was a very good thing, but religion was a better',[71] and in 1901 Dan Boyle, prominent Irish political leader in the city, declared that

> He was sure they all, in common with himself, regretted that the national celebrations should have to assume the tone of being political. They would prefer very much that the day had arrived when Irishmen of all shades of thought should meet together to celebrate St. Patrick's Day – (Hear, hear). But that condition of things was impossible until one thing was secured. Until Ireland obtained for herself the right of self-government they must be political even on St. Patrick's Day. – (Cheers).[72]

What all had recognised was that, since the growing confidence and energy of the Irish nationalist movement had brought the question of self-government onto the political agenda, it would inevitably become an issue in any large public gathering of Irish people. Henceforth the case for Irish self-government and the affairs of its chief political vehicle, the Irish Parliamentary Party, were to be staple fare in the speeches at the public meeting and sometimes at the banquet as well, their tone and content reflecting the current fortunes of the cause. Mitchell Henry in 1877 had been the first MP to put the case at a St Patrick's Day event, but by the late 1880s members of the Irish Parliamentary Party were almost always amongst the guests and even the occasional clerical speaker often ventured into overtly political territory. Speakers argued the case for home rule on a combination of Ireland's historic distinctiveness, the past and present inadequacies of government from London and the general right of self-determination as enjoyed by other peoples. But there was also a recurring emphasis on the need for unity amongst Irish people. The split in in the Irish party in December 1890 following the divorce case involving the party leader Charles Stewart Parnell was by far the greatest though by no means the only source of strain. At the 1891 gathering 'The Chairman … opened proceedings with a speech that called forth great enthusiasm. He declared they would no longer follow the fortunes of a disgraced and fallen man. (Loud applause and "cheering for the Grand Old Man.").' At the urging of Councillor Dan McCabe, the leading Manchester Irish spokesperson, the meeting went on to adopt a resolution which reflected the agonising dilemma that the crisis had posed for the home rule movement:

> we emphatically endorse the policy of maintaining the alliance with the great English Liberal Party, of whose sincerity of purpose and determination to satisfy the claims of Ireland for self-government we are fully assured … considering the near approach of the general election and the consequent necessity for unity amongst Irishmen, we, as Irish exiles, whose primary consideration is for the welfare of our mother land, denounce as criminal the conduct of those who are attempting to disunite the Irish people in the interests of a man whose leadership is no longer possible.

McCabe dismissed 'the few Parnellites of the district … drinking his health in a little place in Ancoats about the size of a 6d house, and it would well hold them all. (Applause)'. The next speaker referred to Parnell as someone who would 'have crushed their hope to gratify his own ambition', and another described him as 'a ruined and desperate politician … [who] would never again be a power in the land'.[73] The following year the organisers took a major risk by inviting T.M. Healy MP, Parnell's bitterest foe, as the main speaker and presenting him with an address and casket in memory of his early days in Manchester. However, possibly because C.P. Scott was also a guest, he was on his best behaviour, admitting that in the past year 'They had been engaged … upon a terrible and, he might say, almost a loathsome task. Its discharge had been one of the most painful proceedings of his lifetime.'[74] As tempers cooled, especially after the rejection of the second Home Rule Bill in the Lords in September 1893 and the defeat of the Liberals in the general election of July 1895, there were increasingly numerous expressions of regret at successive St Patrick's Day gatherings at the continued disunity of Irish parliamentary forces. This was particularly strongly expressed in 1896 by Fr Lynch, who was repeatedly applauded when he deplored the splits amongst the various factions, arguing, 'No question of principle divided them: they were all Home

Rulers'.[75] Consequently the reunion of the party under the leadership of John Redmond in 1900 was hailed with great satisfaction,[76] though after the years of bitter vituperation some wounds never totally healed and there was always a sense of nervous fragility in party ranks.

There were additional sources of tension. At various times Tim Healy and William O'Brien MP broke with the party, rejoined and then left again to lead small groups of independent MPs., sometimes in alliance with each other, and the appeals for unity periodically resurfaced. In 1909, when the internal stresses were particularly acute,[77] several speakers went out of their way to warn of the need for a sustained focus on home rule. Dan McCabe called on Irishmen 'to maintain their solidarity of organisation and not permit themselves to be decoyed by any other issues from their duty to the sacred cause of Ireland's freedom'. John Hayden, MP for South Roscommon, deplored the activities of dissidents, who, he declared, were 'doing the enemy's work though they might appear honest',[78] and William O'Malley, MP for Galway Connemara, found it 'sad to find some of their countrymen criticising the party, finding fault with its work, differing from its policy, speaking words almost of insult against their leaders'.[79] But there were also new challenges arising from social and cultural changes on both sides of the Irish Sea. Speaking to the public meeting in 1906, John Redmond was at pains to acknowledge the extraordinary growth of interest in Ireland's Gaelic tradition and tried to reach out to it when he expressed deep sympathy for the work of Gaelic League:

> I have always ... for many years past regarded my friend Dr. Douglas Hyde as one of the greatest patriots produced by Ireland, and I sincerely hope all the Irish men and women and children in Manchester will support the Gaelic League movement, and in that way learn something of the poetry and the songs of our old country. I hope that in time the movement will rescue from the oblivion that was overtaking it the beautiful old language that the poets and sages of our country though and spoke and wrote in the past.[80]

As early as 1894 Matthias Bodkin, MP for Roscommon North, drew attention to another development common to both Ireland and Britain and showed his lack of understanding and sympathy: 'He had heard ... that some Irishmen had joined the Independent Labour Party in Manchester. He could not believe it. It had always been the dictum of the Irish people that the Irish cause stood first, and the rest nowhere.'[81] Others demonstrated a better grasp of newly emerging political realities and strove to make an ally of the new movement. At the 1906 celebrations Redmond also went out of his way to welcome the Labour contingent in the recently elected parliament: 'I heartily congratulate the Irishmen of Great Britain on the share which they had in the election of that Labour party ... Every man in that Labour party is a friend of Ireland.'[82] For their part McCabe and Boyle, whose Manchester Council seats were in the most working-class districts of the city, repeatedly demonstrated their awareness of social problems and developed an outlook best described by a composite label of Liberal-Nationalist-Labour.[83] Successive speakers on 17 March acknowledged the new movement. In 1909 John Hayden asserted that the Irish party had made every effort to assist 'the uplifting of the labouring classes in England' and was 'prepared all the time to support every just demand of the British labourer'.[84] On the same occasion McCabe argued that 'In Parliament they had always been on the side of the worker in this country, and had been advocates of the rights of the people' and that it was the Irish party which had taught working people how to organise themselves and set about using parliamentary methods for the improvement of their conditions.[85]

Given the alignment of British party politics after 1885, the long periods of Conservative rule between 1886 and 1906 saw little practical prospect of home rule, and the political speeches on 17 March were essentially efforts to maintain faith and morale. Consequently the rhetoric was at times repetitious and unconvincing. But the *Courier* was surely indulging in wishful thinking when, in 1905, it reported that there was no great demand for shamrock, 'a large quantity of which, by the way, came from Jersey' and concluded, 'Throughout the city, and especially in the Irish quarters, it was plainly evident that the custom of "keeping up" St. Patrick's Day is dying away.'[86] By 1906 a Liberal administration had been elected with an overwhelming parliamentary majority, and in Manchester that year Redmond doubtless expressed the hopes of many nationalists when he said, 'you have in office today a government and a majority publicly pledged to the principle of self-government in Ireland ... and we have received a public promise from the government ... that a bill will be introduced as soon as it is possible'.[87] In fact the government majority was so large that it had no need of Irish support. In 1907 an Irish Council Bill intended to provide a form of devolution was tabled, but it was a woefully weak piece of legislation; the Irish party rejected it and it was withdrawn, generating a deep sense of disappointment after the long years of patient waiting. Efforts were made to stress the achievements of the parliamentary party despite this unpromising experience.[88] When he addressed the meeting in 1908, Redmond was doubtless trying to prove that the Irish had got something for their efforts when he pointed to the setting up of a National University of Ireland, drew attention to improvements in rural housing, called for similar measures in urban areas, especially Dublin, argued for higher salaries for teachers and, referring to an Education Bill then before parliament, argued for fair treatment for Catholic schools,[89] whilst stressing that 'the Irish Party is not a Catholic Party, it is a National Party'.[90]

But after the general elections of January and December 1910 the comfortable independent Liberal majority disappeared, and the government was now dependent upon the Irish (and Labour) for its survival; the historic obstacle of the House of Lords was about to be overcome and the prospects for home rule had improved enormously. The tone and content of the St Patrick's Day celebrations were transformed. By March 1911 Dr John Esmonde MP (Tipperary North) was sure that 'never in the whole history of the Irish race had she stood in such a proud and noble position as at the present moment'.[91] The following year confidence was clearly building. Dan Boyle was sure that 'There had never been a St. Patrick's Day when they had met in more hopeful circumstances'; Joe Devlin MP (Belfast West) described the position as 'a moment of national hopefulness'[92] and declared, 'the Irish Parliamentary Party ... was today without fear or weakness on the brink of victory'.[93] By March 1913 the tempo was increasing – the Home Rule Bill had passed the Commons twice and had been rejected once by the Lords but would become law even if rejected three times, and unionists opposed to home rule had organised the signing of the Solemn League and Covenant against Home Rule in September 1912 and founded the Ulster Volunteer Force in January 1913. The Free Trade Hall was filled for the usual public meeting, and an overflow meeting was necessary. The chief guest was William H.K Redmond MP (West Clare), younger brother of the party leader. One speaker declared, 'In all [probability [this] was about the last occasion that they would hear Mr. Redmond in that hall, for the reason that before many months were over he would be a member of the Irish government sitting in Dublin', and another that 'Mr. Redmond had never before brought a message of joy such as he had brought to them that day ... [he] had helped to bring them within sight of the promised goal'.[94] A speaker at the banquet was sure that 'the long dreary chapter in Irish history was about to be closed for ever' and expressed the hope that 'Catholic, Protestant and Methodist would recognise that they were all welded together as a nation to work together hand in hand as one brotherhood.' Redmond for his part was somewhat more realistic, possibly because he had witnessed the ferocity of Tory and unionist opposition in the Commons. Whilst he did profess a belief that 'God was on their side' and predicted that 'Within twelve months there would be the opening of an Irish Parliament in Dublin', he also confessed that the measure was not quite what had been hoped for and noted one option which had surfaced: 'It was not a Bill which, had they had the drawing of, they would not have altered in some respect. But it was a measure which they could accept with the full hope and belief that it would work well both for Ireland and Great Britain. At any rate, it gave them a Parliament of their own, with wide control over all affairs that were their own.' He then warned, 'Whether there would be any offer of compromise about Home Rule he did not know ... But it was the resolve of the Nationalist Party, while willing to do almost anything to disarm the honest suspicion of their Protestant fellow-countrymen, never to accept Home Rule for Ireland at the price of cutting Ireland in two. (Cheers).'[95]

By March 1914 the bill had been rejected for the second time by the Lords, the Irish Volunteers had been formed in November 1913 to strengthen support for home rule, and talk of special arrangements for the north had been aired. Excitement and rhetoric reached a new peak. It was estimated that four thousand people filled the Free Trade Hall; an overflow meeting was full, and many more could not be admitted. The main speakers at the packed public meeting and the overflows were Richard Hazleton MP (Galway North) and William Archer Redmond MP (East Tyrone), the leader's son. The chairman was sure that 'Never in the history of the national struggle had they celebrated St. Patrick's Day with such hope and joy and pride ... Whatever temporary arrangements may be made the result must be, and will be, self-government for the whole of Ireland.' Hazleton declared, 'We shall concede no shred of nationhood' and promised that if the concessions on offer were rejected 'we shall put away the flag of truce, sound the call to arms and against straight to victory against the foe'.[96] Redmond, not to be outdone, made it clear that 'Even the proposal for temporary exclusion was nauseous to us and it could never be construed into a proposal for permanent exclusion'[97] and went on to say that if current proposals were turned down 'the Bill goes through as it stands. And we shall face the consequences. We shall be ready for their civil war.'[98]

The First World War transformed the political landscape of Ireland every bit as much as it transformed Europe. On 3 August 1914 John Redmond had come out in favour of the British stance and pledged that Britain could confidently remove troops from Ireland and leave the defence of the country in the hands of the Irish Volunteers. On 18 September the Home Rule Act had been passed, though it was suspended for the duration of the conflict, and on 20 September Redmond had committed the Volunteers to serve with British forces wherever the firing line extended and had begun to address recruiting meetings. When he came to Manchester in March 1915 it was noted that the visit 'would in ordinary times have been a celebration of the festival with a good deal more in the speeches about Irish politics than about the saint. The war gave the meeting a new tone and a new significance.'[99] On rising to speak '[he] received a remarkable ovation from the vast audience which thronged the Free Trade Hall ... Many thousands were unable to gain admission even to the overflow meeting in the Grand Theatre ... Irish airs were played on the organ and national songs were sung.' Redmond remarked that he had often spoken at such events in the city 'but I have spoken only to the Irish people in Manchester ... today I am glad and proud to know that this is a meeting not of Irishmen alone, but of Irishmen and Englishmen firmly united in a common purpose',[100] and, in a passage replete with ironies he could never conceive, he went on, 'When the war is over we shall go back to the consideration of political questions in a new political world.' He then launched into 'a great recruiting speech',[101] and the meeting closed with the singing of both 'God save Ireland' and 'God save the king', presumably without any sense of irony. There are no reports of a banquet or concert. The following day the Redmonds visited a textile firm and were entertained to lunch at the Town Hall.[102]

There are no traces of celebrations in March 1916 but the following year, when the political context had been revolutionised by the Easter Rising of 1916 and Sinn Féin had scored its first by-election victory in Roscommon (5 February 1917), there was a somewhat subdued event described as 'a reunion' with 'a vocal programme' at a local hotel with Sir Dan McCabe the main speaker. The rhetoric was decidedly dated in view of the steadily accelerating shift of political opinion in Ireland. McCabe declared that 'Ireland was quite willing to remain a part of the Empire ... No people had clung more to the double faith – nationality and religion – than Ireland.'[103] In 1918 celebrations were confined to a concert, but in 1919, with the war over, they were somewhat more elaborate. Shamrock was blessed and distributed at churches, there was a banquet at a local hotel, the Irish National Concert Society gave concerts over two nights with proceeds going towards a scholarship at the National University of Ireland, and the Foresters held their church parade, but without a procession or bands. They assembled at St John's cathedral in Salford and 'Mass was said for the souls of those members of the Order who had been killed or died of wounds in the war'.[104] On this occasion there is no trace of political speeches, but the picture in 1920 was notably different. By then Sinn Féin was well established as the dominant force in Irish politics and the War of Independence had been raging for over a year. There were two parallel events in Manchester, thereby demonstrating the cleavages within Irish opinion. One was attended by the Lord Mayor, but another was organised by the ISDL, the support group for Sinn Féin in Britain. The Irish-born Manchester councillor Hugh Lee and the Irish second-generation mayor of the nearby town of Altrincham were present, the health of the members of Dáil Éireann was drunk, although that body had been declared illegal by the British government in September 1919, and, as already noted, at the conclusion the party chose to sing 'A soldier's song', the IRA marching anthem which would be adopted as the national anthem of the Irish Free State in 1926.[105]

By 1921 the Irish War of Independence had reached such an intensity that 'In the opinion of the Irishmen of Manchester the present was no time for banqueting and celebrations. They therefore decided to abandon the customary banquet and contented themselves with a smoking concert in the Grosvenor Hotel. In all parts of the city the day seemed to be observed by Irish people in a prayerful manner, and as they wore shamrock they were no doubt reminded of what was happening in the land from which it came. Prayers for peace were offered at the Catholic churches.'[106] There was no mention of politics. In March 1922 the celebrations reflected the fact that the political situation had been transformed once again. By then the War of Independence had ended and the Anglo-Irish Treaty of December 1921 had been signed and ratified, however narrowly, by Dáil Éireann in January 1922. The emphasis was exclusively on celebration and enjoyment:

> In Manchester concerts and dances were held during the weekend in almost all the parishes, and at some of the churches there was the blessing and distributing of the shamrock. Sermons were preached on the life of St. Patrick. Though in all parts of the city shamrock was in evidence on the feast day, its wearers seemed far more numerous on Sunday, and a noticeable fact was the prominent place it had with many of the tram drivers and guards.[107]

## Performance and multiple audiences

To some extent the changes of emphasis which can be traced in these celebrations reflected the fact that they were the performance of Irishness before a multiplicity of audiences, some of which had contrasting expectations. At the immediate local level they were communal gatherings with a strong celebratory social dimension, events where Irish people could relax, renew friendships, network and indulge in nostalgia for the homeland in a purely Irish setting. At a more formal level they were an opportunity for local notables to renew their leadership roles, boost morale and exhort the faithful to remain true to Irish causes, especially when the national political outlook was gloomy.

But the Irish in Britain also had to present themselves before a wider audience if they were to achieve their political aspirations. It was therefore most important that Irish public events were conducted in decorous fashion in accordance with prevailing social norms, hence the clerical emphasis on sobriety and the adoption of the conventional forms of banquet, concert and orderly public meeting. At the local level there was a desire to demonstrate that the migrant Irish were a civilised, respectable and sensible people loyal to both the land of their origin and the city where they lived. The most vocal spokesperson of this dual loyalty was Dan McCabe, who expressed his outlook in 1897:

> Irishmen in that great centre of commerce and industry were as anxious for the prosperity of the city of their adoption as any section of the community. He believed there was to be found amongst the Irishmen of Manchester as much civic patriotism as in any other portion of the people … he believed their progress was equal to that of any of their fellow citizens. But whilst they were loyal citizens of Manchester, and anxious for its progress and development, they had deeply rooted in their hearts the desire to see Ireland a nation … it was an idea that had never been obliterated from the Irish mind and the Irish heart.[108]

Some speakers reminded hearers that there was also a British national audience. In 1890 Timothy Harrington MP (Dublin Harbour) argued that 'Irish men and women must not only look at the past history of their country; they had to act in the "living present", and to show those amongst whom they lived that they were fitted for the native government which they claimed'.[109] In 1900 T.F. Kelly was much more specific in recognising that without English allies the Irish alone simply could not achieve home rule when he pointed out 'the intellect of England was now open to conviction on the Irish question. Irishmen, therefore, should seek by temperance in conduct and in speech to win the goodwill of their fellow subjects in England, for they knew it was impossible for a small people like the Irish ever to obtain their liberty except by the favour of the people among whom they lived'.[110]

But there was a further dimension to these celebrations which served to remind both the local Irish and any onlookers that they were not alone in their proclamations of Irish loyalties and aspirations. By the early 1900s there were increasingly frequent references to the strength of the Irish in other parts of the diaspora. In March 1911 John Dillon MP (Mayo East), one of the dominant figures in the Irish party and John Redmond's eventual successor as leader in March 1918, reminded the various audiences that the party:

had not only united the people of Ireland, but they had united the scattered children of their race throughout the world – (cheers) – and they had made England understand, and the world understand, that when they were dealing with the people of Ireland they were not dealing with a miserable remnant of an oppressed and conquered people, but with a mighty race numbering twenty millions, scattered throughout the world, and able to influence – as England had found out and realised at last – great and mighty nations, mightier than England herself, nations whose friendship was worth cultivating, and whose hatred was a dangerous thing.

Dillon pointed out that the imminent coronation of King George V would bring to London the premiers of the various dominions, 'every single man of whom was a strong and pronounced Irish Home Ruler'.[111] When he joined the Manchester celebrations in 1913, Joe Devlin MP recalled that when in Melbourne, Australia, in 1906, he had attended a gathering of Irish people, none of whom had been born in Ireland, 'and yet twelve thousand miles away from the homeland of their race they gathered in that great city with love so deep-rooted and hearts so faithful and loyalty so intense as those on the plains of Tipperary or the mountains of Kerry and were praying and fighting that Ireland might be free'.[112] Both speakers were seeking to remind their local audience that they were not alone, thereby invoking an imaginary sense of fellowship not only with the Irish across the Irish Sea, but across the globe. At the much more practical level, they were also reminding British governments that they were faced with political pressure not only from the Irish in the United Kingdom but from the many millions in the USA, the dominions of the British Empire and elsewhere in the diaspora.

## Conclusion

In Manchester the public celebration of St Patrick's Day during the period under discussion was a multi-dimensional festival which underwent some significant changes of theme and emphasis. Some features endured, most notably the sense of relaxation in convivial fellowship with the likeminded, the wearing of Irish symbols, especially shamrock, the colour green in various manifestations, Irish music and song, special guest speakers and the consumption of food and plentiful alcohol. However, one of the marked changes was the increasing sobriety and respectability of the gatherings. The rowdy processions and occasional group conflicts of the 1830s and 1840s died out, and by the early 1880s the gatherings were decorous, sober and eminently respectable.

The earlier events had been markedly inclusive in political and religious terms, with constant reference to their non-sectarian nature and invocations of unity. But with the resumption of public celebrations in the early 1860s the tone became steadily more and more Catholic and from the early 1880s more overtly nationalist. In the 1840s both Catholic and Protestant clergy had been regular attenders, but by the late 1870s Catholic clergy and concerns were overwhelmingly dominant. However, from the mid-1880s onwards even they had to make room for the growing salience of the home rule issue, though Catholic education was a recurring theme. During the war celebrations were muted and from 1916 onwards the political tone was by turns downbeat and militant and then faded until by 1922 it was entirely absent, being overwhelmed by simple relief and celebration at the end of the War of Independence. Throughout the period countless private celebrations undoubtedly went on in public houses and private homes with much socialising, food and drink and practice of popular religious devotions. By 1922 events seem to have reverted to something like what had occurred a century earlier, with the absence of politics and the emphasis on church services, dances and parties – but clearly this was still the distinctive Irish national day.

But one of the most notable challenges to this sense of Irish difference was the development of political issues in Manchester and Britain as a whole, which at times ran parallel with, and at other times conflicted with, Irish concerns and could therefore exert sometimes conflicting pulls on Irish loyalties.

## Notes

1 Mervyn Busteed, 'Nationalism, historical geography of', in Rob Kitchen and Nigel Thrift (eds), *International encyclopaedia of human geography*, vol. 7 (Oxford: Elsevier, 2009), pp. 255–60.
2 Sean Duffy, 'The arrival of Christianity' in S. Duffy (ed.), *Atlas of Irish History* (Dublin: Gill & Macmillan, 1997), pp. 16–17.
3 Patrick Corish, *The Irish Catholic experience: a historical survey* (Dublin: Gill & Macmillan, 1986), pp. 1–2.
4 Vincent Comerford, *Ireland* (London: Arnold, 2003), pp. 85–8.
5 Mike Cronin and Daryl Adair, *The wearing of the green: a history of St. Patrick's Day* (London: Routledge, 2002), p. 1.
6 Comerford, *Ireland*, p. 90.
7 Cronin and Adair, *The wearing of the green*, pp. 8–9.
8 Jacqueline Hill, 'National festivals, the state and "Protestant ascendancy" in Ireland, 1790–1829', *Irish Historical Studies*, 24 (1984), pp. 30–51.
9 *Manchester Guardian*, 19 March 1866.
10 Marianne Elliott, *When God took sides: religion and identity in Ireland – unfinished history* (Oxford: Oxford University Press, 2009), pp. 99–102.

11  Neil Jarman, *Material conflicts: parades and visual displays in Northern Ireland* (Oxford: Berg, 1997), pp. 50–1.
12  *Manchester Guardian*, 18 March 1890.
13  *Manchester Guardian*, 19 March 1825.
14  *Manchester Guardian*, 23 March 1842.
15  *Manchester Courier*, 19 March 1842.
16  *Manchester Courier*, 20 March 1830.
17  *Manchester Guardian*, 20 March 1830.
18  *Manchester Courier*, 20 March 1830.
19  *Manchester Courier*, 24 March 1832.
20  *Manchester Courier*, 19 March 1838.
21  *Manchester Guardian*, 20 March 1844.
22  *Manchester Courier*, 18 March 1844.
23  *Manchester Guardian*, 13 November 1847. 'Caffres' is presumably a form of 'Kaffirs', a term widely used by white colonists in South Africa to refer to the native population.
24  *Manchester Courier*, 18 March 1848.
25  *Manchester Guardian*, 18 March 1848.
26  *Manchester Guardian*, 20 March 1850.
27  *Manchester Guardian*, 20 March 1852.
28  Gerard Moran, 'The National Brotherhood of St. Patrick in Great Britain in the 1860s', *Irish Studies Review*, 7:3 (December 1999), p. 326.
29  Gerard Moran, 'Nationalists in exile: the National Brotherhood of St. Patrick in Lancashire, 1861–5', in R. Swift and S. Gilley (eds), *The Irish in Victorian Britain: the local dimension* (Dublin: Four Courts Press, 1999), pp. 21–35.
30  *Manchester Guardian*, 19 March 1866.
31  *Manchester Courier*, 19 March 1866.
32  *Manchester Guardian*, 18 March 1867.
33  Mervyn Busteed, '"Plentiful libations of whisky, perfervid Irish oratory and some religious sentiment": celebrating St. Patrick's Day in Manchester, 1825–1922', in J. Strachan and A. O'Malley-Younger (eds), *Ireland: revolution and evolution* (Oxford: Peter Lang, 2010), pp. 81–100.
34  *Manchester Guardian*, 17 March 1908.
35  *Manchester Courier*, 19 March 1877.
36  *Weekly Herald*, 22 March 1889. Founded in 1888 by the Derry-born Charles Diamond, later renamed the *Catholic Herald* – strap line 'Home rule for Ireland and for England, Scotland and Wales. For faith and country, Catholic and Irish. Irish and Catholic.' Diamond served as nationalist MP for North Monaghan in 1892–95, and later joined the British Labour Party. See Owen Dudley Edwards and Patricia J. Storey, 'The Irish press in Victorian Britain', in R. Swift and S. Gilley (eds), *The Irish in the Victorian city* (London: Croom Helm, 1985), pp. 158–78.
37  *Catholic Herald*, 20 March 1903.
38  Letter from Gaelic League to Chief Constable, 7 March 1908, MCLAD, Watch Committee Minutes, vol. 38: 19 December 1907 – 27 February 1908.

39 *Manchester Guardian*, 17 March 1913.
40 *Catholic Herald*, 21 March 1914.
41 Angela Moran, 'Hail ambiguous St. Patrick: sounds of Ireland on parade in Birmingham', *Irish Studies Review*, 20:2 (May 2012), pp. 157–78.
42 *Manchester Courier*, 18 March 1879.
43 *Manchester Guardian*, 18 March 1890.
44 *Catholic Herald*, 21 March 1890.
45 *Catholic Herald*, 20 March 1920.
46 *Manchester Guardian*, 18 March 1890.
47 *Weekly Herald*, 22 March 1889.
48 Lawrence McBride, *The Reynolds letters: an Irish emigrant family in late Victorian Manchester* (Cork: Cork University Press, 1999); *Weekly Herald*, 22 March 1889.
49 'Mr. Daniel Melia', *The Harvest*, 20:241 (1907), p. 230.
50 *Manchester Guardian*, 18 March 1875.
51 *Catholic Herald*, 20 March 1903.
52 *Manchester Courier*, 19 March 1900.
53 *Manchester Guardian*, 19 March 1900.
54 *Manchester Guardian*, 18 March 1902.
55 *Manchester Guardian*, 19 March 1906.
56 *Manchester Examiner*, 18 March 1875.
57 *Manchester Courier*, 19 March 1877.
58 *Manchester Courier*, 18 March 1879.
59 *Manchester Courier*, 20 March 1880.
60 *Manchester Guardian*, 18 March 1882.
61 *Manchester Examiner*, 18 March 1884.
62 *Manchester Guardian*, 18 March 1887.
63 *Weekly Herald*, 22 March 1889.
64 *Weekly Herald*, 22 March 1889.
65 *Manchester Guardian*, 19 March 1895.
66 *Manchester Examiner*, 18 March 1884.
67 *Manchester Guardian*, 18 March 1882.
68 *Manchester Examiner*, 18 March 1885.
69 *Manchester Guardian*, 18 March 1904; *Catholic Herald*, 25 March 1904.
70 *Manchester Courier*, 19 March 1877.
71 *Manchester Guardian*, 18 March 1882.
72 *Manchester Guardian*, 18 March 1901.
73 *Catholic Herald*, 20 March 1891. 'The Grand Old Man' (or GOM) was by then a commonly used term for the eighty-two-year-old Liberal leader William Ewart Gladstone.
74 *Catholic Herald*, 18 March 1892.
75 *Manchester Guardian*, 18 March 1896.
76 *Manchester Guardian*, 20 March 1900.
77 Alvin Jackson, *Home rule: an Irish history 1800–2000* (London: Phoenix Press, 2004), pp. 109–21.

78 *Catholic Herald*, 20 March 1909.
79 *Manchester Guardian*, 17 March 1909.
80 *Manchester Guardian*, 19 March 1906. Douglas Hyde was one of the founders in 1893 of Conradh na Gaeilge (the Gaelic League), which was dedicated to the preservation and expansion of traditional Irish Gaelic culture, especially the Irish language. He served as the first President of Ireland, 1938–45. See Janet and Gareth Dunleavy, *Douglas Hyde: a maker of modern Ireland* (Berkeley: University of California Press, 1991).
81 *Catholic Herald*, 23 March 1894.
82 *Manchester Guardian*, 19 March 1906.
83 Steven Fielding, 'Irish politics in Manchester 1890–1914', *International Review of Social History*, 33 (1988), pp. 261–84.
84 *Catholic Herald*, 20 March 1909.
85 *Manchester Guardian*, 17 March 1909.
86 *Manchester Courier*, 18 March 1905.
87 *Manchester Guardian*, 19 March 1906.
88 Alan O'Day, *Irish home rule, 1867–1921* (Manchester: Manchester University Press, 1998), pp. 210–16.
89 *Manchester Guardian*, 16 March 1908.
90 *Catholic Herald*, 21 March 1908.
91 *Manchester Guardian*, 17 March 1911.
92 *Manchester Guardian*, 18 March 1912.
93 *Catholic Herald*, 23 March 1912.
94 *Catholic Herald*, 22 March 1913.
95 *Manchester Courier*, 17 March 1913.
96 *Manchester Courier*, 21 March 1914.
97 *Manchester Guardian*, 16 March 1914.
98 *Catholic Herald*, 21 March 1914.
99 *Manchester Guardian*, 15 March 1915.
100 *Catholic Herald*, 20 March 1915.
101 *Manchester Guardian*, 15 March 1915.
102 *Catholic Herald*, 20 March 1915.
103 *Catholic Herald*, 24 March 1917.
104 *Catholic Herald*, 23 March 1919.
105 *Catholic Herald*, 20 March 1920.
106 *Catholic Herald*, 23 March 1921.
107 *Catholic Herald*, 25 March 1922.
108 *Manchester Guardian*, 17 March 1897.
109 *Manchester Guardian*, 18 March 1890.
110 *Manchester Guardian*, 20 March 1900.
111 *Catholic Herald*, 25 March 1911.
112 *Catholic Herald*, 22 March 1913.

# 5

# Revolution and reform: 1790s to 1850s

From the late 1790s to the early 1850s the Manchester Irish were involved in a variety of political activities, some dedicated to violent separatism, some to peaceful reform, some focused on Ireland, at other times concerned with issues preoccupying British society in general. This meant that they were on occasion torn between a focus on Ireland and its affairs and the appeal of broader issues. This conflict of interest and loyalties was particularly acute during the Chartist campaigns, when at times the potential of a class-based alliance between Irish and British workers excited radicals and deeply alarmed the ruling authorities of both the Catholic Church and the British state. In Manchester the alliance did achieve a brief but fleeting reality.

## United Irish and English

During the 1790s, as Catholic numbers in Manchester began to rise with a growing Irish influx, some became involved in the political life of the city. Some of the more prosperous became trustees of the city infirmary and some were members of anti-slavery groups, but the outbreak of war with France in 1793 brought new challenges. The movement for parliamentary reform and the French revolution of 1789 had inspired the foundation of a number of radical groups in Manchester, including the largely middle-class Manchester Constitutional Society in October 1790 and the Patriotic Society and Reformation Society in 1792, both of which included a more working-class element than their predecessors. Joint meetings were held, and in March 1792 a radical newspaper, the *Manchester Herald*, was launched. But there was also a decidedly loyalist element in the city population, as demonstrated by a meeting of local publicans in 1792 who pledged themselves not to hire out their rooms for meetings of radical societies, the sacking of the *Herald*'s offices during riots on 10 December and the burning of an effigy of the revolutionary writer Tom Paine, author of *The Rights of Man*, in January 1793. That same month, a declaration of loyalty had been signed by 496 local Catholics, and some joined loyalist organisations.[1]

In February 1793 France declared war on Britain, and the government, which had already taken steps to curb radical publications, embarked on increasingly severe repression. Following a series of meetings of reformers and radicals in Edinburgh in late 1793, the leaders were arrested and a series of trials held. Amongst those detained and tried were several prominent Manchester reformers, including Thomas Walker, a former boroughreeve. He and others were tried at Lancaster on charges of conspiracy and treason but were found not guilty and returned to the city in triumph. However, the government was not deterred, and its increasingly repressive measures, including suspension of Habeas Corpus in May 1794, extension of the law on treason and prohibition of mass meetings in late 1795, led the more moderate elements to withdraw from the reform movement, which went underground, becoming more militant and increasingly inclined to look to France for help in planning insurrection. The Manchester Corresponding Society, notably radical in outlook and largely working-class in membership, had been formed in 1796 but was outbid in militancy by the secret Society of United Englishmen, formed early the following year, which attracted many of the more radical spirits. It was modelled on the Society of United Irishmen formed in Belfast in 1792, who, though originally dedicated to peaceful parliamentary reform, were increasingly driven into secrecy and militancy by government repression. It has been claimed that 'Manchester was to become England's Belfast', and many Ulster migrants were active in setting up the society in the city and its extension into nearby towns; James Dixon of Belfast was swearing in members from November 1796, and by the following May there were reports that nine hundred members had joined.[2] The society absorbed many of the more active members of existing radical groups; although migrant Irish constituted the largest element and there were close links with the Ulster United Irishmen, local English radicals were also notable. The leading United Irishman Fr James Coigley visited the city in June 1797 en route to Paris and was given funds to help him on his way. When he returned in February 1798, again on his way to France, he spent three days in secret discussion with local radicals, many of Ulster origin. At this time it was estimated there were between three and four thousand members in the society.[3]

After Coigley resumed his journey he was arrested in Margate later that month and executed in June.[4] The combination of the naval mutinies of mid-1797, the Irish rebellion of May–June 1798 and the attempted French invasions of Ireland later that year had provoked a further series of repressive measures, including the suppression of the London Corresponding Society, which crippled radical groups in general. There were sporadic efforts to revive the Society of United Englishmen in the early 1800s, but the arrest of Colonel Edward Despard and his associates and his execution in February 1803 and the premature and totally unsuccessful rising organised by Robert Emmet in July 1803 devastated what was left of the various organisations concerned, though details remain obscure and confused.[5]

## Trade unions and parliamentary reform

These events took place within a context of periodically severe economic hardship. Unrest over food shortages and high prices was a frequent occurrence in Manchester from the second half of the 1790s until the closing years of the wars with France, with especially severe outbreaks in July 1795 and April 1812. The situation was aggravated by changes in the technology and organisation of industry, which caused further unemployment. Consequently, embryonic trade unions appeared in the city, with the mule spinners of the cotton industry leading the way.[6] During the French wars government repression had been extended to cover these early unions with the Unlawful Oaths Act of 1797 and the Combination Acts of 1799 and 1800, which remained on the statute book until 1824. But sporadic efforts to organise labour persisted, resulting in periodic clashes with the authorities and employers, especially at times of economic stress. In May 1808 weavers organised a strike: a public meeting on 25 May was broken up by cavalry charges which left one dead, but the weavers did gain a rise in wages. It was one of their few successes. In 1810 spinners attempted to set up a county-wide union and struck for higher wages but after four months were forced back to work at the old rates. In June 1812 there were prosecutions for administration of illegal oaths in the city, and at Lancaster Assizes the same month, eight Manchester people were executed: four for mill burning in Manchester, three for breaking into a house in a search for food and a woman for stealing potatoes. The economic depression following the end of the French wars in 1815 led employers to enforce reductions in wages. In response there was a series of strikes beginning in June 1818, culminating in an outright clash with the military in August when one person was killed, several injured and strike leaders imprisoned.

Alongside and interacting with these developments, the campaign for parliamentary reform revived and in the years immediately after 1815 rapidly gathered momentum, demanding extension of the franchise and annual elections. The newly formed radical Hampden Clubs were in the forefront, and Manchester was a notable stronghold. Open-air meetings in October, November and December 1816 heightened tension and led to the suspension of Habeas Corpus in February 1817. The following month a large crowd gathered to see off a procession intending to march to London to present their case for economic and political reform. Equipped with blankets for sleeping along the way, the 'blanketeers' were stopped by the military, who also cleared the crowd. The Hampden Clubs were banned but were replaced by a network of Union Clubs, and meetings were held in January and June 1819. On 23 January there was a conflict at the Theatre Royal between supporters of the radical orator Henry Hunt and army officers. It was a portent of things to come.

On 16 August contingents from Manchester and surrounding towns and villages gathered at St Peter's Fields in the city to hear Henry 'Orator' Hunt speak on parliamentary reform. It was estimated that upwards of sixty thousand were present. Nervous magistrates had summoned local yeomanry cavalry, and the 15th Hussars were also present. In their efforts to arrest Hunt and the rest of the platform party the ill-disciplined yeomanry energetically used their sabres to force their way through the crowd, but they became scattered and the Hussars charged to their relief. Hunt and several others were arrested, and he was eventually sentenced to two years and six months in prison. At least eleven people were killed and over 650 injured, and the incident became notorious as the 'Peterloo Massacre', an ironic reference to the achievement of the military in charging an unarmed crowd of fellow citizens with large numbers of women and children present.[7] Feelings ran high in the city and there were clashes between police, troops and demonstrators in the strongly Irish New Cross area over the next few days, but Hunt's pleas to his followers to avoid conflict and the imposition of the 'Six Acts', which extended the rights of magistrates to ban public meetings, prevent public drilling and search for arms, meant there was no general recourse to violence. However, the memory of Peterloo entered the city's history and folklore and became an inspiration for future radical generations. The 'Cato Street conspiracy' of February 1820 to assassinate the Cabinet was used to justify further government measures, and these, plus a gradual economic upturn in the early 1820s, combined to take the edge off Manchester radicalism. This was exemplified in the fate of the *Manchester Observer*, which, launched in January 1818 to publicise radical causes, ceased publication in June 1821. Revival came when the campaign for parliamentary reform gradually built up a new momentum later in the decade.

The Irish were actively involved in both early trade unionism and the campaign for parliamentary reform, though there could be a clash of loyalties at times. This was well illustrated by their involvement in the early unions. The Catholic Church was always wary of secret, oath-bound organisations, particularly the Masonic Order, which held an impressive public procession in the city under County Grand Master John Allen in 1788 and had fifteen lodges by 1799. Early in the following century this resulted in an interdict on clergy giving the sacraments to members of any clandestine oath-bound group, and the increasingly prominent Irish leader Daniel O'Connell reinforced this by requesting the Manchester Irish to avoid such organisations. However, some clergy made a distinction between secret societies and openly organised trade unions, and gradually an attitude of 'uneasy toleration' evolved, but latent tensions persisted.[8] In John Doherty Manchester had an organiser who has been described as 'the most outstanding trade union leader … of the early nineteenth century'.[9] Born probably in 1798 in Buncrana, Co. Donegal, he migrated to Manchester in 1816 and worked in a spinning mill, making up for a lack of formal education by private reading and discussion. In the years which followed he became successively a union secretary, a founder of unions, the editor of a series of short-lived newspapers, a bookseller and a printer. He was also active in support of parliamentary reform, repeal of the union between Ireland and Britain, working-class education and temperance and served two prison terms for his various activities. A devout Catholic, he actively championed Catholic rights, including the emancipation campaign, though working-class interests clearly took precedence. His effort to set up the Manchester and Salford Catholic Association in May 1824, linking Irish, Catholic and radical class interests under one umbrella, was quickly elbowed aside within a matter of weeks by a similarly named organisation dominated by clergy and middle class English-born Catholics.[10] That the Irish continued to be active in union affairs is shown by their presence at public meetings, as in May 1832, when an outdoor gathering was addressed by one 'James Whittle, just returned from Ireland', who reported that a notable number of Irish MPs had been nominated and returned by trade unionists and were in favour of parliamentary reform.[11]

Clearly, some Irish were prominent as leaders or public speakers, but the strength of Irish grass-roots support for trade union and radical causes is difficult to gauge. One of the few indications is provided by the Irish crowds which turned out to greet the contingents passing along Rochdale Road on their way to the Peterloo meeting in August 1819, but some further evidence is provided by the lists of people given assistance by the various charities which sprang up to help those injured by yeomanry and police. One estimate is that at least 22% of the casualties had Irish names, a proportion well above the likely Irish percentage in the population at large.[12] Amongst those casualties with Irish names Owen McCabe of 9 Old Mount Street in Angel Meadow is described thus: 'A dreadful wound on the hip, trampled on, walks on crutches ever since, a poor (?) man', and Mary McKenna of nearby Nicholas Street as 'An interesting girl, much bruised in the back part of the head by being trampled on'.[13]

## Catholic emancipation

Both the campaign for trade union rights and that for parliamentary reform clearly drew on Irish support and saw both migrant Irish and Mancunians making common cause. But there were also issues which particularly affected the Irish and could at times set them apart. One of the most divisive was the campaign in the 1820s led by Daniel O'Connell for Catholic emancipation, the right of Catholics to become MPs. A somewhat genteel lobby group known as the Catholic Committee had existed in Ireland since 1760, but it was reconstituted in 1807 with O'Connell as a member, and he rapidly made his mark as a more vigorous and much less deferential advocate. Around the same time, the British government indicated that it would be open to discussion of the emancipation question if granted a veto on the appointment of Catholic bishops, and some of the more conservative members of the Committee were in favour. O'Connell, however, argued eloquently and passionately against the measure, and this 'Veto Controversy' brought him to national prominence as a leading Catholic spokesman.[14] In subsequent years there were vain efforts to pass an emancipation bill at Westminster, though the votes in favour steadily increased. In May 1823 O'Connell founded the Catholic Association, which was subsequently restructured in July 1825 to avoid prosecution. It was a historic departure. Using the Catholic parish as the basic spatial unit and the priest as a key organiser, it mobilised the grass roots of the Irish Catholic population in support of a popular cause. The first effort to launch a support group in Manchester took place in September 1824 when the Manchester and Salford branch of the British Catholic Association was founded, though it had to be reconstituted in October when O'Connell himself pointed out that in establishing a formal link with the London Catholic Association, it was in breach of the law against corresponding societies. It was noted that at the first meeting the proceedings 'were marked with great temper and moderation' and that one of the aims was 'to promote concord and confidence amongst all classes of Catholics and to rebut whatever calumnious imputations might be cast upon them'.[15] At the reconvened meeting on 27 October it was noted that 'amongst the speakers were a number of the most respectable Catholic inhabitants of the town and neighbourhood'. The resolutions passed noted that the meeting had been recalled because 'the principles of the Catholic religion do not permit its members to offend against the laws of the country'. In a clever piece of drafting, clearly devised to reassure observers that they merely wished to share established freedoms, they went on to declare not only that the purpose of the association was to 'promote concord and mutual confidence amongst all classes of Catholics' but that their sole purpose was 'the restoration of our constitutional rights on such terms only as guarantee the integrity of our holy religion'. But they also acknowledged that 'the thanks of this meeting are due, and are hereby given, to the Irish Catholic Association, for their extraordinary and successful efforts to promote the common cause'.[16]

Meetings for and against emancipation were held in the lead-up to the defeat of the bill in the Lords in May 1825. A mass meeting in support was held early in May 1825. To the *Manchester Guardian* the gathering was 'most numerous and respectable', and though there were opponents of emancipation present who put their case and some confusion erupted at the end of the meeting, it was clear that supporters won the day.[17] For the *Manchester Courier*, however, the occasion provided ammunition for the case against. The account focused on the confusion, and reported at one point 'immense tumult, and an exclamation of '*Oh, de tief o' de world!*' from an unshaven *Patlander* in the crowd'. In an accompanying editorial it was alleged that the meeting had been packed by 'a very considerable body of Roman Catholics, including a numerous assemblage of Irish hodmen and operatives of the lowest class, who had been waiting without the doors for some time, and who rushed in the moment they were opened, and filled the room to the prejudice of more respectable persons who were unable to obtain admittance'. What was described as '[the] fierce and intolerant spirit they manifested' was condemned, and it was asserted that 'The general belief appears to be that the majority of Protestants unfavourable to the Catholic Relief Bill, at this meeting, was in the proportion of two to one' without saying how this judgment was arrived at. The same issued alleged that Catholics in the New Cross area had intimidated the organiser of an anti-emancipation petition, who had to be rescued by the police.[18] Later that month the *Courier* returned to the fray, holding the petition up to ridicule on the grounds that it had been signed 'by the lowest rabble, including Irish labourers and Irish hodmen' and that of the names on the first page most of those 'that were legible began with an "O"'. It went on to put the label 'Patlander' against ten of the first twenty-five names, clearly regarding these as damning facts.[19]

## Repeal of the union

With the passage of emancipation in April 1829 and the entry of O'Connell and a group of supporters into Westminster, political excitement amongst the Catholic population waned, but there was now a new level of political consciousness, and there had been a clear demonstration of what could be achieved by mass organisation and agitation. Repeal of the union between Ireland and Britain began to edge onto the political agenda and found its echo amongst the Manchester Irish. A meeting in January 1831 attracted considerable attention and hostility from local press. The *Guardian* noted that 1,200 attended and went on, 'This meeting, it is hardly necessary to say, was composed almost exclusively of the lowest order of Irishmen, whose want of knowledge and generally distressed situation render them particularly liable to become the dupes of political quacks and projectors.' It was also noted that almost all the speakers were Irish. During the meeting Fr Kay, a local Catholic priest, described how he had encountered 'the deplorable distress pervading the working class of his countrymen in the town' and argued that the solution was 'the repeal of the legislative union'. Another speaker broadened the argument and asserted that not only the distress in Ireland, but also the distress in England had been caused by the union, 'which, by driving the impoverished Irish to this country, and compelling them in their necessity to accept the barest wages that could afford them the means of living, had reduced the condition of the labouring classes by their competition.'[20] The *Courier* drew attention to the fact that 'The meeting was almost as exclusively Irish as if it had been held in Dublin or Limerick; and a Popish priest ... was the Chairman ... [it] consisted exclusively of the lower orders of Irish, and ... the individuals who addressed the meeting were the only persons of respectability – even of appearance – who were present.' Much was made of the fact that it was difficult for the chairman to keep order at times because of 'the yells, vociferations and tumult' and that the speakers were not of one mind in their solutions for Ireland's problems; the report particularly noted that one speaker got a hostile reception when he argued that the Irish were putting the cart before the horse by campaigning for repeal before parliamentary reform. Overall it was concluded that 'Our readers will probably be more amused than edified by the uproarious discussion.'[21]

In the general election of December 1832 O'Connell and thirty-nine supporters pledged to repeal of the union were returned, though in the ensuing months they focused on issues such as the government's Coercion Bill for Ireland and tithes rather than repeal. However, from early 1834 O'Connell began to give the issue greater prominence, local repeal associations appeared in Manchester and other cities in Britain, and meetings were held. The gathering of about a thousand people in Manchester's St George's Fields near St Patrick's church on 17 March was addressed by John Doherty amongst others. It was noted that the carriages had been provided by 'a *gentleman* of colour known by the cognomen of "Black Joe" (and used by him for the exhibition of pugilistic feats)'. A series of resolutions was passed but the meeting was dismissed as 'quite contemptible in point of numbers … and still more so in point of intelligence and respectability … having occupied, in delivering abusive harangues, about four hours'.[22] On 22 April 1834 O'Connell made history by putting the first motion for repeal to the House of Commons – it was inevitably lost, by 523 votes to 38. In advance of a further meeting in Manchester in December, it was announced that membership of the local repeal association was available for a fee of a penny per month, three pence for three months, six pence for six months or a shilling for a full year.[23] Thereafter interest flagged, especially when O'Connell negotiated the 'Lichfield House Compact' with the Whig administration in February 1835. The general election in January had left O'Connell and his followers holding the balance of power, and in return for reform of the tithes system and local government, appointment of more Catholics to government places and a generally more enlightened administrative regime in Ireland, he promised to support the Whig government.

This arrangement was not without its problems, but generally worked until the election of July 1841 returned a Tory government under Sir Robert Peel. During the interim repeal had dropped down the order of priorities, but O'Connell was increasingly aware that this had eroded his standing and popularity, and in April 1840 he had launched the Repeal Association with the aim of using the techniques of grass-roots organisation and mass mobilisation which had proved so successful in the emancipation campaign.[24] After a slow start, the movement took off; O'Connell announced that 1843 would be 'Repeal Year' and launched a series of highly theatrical 'monster meetings'. Local branches of the movement multiplied both in Ireland and amongst the Irish in Britain. In Manchester by 1842 there were at least eight branches with reading rooms taking national and Irish newspapers, and some Catholic clergy were notably active supporters. The city was organised into 'repeal wards', some centred on a Catholic church and often named for an Irish saint, each with a warden or organiser, and a 'repeal rent' was regularly collected for campaign funds.[25] However, when in October 1843 O'Connell yielded to a government ban and cancelled a climactic 'monster meeting' planned for Clontarf outside Dublin, his standing suffered a blow from which it never fully recovered.

## Chartism and Chartists

But this was by no means the only cause appealing for support amongst the Irish in Manchester in the early 1840s. Two organisations were founded in 1838 which for a time were to pull the migrant Irish in opposing directions. By the late 1830s disappointment with the rather limited 1832 Reform Act was building up into a movement for much more thoroughgoing parliamentary reform. In November 1837 the *Northern Star* newspaper was launched to publicise the cause, with the Irish MP Feargus O'Connor as one of its leading contributors. In May 1838 the movement crystallised around the 'People's Charter' with its demands for universal male suffrage and annual elections. This was followed by a series of massive outdoor meetings across the country, including a gathering on Kersal Moor, three miles outside Manchester, in September.[26] The first Chartist petition for reform was presented to parliament (and rejected) in July 1839.

Meanwhile, in September 1838 the Anti-Corn Law League had been founded in Manchester under the leadership of George Wilson, Richard Cobden and John Bright to campaign for the abolition of tariffs on imported food grains. It rapidly expanded until in March 1839 it was launched as a nation-wide organisation. Trade unions, repeal, Corn Law agitation and Chartism were therefore causes competing for Irish support, and on occasion the result could be either alliance or conflict, depending upon time, place and personality. O'Connell was a supporter of the anti-Corn Law campaign on the grounds that it would remove a restraint on trade, and when the league held a two-day gathering in a specially built timber pavilion named the Free Trade Hall in Manchester on 13–14 January 1840, he was one of the guest speakers at the banquet. His carriage from the station was escorted by a vast procession, and when he rose to speak he was greeted with 'loud and continuous cheering'.[27] But O'Connell was an opponent of Chartism, partly on the grounds that he was wary of any organisation which might serve to restrain individual choice, and partly because he feared that some of its more extreme manifestations might provoke the physical violence he abhorred. There was also a personality factor at play. Feargus O'Connor had originally been elected as a repeal MP for Co. Cork in 1832 and vigorously upheld that cause, but when O'Connell devised the 'Lichfield House Compact' with the Whigs in February 1835 he deplored the fact that repeal was being allowed to slip down the order of priorities. Unseated on petition that year, he increasingly involved himself in British working-class politics, became a leading light in the Chartist movement and from 1837 onwards diverged ever more markedly from O'Connell.[28] By September 1841 they had parted company to the extent that O'Connell issued a strong warning to his followers in Ireland and Britain that they should ban Chartists from repeal meetings. Given his hold on Irish popular opinion, his stance was a significant obstacle to large-scale Irish involvement in Chartism on both sides of the Irish Sea. Moreover, the Catholic Church, always suspicious of any mass movements founded and organised by those who were not under its guidance, was also opposed. In Manchester it was notable that Fr Hearne, always ready to champion the interests of his overwhelmingly working-class parishioners, supported repeal of both the union and the Corn Laws, but strongly condemned Chartism.

The question of the relationship between Irish migrants in Britain and Chartism has generated lively academic debate, though researchers do agree that there is a dearth of contemporary material on the outlook of rank-and-file Irish migrants during this period.[29] Certainly there were prominent Irish such as O'Connor and Bronterre O'Brien amongst the national leadership and at the local level. Some have pointed out that from quite early on the Chartist movement expressed sympathy and support for Irish issues, and speakers often used the argument that parliamentary reform and repeal of the union would create a prosperous Ireland, which would mean the Irish would remain at home and not migrate to Britain, and lower wages through competition with British labour. It has been argued that this resulted in a class-based alliance between native English workers and their Irish migrant counterparts at the grass-roots level.[30] Others have pointed out that the flimsy sources which exist do not bear out this contention and that anti-Irish and anti-Catholic prejudice, plus fear that the violence popularly associated with the Irish and Irish affairs would spread to Britain in the wake of a Chartist agitation in which Irish leaders were prominent, combined to repel many English of all class backgrounds and was used to justify harsh government repression.[31] It is also true that Irish migrants were not a homogeneous group and that relationships between the various movements varied with time, place, personality and national and indeed international events.[32]

In Manchester there were certainly some local Irish prominent in the Chartist movement such as Daniel Donovan from Cork, an active trade unionist who for a time served on the movement's national council. Others, such as Edward Curran, Christopher Doyle, John Murray and John Finnigan, at various times combined their Chartist activities with support for the Anti-Corn Law League and repeal of the union. But for the Chartist leadership, Corn Law repeal took second place to parliamentary reform since, they argued, justice on any issue, including Irish matters, could come only from a drastically reformed parliament and until then the argument that tariff reform would mean cheaper bread would merely divert energies from reform and provide employers with an excuse to reduce wages. The shifting complexity of loyalties and affiliations was demonstrated by a series of clashes between the League, Chartists and repealers in the early 1840s. A large open-air anti-Corn Law meeting was planned for 2 June 1841 in Stevenson Square with the Manchester Mayor, Sir Thomas Potter, and Richard Cobden as the main speakers and Fr Daniel Hearne on the platform, but for days beforehand placards had been posted urging Chartists to demonstrate against the event. Edward Watkin, one of Cobden's associates, took the precaution of hiring 'League Police' in case of trouble. They were mostly Irish with blackthorn sticks, referred to ironically as 'Irish Lambs' and led by John Finnigan amongst others, an arrangement endorsed by both Cobden and O'Connell. One hostile source described them as 'two or three hundred of the biggest and most savage Irish ragamuffins, from the purlieus of St. George's road and Little Ireland ... primed with bad gin and Irish whiskey'.[33] By 10.30 a.m. there were an estimated twenty thousand in the square, and as soon as the first speaker rose to speak, it became clear that Chartists had packed the area immediately in front of the platform. They hoisted banners and flags which obscured the speakers, the 'Lambs' moved in, Chartists produced staves, and there was a violent clash with the result that, as a more sympathetic source noted, 'the disturbers were driven from the square, but not without having given and received a considerable number of broken heads'. The same source suggested rather unconvincingly that local Tories had contrived the disturbance, though the Irish may have been roused by rumours circulating beforehand that the Chartists planned to burn O'Connell and Fr Hearne in effigy.[34]

A Chartist meeting in October 1841, in which Feargus O'Connor processed through the city streets with banners and made a speech stressing how repeal of the union was an integral part of the Chartist programme, passed off peacefully even though 'the hirelings of the anti-Corn League threatened a disturbance'.[35] The same cannot be said of a meeting he addressed in Manchester in early March 1842. O'Connor was to speak on repeal of the union, but when he arrived the room had been occupied by a large number of supporters of the Anti-Corn Law League, who tried to take over the meeting and impose their own chairman and agenda. At this point

> the repealers, finding themselves beaten ... immediately resorted to a display of physical force ... and a general melee took place on the platform ... most of those present being Irish, everyone characteristically began to lay about him on all within his reach ... all discussion was evidently at an end. In addition to the bludgeons with which they were armed, the infuriated Leaguers tore up the rail, benches, and gas pipes in the hall, as well as the banisters and rails of the staircases, using them as weapons, with the greatest fury, against their opponents ... some of the wretches in the room had actually carried large stones in their pockets ... a constant shower of missiles was kept up in the direction of the platform, and several persons were severely hurt ... Mr. O'Connor's countrymen were quite at home.

O'Connor himself was injured in the fracas and was summoned to appear in court, though charges against him were dismissed. One witness in the ensuing court case alleged that the crowd who had occupied the meeting place early on consisted of 'a body of Irishmen who rushed into the room by force ... The first breach of the peace was caused by a person springing from the body of the room, from among the low Irish repealers.'[36]

The year 1842 was to be a time of extreme economic depression and distress in Britain, and the manufacturing regions in particular suffered from rising unemployment and high food prices. There were riots in Manchester, and the new police force, both mounted and on foot, was deployed, reinforced by special constables. On 16 July, 200 constables were dispatched to Little Ireland, where they were greeted by a large crowd who threw stones and brickbats. The crowd was dispersed and ten cart loads of missiles confiscated.[37] The following month strikers tried to disable mills and factories by removing the plugs of boilers in what became known as the 'Plug Strikes'. The strikers combined with Chartists, and the idea of more widespread joint action took hold. By then troops had been quartered in the city, and when a series of demonstrations took place, they were carefully shepherded away from Irish districts. Further processions during the following week were also shadowed by troops and police, and in the face of this overwhelming force, support ebbed until by the end of the month an uneasy quiet had descended.[38] The authorities took the opportunity to arrest and try many Chartist leaders, though O'Connor and others were acquitted the following March. The second Chartist petition for reform had been rejected by parliament in May 1842, and thereafter the movement ebbed in the face of government repression and a gradual improvement in economic conditions.

There were Chartist conventions in Manchester in April 1844 and December 1845, the latter on the land issue, but it was clear that the movement had lost its earlier impetus. It was equally clear that the repeal movement had similarly lost momentum following O'Connell's acquiescence in the ban on his Clontarf meeting. His prestige was somewhat restored when he was arrested and sentenced to a fine and twelve months' imprisonment and then had the verdict quashed by the Lords in September 1844, but he never quite recovered his dominance of Irish nationalist opinion. The consequent loss of momentum and focus was vividly demonstrated by a meeting to discuss the state of Ireland and devise a petition to parliament held in the Free Trade Hall in early March 1844. The hall was quite full, with an estimated two thirds of the audience believed to be Irish, but the lack of unanimity on the causes and possible solution of Irish problems was widely noted. However, some indication of O'Connell's lingering support was given by the fact that, though none of the speakers put the case for repeal, each time the cause was referred to in passing there was 'Immense cheering for some minutes, the people rising and waving their hats'. When one speaker declared he was not a repealer, there were cries of 'I am' and 'we all are here' from the floor. Finally, when the gathering ended after four hours there were three cheers for O'Connell.[39]

But strains had appeared within the movement which O'Connell had dominated for so long. A new, younger element had appeared which showed increasing impatience with the way in which the ageing O'Connell dominated the repeal organisation, determined policy, placed family members of very limited ability in significant positions and showed undue deference to the Catholic Church and its susceptibilities. To some extent it was the impatience of a younger generation leading O'Connell to dub them 'Young Ireland', but there was also a difference in mindset and outlook. In some ways the newcomers had more in common with the secular, liberal-minded, romantic cultural nationalists of contemporary Europe than with the mass movements O'Connell had led, which were based on the Catholic parish and often dependent on the support and organising energy of the local parish priest. Moreover, several of the leading Young Irelanders, most notably the widely admired Thomas Davis, were Protestant. In October 1842 three of the most gifted, Davis, Charles Gavin Duffy and John Blake Dillon, launched a new weekly paper, *The Nation*. In political terms it was all for repeal, but it went far beyond the traditional preoccupations of the movement in its emphasis on the cultural dimensions of Irish nationalism. In addition to political commentary its columns were filled with Irish history, poetry, songs and ballads with the aim of stimulating a pride in things Irish that could appeal to all regardless of class or creed. The paper was a runaway success. It became a standard item in the reading rooms organised by the Young Irelanders and was often read aloud in public for the benefit of the illiterate. Altogether its readership was over one million, a remarkable total in a population of just over eight million with a high proportion living in poverty.[40]

## Confederates, Chartists and the Manchester moment

From the outset O'Connell had regarded *The Nation* with deep suspicion, and as his political grip and personal powers gradually waned, suspicion evolved into outright antagonism as the various contributors became increasingly irreverent and adventurous in the tone and language of their writings and publicly differed from him on issues such as non-denominational education. The death of Davis from scarlet fever at the age of thirty in September 1845 was a devastating blow, but the momentum of the group was maintained by an influx of new writers, of whom the most notable were Thomas D'Arcy McGee and John Mitchel. By early 1846 O'Connell's patience was fast running out and he decided to force the issue at a meeting of the Repeal Association committee. A series of resolutions was prepared which involved calling on all members to forswear the use of violence for political purposes. In fact no one at this stage was urging a rising, but the topic had been chosen to wrongfoot and embarrass the Young Irelanders by forcing them to accept or reject O'Connell's leadership on such a delicate issue. They recognised the ploy and accepted the challenge at a series of fiery unrestrained debates in mid-July 1846. The result was a bitter split in which some of the most talented and energetic Young Irelanders parted company with the Repeal Association, taking control of *The Nation* with them. During the ensuing months there were increasingly vitriolic exchanges between the former colleagues; reconciliation became clearly impossible and in January 1847 the seceders formed the Irish Confederates. The new group was governed by a council, including Thomas Francis Meagher, who had made his name as a particularly eloquent defender of the Young Ireland vision in exchanges with O'Connell's son John. The Confederates were dedicated to obtaining an Irish parliament by constitutional means totally independent of the support and favours of both Whigs and Tories. In the ensuing months Duffy and McGee took the lead in organising a network of clubs, which incorporated reading rooms stocked with books and newspapers and hosted lectures intended to educate members in Irish affairs and help realise their vision of an almost mystical cultural renewal of Ireland

and all its people regardless of creed and background. The clubs offered a mix of instruction, inspiration and social contact with the like-minded, and by the height of their popularity in mid- to late 1848 they numbered perhaps 45,000 members in 224 clubs in Ireland, whilst 'Another dozen clubs existed amongst the Irish living in cities in Britain', including Liverpool, Manchester, Birmingham, Sheffield, London, Glasgow, Greenock and Airdrie.[41]

By September 1847 there was sufficient strength in Manchester for the Confederate Secretary, D'Arcy McGee, to come over from Dublin and address a meeting of two hundred local supporters, one local observer noting that they were indeed predominantly 'Young Ireland'. The chairman declared that their purpose was 'the repeal of the union and the regeneration of their country'.[42] McGee, who was greeted with loud cheers when he rose to speak, took pains to assure the audience that he had not come to the city 'to excite any improper feelings or create animosity'. Instead, he declared, the prime purpose of the organisation was repeal of the union, a just cause which he believed would be achieved by its own efforts to bring about the triumph of mind over prejudice. He argued that the Irish had no hostility against the English people, who had suffered as much as any from the actions of the English government. O'Connell had died in May, and to loud applause McGee ended with a tribute to him and his achievements and commended the new Confederate movement as his natural successors, declaring that if O'Connell had not quite bequeathed a nation 'he had left the materials of a nation and those materials would never be united on any narrower principles than those of the Irish Confederation'.[43]

But in the ensuing months a succession of events created a momentum for more extreme views and the forging of an alliance between Confederate elements and some of the reviving Chartists. As already noted, from 1845 onwards the famine had been following its murderous course, and 1847 was a year of great suffering. Some argued that the situation was worsened by British government policy, and John Mitchel in particular began to develop a critique which would drive him to place the blame for much of the famine suffering on the mendacity and calculated cruelty of the British administration and to argue that the solution was an independent republic achieved by force of arms. By early 1848 he had so far diverged from the majority of the Confederates that he founded a notably successful new newspaper, *The United Irishman*, in which he openly urged training in the use of arms, guerrilla warfare and insurrection.[44] The final break was to come in May but in the interim he and his supporters argued their case in Confederate Club meetings. Disillusioned by the stance of landlords on famine relief and their support for government coercion measures, he also signalled a significant departure in his usually conservative social views by arguing that the natural allies for the Irish people were to be found in the more militant elements of the British Chartist movement.

The general distress which marked living and working conditions in Britain in the mid- to late 1840s had fuelled a Chartist revival, leading to a build-up of support for a third petition to parliament in early 1848. As already noted, the possibility of an alliance with the migrant Irish in Britain had been unsuccessfully touted by Chartist leaders from early on in the movement, and the right of Irish self-government had been incorporated in a succession of Chartist public declarations. But the project had been stillborn, thanks to the combined opposition of O'Connell and the Catholic Church and the impact of traditional anti-Catholic and anti-Irish sentiment. The death of O'Connell removed one obstacle, and the process of accommodation was also assisted by the fact that James Fintan Lalor, one of the contributors to *The Nation*, had been arguing eloquently for land reform to be incorporated in the Confederate programme. Since, under O'Connor's urging, that topic had become a notable theme in the Chartist programme, there was clear potential for a meeting of minds. The process was further accelerated by the rapid succession of revolutions across Europe in 1848, which excited liberals and terrified conservatives everywhere.[45] The French monarchy was overthrown on 24 February 1848; this was followed by a rising in Vienna on 13 March which led to the dismissal of Prince Metternich, long seen as the *éminence grise* of conservative hegemony. A succession of outbreaks followed in Milan and Venice later in the month. Liberal and nationalist excitement knew no bounds in this 'springtime of peoples'. In Ireland even William Smith O'Brien, MP for Limerick, the moderate leader of the Confederates, called on 11 March for an Irish 'National Guard' on the French model.

It was only in Manchester that the proposed alliance of Chartists and Irish repealers became a reality, and even then only for a few weeks.[46] Plans were laid for a great symbolic public meeting at the Free Trade Hall on St Patrick's Day, when, as one speaker at an earlier meeting declared, it was intended that 'the marriage ceremony would be performed between the working men of England and those of Ireland'. He then led the crowd in 'Three cheers for O'Connor, Repeal and the Charter'.[47] As noted earlier, the prospect of the meeting planned for 17 March deeply alarmed both secular and Catholic authorities, but in fact it was conducted in a quiet and orderly manner. The Catholic clergy of the area held a special meeting at which they agreed an appeal to their parishioners; this was signed by sixteen priests, printed and distributed widely throughout the district:

> To the Irish Catholics Residing in the city of Manchester and the borough of Salford and the Neighbourhoods ... We, the Catholic clergy, residing in Manchester and Salford, having understood that efforts are being made to induce you to assemble in large numbers, on an early day, under circumstance that are calculated to disturb the peace of this neighbourhood, deem it our duty to warn you against being led into illegal and immoral acts. We can assure you that it is far from our wish to interfere in party politics; we are anxious, however, to prevent our flock in any way becoming parties to a movement, having a tendency to lead to a breach of the peace, or likely in any way to annoy the well-disposed portion of our fellow citizens. We, therefore, earnestly implore all Catholics to refrain, for the present, from taking part in any processions or promiscuous meetings where large bodies of men assemble. Our religion teaches us to obey the law, and to respect the civil authorities; and it would be sinful for any person to take part in proceedings which the law prohibits or which the authorities pronounce to be illegal. We observe that a meeting is advertised to be held on the 17th of this month, the feast of the glorious apostle of your beloved country. By your veneration for the virtue of that great saint, we urge you to be more than usually cautious to do no act on that day which, in the remotest degree, is calculated to dishonour the festival or to bring scandal upon our holy faith.[48]

The appeal doubtless contributed to the remarkable quietness with which St Patrick's Day as a whole was celebrated in the city, but it is also highly likely that it caused many of the more devout and cautious Irish to pause and reconsider their attitude towards the meeting and the overall project of the planned alliance.

It was estimated that about eight thousand attended; a band played 'St Patrick's Day in the morning' and other tunes, many wore tricolour rosettes of green, white and orange, and the analogy of marriage between repealers and Chartists was frequently invoked. O'Connor and Thomas Francis Meagher shared the platform, and the latter took the opportunity to recant and apologise for previously keeping Chartists and British working people at a distance and to appeal for 'a holy alliance of democracy'. The meeting proceeded to adopt '*An address of the Irish and English Repealers of Manchester to the Sovereign People of France*' congratulating the French people on their recent revolution and pledging themselves to ensure that 'Ireland shall have her parliament restored and England shall have her idolised charter'.[49] At a tea party the following evening speakers were at pains to keep up the momentum. The chairman described the event as

> the meeting of the democrats of Manchester, assembled for the purpose of showing to the delegation from the Irish Confederation that the democracy of this part of England at least were in favour of a repeal of the legislative

union .... he had no doubt that they would have ... the democracy of the people of England with them in their struggle for the independence of Ireland. (Applause).⁵⁰

O'Connor declared that the previous disunity of the people of Ireland and England had facilitated their oppression, which would now be ended by their fraternisation.⁵¹

A series of meetings followed in quick succession at which speakers strove to drive home the significance of the new alliance. At one gathering John Finnigan noted that there had been bad feeling between himself and Chartists in the past, but 'he begged pardon for any offensive acts of which he had been guilty, and he freely forgave those who had opposed him and others, in their efforts to obtain the repeal of the union'. At an open-air event outside Oldham, described as 'a camp meeting of English Chartists and Irish repealers', a crowd estimated at up to fifty thousand passed resolutions in favour of both the Chartist programme and repeal, declaring, 'we pledge ourselves to assist our Irish brethren in the accomplishment of that desirable project'.⁵² From the Manchester meeting Meagher had returned to Dublin, where he again emphasised the newly found sense of solidarity with the Chartists of Britain. At the end of March he proceeded to France with Smith O'Brien and four other members of the leadership, where they presented the compliments of the Confederates to the newly installed President Lamartine on 3 April, Meagher being reported as presenting the address from 'the repealers of Manchester'. Lamartine, under pressure from the British government, greeted the delegation in polite but non-committal fashion.⁵³ However, he did make one historic gesture when he presented the delegation with a new flag on the model of the French tricolour, incorporating three vertical panels of green, white and orange to symbolise reconciliation within Ireland.⁵⁴

O'Brien and Meagher had been able to make the trip to Paris only with the special permission of the British government, since they had been arrested on 23 March along with Mitchel and were on bail. The arrests provoked furious indignation in Ireland and amongst Irish migrant communities and led to a series of public meetings at which the language became increasingly militant, further stoking the febrile atmosphere. At the end of March a meeting of Chartists and repealers in Salford, attended by eight hundred 'working men', was reminded that on 17 March 'the chartists of Manchester and the chartists of Salford pledged themselves that if the government of this country attempted to put down the expression of public opinion in Ireland, they, the chartists of England, would resist them to the utmost of their power'. Other speakers argued:

If the English would stand by Paddy for the repeal of the union, the Irish would stand by the chartists ... The time had come for action, and Mitchel said there was nothing like the forcible action of the pike, the bayonet and the sword ... when the people had had a musket in their hand and made a demand upon the government, the government had always conceded it sooner than they would without.[55]

The chairman tried to stop a resolution in favour of forming a national guard, in the belief that moral force of argument was sufficient, but there was strong support for another speaker who urged all to provide themselves with arms and enrol.[56]

The third Chartist petition was the focus of a mass meeting on London's Kennington Common on 10 April. It was widely noted that one of the largest contingents consisted of five thousand Confederates marching as 'The Emmet Brigade' behind a green banner edged in orange with a harp in the centre.[57] However, the plan to proceed to parliament to lodge the petition was thwarted by a government ban which, to the disappointment of his followers, O'Connor accepted. On proceeding to take his seat in the Commons and present the petition he was howled down in derision, but again advised his followers to accept the decision and disperse quietly. From this point onwards the Chartist movement began to go into gradual decline, but the minority who had always favoured direct action were more convinced than ever of the justice of their outlook.

The conflict of forces and influences was reflected in a series of meetings in Manchester and district. A gathering of a thousand 'repealers and chartists' at the Manchester Hall of Science agreed to a collection to support O'Brien, Meagher and Mitchel and were told that, in the circumstances, resistance was a virtue. Another thousand gathered in Stevenson Square to protest at government restrictions on public gatherings. One speaker pledged that he would be 'a second Emmet in the cause of freedom', and a Chartist meeting at the Peoples' Institute was attended by four hundred largely younger men. Though they were united in condemnation of the arrests in Ireland, there was considerable dissent over a resolution supporting O'Connor's stance in ordering peaceful acceptance of the rejection of the petition, with some speakers from the floor urging collection of arms.[58] This tone of militancy was taken up at other gatherings. At a Chartist meeting in Stevenson Square three days later one speaker pointed to the biblical injunction 'Let him that hath no sword, sell his garment and buy one', and another declared, 'If it was necessary, he would get pikes and advise the people to do the same'; at yet another Chartist gathering there was wide support for the idea that troops should refuse to serve in Ireland, and it was declared that 'Never before were the people of England and Ireland up at the same time, struggling for their liberties.'[59]

The Treason/Felony Act, passed on 22 April 1848, had widened the definition of treason and was used to prosecute O'Brien, Meagher and Mitchel. Another protest meeting was called in Stevenson Square at which a resolution was passed stating that 'in the city of Manchester there are thousands of strong determined men, ready at a moment's notice, to lay down their lives in defence of the land of their birth', and one speaker shared his conviction that 'The day of Ireland's redemption was at hand. Now was the time, now was the day for Ireland.'[60] In fact O'Brien and Meagher were acquitted, but Mitchel was sentenced to fourteen years' transportation. This was interpreted as a piece of personal malice and led to even further Irish anger. One of the most remarkable meetings took place in Stevenson Square on 29 May, attended by about eight hundred 'mostly Irish' people, when one speaker urged the organisation of joint Chartist and Confederate clubs. But the most striking contribution came from a Mrs Theobold, 'an Irishwoman', who said that 'if the men were not prepared to do their duty ... she could tell them that the women, though "the weaker vessel", were determined, in the name of God, to do their duty, and one and all, to raise the standard of liberty ... The repealers for their part were determined to go back to *Erin-go-bragh* ... They were prepared to take the field by storm.' At another meeting a few days later the John Mitchel Club marched in procession to the square to hear condemnation of Mitchel's sentence and arrangements for a mass gathering of supporters from across the region later that week, though this was quickly banned by the authorities.[61] Two events in early June showed how feelings in more radical circles were approaching boiling point. At a meeting in the City Music Hall, Ernest Jones, the prominent local Chartist leader, stated that 500,000 men could be easily raised to free Mitchel. The details of an arrest around that time give a glimpse of the clandestine preparations in which some were involved. Fourteen men, mostly Irish, who were reading newspapers, were arrested at the premises of John Downey, a shoemaker of Rochdale Road, which were used as the venue for the John Mitchel and Brian Boru Confederate Clubs; swords, a blunderbuss, pikes and two muskets were seized.[62]

In Ireland events were clearly building towards some sort of climax. From mid-July the government began to bear down increasingly heavily, arresting radical journalists and leading Confederates, imposing martial law and curfews on parts of the country and suspending Habeas Corpus. But for the authorities in Manchester the most alarming event to date was a parade which took place on the evening of 25 July. About two thousand

Confederate members marched from their club rooms to an open space on the north side of the city, where they formed ranks for inspection, then gave three cheers and proceeded back to their meeting rooms via the New Cross district. By the time the military – including the Irish Dragoons – arrived, they had dispersed. No arms had been seen, but the general feeling was that this was a test run for something much more serious in the near future. The previous day a man had been arrested and charged with manufacturing 'pikes similar to those recommended for use by the chartists and repeal agitators'.[63]

On 29 July there was a very limited insurrection at the village of Ballingarry in Co. Tipperary in which two insurgents but no police were killed, and the entire project collapsed within two hours.[64] Excited crowds began to gather regularly in Manchester's New Cross and Rochdale Road in anticipation of news. The authorities feared that 'violent excitement among the Irish part of the population … might probably embolden them to turn their secret plotting into open violence'. The air of febrile tension was increased by the news that Smith O'Brien had been arrested on 5 August. As defence against possible attacks, stores of cutlasses were laid in at police stations, but it was felt that arson attacks on mills and warehouses were more likely. There were reports that the leaders of the fourteen or fifteen Confederate Clubs believed to exist in the city had met, but there was no public demonstration, and when news of the failed rising finally filtered through, the earlier crowds drifted away.[65]

In fact some sort of local rising seems to have been planned for mid-August, but thanks to spies and informers the authorities were on the alert.[66] By this time much of the urban north of England was for practical purposes almost under martial law. In Manchester twelve thousand special constables had been recruited and infantry and cavalry units deployed.[67] This may explain why the disturbances which did occur were not in the city but in nearby towns. The most notable occurred in Ashton-under-Lyne, a few miles to the east. Rumours of some form of trouble had been circulating, and around midnight on 13 August a company of men variously estimated at between fifty and a hundred turned out 'with a celerity denoting the utmost degree of organisation'. Armed with pikes and guns they marched through the town six or seven abreast 'keeping the step admirably', pikes gleaming in the moonlight.[68] The intention seems to have been

> that the various chartist organisations and Irish confederates clubs, with numerous bodies of colliers and others, throughout a district embracing several of the principal manufacturing towns of Lancashire … were in a conspiracy for the purpose of assembling in all their strength; and every

man armed … to march upon Manchester … They were assured that an overwhelming force of their 'brethren in arms' the Irish confederates and repealers, and the English chartists of Manchester, would be in readiness to receive them.

It was rumoured that on arrival in Manchester a first task would be to set fire to a half-dozen of the largest cotton mills and then take on the police and troops. However, when the group which turned out in Ashton encountered a police constable and he was piked and shot to death, the rest of the company dropped their weapons and scattered. News of the killing, together with a rapid response by the authorities, was enough to cause the planned insurgency, such as it was, to melt away.[69]

In Manchester there had been plans for a gathering of Confederate Club members on 15 August, but the authorities had the city under tight control, and the non-arrival of the club contingents from nearby towns caused them to disperse quietly. That same evening three hundred police and troops in five groups descended on the known meeting places of Confederates and Chartists and made the first of forty-six arrests, with the result that 'a decisive blow was struck at the hot-beds of Chartist and Repeal in this city, by the arrest of a number of those who have figured as the leaders of the rebellious movements of the last few months'.[70] There was no resistance. Of the first fifteen arrested that evening it was noted that 'Several of them are members of both chartist and confederate clubs'. In all, eight of the fifteen were Irish-born.[71] Eventually, twenty-eight people were accused of crimes including conspiracy, incitement to arms and seditious language, but witnesses proved totally unreliable and in the end only ten were sentenced, of whom six were given one year and four nine months in prison.[72]

In Ireland, Meagher was arrested on 15 August and was eventually sentenced to death with Smith O'Brien and two others, though this sentence was later commuted to transportation. There were sporadic outbreaks of disorder in Ireland for the following twelve months, but in Britain excitement quickly died away. The Chartist movement lingered into the early 1850s but the last national Chartist convention was held in February 1855, and in August O'Connor, by then a sad and pathetic figure, was dead. The class-based alliance of those heady few weeks in 1848 was a fleeting episode doomed to failure from the outset. It was beset by a combination of popular anti-Catholic and anti-Irish prejudices and a recent history of mutual suspicion which could not be overcome in such a short time. Moreover, direct action appealed only to a small militant minority in both organisations and was crippled by the absence of coherent strategy and agreed leadership. Since the rising in Ireland had been crushed in July there was no clear reason for an insurgency in Britain in August beyond a desire to be seen to be doing something in this year of European revolution. It has been argued that 'The Irish confederates disappeared almost without a trace in Lancashire, along with virtually all public recognition of Chartism.'[73]

## Conclusion

From the late eighteenth century onwards the growing number of Irish in Manchester increasingly engaged in the life of the city at all levels. Paradoxically, this could tend to integration or differentiation. Issues such as parliamentary reform, trade union rights and anti-Corn Law agitation could provide a common platform with others in the city and see them working towards common aims. However, other issues, such as Catholic emancipation and repeal of the union, underlined the differences from the rest of the population. The various Chartist campaigns illustrated the stresses and strains on the basis of religion and political priorities, with the result that the Chartist–Confederate revolutionary alliance feared by the Catholic Church and the authorities was chiefly notable for its very limited duration and appeal. By the mid-1850s there was something of a lull in Irish politics in Manchester, but in the following decades both the tradition of peaceful political activity so skilfully pioneered by O'Connell in his various campaigns and expressed in electoral activity and the clandestine separatism embraced by some of the Confederates would receive powerful reinforcement, not least in Manchester itself.

## Notes

1 Gerard Connolly, 'Catholicism in Manchester and Salford: the search for "Le Chrétien quelconque"' (Ph.D. dissertation, Department of History, University of Manchester, 1980).
2 Marianne Elliott, *Partners in revolution: the United Irishmen and France* (New Haven: Yale University Press, 1982), p. 145. The boroughreeve, appointed annually, had oversight of finance and policing.
3 Marianne Elliott, 'Irish republicanism in England: the first phase', in T. Bartlett and D. Hayton (eds), *Penal era and golden age: essays in Irish history 1690–1800* (Belfast: Ulster Historical Foundation, 1979), p. 221.
4 Elliott, *Partners in revolution*, pp. 145–84.
5 Marianne Elliott, 'The "Despard Conspiracy" reconsidered', *Past and Present*, 75 (1977), pp. 46–61.
6 Alan Kidd, *Manchester* (Keele: Ryburn, 1993), pp. 81–92.

7 Malcolm Bee and Walter Bee, 'The casualties of Peterloo', *Manchester Region History Review*, 3:1 (1989), pp. 43-5; Michael Bush, *The casualties of Peterloo* (Lancaster: Carnegie Publishing, 2005); Joyce Marlow, 'The day of Peterloo', *Manchester Region History Review*, 3:1 (1989), pp. 3-7.
8 Gerard Connolly, 'The Catholic Church and the first Manchester and Salford trade unions in the age of the industrial revolution', *Transactions of the Lancashire and Cheshire Antiquarian Society*, 83 (1985), p. 155.
9 R.G. Kirby and A.E. Musson, *The voice of the people: John Doherty 1798-1854, trade unionist, radical and factory reformer* (Manchester: Manchester University Press, 1975), p. vii.
10 Connolly, 'Catholicism in Manchester and Salford', pp. 16-20; Teresa Moriarty, 'John Doherty', in J. McGuire and J. Quinn (eds), *Dictionary of Irish biography* (Cambridge: Cambridge University Press, 2009), pp. 357-8.
11 *Manchester Guardian*, 10 May 1832.
12 Bush, *The casualties of Peterloo*, p. 29.
13 'Peterloo Relief List', John Rylands Library, Deansgate, Manchester, English MS 172.
14 Peter Geoghegan, *King Dan: the rise of Daniel O'Connell 1775-1829* (Dublin: Gill & Macmillan, 2010), pp. 106-9.
15 *Manchester Guardian*, 2 October 1824.
16 *Manchester Guardian*, 6 November 1824.
17 *Manchester Guardian*, 7 May 1825.
18 *Manchester Courier*, 7 May 1825.
19 *Manchester Courier*, 21 May 1825.
20 *Manchester Guardian*, 29 January 1831.
21 *Manchester Courier*, 29 January 1831.
22 *Manchester Guardian*, 22 March 1834.
23 *Manchester Guardian*, 18 December 1834.
24 Peter Geoghegan, *Liberator: the life and death of Daniel O'Connell 1830-1847* (Dublin: Gill & Macmillan, 2010), p. 133.
25 Connolly, 'Catholicism in Manchester and Salford', pp. 391-2.
26 Paul Pickering, *Chartism and the Chartists in Manchester and Salford* (London: Macmillan, 1995).
27 *Manchester Guardian*, 15 January 1840. This was the first event to be held in the building, which was put up in six weeks. In 1843 it was rebuilt in brick, and in 1853 this building was replaced by a stone structure designed by Edward Walters. See Kidd, *Manchester*, pp. 69-72.
28 Geoghegan, *Liberator*, pp. 45-7.
29 Don MacRaild, *Irish migrants in modern Britain 1750-1922* (Basingstoke: Macmillan, 1999), p. 134.
30 Rachel O'Higgins, 'The Irish influence in the Chartist movement', *Past and Present*, 20 (1961), pp. 83-96; Dorothy Thompson, 'Ireland and the Irish in English radicalism before 1850', in J. Epstein and D. Thompson, *The Chartist experience: studies in working class radicalism and culture 1830-1860* (London: Macmillan, 1982), pp. 120-51.

31 J.H. Treble, 'O'Connor, O'Connell and the attitudes of Irish immigrants towards Chartism in the north of England', in J. Butt and I.F. Clarke (eds), *The Victorians and social protest* (Newton Abbott: David & Charles, 1973), pp. 33–71, especially pp. 34, 41.
32 John Belchem, 'English working class radicalism and the Irish, 1815–50', in R. Swift and S. Gilley (eds), *The Irish in the Victorian city* (London: Croom Helm, 1985), pp. 85–97; Graham Davis, *The Irish in Britain 1815–1914* (Dublin: Gill & Macmillan, 1991), chap. 5: 'Chartism'.
33 *Manchester Courier*, 2 June 1841.
34 *Manchester Guardian*, 5 June 1841; Pickering, *Chartism and the Chartists*, pp. 86–94.
35 *Manchester Examiner and Times*, 2 October 1841; *Manchester Courier*, 2 October 1841.
36 *Manchester Courier*, 12 March 1842.
37 *Illustrated London News*, 16 July 1842, p. 232.
38 Kidd, *Manchester*, pp. 99–100.
39 *Manchester Guardian*, 2 March 1844.
40 Richard English, *Irish freedom: the history of nationalism in Ireland* (London: Macmillan, 2006), pp. 142–4, 160–1; Christine Kinealy, *Repeal and revolution: 1848 in Ireland* (Manchester: Manchester University Press, 2009), p. 29.
41 Gary Owens, 'Popular mobilisation and the rising of 1848: the clubs of the Irish Confederation', in L.M. Geary (ed.), *Rebellion and remembrance in modern Ireland* (Dublin: Four Courts Press, 2001), p. 56.
42 *Manchester Courier*, 15 September 1847.
43 *Manchester Guardian*, 15 September 1847
44 Gerry Kearns, '"Cultivate that holy hatred": place, trauma and identity in the Irish nationalism of John Mitchel', *Political Geography*, 20:7 (2001), pp. 885–911.
45 Mike Rapport, *1848: the year of revolution* (London: Abacus, 2008).
46 John Belchem, 'Liverpool in the year of revolution: the political and associational culture of the Irish immigrant community in 1848', in J. Belchem (ed.), *Popular politics, riot and labour: essays in Liverpool history* (Liverpool: Liverpool University Press, 1992), p. 79.
47 *Manchester Guardian*, 15 March 1848.
48 *Manchester Courier*, 18 March 1848.
49 Kinealy, *Repeal and revolution*, p. 148; *Manchester Examiner and Times*, 18 March 1848; *Manchester Courier*, 23 March 1848.
50 *Manchester Courier*, 23 March 1848.
51 *Manchester Courier*, 22 March 1848.
52 Christine Kinealy, '"Brethren in bondage": Chartists, O'Connellites, Young Irelanders and the 1848 rising', in F. Lane and D. Ó Drisceoil (eds), *Politics and the Irish working class, 1830–1945* (Houndmills, Basingstoke: Palgrave Macmillan, 2003), p. 100; *Manchester Guardian*, 22 March 1848.
53 Kinealy, *Repeal and revolution*, pp. 140–5.
54 Kinealy, 'Brethren in bondage', p. 98.

55 *Manchester Examiner and Times*, 28 March 1848.
56 *Manchester Courier*, 29 March 1848.
57 *Manchester Guardian*, 12 April 1848.
58 *Manchester Guardian*, 15 April 1848.
59 *Manchester Guardian*, 18 April 1848.
60 *Manchester Guardian*, 20 April 1848.
61 *Manchester Guardian*, 31 May 1848; Kinealy, 'Brethren in bondage', p. 104.
62 *Manchester Guardian*, 7 June 1848.
63 *Manchester Guardian*, 26 July 1848.
64 Kinealy, *Repeal and revolution*, p. 199.
65 *Manchester Guardian*, 29 July 1848.
66 Belchem, 'English working class radicalism', p. 92.
67 Kinealy, *Repeal and revolution*, p. 194; Pickering, *Chartism and the Chartists*, p. 176.
68 *Manchester Guardian*, 16 August 1848.
69 *Manchester Guardian*, 19 August 1848.
70 *Manchester Courier*, 16 August 1848.
71 *Manchester Guardian*, 19 August 1848.
72 William J. Lowe, 'The Chartists and the Irish Confederates: Lancashire 1848', *Irish Historical Studies*, 24 (1984), pp. 193–5.
73 William J. Lowe, *The Irish in mid-Victorian Lancashire: the making of a working class community* (New York: Peter Lang, 1989), p. 189.

# 6

## Elections and meetings: 1870–1921

In his survey of the Irish in Britain published as a series of letters in *The Nation* in 1872, Hugh Heinrick argued that they were not making the best of their voting strength, and was equally sure they had no one but themselves to blame. In north-west England in particular he was sure that, given their numbers, 'if the Irish people do not hold the key of the position in every urban constituency, the fault must be their own. They have the numbers, the votes, the influence sufficient to dictate terms to political rivals.' This power, he argued, could be used to tip the balance between the contending British political parties, punishing them when Ireland was maltreated and putting them into power when they promised justice and home rule. In particular he suggested, 'Take Manchester as an instance of what may and should be done if the national question is to be advanced.'[1] Estimating the Irish population to be 100,000 of whom 12,000 had the vote, he argued, 'Provided there is organisation and union, what party can presume to represent this great city in opposition to the will of the Irish people?' Indeed, he went on,

> There is no doubt in my mind that, if the relative estimate of population furnished me be within any reasonable limit correct, the Irish people of Manchester have sufficient power, not alone to exact terms for Ireland from English parties, but to call on an Irishman to stand in their name and carry his election triumphantly. Unite and organise – canvass and act – and the thing is done. If I have a doubt on the point, it is that the voting power may be overestimated.[2]

He was right to be cautious. The Irish-born of Manchester in 1871 actually numbered 34,066 or 8.6% of the population, and they were never strong enough to elect a public representative standing under an exclusively Irish party label. But he was far from being the only public figure to exaggerate, knowingly or in ignorance, the strength and impact of Irish voters in nineteenth-century British elections. In the mid-1880s various authorities estimated that Irish voters in Britain could decide the result in anything from twenty-five to ninety-seven parliamentary seats.[3] Since then it has been argued that the Irish impact was diluted by lack of community cohesion, poor organisation, failure to be registered for the franchise and the fact that anti-Irish and anti-Catholic sentiment would tend to cancel out Irish voting strength. In fact, the Irish in Britain were a notably compact community group marked by loyalty to Catholicism and Irish nationalism; both the church and nationalist politicians had the motivation to organise them for political purposes and did so with some skill. At the parliamentary level, only the Liverpool Scotland Road constituency had enough Irish voters to elect a nationalist MP, and the same city had an Irish nationalist group on the council until the 1920s. Elsewhere, however, it has been argued that the Irish were never strong enough to swing parliamentary elections, even in London, where there was the greatest concentration of Irish in Britain, and that in any case they were generally allied with the Liberal Party in a relationship which, though troubled, never totally fractured.[4]

It has been suggested that the Irish impact was most notable at the local level.[5] In this chapter it is proposed to examine the role of the Irish in Manchester politics through the medium of council, School Board and parliamentary elections and to trace the development of local nationalist thought and tactics on the two issues which particularly concerned the Irish population, namely Irish self-government and church-based education, through the elections and the themes of the public meetings which took place in the city between 1870 and 1921.

## Manchester municipal elections

Manchester received its first two MPs in 1832 and its borough charter in November 1838 after a bitter battle against a combination of traditionalist Tories and aggrieved working-class reformers. Thereafter it steadily acquired additional powers and recognition but remained the same in area until 1885. In August 1839 the Manchester Police Act allowed the organisation of a full-time police force, and in October 1839 a Police Commissioner was appointed. In 1843 the corporation took over responsibility for the force. Two years later the first Church of England Bishop of Manchester was installed, and in July 1851 the first Catholic Bishop of Salford.[6] In 1853 city status was granted. Following the 1868 Reform Act the city acquired three MPs, and in 1885 further reform saw it subdivided into six parliamentary constituencies. From 1885 onwards the area and population of the city grew steadily in a series of boundary extensions as it took over small neighbouring entities which found themselves unable to bear the growing responsibilities and costs of local government, particularly in the fields of policing, housing, gas and water provision and, after 1902, education. By 1913 the city had essentially completed its 'imperial' phase.[7] From 1838 to 1913 it had grown from a population of 242,357 people in 4,293 acres to 714,281 inhabitants and 21,690 acres.[8]

Following their bitter fight against the granting of the town charter and their persistent challenges to its validity down to 1841, Conservatives as a party largely stood aside from municipal politics until well into the second half of the century. Consequently for much of the period the city was dominated by middle-class councillors who were Liberal in outlook,[9] though until the late 1870s there was a certain reluctance for candidates to be seen as fighting under party labels. The local council chamber was seen as a venue where people of good will gathered to consider what was best for the community regardless of their personal politics. In reality, this was something of a conceit, since the affiliation of candidates was an open secret, even if not officially referred to or reported in the press. Certainly, by the last quarter of the nineteenth century council elections were widely accepted as party contests.

In contrast to the situation in Liverpool, the Manchester Irish lacked the numbers to organise a separate political party which could win council seats or elect an MP on their own.[10] Consequently, to obtain some form of representation they had to ally with one of the existing parties. Traditionally, the Liberals had been more sympathetic to Irish demands and the Irish were generally, though not invariably, to be found in alliance with them, particularly after Irish home rule became party policy in late 1885. Most Irish voting strength concentrated in the council wards of New Cross and St Michael's on the north side of the city, taking in the strongly Irish neighbourhoods found in Angel Meadow and Ancoats.

Down to 1869 there are no traces of issues of particular interest to Irish voters. Indeed contemporary reports suggest that observers sometimes queried why there should be any contests at all. In 1864 for example, it was remarked that 'No local question is attracting much attention at present, and such contests as occurred were, for the most part, struggles between individuals ambitious of municipal honours.' The issues mentioned during campaigning in St Michael's were 'less taxation … economy and efficiency' and temperance.[11] In 1869 however, the contest in the same ward was close, and it was noted, 'The Roman Catholic interest is very strong in this ward.' The successful candidate declared, 'The election had been a religious question and the minds of the Roman Catholic voters had been influenced against him by misrepresentations', though his opponent denied any 'improper practices'.¹² Such sentiment had clearly been latent, because from this point onwards it surfaced with increasing frequency as national issues such as denominational education and then specifically Irish issues such as land reform and home rule came onto the political agenda.

In the 1870 contest in St Michael's, both party and religious sentiment were openly invoked. The Liberal candidate presented himself as a free and independent friend of the working man, whilst the main Conservative candidate, William Touchstone, campaigned on the grounds of his personal qualities and support for religious education. But his opponents drew Roman Catholic attention to the fact that he was a prominent member of the Orange Order, and alleged he 'would destroy their religion "root and branch if he could"'. The victorious Liberal acknowledged that 'he had more especially to thank the Roman Catholics for his election'.¹³ The following year both wards were marked by intense sectarian feeling. In New Cross, with two seats at stake, it was reported: 'The contest in this ward was essentially political, or rather religious and political. A great portion of the ward being Roman Catholic, an election cry was "religious education". The Roman Catholics, almost to a man, voted for "Shaw [Conservative] and religious education".'¹⁴ An Irish observer based in Manchester noted the irony that Shaw's victory was celebrated by an Orange procession led by bands playing traditional sectarian tunes as they passed Catholic churches and convents.¹⁵ Proceedings in St Michael's ward were rancorous and boisterous. The incumbent Liberal councillor Dyson had originally decided to stand down but, on learning that the party had nominated a Catholic to succeed him, changed his mind. The resulting contest roused strong sectarian feelings: 'So far did this element prevail that it served to divide party interests, and secured for Mr. Dyson the support of a number of Conservatives as well as a large portion of the Liberal party.'¹⁶ The Orange Order issued a manifesto to the effect that 'We don't contest for Dyson so much as against Popery and priestcraft', and placards appeared with references to home rule and 'Hyde Road Murderers'.¹⁷ When Dyson's victory was announced, 'The proceedings at the close of the poll were of the most uproarious character' and the customary speeches were cut short.¹⁸

The moral drawn by an Irish reporter was that 'our people should abstain from all interference with elections in places where they are imperfectly organised, and that, instead of being any longer the tool of

English political parties – Tory, Whig or Radical – immediate steps should be taken to from branches of the Home Rule Association.' In fact this same newspaper carried a notice that a local branch meeting was shortly to be held and that 'Other branches are in course of formation.'[19] Isaac Butt, MP for Limerick City, had founded the Home Rule Association at a meeting in the city in January 1873 and had addressed another gathering in January 1874. In Manchester municipal elections that year the general feeling was that 'the election has ... been the dullest that we have known for some years'. The sole exception was St Michael's, where, it was noted, 'The ward includes about 12,000 voters, amongst whom are a very large proportion of Irish; and it was here that the antagonism of classes and creeds came most distinctly into prominence ... it was obvious that the issue depended upon the Catholic vote.' Both Liberals and Conservatives made strenuous efforts to gain the public support of clergy, and in the end 'the Conservative and friend of religious education' was the victor.[20]

Over the next ten years feeling seems to have ebbed: on occasion incumbent councillors were returned unopposed, as in 1877 and 1878, and when there were contests, they were conducted in low-key fashion. In 1876, when the general verdict was that 'We do not remember an election in which there was so little party feeling exhibited on one side or the other', the apathy even infected St Michael's and New Cross wards. There the efforts to play on sectarian feeling were somewhat half-hearted, and in both wards the dominant issues were generalised appeals to 'justice', 'truth', 'honesty' and mundane matters such as baths and washhouses.[21] In 1879 there were only two contests in the entire city, but on this occasion passions did run high in St Michael's. The incumbent Liberal, correctly sensing a strong Conservative challenge, went to considerable lengths to cultivate the Catholic and Irish vote, visiting schools and advocating temperance, 'and in addition to getting priests to advocate his cause on the platform, he secured the services of some of them on the day of election. His cabs ... were smothered with bills, printed in red and green, the latter asking the voters to poll for "Brown and Home Rule."' His efforts paid off with a narrow win.[22]

The organisation and administration of municipal elections underwent considerable reform in the 1870s and 1880s. Parties had traditionally employed large numbers of cabs to bring voters to the polls, sometimes causing hilarity, as in 1870, when it was reported, 'It was very amusing to observe the great gratification exhibited by some rather ragged and dirty looking women, from the poorer parts the ward [St Michael's] at the enjoyment of a luxury so rare to them as that of being driven in a carriage.'[23] Following the Secret Ballot Act of 1872, it was noted that two years later 'The polling was conducted with greater ease and expedition than could reasonably have been expected, when we consider the great number of illiterate and women who are upon the register. The women had a very hazy idea of the secrecy which the Ballot Act is supposed to have ensured.'[24] It had been customary to have only one polling station per ward, but for large and populous divisions such as New Cross and St Michael's this created obvious problems which were not solved until additional facilities were provided in 1879. Women had been qualified to vote in local elections since 1870, and the franchise was further extended with the abolition of the property qualification in 1882.[25] The Corrupt Practices Act of 1884 laid down regulations for the conduct of elections on polling day. Party committee rooms could not be located in public houses or clubs, canvassers and cabs could not be hired, the hours of polling, formerly from 8.00 a.m. to 4.00 p.m., were extended to 8.00 p.m., bribery and impersonation of voters were made criminal offences, campaign expenditure was capped, and expense returns had to be lodged with local authorities within twenty-three days of the election.[26]

In 1884, in the first elections held under the new regime, New Cross and St Michael's were vigorously contested and the Conservatives were successful in both. In New Cross, Liberals and Irish nationalists could not agree on a candidate, and placards in the name of T.P. O'Connor MP, President of the Irish National League of Great Britain, urged Catholics to vote Conservative, though it was noted that 'there was an entire absence of mud-throwing and … on both sides the best of feeling was displayed'.[27] In St Michael's the contest for the Irish vote was particularly intense, because for the first time in Manchester local elections, an independent Irish candidate was standing. In his address he declared he believed that the Catholic and Irish voters of the area 'should assert their right to a proportionate share in the municipal government of the city'. In the event the incumbent Conservative was re-elected and the Irish candidate came third with 1,305 votes, but it was notable that the Irish vote far exceeded the Conservative majority of 388. The reasoning behind the candidature may well have been summed up by a local reporter: 'it may be that in view of the changes which are to be effected by the proposed redistribution bill, the running of a candidate was decided upon to ascertain the strength of the party'. The same newspaper noted that despite the presence of such a large number of 'the Irish labouring class … not a single individual was locked up for drunkenness'.[28] This first test of the new regulations had provided some idea of the relative strength of the various parties.

In 1885 it was remarked that the election was 'carried out in a thoroughly business-like fashion', though it was noted that there were problems with the high rate of illiteracy amongst voters in St Michael's ward.²⁹ There were only six contests in the local elections, including St Michael's, where the long-serving Liberal incumbent, William Brown, was returned, assisted by a leaflet from the local branch of the Irish National League addressed to 'the Irish and Catholic electors of the ward'.³⁰ The result was that when the new council convened and elected Brown to the rank of alderman, this created a vacancy in the ranks of ward councillors, which was filled unopposed by Charles O'Neill, the first Catholic member of Manchester Council in modern times.³¹ A similar process in New Cross did create a by-election, and here local Irish nationalists decided to test the water with a candidate who came second to a Conservative with 1,277 votes, though in the absence of a Liberal these cannot be taken as a measure of Irish votes alone.³²

Given that by early 1886 the Liberal Party had adopted Irish home rule as party policy, the broad pattern of Irish allegiances in Manchester was now set until the early twentieth century. Previously the Conservatives had often been able to appeal to some Irish through their support of public funding for religious education, and this would continue to strain the nationalist–Liberal alliance, but henceforth it was the issue of home rule which dominated the Irish political agenda in the city. There was also a growing intensity in the main party contest. The Conservatives had been steadily building up support following the 1868 Reform Act. Their increasingly effective populist appeal for loyalty to church, crown, constitution, the empire and the union with Ireland, mixed with judicious measures of social reform, created a strong base of working-class Toryism which served them well at elections. The Liberals suffered from the split in the party following the adoption of home rule, but the extent of the damage varied from place to place. It has been argued that the impact on Manchester was less than might be expected, with signs of strong recovery by late 1886 in terms of finance and branch activity. Moreover it has been pointed out that many of the leading personalities who left the party at this time had long been uneasy at its drift towards a more radical social programme and that any losses in voter support may well have been made up by the much stronger support from the Irish.³³ The greatest damage was at municipal level, where by 1885 the Conservatives already had a majority of elected members and the Liberals retained their control only through the votes of aldermen. The defection of three Liberal aldermen and four councillors as Liberal Unionists robbed the Liberals of overall control for the first time since incorporation, and they were not to regain a majority until the mid-1890s. There was also a series of scandals over council maladministration during this time, and given the long history of Liberal hegemony at the town hall, this weakened their position still further.³⁴ The Irish for their part were better organised than ever before. At parliamentary level the advance of Charles Stewart Parnell to the leadership of the home rule movement from 1877 onwards led to radical reorganisation, including the imposition of strict discipline at the parliamentary level and the organisation of a strong grass-roots support base. At the local level branches of the Irish National League under the chairmanship of T.P. O'Connor were found in all urban centres where the Irish had settled in Britain. The rapid growth of the nationally minded Irish National Foresters mutual insurance society also helped mobilise the Irish more effectively than ever before.

By October 1886 Manchester Council consisted of thirty-nine Liberals and thirty-six Conservatives. Whilst it was remarked that there was relatively little public excitement during the 1886 local election campaign, it was also noted that 'The wards in which public interest was most conspicuously shown were St. Michael's and New Cross.' In both cases the Irish vote was now being mobilised for the Liberals. In New Cross 'The Liberals … probably thinking that they might succeed in snatching the second seat with the aid of the Irish vote … forced a contest' and were rewarded with a gain. In St Michael's the Liberals nominated John Ashworth known as 'a Liberal Roman Catholic'. The Conservative incumbent appealed for a vote against 'dictation from the National League' and narrowly retained his seat.³⁵

Henceforth both wards generally, though not invariably, returned Liberals to the council, and in some years the incumbent councillors were returned unopposed. During this period a local electoral alliance was devised which generally proved fruitful but did not always run smoothly. A succession of candidates stood on a joint Liberal and Irish nationalist ticket and were elected. Amongst these was Dan McCabe, well known as a second-generation Irish Catholic, whose victory in St Michael's in 1889 was reported as 'a majority of 471 for home rule'.³⁶ By 1892, when he was up for re-election, the same (Conservative) source scolded a maverick Liberal who stood against him on the grounds that 'Mr. McCabe has given substantial satisfaction to every section of his constituents and even those who differ from him in politics did not consider that there were proper or reasonable grounds for opposing him.'³⁷ The *Guardian* drew attention to the fact that 'The Conservatives of the ward were advised by [incumbent councillors] to vote for Mr. McCabe.'³⁸ It was typical of a career which was to culminate in McCabe becoming the city's first Catholic Lord Mayor and eventually being knighted by both King George V and the Vatican (Figure 12). Several other Irish nationalists followed the same path in both

St Michael's and New Cross. By the early twentieth century Liberals and nationalists had arrived at an arrangement in St Michael's: 'The custom followed with these parties in the ward for some years had been that the Radicals [Liberals] nominate one year, the Irish the next year and the two sections combined in the third year.'[39] But the arrangement did not always run smoothly. F.J. Farley, a popular local nationalist, was defeated in both 1902 and 1904, owing to what were diplomatically described as 'misunderstandings' with local Liberals.[40] The consequent anger amongst committee members of the local nationalist club led them to resolve that

> at all future municipal elections the gentleman chosen by this Branch must be nominated principally by Nationalists and in a spirit sufficiently National to meet the approval of this Committee. In the event of a 'candidate' being chosen by this club, and who, after nomination fights on 'Liberal' lines, it will be the duty of this Committee to inform the Irish electors, by placing posters throughout the ward, that this candidate does not meet with the approval of the local branch of the United Irish League.[41]

Relations were repaired, but were not always easy.

Additional problems arose when the burgeoning Labour movement began to contest local elections. At the St Patrick's Day celebrations of 1894 Mathias Bodkin MP had expressed incredulity on being told that some local Irish had joined the Independent Labour Party, since 'It had always been the dictum of the Irish people that the Irish cause stood and the rest nowhere.'[42] But, given the nature of St Michael's and New Cross wards, it is hardly surprising that the Liberals and nationalists of the area had from the outset taken a radical stance on issues such as housing, social reform and the provision of municipal facilities.[43] In fact this outlook was quite in accord with the Progressive Municipal Programme adopted by the Manchester Liberals, in which they committed themselves to an eight-hour day for the corporation workforce, large-scale slum clearance, reform of local finance and greater representation for working people on public bodies.[44] Nonetheless relations between the labour movement and the local Irish were not always easy. When McCabe and fellow members of the Union of Gasworkers and General Labourers turned up at a demonstration there were efforts to relegate their deputation to the tail end of the procession, upon which they returned home.[45] Despite this, local nationalists and Liberals persisted in their generally successful appeals to the local working-class vote. When Dan Boyle, organiser of the Irish National Foresters and later nationalist MP for North Mayo, first stood for election in New Cross ward against an incumbent Liberal Unionist, he explicitly made a strong pitch for the Labour vote. At one meeting he nailed his

THE RIGHT HONOURABLE DANIEL McCABE,
LORD MAYOR OF MANCHESTER, 1913-14.

12  Alderman Daniel McCabe on his election as Manchester's first Catholic Lord Mayor

colours to the mast: 'While he wished to confine himself to municipal questions, at the same time he wished no one to vote for him without first knowing that he was an Irish Nationalist. He claimed, moreover, to be a Labour man. He had not a word to say against the Labour party and sympathised with much of what they were fighting for.'[46] On another occasion it was reported, 'he endorses the Labour programme as identical with that of Liberals.'[47] Liberals won both seats and Boyle went on to be re-elected, despite Conservative efforts to make an issue of his Catholicism and his Irish nationalism, until he stood down from the council in 1917 (Figure 13). When F.J. Farley was again adopted as a candidate in late 1904 the local nationalist club noted, 'The deputation to meet the Liberals having given their report it was carried "unam" to adopt the Committee's suggestion to approach Mr. F.J. Farley to stand as the Nationalist and Labour candidate at the forthcoming November election.'[48] However, he again went down to defeat by a Conservative.[49]

MR. COUNCILLOR DANIEL BOYLE.
(*From a Photograph by Mr. Franz Baum, Manchester and London.*)

13 Daniel Boyle, Manchester alderman, Nationalist MP for North Mayo and notable organiser of the Irish vote

Subsequent Conservative successes may have been due to the fact that from about 1909 onwards the two wards were sometimes witnessing lively three-way contests as the national political temperature rose in the wake of Lloyd George's 'People's Budget', reform of the House of Lords, the two general elections of 1910 and the introduction of the Irish Home Rule Bill in April 1912. But it is also possible that some of the Liberal and nationalist failures came about because the issue of religious education, always likely to strain the alliance, had returned to both the local and the national political agenda.

## School Board elections, 1870–1900

Under the 1870 Education Act there was to be a dual system of educational provision in Great Britain. One stream consisted of the approximately twenty thousand voluntary or church schools, almost all run by the Church of England and the Catholic Church. Henceforth these would receive no public funding. A parallel stream consisted of schools overseen by School Boards elected every three years on what was virtually a household franchise, financed partly by a property tax and partly by fees levied from wealthier families. The function of the new boards was the provision of mass primary education through the building, maintenance, staffing and equipping of schools for children not in the church schools. One motivation behind these arrangements may have been to siphon off from local council affairs what was proving to be a notably contentious issue. To some extent this succeeded, though as has been seen the issue did still periodically surface in municipal elections. It dominated elections to the School Boards and led to some notably revealing electoral patterns and tactics in which the overwhelmingly Catholic Irish played a key role, with implications beyond the question of education.

School Boards had no control over the voluntary schools, but they could provide religious instruction on a non-denominational basis. This was enough to attract the attention of both the main Christian denominations and those, including Nonconformists and secularists, who opposed the idea of any publicly funded religious instruction. For the two main churches there was a dual concern. One was the fact that, try as they might, they did not always have the resources to provide schooling for all their adherents, who therefore had to attend Board schools. This concern increased after attendance was made compulsory by the 1880 Education Act. In addition, Anglicans and Catholics were at one in arguing for religious instruction as an integral part of the curriculum, though they differed in exactly what was to be taught. Nonconformists were opposed in principle to religious instruction, which they feared would differ radically from their outlook, and secularists were against any form of religious teaching in publicly funded schools. These last two fought under a variety of labels down the years, including 'Unsectarian', 'Free School Board', 'Progressive' and 'United Education', and in the 1890s the Labour Party began to put up candidates. Since there were fifteen members on the Manchester School Board and each voter had up to fifteen votes, there was the possibility that electors would spread their votes across a range of candidates. The contending groups were therefore faced with the work of locating their supporters, ensuring that they registered to vote and then at elections instructing them to concentrate their votes on appropriate candidates.[50] All this clearly demanded considerable organisation and energy.

At the first Manchester School Board elections in 1870 there were forty-four candidates for the fifteen places, of which six were captured by Church of England members ('the Church party'), five by Nonconformists, two by Catholics and the balance by independents.[51] Local observers were unanimous that there had been some very skilful vote management by both the Church party and Catholics. One of the organisers of the Church party campaign outlined their approach and in so doing described techniques probably common to all groups:

> The [Anglican] Church party directed their efforts to the return of five candidates. Their organisation was very perfect ... communications had been sent to all the clergy asking them to open their schoolrooms every night, and to form a staff of lay helpers to instruct voters as to how, when and where to vote. Seventy-two thousand handbills had been distributed, most of which had the names of the rectors, vicars and incumbents of the city of Manchester attached. Meetings were held ... 42,000 voting papers were sent to the local committee rooms and a huge number was also distributed. Thirty-six school rooms were put at the service of the committee, in which were located auxiliary committees ... the cost would be at least £1,000 ... On the day of the election, canvassers on behalf of the Church party were present at many of the polling booths and assisted or induced (in most cases quietly and unobtrusively) to cast their votes in favour of the five Church candidates.[52]

Amongst those who supported the Church party effort was the local Orange Order.[53]

Considerable comment focused on the success of the two Catholic candidates who topped the poll in the city: 'The organisation among the Roman Catholics appears to have been equally perfect, but their method of working was quite secret.'[54] Others were quite sure how it had been done: 'This was accomplished, under the published advice of leading members of that body, by the concentration of all the Catholic votes upon their candidates.'[55] The best-known Catholic candidate was the redoubtable Canon Toole of St Wilfrid's church in Hulme. He topped the poll, and it was notable that 52.5% of his total vote came from St Michael's and New Cross wards.[56]

Given the novelty of the system, it is hardly surprising that there were teething troubles. In 1870 it was reported that votes were most commonly spoilt by failure to indicate any preference at all on the ballot, more than fifteen marks on the paper, lack of identification of the voter and impersonation of another voter.[57] But the most frequently recurring complaint was the illiteracy of would-be voters. Illiterate voters could request the returning officer to complete the ballot on their behalf, and in 1873 it was recorded that there were 2,685 votes in this category, 9.9% of the total.[58] In New Cross and St Michael's it was reported: 'A large proportion of the voters in these wards are illiterate Irish, who, as had been anticipated, were a source of some difficulty to the presiding officers ... In a large number of cases the voters (evidently Roman Catholics) had marked simply one cross against each of the three candidates they intended to support.' This was supplemented by amusing anecdotes of elderly women bemused by the process, one of whom, on emerging from the polling booth in St Michael's, declared 'That would puzzle a horse.'[59] Such complaints died away as voters became accustomed to the process and compulsory education raised literacy levels.

The general issue for the contending groups over the next thirty years was the place of religious instruction in the developing state school system, but as time went on there were some intriguing shifts of emphasis. From the outset the Manchester School Board proved to be quite enlightened on general educational matters, taking a generous approach to the provision of meals, evening schools and education for the mentally handicapped.[60] On strictly religious questions, however, it was notably orthodox, devising a syllabus on religious education which, though nominally non-denominational, attracted praise from Anglican clergy across the country.[61] At the very end of the period under discussion a candidate supporting secular education made the quite valid point that in some respects the voluntary school supporters elected to the board were more interested in defending their own schools, which were outside board control, than in running the state schools.[62] Catholic candidates and supporters throughout the period declared that 'They represented the Catholic cause and went on the School Board to defend Catholic interests'.[63] Church candidates argued that supporters of secular education 'desired to close the voluntary schools and thus "double the rates"', and secularists in turn charged that 'The whole intention and aim of the Church party and the Roman Catholic party was not to teach religion so much as to teach those differential things which brought about disunion between one branch of religious people and another'.[64] Anglicans, Nonconformists and secularists periodically attacked what they alleged were Catholic machinations and intentions. In 1882 secular candidates reminded supporters that

> they knew well that the Roman Catholics had an admirable way of manipulating their voters ... the Roman Catholic priesthood ... claimed all control over the faith and morals of their people, and denounced all education that did not came from their own hands ... the obedient sons of the church must follow the course marked out for them ... They at all events could have no part nor parcel with the monstrous claims of the Roman Catholic priesthood over the souls of men.[65]

In 1891 the first Labour candidate tried to set a different agenda when he argued that 'The Churchmen, the Nonconformist and the Roman Catholic had hitherto used working men like pawns for their own purposes: now it was time that the working man took the bull by the horns, did his own work, and carried out his own principles for himself.'[66] In the campaign of 1897, when Labour elected its only board member, it was stressed that its programme was distinct in that 'no reference whatever was made to the question of religion'.[67]

Whilst anti-Catholic sentiments were not unknown amongst Church candidates, it gradually became clear that in their support for inclusion of some form of religious teaching in publicly funded schools, Church and Catholic candidates shared common concern. As early as 1882 it had been remarked that both the Church party and Catholics were 'the friends of religious education',[68] and from the early 1880s onwards there emerged a pragmatic alliance between the two groups in the organisation and structuring of the work of the board. There was also a growing concern with costs and efficiency and less squabbling over purely denominational concerns. This was noted in the aftermath of the 1885 election, when it was suggested, 'four of the Church members … are, in respect of school work, … practically at one with the Roman Catholic members and will no doubt enter into an alliance with them for the purpose of checking educational effort on the part of the board … they will be able to elect the chairman and control the policy of the Board.'[69] By the end of the 1890s it was becoming clear that there were moves towards a new settlement of the education question. In a speech during his 1897 campaign, Canon Lynch, one of the Catholic candidates, suggested that 'They were drawing near to final and satisfactory solution of this difficult [education] problem.'[70] In his final campaign before the abolition of School Boards in 1900 he paid tribute to the sympathetic way in which the School Board had dealt with orphaned or neglected Catholic children and described the Catholic members of the Board as 'a portion of the Voluntary party on the Board', indicating the degree of practical cooperation between the two religious groups.[71]

Despite all the energy invested by the contending parties, there was persistent concern over the low level of voter participation. In 1870 it had been 42.8%, but thereafter it gradually declined, to 40.8% in 1873 and 35.7% in 1879,[72] and it persisted at that level throughout the period, despite increases in voting hours and numbers of polling booths. All parties realised that victory could go to whoever located, registered and got their supporters to the polls and instructed them on how to operate the voting system. For Catholic voters the point was driven home by the varied fortunes of their candidates over the years. Over the period 1870–1900 the Catholic vote averaged 20.6% of those cast.[73] The challenge was not only to ensure that Catholic voters turned out but that they divided their fifteen votes equally amongst the Catholic candidates. When this was done, Catholics could usually take three or even four seats, but poor voting discipline could be costly, as in 1891, when two incumbent Catholic Board members lost their seats and one of the two survivors was the last person elected. This result focused the minds of local Catholic leaders on the whole process of locating and organising the faithful. Catholic Registration Societies had been set up in London in the mid-1870s, but most provincial cities had been slow to follow.[74] As early as 1889 the president of a local branch of the Irish National League had pointed to the need for 'an Irish registration office in Manchester',[75] and there were increasingly strong admonitions for Catholics to participate and detailed printed instructions on how to allocate their votes. In the run-up to the School Board election of 1894 Bishop Bilsborrow sent a letter to all parish priests in which he wrote:

> I request that you will bring to the notice of your people on Sunday next, as clearly and forcibly as you can, the extreme importance to Catholic interests of the School Board Election, on Saturday next ... Let the Catholic Registration Society and every Local Committee canvas every Catholic voter ... The Catholic candidates, both for Salford and Manchester, are the choice of all the congregations – they are the elect of all the Catholic body. Let us therefore, go to the poll in one solid phalanx ... I request that you will convey to all your people at all the Masses next Sunday the substance of this letter, and that you will promote, with dutiful zeal, its circulation everywhere amongst them.[76]

The candidates had been chosen at a meeting chaired by the bishop and consisting of six lay delegates and one cleric from each of the twenty-four parishes.[77] In their literature they reminded readers that 'At the last election [1891] Catholics suffered a severe defeat for the first time' and warned, 'There must be no frittering away of our strength by giving a single vote to anyone except the Catholic Candidates' (Figure 14).[78] The pleas clearly worked, since the Board election of that year saw the Catholic vote tightly bunched around their three successful candidates, with the lowest level of variation in the entire period.

The following year the Registration Society adopted a constitution, but it clearly faltered, because by early 1897 an anonymous writer was anxiously explaining the structure and work of the organisation and encouraging support,[79] and in August 1900 the bishop again wrote to all parish priests: 'As the Catholic Registration Association of Manchester has practically ceased to exist, it is of the utmost importance for Catholic interests that it be revived immediately ... Will you therefore call a meeting of your congregation ... and at that meeting elect six laymen to represent your

# TO THE CATHOLIC ELECTORS
## OF MANCHESTER.

LADIES AND GENTLEMEN,

At a meeting of the Clergy and representative laity of Manchester, held under the presidency of his Lordship the Bishop, we, the undersigned, were requested to allow ourselves to be nominated for the Manchester School Board.

We willingly acceded to that request.

The present election is fraught with grave issues for Catholics.

We claim in justice to ourselves as citizens, and in the interests of Education, an equitable share in the Education rate.

A heavy Catholic vote in Manchester would be an object lesson to Parliament that a large and influential party, whose strength must be reckoned with, exists in one of the most important cities in England.

We can no longer tolerate that our Religion as Catholics should be regarded as an obstacle to the attainment of our full civil rights. Our Catholic schools must stand before the law on the same footing as the unduly favoured Board Schools.

We shall do our utmost to defend the sacred rights of Catholic parents which the great law of Nature confers on them, to educate their children in their own schools and in their own Religion.

Our policy on the Manchester School Board will be to safeguard parental rights, and in the interests of religious equality to defend Voluntary schools; to reduce the rates as far as is consistent with the progress of education, and to advocate the abolition of the seventeen-and-sixpenny limit in the education grant.

If returned, we shall vote in favour of the Board entering into contracts only with those firms who pay their workmen standard wages.

At the last election Catholics suffered a severe defeat for the first time. To ensure the return of the three Catholic Candidates on the present occasion, every effort must be strained to the uttermost, and nothing must be left undone until every Catholic vote without exception has been polled.

There must be no frittering away of our strength by giving a single vote to anyone except the Catholic Candidates,

**We ask you to give 5 votes to each Catholic Candidate.** Giving all your votes to one only would seriously imperil the success of the others.

**The election will take place on Saturday, November 17th**

We have the honour to be, Ladies and gentlemen,

Your obedient servants,

**BRUNO CANON DE SPLENTER, J.C.D.,
PATRICK LYNCH,
THOMAS FREEMAN KELLY.**

*Manchester, October 30th, 1894.*

Cards giving directions how and where to vote will be given you before the polling day.

Printed and Published by T. H. SALE & Co., Stevenson Square, Manchester.

*14 Rallying the faithful for the 1894 School Board election*

Congregation on the General Association.'[80] The society clearly entered a new phase of life, since it issued a revised constitution in May 1901 stating that its objects were 'to guard and strengthen the Catholic vote, to preserve the unity of Catholics, and to support and advance all questions affecting the Catholic religion'.[81] This time it thrived. One reason was that School

Boards had been abolished and control of schools vested in local authorities, making council elections even more relevant to Catholic interests. A data bank of Catholic voters was therefore of great electoral value not only for Catholic purposes but also to Liberal candidates, especially in St Michael's and New Cross and to parliamentary candidates. Consequently it was notable that some of the most prominent of the Irish nationalists who eventually became Liberal councillors made it their business to become involved in the work of the School Board and the Registration Society. Charles O'Neill, the first Manchester Catholic councillor in modern times, was a Board member in 1879–91; Dan McCabe, the first Catholic Lord Mayor, was a vice chair of the Registration Society, as was Dan Boyle, alderman and MP for North Mayo. From 1902 onwards, as education became a local council responsibility, the return of a Liberal government became increasingly likely, and reform of both education and Irish government were on their political agenda, attention turned more frequently than was usual to national parliamentary politics.

## Parliamentary politics

As noted earlier, the Manchester Irish were never sufficiently numerous to elect a nationalist to one of the city's parliamentary seats, but this did not stop rumours circulating about the possibility of an Irish candidate who might impact on the fortunes of the main parties. At the founding meeting of the Home Rule Confederation in the city in January 1873 Isaac Butt had announced that earlier in the day there had been a meeting of representative Irish from all over England who had decided that 'it was highly necessary that the Irish electoral power in England should be organised, concentrated and used … that there should be in Manchester, and every town, an Irish vote, composed of Irishmen determined to vote together as one man for the interests of their country'. He clearly shared the notion that this vote was larger and more strategic than it actually was, since he went on to estimate that 'There were some 60 English towns – and those towns the very strongholds of Liberalism – where the Irish vote was so powerful that no representative of either of the rival parties could be returned to parliament without the concurrence and assistance of the Irish people.'[82] Just over a year later placards were distributed urging Irish voters to reserve their vote in the imminent general election for a home rule candidate, and rumours circulated that Butt himself would be standing. However, when he addressed a meeting in the city he assured the audience that he had no intention of standing and urged them to support Jacob Bright, an incumbent Liberal, who had expressed his support for Irish self-determination. Despite this, the meeting passed a resolution that Butt be nominated as 'the Home Rule and working men's candidate', though the idea came to nothing.[83] By the mid-1870s there was a Home Rule Association in the city which held regular meetings, and leading Irish nationalist parliamentarians visited and spoke not only on St Patrick's Day and at the Manchester Martyrs' commemoration events (described in Chapter 7 below), but at grand public meetings designed to publicise the cause of home rule and encourage the faithful.

Despite Butt's remarks, at this early stage the relationship with the Liberals was decidedly fragile, as was demonstrated when the same Jacob Bright commended by Butt held an annual open meeting for constituents in January 1882. By this time Parnell was leader of both the nationalist movement and the Irish National Land League, which was overseeing a militant campaign of agrarian agitation in Ireland. The incumbent Liberal government had passed an Irish Land Act in August 1881, but this had received a cool reception from nationalists, and any lingering gratitude had been dissipated when the government, exasperated by the challenge to law and order mounted by Land League campaigns in several parts of Ireland, ordered the arrest of Parnell and outlawed the Land League in October. In early January 1882 a meeting of local Irish passed a resolution of protest against government coercion policy, and this was taken to the Liberal meeting at the Free Trade Hall but voted down. Bright was heard in relative quiet, but when his fellow MP John Slagg tried to speak he was constantly interrupted by shouting and singing of 'God save Ireland'. Fights broke out in which sticks were used, blood was shed, and ladies were ushered onto the platform for safety; one speaker described the affair as 'more disturbed than any Liberal meeting, within his recollection, held in Manchester'.[84] One traditionally Conservative source described the proceedings as 'a complete bear garden … a tumultuous assembly of the type which we had hoped had become extinct in Manchester' and gleefully predicted: 'Messrs. Bright and Slagg went into parliament on the strength of the Irish vote … the uproarious proceedings … of the evening afford indications of the probability of their losing their seats by the same means.'[85]

Relations improved somewhat with the release of Parnell in May 1882 and the informal 'Kilmainham Treaty', under which he agreed to tone down agrarian agitation and Gladstone agreed to revisit the land question. However, in 1883 there was talk of putting up T.B. Kiernan, a local commission agent and merchant, as an Irish candidate in the next general election, but this was withdrawn on instructions from Parnell and the Land League founder Michael Davitt when the prospective Liberal candidate proved satisfactory.[86] The prickly relationship resurfaced when the

Liberals chose R.P. Blennerhassett as a candidate in the 1885 general election. A Protestant supporter of Butt, he had originally been returned as home rule MP for Kerry in a significant by-election in February 1872, but he was increasingly uncomfortable with the growing militancy of the agrarian agitation and the nationalist movement under Parnell and sought to transfer to a Manchester seat in time for the 1885 election.[87] He was adopted as Liberal candidate for Manchester North East but faced bitter recrimination from the local Irish, who strongly opposed his adoption, disrupted his meetings and were advised by one observer to adopt a policy of 'Silent contempt and a solid vote against … one whom they not unnaturally consider a "renegade" and a "Judas" to their cause'.[88] Overall, the election was something of a disaster for Manchester Liberals, the Conservatives taking five of the six seats, including North East. Since Parnell and O'Connor had advised the Irish in Britain to vote Conservative, there was a clear temptation to put the losses down to Irish voters deserting the Liberals. By the time of the next election in July 1886 home rule was Liberal policy, and though the national result was a Conservative victory, in Manchester the Liberals recovered two seats, which again were attributed to a switch in the Irish vote. Certainly relations between local Irish and the Liberals had entered a new phase. During the campaign the Liberal association staged a massive public meeting to which they invited Parnell as main speaker. Jacob Bright, presiding over the event, declared, 'they were united together for a common purpose … not in a paper union, but in a union of hearts and minds', and Parnell declared, 'The union now begun would be a permanent union, because it was based upon a union of feeling, upon an accord of principle and conviction.'[89] At election time the two parties could work quite well together. In the Manchester North East by-election of October 1891 a home rule van toured the constituency, and it was noted that 'The work of bringing up the Irish who are voters in the constituency was undertaken by their own organisation, and they had three separate committee rooms … [the] secretary of the National Home Rule League took charge of the arrangements, and he was ably assisted by Mr. D. Boyle, the local secretary.'[90]

In reality, the relationship was never as close or as comfortable as the rhetoric of these early days would suggest. Moreover, there were elements within the Liberal Party who always looked upon the commitment to home rule as a decided electoral liability at the national level and a major factor in the Conservative dominance and the almost total exclusion of Liberals from office between 1886 and 1906. Gladstone had retired as Liberal leader early in March 1894, and was succeeded by the Earl of Rosebery. In his first speech as Prime Minister on 12 March Rosebery seemed to be distancing the Liberals from their commitment when he stated that home rule could come about only when England, as 'the predominant partner' in the United Kingdom, was convinced of the merits of the case.⁹¹ On 17 March he sought to reaffirm party commitment to home rule, but the episode confirmed the suspicions of nationalists that some Liberals were decidedly lukewarm on the question. The relationship had been placed under considerable strain; at the St Patrick's Day celebrations in Manchester it was notable that whilst Mathias Bodkin, MP for Roscommon North, reaffirmed loyalty to the alliance, he was applauded when he also made it clear that 'much confidence as they had in the Liberal party, they had still greater confidence in themselves'.⁹²

During the 1890s the Manchester Irish, like nationalists throughout Ireland and Britain, were preoccupied with the issue of Parnell's leadership and the split in the parliamentary party. Though the majority in the city were anti-Parnell, there was a small but vociferous Parnell Leadership Club.⁹³ However, even in their disunity they were able, and possibly eager, to come together in defence of Catholic schools and increasingly used public meetings and demonstrations to express their views on the issue. An education bill was expected from the new Conservative government elected in 1896, and a national campaign of public meetings was launched in the city. In January 1896 it culminated with a gathering in the Free Trade Hall addressed by the Irish party leader, John Dillon. When he rose to propose a motion supporting the bill he remarked that

> there was something peculiarly fitting in calling upon a member of the Irish nationalist to propose it ... For he came there as the representative of a race which through long and dark and stormy centuries of persecution of which few nations of men had passed through, had remained faithful to the cause of the Catholic faith ... There was a very particular reason why they should take a particular interest in those schools. He supposed that at least nine-tenths of the children attending them were of his own blood ... The Irish party ... are counted in most estimates as opponents of the government ... when it comes to being a question of doing justice to the Voluntary schools we shall be with the government ... Those were the views of every Irish Nationalist member.⁹⁴

In 1902 the government attempted what it hoped was a final settlement of the schools question with a proposal to provide public funding for voluntary schools. Again a public meeting was held to express support for most of the measure, and there are traces of some embarrassment amongst Irish nationalists at having to encourage public support for a Conservative measure. Dan McCabe expressed faint praise: 'This bill he regarded as a good bill – as good a bill as they could expect from the present government.' Dan Boyle provoked laughter and applause when he spoke in similar vein: '[this] was the first time he had been on a platform in support of anything done by this government ... But he was an Irishman, and Irishmen were a discriminating people. If the government, even by accident, should do something right, they were prepared to support the government and to avail themselves to the fullest extent of the accident.'[95]

As the political tide began to flow away from the Conservatives, nationalists began to anticipate a Liberal government and the possibility of another home rule bill. However, it was also widely expected that any future Liberal government would seek to respond to the grievances of their Nonconformist followers by revising the 1902 Act. Since this had provided Catholic schools with public funds, and since religious education was such a key issue for Catholics, the potential for conflicting pressures on the Irish was obvious. Conservatives sought to exploit this potential cleavage whilst Irish leaders responded with assurances to their followers that they were reliable stewards of both the cause of home rule and the cause of Catholic schools. As early as 1902 John Redmond noted how, in a recent by-election which the Liberals had won, an attempt had been made 'to induce the Irish voters ... to vote against a Home Ruler because the man who opposed the Home Ruler took views on the education question which were more in harmony with Irish views than those of the Liberal candidate. An attempt was made, in other words, to set up the education question as above the question of Home Rule.' On education he went to some length to make it clear that 'The Irish party may be trusted to safeguard those interests ... we do not believe [that this] ... clashes in the slightest degree with our duty to the national cause.' Redmond then took the opportunity to share his vision of Ireland's future relationship with Britain under home rule, enjoying self-government within an empire characterised by 'the happiness and freedom of its citizens', founded upon 'the contentment and loyalty which always flow from justice and from right ... an Imperialism founded upon the friendship and the goodwill of Ireland', and he went on to argue that 'the contentment and goodwill and reconciliation of Ireland were of infinitely more value to the empire than the peace, contentment and loyalty even of Canada or Australia'.[96]

The approach of the general election meant that the education issue surfaced more frequently; at the 1904 St Patrick's Day celebrations Canon Lynch pressed for a united outlook amongst Catholics and wondered whether 'surely it was not beyond the statesmanship of the Catholic Church in England and the leaders of the Irish party to discover a common platform, so that voting for Home Rule would not be antagonistic to Catholic education interests'.[97] At the same event, Redmond returned to the issue, this time adding a warning to any new government. He informed his audience: 'I do not share in the remotest degree the fears of those who think that a Liberal government ... would immediately attack the interests of the Catholic schools of Great Britain. Even if they did they would not be likely to succeed ... Any attempt to injure those religious interests of our people by any Liberal government would mean their instant defeat by us, or at any rate, would mean our bitter opposition.'[98] In January 1906 a Liberal government was indeed elected, but with a large majority independent of the need for Irish support. In Manchester the Liberals recovered fully from their total defeat in the 1900 election, when patriotic fervour generated by the Boer War had seen them take only one seat. This time they took four and, in a novel development, Labour took the remaining two, including Manchester North East, where the victor was the second-generation Irishman J.R. Clynes.

Anticipating an education bill, in March 1906 a meeting in the Free Trade Hall addressed by Bishop Casartelli overflowed into the nearby Grand Theatre and the seven thousand people present heard impassioned speeches. The bishop, never known for political subtlety, condemned the Labour Party as bent on totally secular education and queried how long Catholics could cooperate with them.[99] As for the Liberals, he noted that it was common knowledge that in the recent general election they had received the greater part of the Catholic vote and was applauded when he warned that if Liberal policy were deemed hostile to Catholic education, 'then I need not suggest to them what will become of the Catholic vote at the next election and many more elections to come'. Another speaker cheekily adapted a Protestant Unionist slogan with the cry 'Catholicity for Catholic children, and no surrender', but also made a great effort to link the Irish and the Catholic education issues when he argued that 'The case of the Catholic school was to a large extent part of the Irish question. If the government settled the question all Christendom would bless them, but did they think they would succeed if, while they remembered the ills of Ireland, they heaped up fresh wrongs upon Irishmen in Great Britain? He would say to the government, "Whatever you do, do not touch the religion of the Irish people".'[100]

The anticipated bill was introduced on 9 April 1906; it seemed that Catholic fears had been justified, because it was proposed that the power to appoint teachers to church schools funded by the local authority would pass from the church concerned to the local council. As the bill moved through parliament, Catholic opposition steadily mounted. When the annual convention of the United Irish League was held in Manchester in June 1906, T.P. O'Connor made it clear that the Irish party had some severe reservations, promising that 'When the time comes, we shall be prepared to fight as one man for Catholic schools.'[101]

Manchester Catholic feeling climaxed in a massive demonstration at the city's Bellevue Gardens on Saturday 13 October 1906, when estimates of those present varied from 40,000 to 75,000, with claims there were representatives from all of the 137 parishes and missions in the diocese.[102] Speeches were made from three platforms, and speakers made it clear that if the bill were passed both the Labour and Liberals parties would feel their wrath at the next election. Listeners were assured that 'The Catholics of England and of Ireland were never more united than on this question.' One speaker told the audience that 'Henceforward he believed that as every Irishman he had ever spoken to detested the name of Cromwell, the name of Birrell [the education minister] would also be detested.' Councillor Dan Boyle declared that any government which 'filched away' the schools from the Catholic population was 'guilty of a gross and immoral transaction'.[103] Given the subject matter and the presence of the bishop and clergy, who led in prayers and hymns, it is hardly surprising that there was an atmosphere of deep religious fervour, with the spontaneous singing of favourite hymns such as 'Faith of our fathers' and 'Hail glorious St Patrick'.[104] In the subsequent parliamentary manoeuvrings, John Redmond led the assault in the Commons with considerable skill, ensuring that in everything he did he kept in close contact with the hierarchy, thereby wrong-footing the Conservative Catholic peers in the Lords, who tended to be too politically partisan in their stance.[105] The combination of extra-parliamentary Catholic opposition and Conservative obstruction in the Lords led the government to withdraw the bill in mid-December 1906.

The October 1906 rally had been the first public outing of the Catholic Federation, a lay organisation founded earlier in the year in response to the fact that 'many of our Catholic working men were feeling the necessity, in face of the growth of secularist and socialist principles in various trade unions, of combining their forces in some sort of federation ... permanent and stable in view of future needs ... its work being the promotion and defence of Catholic interests ... chiefly by cooperation amongst ourselves so as to organise our forces for elections'.[106] The intention was to have a branch in every parish, overseen by a diocesan committee, with sub-committees to organise debates, social events and voter registration and the interrogation of election candidates on questions of interest to Catholics, but especially religious education.[107] The organisation spread into a number of northern cities, and in the Salford diocese a monthly journal, *The Federationist*, was launched in 1910. However, it never outgrew the shrill defensive tones of its early days and, despite its strong support for female suffrage and workers' rights, it failed to adjust to the shifts in Catholic social teaching which in time successfully accommodated the church to the reformist and Christian socialist strands of the emergent Labour Party. By the early 1920s it was preoccupied with what it saw as threats to traditional moral values, quizzing Manchester Council candidates on their attitudes towards public bathhouses in 1921.[108] It was wound up in 1929.[109]

The defeat of the 1906 Education Bill was described by T.P. O'Connor at the 1907 St Patrick's Day celebrations as 'a complete victory for Irish convictions',[110] and the Irish party took a similar stance on the three equally unsuccessful attempts to modify the 1902 Act in 1907 and 1908, because, as Redmond explained at a public meeting in the latter year, 'we feel the duty thrown upon as, as a National Party, of looking after, as far as we can, the educational interests of the Irish parents and children of Great Britain'.[111]

Later that year a famous by-election created an outright clash between the religious and political loyalties of the Manchester Irish. In 1906 Winston Churchill had been elected Liberal MP for Manchester North West. On his appointment to his first Cabinet post, as President of the Board of Trade, he had to follow the custom of the time and stand for re-election. The Catholic population was advised by Bishop Casartelli to vote Conservative because of the Education Bill making its way through parliament, and at one point Redmond advised the Irish to withhold their votes.[112] However, after reassurances from the Liberal leadership he advised support, and local Irish leaders argued carefully for a Liberal vote because of party policy on home rule. At a meeting on 22 April Churchill pledged the government to ensure the Irish people were 'contented and prosperous ... in a true union of hearts', and at that gathering it was reported that 'for the first time [he] had the assistance as speakers of Mr. Councillor D. Boyle and other Irish Nationalists'. Dan McCabe stated he believed the government would do a great deal for Ireland and that it was close to a settlement of the education question. Boyle attempted an adroit balancing act in appealing to both the working-class and the Irish Catholic vote. He appealed to the Irish, first, on the grounds of national loyalty, stating that because of recent Liberal commitments on home rule 'From the point of view of Ireland I am satisfied.' He went on, 'But I am also a citizen of Manchester. Living here for thirty years and having my interests here, I am interested in everything that makes for the well-being of the working-classes amongst whom I work and belong ... Therefore I am here to speak for [Mr.Churchill] not only as an Irish Nationalist, but as a man keenly interested in the reforms we require.' However, he could not avoid the question of education and recent clerical intervention. He continued: 'I want to enter into no conflict, I want to use no words of disrespect or discourtesy, or anything but admiration and sincere respect for every priest and bishop of our Church … I claim that, politically, I must be allowed to speak and move and act animated by as keen a sense of justice to my religion, and above all to my country, as any man, whether lay or cleric.' He informed the meeting that the advice of the Irish party was 'vote for Winston Churchill', assuring the audience that if church schools were ever in danger the party would again be foremost in their defence, and ended by declaring that he would follow party advice 'in the name of Irishmen, in the name of religion, of my religion, and to vote for the best interest of my country and religion as my political leaders have asked'.[113] In the event the Conservatives captured the seat by 429 votes, the victor publicly acknowledging, 'we had tremendous assistance from the Catholic Federation … who preferred to put the souls of the children before the dictates of Mr. John Redmond', and Churchill himself was convinced that the Irish were responsible for his defeat.[114]

In the two elections of 1910 efforts were once again made to coax the Irish away from the Liberals on grounds of the schools question. The *Manchester Courier*, in accordance with its traditional Conservative stance, pointed out that the recent efforts at educational reform had largely been foiled by the House of Lords, that a Liberal victory would lead to the abolition of the Lords' veto and therefore that Catholics should vote Conservative as the best guarantee of the continued safety of Catholic schools. But it also noted that 'an attempt will be made to divert the issue by Irish politicians'.[115] In fact the two elections of that year saw electoral arrangements between Liberals and nationalists in Manchester work notably well. This was partly because the Liberal appeal that year had an attractive simplicity for all the elements of the Liberal–Labour–Irish alliance. The Lords' obstruction of the 'People's Budget' was represented as a historic clash between people and peers, with the latter wilfully blocking all progressive reform of living and working conditions in both urban and rural Britain and constitutional change in Ireland. As John Redmond put it, after a long struggle 'for the first time the interests of the English working classes and the interests of the Irish people are identical'.[116] Arrangements were made for the allocation of votes and seats within the city. Liberals and Labour had arrived at another agreement to share out the parliamentary seats. Irish nationalists received instructions from the United Irish League on how to allocate their votes in each constituency, and these generally worked.[117] This time, belatedly aware of the resentment caused by his stance in the 1908 by-election, Casartelli was much more circumspect, recognising that constitutional issues were paramount.[118] The result was that Liberals and Labour took five of the six seats in January 1910 and captured the last one in December.

By the 1918 general election the political landscape and the political system in both Britain and Ireland had been transformed, with the enfranchisement of all women over thirty, the redistribution of parliamentary seats, Conservatives and some Liberals fighting the election in coalition, the steady decline of the Irish Nationalist Party and the rise of Sinn Féin. The city now had nine parliamentary seats, of which Coalition candidates took seven and Labour two; one of the latter went to J.R. Clynes, who was returned unopposed in the new seat of Manchester Platting. Given the excited atmosphere of the immediate post-war weeks and the strength of Coalition resources, the Irish vote was swamped, but it was suggested that in Blackley, where it was estimated at 2,500, and Clayton it would go to the Labour candidates, though in both cases the Conservative won.[119] There were indications in a series of meetings held in 1918 and 1919 of how Irish opinion in the city had shifted. In October 1918 the United Irish League of Great Britain held a convention, its first one since the outbreak of war, in Manchester under the chairmanship of John Dillon, who had succeeded Redmond upon Redmond's death in March that year. When he rose to speak at the public meeting in the Free Trade Hall, the gathering was disrupted for twenty minutes by Sinn Féin followers with songs, shouts and fighting, and the meeting could continue only after their forcible expulsion.[120] By contrast, when Arthur Griffith, the founder of Sinn Féin, visited Manchester one year later, it was estimated that the crowds in the same hall, a nearby cinema and the streets outside numbered between ten and twelve thousand.[121] The following year there were even greater crowds when Countess Markievicz, Sinn Féin MP for Dublin St Patrick's, Hanna Sheehy-Skeffington, widow of Francis Sheehy-Skeffington, who had been murdered by a crazed British officer during the suppression of the 1916 rising, and Ida Connolly, daughter of James Connolly, the Labour leader executed during the rising, visited the city to raise funds for a college in Connolly's memory. It was estimated there were up to 15,000 people at the meetings in the Free Trade Hall, the nearby Queen's Theatre and the overflow in the surrounding streets. Both events were under the aegis of the ISDL, which was rapidly replacing the UIL as the political arm of the Irish in Britain.

In local elections the traditional alliance of Liberals and nationalists was fast disintegrating. For the Irish, Liberals were now as closely associated with English repression in Ireland as Conservatives since most of their MPs were supporters of the Coalition government. Moreover, at the local level Liberal associations were divided between supporters of Lloyd George and of Asquith and were being replaced in working-class areas such as St Michael's and New Cross by the Labour Party. However, there was not always a seamless switch of allegiance, since some thought the Labour Party in general and Clynes in particular to be less than enthusiastic on both Irish self-government and religious education. At one point it was suggested that Dan Boyle should contest his seat, but he gave strong pledges on the issues and Boyle did not stand.[122] In April 1920 came an actual electoral test of the strength of the Irish parliamentary vote in British urban areas at a by-election in nearby Stockport. William O'Brien, Secretary of the Irish Labour Party and currently on hunger strike in Wormwood Scrubs prison, stood as an Irish 'Workers' Republican' candidate, coming last of seven candidates with 2,336 votes, which were estimated as 'substantially the whole Irish vote'.[123] It was in some respects a derisory vote, but in a close contest in a single member constituency it could have made all the difference, and as such it perfectly summed up the chronic ambiguity about the significance of the Irish vote in British elections during the period under discussion.

## Conclusion

It is worth bearing in mind that interest and participation in politics are always something of an acquired taste, and there were factors which may well have inhibited the Irish from participation in politics in Britain. The great majority were preoccupied with making a living in the difficult circumstances that all migrants encounter. Moreover, they were a mobile population who moved frequently in search of work, and this, together with the fact that relatively few met the property qualification, meant that for quite some time a considerable proportion did not qualify for the vote. Of those who did, not all were registered. Some did not use the vote, and of those who did, not all voted the same way.[124] In addition, membership of the variously named groups which tried to rally the Irish vote in Britain always had a significant social dimension which may well have outweighed any political considerations, especially when public houses were used as meeting places. Even when separate club rooms were acquired, the attractions of billiards, smoking concerts, socials, picnics and the bar were powerful. When in 1905 it was proposed that the Michael Davitt Club of the Manchester UIL should ban alcohol and run on temperance lines the proposal was 'beaten by a large majority, the motion attracting only 12 votes'.[125]

Participation in the electoral process can be viewed as both a means of incorporating the Irish into the British body politic and simultaneously a means of differentiating them from the rest of the population. The mere act of putting forward candidates was an act of formal participation, and the alliance with the Liberals, which, though never cosy, endured for almost a quarter of a century, bound the Irish even more closely into the political system. However, the element of discomfort within that alliance was due to the two issues which particularly concerned the Irish for most of the period, namely home rule and religious education. Both marked the Irish as distinctive in Britain. The Liberal adoption of home rule as party policy in 1885 in some senses drew the Irish into a closer alliance within the political system. However, the adoption of a sometimes strident anti-home-rule stance by the Conservatives drew attention to the Irish as an element which did not quite fit into the constitutional mainstream. Moreover, even within the Liberal alliance there were always some who were less than enthusiastic about home rule. Nonetheless, local and, to a lesser extent parliamentary elections in Manchester enabled the Irish to enter and use the system.

School Board elections also worked in both ways. As the overwhelming core of the Catholic population, the Irish were organised and marshalled for voting purposes from quite early on. Once again this enabled their participation in public affairs, particularly in educational matters, but by encouraging the identification and use of the Catholic vote as a specific, disciplined bloc, it also marked them out as a distinctive group. Moreover, voter location and registration fed into local and parliamentary electioneering, again marking out the Irish as a distinctive voting bloc. The takeover of education by local authorities in 1902 and the subsequent Liberal efforts to bring about educational reform returned the schools issue to the broader local and national agenda. Together with the revival of home rule as an issue, particularly by 1910, the combined effect was to raise the profile of the Irish as a participating but distinctive group. The 1916 rising and subsequent growth of Sinn Féin saw a demand for a much greater degree of self-determination and a policy of non-participation in formal British parliamentary politics. As the local level, the UIL, the Liberal Party and the alliance between the two were destroyed and rendered irrelevant by the new dispensation. In terms of politics, after 1922 Irish issues gradually faded from the formal Manchester political agenda for all save a small number of devotees, and social and economic concerns, and occasionally education, came uppermost. As with the rest of Britain, it was not until the collapse of the Northern Ireland state in the late 1960s that Irish issues again attracted some sustained attention in Manchester.

## Notes

1 Hugh Heinrick, *A survey of the Irish in England (1872)*, ed. Alan O'Day (London: Hambledon Press, 1990), p. 83.
2 Heinrick, *A survey of the Irish in England*, p. 84.
3 Alan O'Day, *The English face of Irish nationalism: Parnellite involvement in British politics 1880–86* (Dublin: Gill & Macmillan, 1977), p. 110.
4 Alan O'Day, 'Irish influence on parliamentary elections in London, 1885–1914: a simple test', in R. Swift and S. Gilley (eds), *The Irish in the Victorian city* (London: Croom Helm, 1985), pp. 98–105.
5 O'Day, 'Irish influence', p. 104.
6 Manchester was the core of the diocese but the anti-Catholic furore surrounding the restoration of the hierarchy in 1850 inspired legislation preventing the Catholic Church from duplicating Anglican diocesan titles.
7 Alan Kidd, *Manchester* (Keele: Ryburn, 1993), pp. 198–9. Wythenshawe, the last significant boundary extension, was to be acquired in 1931, eventually becoming the site of a large overspill estate and Ringway, later Manchester International, Airport.
8 Shena D. Simon, *A century of city government: Manchester 1838–1938* (London: Allen & Unwin, 1938), p. 119.
9 Kidd, *Manchester*, pp. 67–8.
10 John Belchem, *Irish, Catholic and Scouse: the history of the Liverpool-Irish, 1800–1939* (Liverpool: Liverpool University Press, 2007); P.J. Waller, *Democracy and sectarianism: a political and social history of Liverpool 1868–1939* (Liverpool: Liverpool University Press, 1981).
11 *Manchester Guardian*, 2 November 1864.
12 *Manchester Guardian*, 2 November 1869.
13 *Manchester Guardian*, 2 November 1870.
14 *Manchester Examiner and Times*, 2 November 1871.
15 *The Nation*, 25 November 1871.
16 *Manchester Guardian*, 2 November 1871.
17 *The Nation*, 25 November 1871. 'Hyde Road murderers' was a reference to the Manchester Martyrs incident discussed in the next chapter.
18 *Manchester Courier*, 2 November 1871.
19 *The Nation*, 25 November 1871.
20 *Manchester Guardian*, 3 November 1874.
21 *Manchester Courier*, 2 November 1876.
22 *Manchester Courier*, 3 November 1879.
23 *Manchester Guardian*, 2 November 1870.
24 *Manchester Guardian*, 3 November 1874.
25 Simon, *A century of city government*, p. 402. Women could not stand as candidates until 1907, when Manchester elected its first female councillor.
26 *Manchester Courier*, 3 November 1884.
27 *Manchester Guardian*, 3 November 1884. The Irish National League of Great Britain had succeeded the Home Rule Confederation as the political vehicle

for Irish nationalists in Great Britain. In 1900, following the reunification of the Irish party, it was renamed the United Irish League (UIL).
28 *Manchester Courier*, 3 November 1884. The reference was to the forthcoming Reform Act, which would double Manchester's representation to six parliamentary constituencies.
29 *Manchester Guardian*, 3 November 1885.
30 *Manchester Courier*, 3 November 1885.
31 Neil Smith and Mervyn Busteed, 'A diasporic elite – the emergence of an Irish middle class in nineteenth century Manchester', in C. O'Neill (ed.), *Irish elites in the nineteenth century* (Dublin: Four Courts Press, 2013), pp. 204–5. An alderman was selected by fellow councillors, had to resign from the post of councillor and servedfor a six-year term. The post was abolished in 1974, but the purely honorary title can still be awarded.
32 *Manchester Courier*, 25 November 1885.
33 James R. Moore, *The transformation of urban Liberalism: party politics and urban governance in late nineteenth century England* (Farnham: Ashgate, 2006), pp. 77–81.
34 James Moore, 'Municipal corruption and political partisanship in Manchester', in James Moore and John Smith (eds), *Corruption in urban politics and society: Britain 1780–1950* (Farnham: Ashgate, 2007), pp. 95–112. Liberal Unionists were former Liberals who left the party when it opted to support Irish home rule. They eventually merged with the Conservative Party.
35 *Manchester Guardian*, 2 November 1886.
36 *Manchester Courier*, 2 November 1889.
37 *Manchester Courier*, 2 November 1892.
38 *Manchester Guardian*, 2 November 1892.
39 *Manchester Courier*, 11 April 1902. This Conservative is making a point about the alleged extremism of the local Liberal and Nationalist parties.
40 *Catholic Herald*, 28 September 1906.
41 Minute Book of the Shamrock Hall Branch of the Irish Democratic League, Special Committee Meeting, 18 November 1903, author's private collection.
42 *Catholic Herald*, 23 March 1894.
43 Steven Fielding, 'Irish politics in Manchester 1890–1914', *International Review of Social History*, 33 (1988), pp. 261–84.
44 Moore, *The transformation of urban Liberalism*, chap. 9: 'Manchester and the rise of Progressivism'.
45 Moore, *The transformation of urban Liberalism*, p. 226.
46 *Manchester Guardian*, 23 October 1894.
47 *Manchester Guardian*, 24 October 1894.
48 Minute Book of the Shamrock Hall Branch of the Irish Democratic League, Special Meeting, 28 September 1904, author's private collection.
49 Local elections were suspended during the First World War, and when they resumed there was a steady drift of the Liberal and nationalist vote in both wards towards Labour, though it has been argued that for some time a

distinctive Irish presence was discernible within the local Labour parties. See Fielding, 'Irish politics', p. 283.
50 At this stage the obligation was on the elector to claim the right to vote; later the task of registration was undertaken by local authorities.
51 Amongst those elected was Lydia Becker, the first woman to be voted onto a School Board outside London.
52 *Manchester City News*, 26 November 1870.
53 *Manchester Guardian*, 17 November 1870. For an overview of the Catholic education question in the Manchester area, see Fr David Lannon, 'Catholic education in the Salford diocese, 1870–1944' (Ph.D. dissertation, University of Hull, 2003).
54 *Manchester City News*, 26 November 1870.
55 *Manchester Guardian*, 26 November 1870.
56 Calculation from figures given in *Manchester Courier*, 26 November 1870.
57 *Manchester Courier*, 26 November 1870.
58 *Manchester Courier*, 15 November 1873.
59 *Manchester Guardian*, 13 November 1873.
60 Patricia Hollis, *Ladies elect: women in English local government 1865–1914* (Oxford: Clarendon Press: 1987), p. 142.
61 Marjorie Cruickshank, *Church and state in English education: 1870 to the present day* (London, Macmillan: 1963), p. 44.
62 *Manchester Guardian*, 1 November 1900.
63 *Manchester Guardian*, 9 November 1900.
64 *Manchester Guardian*, 2 and 19 November 1888. 'Rates' was the popular term for the local property tax which financed much of local government.
65 *Manchester Guardian*, 2 November 1882.
66 *Manchester Guardian*, 5 November 1891.
67 *Manchester Guardian*, 4 November 1897.
68 *Manchester Courier*, 13 November 1882.
69 *Manchester Guardian*, 7 November 1885.
70 *Manchester Guardian*, 28 November 1897.
71 *Manchester Guardian*, 9 November 1900,
72 Calculated from *Manchester Guardian*, 26 November 1870; *Manchester Courier*, 14 November 1873; *Manchester Examiner*, 14 November 1879.
73 The Catholic vote for 1882 included that for an unsuccessful Land League candidate.
74 Patrick Doyle, 'Catholic electoral registration societies' (undated), Salford Diocese Archives, PB 293.
75 *Manchester Guardian*, 15 October 1889.
76 Acta of Bishop Bilsborrow, 10 November 1894, Salford Diocese Archives.
77 *Manchester Guardian*, 8 November 1894.
78 Acta of Bishop Bilsborrow, 30 October 1894, Salford Diocese Archives.
79 Anon., 'Catholic United Effort', *The Harvest*, 10:112 (1897), pp. 9–10. Unless otherwise indicated, articles in this journal are anonymous.

80 Acta of Bishop Bilsborrow, 6 August 1900, Salford Diocese Archives.
81 'The Salford Registration Association: Objects, Constitution and Rules', p. 3, Salford Diocese Archives, 181/3.
82 *Manchester Guardian*, 9 January 1873.
83 *Manchester Guardian*, 31 January 1874.
84 *Manchester Guardian*, 17 January 1882.
85 *Manchester Courier*, 17 January 1882. This was an accurate prediction, since both Bright and Slagg were defeated in 1885, though whether the Irish were solely responsible for this was very doubtful, since there was a national swing to the Conservatives.
86 *Manchester Guardian*, 21 and 29 September 1883.
87 Vincent Comerford, 'Isaac Butt and the home rule party, 1870–77', in W.E. Vaughan (ed.), *A new history of Ireland*, vol. 6: *Ireland under the Union, II: 1870–1921* (Oxford: Oxford University Press, 2010), pp. 8–9; Philip Bull, 'Isaac Butt, British Liberalism and an alternative nationalist tradition', in D.G. Boyce and R. Swift (eds), *Problems and perspectives in Irish history since 1800: essays in honour of Patrick Buckland* (Dublin: Four Courts Press, 2004), pp. 147–63.
88 *Manchester Guardian*, 18 June 1885; *Manchester Courier*, 11 November 1885; Moore, *The transformation of urban Liberalism*, chap.1: 'The rise of Manchester radicalism', pp. 44–5.
89 *Manchester Guardian*, 1 July 1886.
90 *Manchester Guardian*, 9 October 1891. The Irish National League is being referred to. The Conservatives held the seat with a drastically reduced majority. The Liberal candidate was C.P. Scott, editor of the *Manchester Guardian*.
91 Leo McKinstry, *Rosebery: statesman in turmoil* (Murray: London, 2005), pp. 307–10.
92 *Catholic Herald*, 23 March 1894.
93 Peter Henderson, 'Manchester, an Irish grandfather and some letters from the 1800s', *Manchester Genealogist*, 30:1 (2003), pp. 31–38.
94 *Manchester Guardian*, 8 January 1896.
95 *Manchester Guardian*, 8 May 1902.
96 *Manchester Guardian*, 19 May 1902.
97 *Manchester Guardian*, 18 March 1904.
98 *Catholic Herald*, 25 March 1904.
99 *Manchester Courier*, 6 March 1906. Bishop Casartelli, son of a Manchester Italian family, had succeeded Bishop Bilsborrow in March 1903.
100 *Manchester Guardian*, 6 March 1906.
101 *Manchester Guardian*, 4 June 1906.
102 Peter Doyle, 'The Catholic Federation 1906–1929', in W.J. Shiels and D. Wood (eds), *Voluntary religion* (Oxford: Basil Blackwell, 1986), p. 461; John O'Dea, 'The Catholic Federation: The mighty protest at Belle Vue', *The Harvest*, 19:230 (1906), p. 243.
103 *Manchester Courier*, 15 October 1906.
104 O'Dea, 'The Catholic Federation', p. 245.

105 John Cashman, 'The 1906 Education Bill: Catholic peers and Irish nationalists', *Recusant History*, 18 (1987), pp. 422–39; V. Alan McClelland, 'Bourne, Norfolk and the Irish parliamentarians: Roman Catholics and the Education Bill of 1906', *Recusant History*, 2 (1996), pp. 228–56.
106 'The Catholic Federation', *The Harvest*, 19:227 (1906), p. 209.
107 'The Catholic Federation', *The Harvest*, 19:229 (1906), p. 224; 'The Catholic Federation', *The Harvest*, 20:236 (1907), p. 103.
108 *Manchester Guardian*, 1 November 1921.
109 Doyle, 'The Catholic Federation', pp. 461–76; Steven Fielding, *Class and ethnicity: Irish Catholics in England 1880–1939* (Buckingham: Open University Press, 1993), pp. 114–18.
110 *Manchester Guardian*, 18 March 1907.
111 *Catholic Herald*, 21 March 1908.
112 Martin Broadley, *Louis Charles Casartelli: a bishop in peace and war* (Manchester: Koinonia: 2006), pp. 178–85.
113 *Manchester Guardian*, 23 April 1908.
114 *Manchester Guardian*, 25 April 1908; Randolph S. Churchill, *Winston S. Churchill: young statesman 1901–1914* (London, Heinemann: 1967), p. 259. Churchill was elected for Dundee on 9 May.
115 *Manchester Courier*, 25 October 1910.
116 *Manchester Guardian*, 10 January 1910.
117 *Manchester Guardian*, 23 December 1909.
118 Broadley, *Casartelli*, pp. 185–6.
119 *Manchester Guardian*, 14 December 1918.
120 *Manchester Guardian*, 28 October 1918.
121 *Manchester Guardian*, 20 October 1919; *Catholic Herald*, 25 October 1919.
122 Fielding, *Class and ethnicity*, pp. 103–4.
123 *Manchester Guardian*, 12 April 1920.
124 Fitzpatrick, 'The Irish in Britain', p. 681.
125 Minute Book of the Shamrock Hall Branch of the Irish Democratic League, 15 March 1904, author's private collection.

# 7

## Fenians, martyrs and memories

Though the 1848 rising had been a military failure, the episode had revived the violent, underground separatist tradition in Ireland and the diaspora. This was to be taken up by subsequent generations, to run in parallel, and interact with, conventional electoral politics. From the late 1850s to the early 1870s the Fenian movement would retain a fair amount of support in Ireland and Britain, especially after the Manchester Martyrs incident of 1867, which was to become the most enduring public commemoration in the nationalist tradition. The incident would become a contested event, with ownership and meaning constantly disputed between the constitutional and separatist traditions, not least in Manchester itself, especially towards the end of the period.

### The Fenian movement in Ireland and Britain

James Stephens had been involved in the Confederate Clubs and the skirmish at Ballingarry in July 1848 and subsequently fled to Paris, where he made a living as an English teacher and came into contact with other Irish refugee veterans of 1848 and the French republican opposition to Louis Napoleon's Second Empire. After returning to Dublin in 1855, he embarked on a tour of the country to collect material for a book, made a living as a French tutor and moved in advanced nationalist circles.[1] On St Patrick's Day 1858, he founded what eventually took the name of the Irish Republican Brotherhood, financed by funds from militant Irish-Americans. Later he travelled to New York and with others set up the American equivalent of the IRB, which, under the inspiration of the Irish-language scholar John O'Mahony, took the name of the Fenian Brotherhood, after the Irish *fianna* ('soldier').[2] The name soon became attached to the entire organisation on both sides of the Atlantic, fusing a variety of pre-existing separatist groups into a single movement. The basic local unit was a 'circle' of about ten members, led by a 'head' who alone knew the identity of his link with the next level of the hierarchy. This was intended as insurance against infiltration and leakage of information, though in fact the movement was to be thoroughly penetrated by informers and government agents. Stephens as the overall head of the organisation was termed the 'Head Centre'. The result was an organisation which may well have merged historic Irish traditions of clandestine organisation with the conspiratorial groups, influenced by the Italian nationalist Mazzini, which Stephens had encountered during his sojourn in Europe.[3] Secretive and oath-bound, it was pledged to the establishment of an independent Irish republic by force of arms, if possible by alliance with any power likely to be at war with Britain. In many ways it can be distinguished from Young Ireland in terms of both aims and methods, but there was considerable continuity with the Confederate Clubs.[4]

Shortly after the founding of the IRB Stephens and Thomas Clarke Luby embarked on a recruiting tour of Ireland during spring and summer of 1858, during which the former displayed his flair for talent spotting and organisation.[5] After his sojourns in the USA and then Paris between late 1858 and early 1861, Stephens returned to Ireland. During his absence the movement had spread widely, recruiting particularly amongst young artisans in the Dublin region and the country towns. Some were undoubtedly attracted by the social camaraderie involved in any such organisation, but others were probably drawn by the flattery and thrill of belonging to a secretive organisation, and some by the exciting prospect of taking part in military action at some point in the future.[6]

Whilst nationalist activity at this stage in Irish history was generally at a low ebb, the Fenians were by no means the only group trying to tap into what popular national sentiment did exist. It was one of the key features of the movement that it could channel such diffuse latent feelings and infiltrate or disrupt competing organisations. As noted earlier, in March 1861 the National Brotherhood of St Patrick had been founded dedicated to the celebration of Irish nationality, the education of the people in its literature and history and the organisation of social events with a nationalist theme, especially on St Patrick's Day. On the Confederate model, reading rooms were set up furnished with Irish newspapers and literature, and meetings were organised: talks were given on aspects of Irish culture, particularly history, debates were held, and Irish language classes were offered. Current affairs in Ireland were publicised and funds raised for causes such as the tenants evicted in a series of incidents in Co. Mayo in early 1861. But the main achievement was probably to help bring together the politically conscious Irish after a period of political quiescence. Lancashire was a particularly notable stronghold, with thirty branches at its peak.[7] From the outset the National Brotherhood was deeply penetrated by Fenians, and as time went on their influence was to grow.

In late 1861 there was a vivid illustration of what would become the Fenians' unsurpassed talent for theatrical political propaganda. In January Terence Bellew McManus, who had been active in the 1848 rising and had been sentenced to death, later commuted to transportation, died in San Francisco and was initially buried in a local cemetery. At Fenian prompting the body was exhumed eight months later; it was shipped to New York and thence to Cork and finally to Dublin in a series of increasingly elaborate corteges orchestrated by local Fenians. An estimated 30,000 came to view the body during the seven days when it lay at the city's Mechanics' Institute and the climax was an enormous funeral procession to Dublin's Glasnevin cemetery in November 1861, when the police estimated there were 8,000 in the cortege and 40,000 spectators. Archbishop Cullen of Dublin had forbidden his priests to participate but nine clergy from elsewhere were present, including Fr Lavelle of Partry, Co. Mayo, who gave an impromptu oration. The event added enormously to the Fenians' prestige and confidence, since it was widely known that they had been responsible for the entire project. A meeting of sympathy in Manchester attracted over four thousand Irish; at this point the National Brotherhood of St Patrick was probably at its height in the city.[8]

But thereafter the Fenians were to come under increasing pressure, both external and internal. Whilst at the local level some individual Catholic priests such as Lavelle were sympathetic to the movement, from the outset the Catholic Church was deeply suspicious and eventually came out in strong opposition.[9] This antipathy was due to a mix of historic and contemporary concerns. The atheistic excesses of the early stages of the French revolution and opposition to all oath-bound organisations, including the Masons, made church authorities wary of any organisation with a secretive revolutionary ethos. Moreover, the Fenian belief in the separation of church and state called into question the Irish hierarchy's aspiration to be the dominant source of mores and morals in any self-governing Ireland.[10] Consequently, in spring 1862 Cullen made membership of the National Brotherhood of St Patrick a reserved sin, and in August 1864 the Irish hierarchy specifically named and condemned it. Lancashire clergy followed suit, and thereafter the organisation suffered from their increasingly severe strictures. It was also true that Stephens, always suspicious of any development which might divert attention from the core aims of the IRB and his leadership, became increasingly antagonistic. Under these combined pressures the Brotherhood went into decline and by 1865 had totally collapsed. However, it had succeeded in raising the nationalist consciousness of the Irish in Britain, facilitated networking amongst those who were politically active and laid the foundation for north-west England to develop into the best-organised Fenian district in Britain, with entire local branches reborn as Fenian clubs.[11]

In late 1863 Stephens took the extraordinary decision for a secret society to launch a newspaper, and *The Irish People*, based in premises within easy walking distance of Dublin Castle, was published weekly from 23 November until its suppression in September 1865. Whilst circulation was around a modest eight thousand, it served as a useful tool for propaganda and a source of information for members and sympathisers, proving especially influential amongst the Irish in Britain. It proved equally convenient for the authorities, who, when they raided the premises on 15 September 1865, were able to seize the presses and a vast amount of documentation. Leading organisers and contributors were arrested the next day.[12] By early October, 187 leading Fenians were in custody in Britain and Ireland. Stephens was arrested on 11 November; he escaped thirteen days later and made his way to Paris in March 1866 and New York in May. By now the movement had spread widely in Ireland and amongst the Irish in Britain, especially in the north-west and amongst the Irish in the British army. There was also a steadily building expectation that there would be a rising in Ireland in the not-too-distant future. However, in December 1865 Stephens had persuaded leading members that the time was not yet ripe, and plans for a rising were postponed. In the next few months there were two further postponements, and latent strains in the movement surfaced in a fatal series of schisms.

In the USA there had been growing impatience with what some regarded as a loss of focus and a diversion of effort into projects such as *The Irish People*. Some elements argued that the American Civil War, which had been raging since April 1861, had brought Britain and America close to hostilities on a number of occasions, especially in November and December 1861, and that these were exactly the opportunities which the Fenian movement should be exploiting. Others were irked by Stephens' dictatorial and conspiratorial outlook and his paranoid suspicion of possible rivals. The Union victory in the Civil War in April 1865 saw the demobilisation of large numbers of Irish-Americans with Fenian sympathies, who drifted across the Atlantic to Ireland and Britain, there to await the signal for a rising. Increasing amounts of funds also found their way across the Atlantic, and the combination led to a steady build-up of expectations in both Ireland and the USA and growing alarm on the part of the British authorities. By October 1865 a third Fenian convention had adopted a policy of immediate military action against Canada in the hope of provoking war between the USA and Britain, a sure sign that Stephens and his allies were losing control of some elements of the American movement. This was confirmed in December 1865 when two rival camps emerged, one led by John O'Mahony, which remained loyal to Stephens, and another led by William R. Roberts, which became known as 'the senate wing' in reference to the constitution it devised for an Irish republic, including a senate modelled on the American model. In mid-June 1866 a series of raids into Canada, sponsored by both groups, were mounted, and, despite the defeat of Canadian militia units at Ridgeway in Ontario, were easily contained without any lasting

15 'Colonel' Thomas J. Kelly, 'Head Centre' of the IRB, rescued from the police van with Timothy Deasy; photograph possibly from the late 1860s

damage to Anglo-American relations.[13] When Stephens arrived in May he assumed leadership of the group which had followed O'Mahony but was shunned by the Roberts organisation. In a series of public meetings he declared the intention to launch a rising in Ireland later in the year, but in early December, realising that the resources and support for such an effort did not exist, he announced another postponement and at the end of the month was replaced as head of the Fenian movement by the Galway-born 'Colonel' Thomas J. Kelly, a former officer in the Union army (Figure 15). Stephens was effectively to be shut out from Fenian affairs for the rest of his life.

Kelly travelled to London, where on 10 February 1867 a 'provisional government of the Irish Republic' was set up and he was declared acting chief executive. A plan for a raid on Chester Castle on 11 February to seize the contents of the arsenal and ship them to Ireland was by now well advanced, and by the appointed date over a thousand Fenians had made their way to the city. However, at the last moment it was discovered that the scheme had been betrayed and the attack was called off. The rising in Ireland was now set for 5 March, but the result was a scattered series of small skirmishes of no military significance which flared on and off for a series of weeks in March and April before dying away. The enterprise had been fatally compromised from the outset by factionalism, procrastination, absence of military strategy and leadership, lack of arms, vigorous action by the authorities, large-scale penetration by informers and government agents and bad weather. The collapse of the projects in Ireland and at Chester had combined to drain much of the energy and morale from the movement, but events were soon to show that Fenianism as both an idea and a movement was far from dead.

On 17 August at a secret meeting of about three hundred delegates in Manchester, Kelly was confirmed as chief executive or 'Head Centre', and efforts were made to devise an administrative structure for the movement. At the conclusion of the meeting, Kelly and Timothy Deasy, another Union army veteran, who had commanded a Fenian unit in Cork during the recent rising, remained in Manchester to deal with some Brotherhood business. Late on 10 September they called at a second-hand clothes shop in Oak Street, near Smithfield Market on the north side of the city, which was used for IRB business. However, the place was under surveillance and when they left they were stopped by the police, found to be carrying revolvers and arrested. At the police station they gave the names John White (Kelly) and Martin Williams (Deasy). Following the first court appearance they were remanded for a week, but the notorious informer John Joseph Corydon was in the city and quickly identified them. The

*Guardian* almost seemed pleased to report that 'the two men who were apprehended on Smithfield market … prove to be Fenians of some consequence'.[14] In IRB circles the arrests were seen as a heavy blow, and plans were quickly made for a rescue.[15] The next court appearance was set for 18 September, when it was planned to ambush the police van on its way back from court to Bellevue jail on the north-eastern side of the city. The actual site selected for the ambush was the point where the railway crossed Hyde Road on an archway. Stones were stockpiled nearby and IRB members were instructed to wait in nearby public houses.

## The Manchester Martyrs

Rumours of some sort of incident had been circulating and the authorities took extra precautions. Police Sergeant Brett, a regular attender at court proceedings, accompanied the van carrying the prisoners as usual, though on this occasion he travelled inside the vehicle carrying the prisoners, with an extra five constables on the outside and a further four following in another vehicle. None were armed. As the van passed under the archway at about 4.00 p.m., it was halted by an armed man, who shot the horses. A crowd estimated at about thirty or forty men with axes, stones and revolvers appeared, scattered the police with pistol shots and formed a cordon between the van and the following cab. Whilst they kept the police and a gathering crowd at bay, wounding two constables and a civilian, others tried to break open the van, but had no success until a shot was fired into the lock, mortally wounding Sergeant Brett in the process. A prisoner took his keys and handed them through a vent to the attackers, who opened the doors and freed Kelly and Deasy. They fled across nearby fields, hid out for a time in local houses and eventually made their way to the USA. The attackers scattered across the nearby brick fields and through the streets, pursued by the police and some of the crowd. The affairs had lasted about thirty minutes.[16]

Whilst the Fenian movement rejoiced at the audacity and success of the rescue, the same qualities provoked shock and anger in Britain. The word 'outrage' constantly recurred in editorials: 'No more lamentable event than this has troubled the heart of England for many a day … for many years no event has so agitated the mind of England.'[17] Another editor declared, 'The indignation – we were going to say alarm – was universal and profound.'[18] The suppression of the *Irish People*, the suspension of Habeas Corpus, the numerous arrests and the total ineffectiveness of the March uprising had led the authorities to conclude that the back of the 'Fenian threat' had been broken. Consequently, the incident at Manchester came as something of a bolt from the blue, and the killing of the well-known and respected Sergeant Brett provoked a panic that the entire social order was under threat. Manchester Corporation offered a reward of £200 for the arrest of Brett's killers, and the government put up £300 for the recapture of Kelly and Deasy. Extensive police raids were carried out in the city's Irish districts, houses were searched, and eventually sixty-two people were arrested. The sense of outraged panic was well expressed by the *Guardian*, which, having listed the thirty people arrested in the first sweep, continued:

> Most of the prisoners are of the lower class of Irish, of imperfect or no education, and out of employment … most of the men who have taken part in this outrage give local addresses. We believe that until this outrage the police had very little idea that the Fenian movement had many promoters in Manchester. The miscreants who attacked the police van on Wednesday will only be a very small portion of what is now feared are a very large body of sympathisers with the Irish sedition. The Ancoats district and 'Little Ireland' contain the majority of the Irish element of Manchester; but so quietly have the discontented residents in those and other parts of the city conducted their meetings the police had little or no information whatever as to the numbers who are supposed in any way to have been connected with the Fenian movement.

An editorial in the same edition drove home the point: 'It is when we find that, in our own industrious and outwardly peaceful cities, widespread political conspiracy can be organised with perfect secrecy and carried into execution with the hardihood displayed in some recent instances, that the real strain upon our credulity begins. The striking illustration just afforded in Manchester of the active existence of this sort of thing in the midst of English society must awaken every honest and intelligent mind.'[19] The *Courier* was not to be outdone in condemnation of what it described as 'a Fenian outrage of the most serious nature … It is evident that the importance of the Fenian conspiracy has been seriously underestimated'; it suggested that the police had not been armed because 'The people of this country are … so habituated to obedience to the law that the idea of arming the police never seems to enter the heads of the authorities.' It went on to castigate those of a 'liberal' disposition who argued that Fenianism was a reaction to British misgovernment of Ireland and asserted that the movement 'bears upon it the marks of its Transatlantic origin in the shape of the vilest rowdyism, and the greatest carelessness of human life.'[20] In a subsequent edition it took a sideswipe at two old foes when it condemned a statement of the Bishop of Salford as inadequate: 'Irish Roman Catholics appear to be doing their utmost to convince the people of this country that their faith is synonymous with disloyalty to the English crown.'[21] In fact Bishop Turner's pastoral had condemned 'the deplorable deed which is now under magisterial investigation in Manchester', seeing it as symptomatic of what he described as 'the lawless spirit of disobedience, insubordination and independence which is spreading through Europe', and he had reminded the clergy of their duty to instruct their flocks on 'the sinfulness of belonging to any of those secret and illegal organisations which are bound by oaths' and pointed out that church teachings 'do not allow you to administer the sacraments to those who obstinately adhere to them'.[22]

The wildest rumours now circulated about future Fenian plans, including a rising to coincide with any future trials, attacks on gasworks to darken the streets and facilitate further disturbances and arson in warehouses and docks. Local authorities throughout the country hurried to strengthen security. The governor of the city jail informed the Manchester Council that he did not think the premises sufficiently secure to hold the prisoners recently lodged there, warders were quickly reinforced by troops, and plans were made to install telegraphic communication between the jail, courts, police stations and town hall.[23] Local leaders hurried to emphasise that firm measures would be taken. At a meeting of Manchester Council on 26 September a councillor declared that these would demonstrate that everyone was 'determined to do their duty, and to put down such outrage at whatever cost', but speakers were also at pains to reassure themselves and the public that such disloyalty was the exception, even amongst the Irish. The veteran radical alderman Abel Heywood declared that:

> He separated altogether the working men of Manchester and a very large proportion of the Irishmen in the city from those who participated in the recent outrage. It had been to him the greatest pleasure within the last twenty or twenty five years to witness the gradual absorption as it were of the Irish portion of the population with the general community, and to observe their adoption of our law and satisfaction with our institutions … He could not think excepting with regard to … a few misguided men, there was any conspiracy within the city of Manchester which embraced any large section of the Irish population (Hear, hear). He could not for a moment believe that any Englishmen that were to be found either in Manchester or its outskirts had the slightest sympathy with such an effort, and therefore that though they might regret the violent and ruthless attack upon the officers of the law, they might take credit in believing that they only had to deal with and lament the existence among them of a few misguided men. He made these observations to prevent, if possible, the spread of the fear and alarm which appeared to prevail.[24]

It was against this background hat the funeral of Sergeant Brett took place on 29 September. It was the occasion for a large-scale display of public grief and anger. The mayor and corporation were present, the procession was over a mile long, and it was estimated that over fifteen thousand spectators lined the route. The inquest on 9 October returned a verdict of 'wilful murder against William O'Meara Allen and others'.[25] The trial was set to begin on 28 October, and security precautions became increasingly elaborate. Police were armed with cutlasses and firearms, a stock of revolvers was gathered in the town hall, and army units were moved into the city.[26] These included a troop of the 10th Hussars and 41 men from the Royal Horse Artillery with two nine-pounder Armstrong field guns. An additional 100 gunners with two field guns followed, plus 700 men of the 72nd Highland Regiment.[27] A special meeting of the city justices passed a resolution rendering all citizens on the city roll liable to be sworn as special constables, and eventually over 2,000 were recruited.[28]

The trial proceeded under a Special Commission as authorised by the Treason Felony Act passed at the height of the multiple anxieties of 1848. Under this any person proven to have been involved in the planning or execution of an offence was as guilty as those who actually carried it out. The commission was presided over by judges Blackthorn and Mellor, and the prosecution was led by the Attorney General, Sir John Kerslake, accompanied by two QCs and two junior counsel, an indication of how seriously the government viewed the case. Four lawyers represented the main defendants. In all there were 23 men to be tried; 57 witnesses were listed for the prosecution and 105 for the defence, and 23 jurors were empanelled.[29] The trial took sixteen days, the sittings usually lasting from 9.00 a.m. to 6.00 p.m., but sometimes longer. On 2 November the jury retired at 6.15 p.m. and returned after eighty minutes to give verdicts of guilty of murder on William Allen, Michael Larkin, Michael O'Brien (tried as William Gould), Thomas Maguire and Edward Shore (actually Edward O'Meagher Condon). All were sentenced to hang in public at the New Bailey prison on 23 November. The condemned spoke from the dock, Gould ending with the cry 'God save Ireland', which was taken up by several others. Of the remaining accused, eight were released without further indictment, one was acquitted of murder, two were found not guilty of murder but later found guilty of riot and assault by another jury, and seven were convicted of riot and assault and sentenced to prison terms.[30]

In Britain there was a widespread sense that justice was being served, but in Ireland it was generally expected that the death sentences would be commuted. In part this arose because there had been no executions for political crimes in Ireland since Robert Emmet in 1803, and the death sentences passed on O'Brien, Meagher and Patrick O'Donoghue for their part in the rising of 1848 had been commuted to transportation. These hopes were reinforced when it became clear that there was no credible evidence against Maguire, a serving Royal Marine, and on 13 November he was granted a royal pardon. Expectations of mercy were further boosted when on 19 November Condon's sentence was commuted to life imprisonment on the grounds of his American citizenship. But it was not to be. Sergeant Brett was a popular family man and devout Anglican serving in the heart of one of Britain's great cities, and his killing appeared an act of calculated defiance. Moreover, there had recently been considerable public alarm over violent urban crime and fears of social disorder. A campaign for mercy was launched, with support from some radical and intellectual circles in Britain and much more widespread sympathy in Ireland. Meetings and petitions were organised emphasising the youth and sincere political motivation of the condemned, but the government's steady refusal of clemency led to a build-up of tension as the execution drew near. Rumours circulated of desperate Fenian plots for another rescue under cover of widespread arson. Military units were deployed within and around the prison, the fire brigade was put on alert, local firms enlisted armed employees to keep premises illuminated and guarded, fires were kept burning on railway bridges on the night before the execution, and the mayor and magistrates remained on duty throughout the night, with the result that 'between midnight and six o'clock in the morning a walk through the streets produced the impression that the city was in a state of siege'.[31] Local Catholic clergy ministered to the prisoners and the families of Larkin and Allen were regular visitors.

To make the hanging visible to the public a section of the outer wall of the New Bailey prison was removed and a platform supporting the three gibbets was inserted. Large crowds of spectators gathered behind barriers patrolled by police; whilst it was reported that 'generally their conduct might be said to be on the side of decorum' it was also noted that there was some jocularity, singing and banter with the police: 'all the public houses in the streets adjacent to the prison, more particularly where the barriers were erected, kept up a thriving trade, and many jovial characters broke from the bars'.[32] The executions took place shortly after eight in the morning of 23 November, when the corpses dropped out of sight to dangle in the pit beneath the scaffold. Allen appears to have died instantly, Larkin shortly afterwards, but Calcraft the hangman bungled the job and O'Brien lingered for about forty-five minutes, tended by a Catholic priest.

When it had become clear that the sentences were to be carried out, newspapers of contrasting outlook were at one. The *Manchester Guardian* declared, 'We know that they attacked the officers of justice, being well aware that the latter were acting under the direction of the magistrates and in the prosecution of their daily duties ... To the letter of the law they are entitled ... but we cannot regret if its most favourable interpretation affords them no refuge from the just consequences of their offence.'[33] For the *Manchester Courier* the moral was obvious: 'The tragic scene was enacted and a terrible lesson conveyed to the lawless and disaffected ... a violent and ignominious death on the scaffold ... the authorities refused to regard the crime as anything less than murder, pure and simple, and for this murder they have paid the penalty of the law.'[34] The episode entered local folk memory, became the subject of frequent reminiscence and was constantly recycled in publications feeding the growing popular appetite for lurid crime stories and also invoked by some as evidence of Fenian and more broadly general Irish savagery.[35] Barely a month after the Manchester executions an unsuccessful attempt to release Ricard O'Sullivan Burke, believed by some to be the organiser of the Manchester rescue, by blowing a hole in the wall of Clerkenwell prison in London killed twelve people, injured over a hundred and wrecked sixty houses in the surrounding working-class district. The episode served to reinforce popular anti-Irish prejudice and public panic.[36]

Reactions in Ireland were very different. Once again an act of the London government designed to impress both British and Irish public opinion as evidence of firmness alienated the Irish and stoked nationalist sentiment.[37] The episode resonated throughout the Irish world but especially in Irish migrant communities because it had occurred within the diaspora. To Irish nationalists the rescue was now seen as a gallant defiance of a harsh regime which had committed judicial murder; three very ordinary working-class Irish men were transformed into the 'Manchester Martyrs' and entered the pantheon of Irish nationalist heroes who had upheld the tradition of armed resistance and given up their lives for their country's freedom.[38] The process of transformation began immediately and was reflected in newspapers of varying outlook. Two days after the executions one Irish newspaper argued that if they had been English they would have been tried for manslaughter rather than treason felony. It described Allen and his companions as 'humble Irishmen ... [who] fearlessly suffered for a cause they believed to be true ... die they did, bravely, piously and silently'.[39] Under the emotive headline 'The Martyrdom at Manchester' another declared, 'three more of the "mere Irish" have been immolated on the scaffold in vindication of the great British dominion in Ireland. The bloody holocaust has been offered … [they] are thereby added to the long list of enthusiastic martyrs, whose memories are a rosary of sorrow and of hope hanging round the neck of beautiful Eire. The old weapon of English rule in Ireland, its most approved minister, is again in force.'[40] Another was angrily prophetic: 'No words can describe the feelings of horror and fierce resentment awakened in the hearts of the Irish people by that savage deed … [which] has produced an indelible impression in the minds of the Irish people … and its results will appear in many a long year of hate and strife between the two nations.'[41]

Various features of the episode readily lent themselves to popular propaganda. The actual morning of the executions was almost gothic. Temperatures were low and a thick mist built up as the time of the hangings drew near. Fog signals on the nearby railway periodically boomed and re-echoed, startling the crowds. The mere fact that this was a triple public execution lent an air of ghoulishness. The whole narrative lent itself to constant retelling since it had all the characteristics of the 'rattling good yarn' found in the lengthy episodic novels enjoyed by the contemporary reading public. It featured clandestine meetings of an oath-bound secret society, schemes and plots, accidental arrest, identification by an informer, dramatic rescue and escape, accidental killing, public panic and wild rumours, an elaborate treason trial, last-minute pardon and reprieve and finally three grisly public hangings. There were also lingering suspicions that there had been a miscarriage of justice. It was widely alleged at the time of the trial that Allen had fired the shot which killed Sergeant Brett, but rumours soon circulated that Peter Rice, who had certainly been amongst the attackers, was responsible.[42] The episode was a rich propaganda gift to the Fenian movement, and its impact was immensely amplified by the stream of songs and ballads which immediately flowed.[43] Of these, the best-known first appeared in the newspaper *The Nation* on 7 December 1867, just over a fortnight after the executions. 'God save Ireland', composed by T.D. Sullivan, brother of the proprietor, was based on Condon's cry from the dock at the end of his trial and sung to the tune of 'Tramp! Tramp! Tramp! The boys are marching!', a marching song of Union troops during the recently concluded American Civil War, in which many Irish had served and which had provided the military training of so many Fenians. It was an instant success, becoming the unofficial anthem of the nationalist movement, sung at the conclusion of Irish political meetings and many social events for several decades. Sketches of the attack on the van, the three men, the courtroom and the execution proliferated and were embellished in a vast stream of pamphlets, booklets and memorabilia. On 14 December 1867 one Irish newspaper argued that the men should be remembered by a memorial cross in the Catholic graveyard of every Irish town, and in March 1868 the first such monument appeared in Glasnevin cemetery, soon to be followed by others throughout the country. But within twenty-four hours of the executions other forms of commemoration had spontaneously appeared which were to endure.

## Commemoration and procession

The period from approximately 1870 to 1914 saw the various nation states of Europe undergo a process of remarkable reorganisation of their peoples and resources.[44] Parallel with this went efforts to define the nature and purpose of the dominant national ideology. Subaltern nationalities underwent a similar process, partly in response to measures introduced by the hegemonic power. As part of this trend there was a remarkable move to commemorate the national past. This was reflected in what has been termed 'banal nationalism', namely the display of instantly recognisable symbols on everyday items such as coins, banknotes, stamps and official documents and the display of the national flag on buildings and on official occasions. Currency and stamps in particular recall iconic heroic personalities, events and places. In their own quiet way these everyday features send signals about national identity, authority and legitimacy. But the trend was also reflected in a much more explicit public manner through commemorative monuments and ceremonies. In Ireland, as elsewhere, the four decades after 1870 saw a proliferation of such events and edifices. This was true throughout the country, but especially in Dublin, where the burgeoning nationalist movement responded to decades of monuments to British imperial heroes with memorials to prominent nationalists.[45] But of all the occasions and people remembered, the Manchester Martyrs episode was to become the most long-running event in the Irish nationalist tradition.[46]

In early December 1867 two newspapers reflected on a demonstration by Irish people in Manchester in support of the recently executed men. One was locally based, one was Irish, and both were gloomily prophetic about the long-term significance of what they witnessed. The *Manchester Examiner and Times* reporter noted the presence of both sexes amongst the participants and went on, 'Another remarkable contingent were a string of boys, apparently from some Roman Catholic school, nearly all of whom wore green neckties or green woollen comforters, and green badges on their arms. To an outside observer the reflection was irresistible that in these youthful processionists the story of recent Fenians was being fostered to trouble the next generation.'[47] The reporter from Dublin was so disturbed that syntax suffered: 'Probably the youthful element in the procession is the worst feature about it. Such a march, bedecked with green as they were, will be an inobliterable epoch in their young lives, and no lapse of time will be able to efface it – more especially as they seemed to glory in the demonstration.'[48] Both had recognised not merely how recent events would resonate in future years, but the role of such public events in transmitting their significance.

Public commemoration is a multi-dimensional event reflecting historic incidents and personalities endowed with particular significance by the participants. Deliberate selection is involved in all such commemoration and indeed in all nationalist versions of history. Such selective remembering, forgetting and revision[49] leads to the creation of what has been termed 'social memory'.[50] At the simplest level an act of commemoration is a regularly repeated gathering of people at an agreed location to recall an event, an individual or a group of people and their actions. There is undoubtedly a strong social dimension to such assemblies, involving like-minded friends, acquaintances and neighbours. There is an established formalised pattern to the occasions, which thereby imbues them with an air of reverential solemnity. Participants follow a formal structured series of acts with an orchestrated sequence of movement, stillness, spoken words and silence. The impact is amplified if the acts are regularly carried out in public space and if the participants are organised in orderly ranks, dressed in distinctive fashion, carry symbolic items such as flags, banners, placards or staffs of office or are accompanied by bands playing significant tunes.[51]

However, despite their apparent immutability, there is in fact a great deal of flexibility embedded within such events. At one level they have an air of ritual setting them apart from daily life to the point of liminality. But they must be organised, rehearsed, publicised and orchestrated. Their appeal is visual, auditory and almost spiritual in that the constant repetition of movement, speech and silence is strongly reminiscent of religious ceremony, and this may be reinforced by the participation of religious leaders. This multi-faceted appeal reaches out to bond spectators to actual participants, blurring the boundaries the two and creating a sense of total communal involvement. This is reinforced when regular repetition of the event at specific dates, times and places makes it a fixed and accepted feature of the cultural calendar.

A further duality arises from the combination of apparent rigidity with flexibility of interpretation. Ritual public events can be made to bear multiple meanings through the ages. At a specific time they may mean very different things to different social groups, but their meaning can also alter with time in response to political, socio-economic and cultural change.

The prime purpose of such gatherings is to recall events and personalities deemed worthy of remembrance. As such, they seek to connect the past with the present – and indeed it has been argued that such group commemoration is always conducted with an eye to the present.[52] At a basic level commemoration implies instruction, in that a moral is drawn from the incidents and personalities being recalled, along with implicit and sometimes spoken exhortation to follow their example in the present day. A sense of dutiful obligation is therefore imposed upon participants and observers. This reaching back to connect past with present implies continuity and therefore legitimacy. If a link can be made with a contemporary political outlook, then the implication is that it is valid and that the group is proceeding along the 'right' path.

Flexibility is also signified by the ways in which personalities and events can be selected for commemoration to justify contemporary attitudes and actions.[53] Conversely, awkward or embarrassing elements will be forgotten in a deliberate bout of convenient collective amnesia, and incidents and people will be viewed in a new light or quietly allowed to fade into the background, whilst previously obscure events and individuals will be highlighted, drawing out lessons designed to justify contemporary attitudes. However, as nationalist movements began to cohere in nineteenth-century Europe, some emerging national groups found that their historical raw material for commemoration was notably thin. In such cases a self-justifying heroic historical narrative was often deliberately devised and a process of 'invention of tradition' took place as events and persons were selected and endowed with all the necessary ritual and iconography designed to instil the desired aura of respect, reverence, age and legitimacy, whereas in reality much of it was of very recent manufacture.[54] However, such events will resonate with a population only if they are carefully crafted to converge with established patterns of behaviour and sentiment[55] and address the current situation of the group in a plausible and credible fashion.[56]

Processions have long been a key feature of commemoration, and they too are inherently flexible in that they can be employed by hegemonic groups to display their power and proclaim their values and by subaltern groups to present an alternative reading. Every feature of a procession, including participants, dress, behaviour, body language and the route followed, is designed to convey a message. For hegemonic groups such events are visual displays of how they believe society as a whole should be organised and structured.[57] The role of those excluded is to look on in deference, be impressed and learn.[58] Nation states quickly realised the value of such events, and from the earliest times processions were adopted as ideal means of publicly proclaiming national values and power relationships. Superficially it would seem that only hegemonic groups would be able to use this means of expression, but in fact there is a long tradition of carnival in Western Europe whereby for a short time alternative outlooks could be presented in jocular satirical form, thereby acting as a sort of safety valve for a specified period.[59]

But alternative processions can also be organised not merely as officially tolerated licensed naughtiness, but in outright defiance of hegemonic authorities. In such cases location and route become central issues. Marginal spaces where official authority is weak or traditionally disputed can provide one type of venue, but the performance of an alternative viewpoint is much more effective if staged in public spaces deliberately designed or adapted for public display. The central districts of large cities are ideal in that they contain the most prestigious buildings and with the passage of time have accumulated an air of historic significance in the civic life of the population. Moreover, in many cases they have been laid out or reshaped to provide long processional ways to accommodate public events and show off participants to best advantage. Even when streets and spaces were not designed with that purpose in mind, certain spaces and routes have often become accepted as the traditional routes for parades and public gatherings.[60] The mere occupation and use of such spaces by any group, hegemonic or subaltern, can be significant.

The roots of public processions in Europe lie in the annual July Corpus Christi processions of the Catholic Church. In time the parades of robed clergy with banners and symbols of office were joined by secular political leaders and representatives of local trade and professional guilds carrying symbols of their trade and status, thereby implying divine approval of the status quo.[61] The procession was quickly taken up as an ideal means of expressing the values and aspirations of the burgeoning nation states of early modern Europe, and official calendars of regular national celebration and commemoration soon developed.[62] In Britain the procession was also one of the traditional means by which those outside the formal political structure expressed their views.[63]

Though they could get out of hand at times, by the mid-nineteenth century the widening of the franchise, the development of municipal police forces and a shift in popular ideas on what constituted acceptable behaviour in public spaces combined to create almost a set of widely endorsed rules on behaviour, dress and deportment in public processions.[64] Any public demonstration would have to negotiate theses cultural ground rules and local traditions on the use of public space.

The Irish tradition of processions and parading also had its roots in

Catholic practice and demonstrations by trade guilds, but evolved in a distinctive pattern reflecting the country's history. By the early nineteenth century there were two elements within the Irish Protestant parading tradition. At the official level there was a series of dates marked by the ruling Church of Ireland elite, commemorating the establishment of their dominance and celebrating a narrative of terrible Catholic threat and timely providential deliverance.[65] But as noted earlier, the establishment and rapid spread of the Orange Order from the mid-1790s onwards led to a pattern of rowdy populist demonstrations on 4 November and, increasingly more frequently, on 12 July.[66] These often led to violent clashes with Catholic nationalists, resulting in the dissolution of the Order in 1836 and the ban on party processions and public display of party emblems.[67] As already noted, the Catholic tradition of religious parading was well established, but specifically political processions came relatively late and are somewhat under-researched, though the diasporic dimension, especially in North America, has received some attention.[68] The earliest nationalist political processions were organised by the early nineteenth-century Ribbon societies to protest about a mix of economic and political grievances. Although nominally secret, on occasion they held impressive public demonstrations and tended to use St Patrick's Day as an occasion for distinctly Catholic and nationalist demonstration.[69] They frequently clashed with the Orange Order, especially in Ulster, and the resulting deaths provided further opportunity for additional public demonstrations, thereby establishing the tradition of the funeral as a political demonstration.[70] 'Monster meetings' and processions with displays of flags, tableaux and emblems were significant features of Daniel O'Connell's campaign for repeal of the union in the early 1840s, and were powerful theatrical performances of 'nationalism without words'.[71]

Commemorative events are a political resource and opportunity. Advocates of a viewpoint can use such gatherings to explain their outlook and justify it as rooted in the values and traditions being celebrated on such occasions. Consequently, ownership of the right to organise the event is worth contesting. In the case of the Manchester Martyrs' commemoration in Manchester, the contending parties were Fenian sympathisers or 'advanced nationalists' and moderate nationalists, but the situation also created serious problems for the Catholic Church. As already noted, the conspiratorial violence of the IRB led the Irish hierarchy under the leadership of the formidable Cardinal Paul Cullen to issue outright condemnations of the movement and its front organisations such as the National Brotherhood of St Patrick.[72] In Salford diocese Bishop Turner had issued a pastoral letter on 3 October 1867 following the rescue of Kelly and Deasy, the shooting of Sergeant Brett and the police raids and arrests in the Irish districts of the city. In this he deplored recent events:

> especially as having happened in our neighbourhood and within the limits of the spiritual jurisdiction assigned to us. It pains us because it is the result of those … anti-Catholic principles which we deplore, and which have been applied to the supposed interests of a Catholic land, whose long borne sufferings are now winning the sympathy of the world; sufferings which can never be alleviated by lawless and sinful deeds … no one can be surprised that such a condition of affairs should produce wide-spread dissatisfaction in Ireland. Still, it can never justify such deeds or courses as those which we deplore … It is to be lamented that the adoption, by some, of these new and irreligious theories, so popular here, and their application to this case should have led to so great a crime.[73]

But it soon became clear that both the church and the moderate nationalists were going to have to accept the fact that there was a lingering well of sympathy for the executed men.

## A tradition invented

The organisation of the rescue and escape of Kelly and Deasy indicated a degree of Fenian support in the area, and in the following fortnight two processions suggested that it extended well beyond a core of activists. The first procession took place on the afternoon of Sunday 24 November, the day immediately following the executions, and has the air of a spontaneous expression of indignation and anger. A crowd of about five thousand Irish gathered in the New Cross district on the northern side of the city. The crowd was composed of all ages and both genders, many wearing green ribbons, and it was noticed that 'The men were all very respectably attired, and conducted themselves with the greatest decorum.'[74] On the south-western side of the city another crowd gathered in Clopton Street in Hulme district and triggered an incident which sharply illustrated the unease of the Catholic Church. The assembly point was next to St Wilfrid's Catholic church, where Canon Toole, the widely respected parish priest, remonstrated with the organisers, trying to persuade them not to proceed. In this he was unsuccessful, but the starting point was moved into another street.[75] The procession formed up, led by a drum and fife band playing the 'Dead march' from *Saul*, and moved in a northerly direction across the city. It was joined by a contingent from Salford and those who had gathered at New Cross, and moved through the strongly Irish streets of Ancoats, passed the houses where the relatives of Allen and Larkin were staying, where men uncovered their heads and silence was observed, and returned to the starting point. It was estimated that 1,200 to 1,500 took part and spectators numbered 2,500 to 3,000. It was noted: 'Throughout the long route taken by the procession the demeanour of those who took part in it was quite orderly. Indeed the marked silence of the processionists gave to the demonstration ... something of the air and quiet of a funeral cortege. In fact, the procession turned out to be much of that nature.'[76]

The procession one week later was much larger and more carefully prepared. Leaflets printed on green paper with black edging appeared the previous week detailing arrangements for the event and exhorting participants, 'The utmost order is requested on the part of the processionists. Remember every improper act gives strength to the enemy.'[77] Clearly alarmed, Bishop Turner convened a meeting of clergy, who agreed to warn their congregations off the event. The address at St Wilfrid's on the morning of the procession followed the general pattern:

> We have heard with regret and anxiety that it is intended to have some kind of funeral procession through the city today ... We advise you, and beg most earnestly, that every person who has any influence in the matter, will make use of it to prevent the procession, and if it should go on, we entreat all of you who have any love for their religion, or for Ireland, or for those from Ireland who are in this country, that they will keep away from it ... It may disturb the peace of the town, because it may afford your mischievous or ill-disposed enemies to break the peace, and then you would be blamed, and would suffer for it. We shall leave the church open all the afternoon, and we entreat those who have a respect for the memory of the dead ... to come to the church and pray for them, instead of joining any procession.[78]

Despite these pleas, the event went ahead and attracted considerable support. The route followed by this procession appropriated the public space and traditions of the city for specifically Irish purposes, a combination of compromise and resistance. The starting point was Stevenson Square on the north side of the city, a traditional Manchester venue for public meetings associated with causes such as parliamentary reform, Chartism and trade union rights. It was also close to strongly Irish districts and the place where Kelly and Deasy had been arrested. The procession travelled in a south-westerly direction and crossed into Salford. As it passed the place of execution 'a demonstration of a singular character was made' in the most emotionally charged incident of the day. Two cabs carrying Allen's mother and fiancée and Larkin's family were drawn up beneath the scaffold site, and as the procession passed men bared their heads in response to shouted commands, many women wept, some sang the 'Litany for the dead', and cheers were given for the executed men.[79] This was to become a sacred site for the Manchester Irish.

Estimates of the number of people in the procession varied from 2,000 to 5,000, of both genders and all age and class groups, and there were also large numbers of spectators, altogether a considerable turnout in the face of the heavy rain and the strictures of the Catholic Church.[80] Observers were impressed by the respectable dress and quiet dignity of participants and onlookers and the striking presence of the colours black and green. Particular note was taken of the disciplined deportment and behaviour displayed: 'They were well marshalled by their leaders ... many of them were old men and women, who trudged along resolutely and with stern countenance; the children walked as though they were taking part in some notable solemnity... [they] dispersed in an orderly manner.' The only untoward incident demonstrated the degree of discipline and control exerted by the organisers. A spectator discovered that his watch had been stolen, but with the help of two plain-clothes police officers he seized the pickpocket. They in turn were assisted by a member of the procession, and when they tried to take their prisoner into the local town hall 'The Fenian procession opened up and formed a lane through which the police officers without further difficulty conducted the pickpocket into the lock up.'[81] Manchester Fenians had clearly succeeded in capitalising on the wave of sympathy for the executed men and organising it into highly effective public demonstrations and inserting these into the traditional public spaces of a city where popular feeling over the recent incidents was still running high.[82] In many ways it was a carefully crafted blend of deference to local custom and a defiant demonstration of Irish strength and sentiment, a technique used elsewhere in the diaspora.[83]

A survey of local newspapers reveals no further traces of public processions in memory of the martyrs in Manchester until 1888. From that year until 1921 there is evidence of processions commemorating the martyrs in twenty-four of the thirty-three years, and by the early 1890s the ritual had become part of the cultural calendar of the Manchester Irish and the city as a whole.[84] A definite structure quickly emerged. The date normally chosen was the Sunday closest to the execution anniversary of 23 November. Down to 1907 the procession formed up at New Cross on the northern side of the city and walked to St Patrick's church for Requiem Mass, followed by a public meeting, often in the parochial hall or the nearby Shamrock Hall of the local home rule club. From 1908 the assembly point was switched to Bexley Square in Salford and the procession proceeded to the execution site where it paused in silence and then moved on to St Patrick's (Figure 16).[85] With the passage of time all the significant Irish organisations in the city came to be represented,

# MARTYRS' SUNDAY

## THE ANNUAL
# Demonstration

In commemoration of the Manchester Martyrs will be held on
## SUNDAY, Nov. 30th

THE first assembly of the procession, headed by North-East Manchester Reed Band, will take place in Bexley Square, Salford, at 9 o'clock, so as to proceed through Bailey-Street, in memory of the execution, where a special halt will be made, and "Dead March" played; then continue via Bridge Street, Deansgate, Market Street, Oldham Street, to New Cross, where a re-assembly will take place, and start at 10 o'clock for St. Patrick's Church, Livesey Street, for 11 o'clock Mass, which will be offered up for the repose of the souls of Allen, Larkin, and O'Brien.—After Mass the procession will re-form in the Churchyard, and proceed along Rochdale Road, to the Shamrock Hall, and back by Reather Street, to the Parochial Hall, where a Meeting will be held.

The Panegyric will be delivered by

## J. T. Donovan, Esq.
(Barrister-at-Law and Secretary U.I.L. of Ireland).

Chairman - - J. P. BYRNE, Esq., P.L.G.

## ALL IRISHMEN AND IRISHWOMEN ARE INVITED.

*MARSHALS:*
Messrs. T. Dalton and J. McMahon.

*TREASURER:*
Mr. F. McCarley.

*SECRETARIES:*
Messrs. John Doyle, E. D. Crowley, J. O'Sullivan.

### "GOD SAVE IRELAND."

16 Details of the 1913 Manchester Martyrs commemoration

including not only local branches of the home rule organisation, but the Irish National Foresters, the Gaelic Athletic Association, the Gaelic League, the Ancient Order of Hibernians and Fianna Éireann.[86]

## The Catholic Church: caution and flexibility

Given the significance of the event in local Irish community life, both the Catholic Church and political groups had an enduring interest in ownership and control of its meaning. Despite its earlier strictures the Catholic Church realised from quite early on that there was considerable sympathy and admiration for the courage and patriotism of the three men. Indeed, there were requests and payments for Requiem Masses in several parishes of the Salford diocese as early as the first anniversary of the executions.[87] The church adopted the tactic of focusing on the Catholic faith of Allen, Larkin and O'Brien, their courage and their devotion to family and country. Procession organisers for their part ensured that Requiem Mass was always integral to the event, that St Patrick's parochial hall was regularly used for the public meeting and that a cleric was occasionally invited to give the address. The fact that all three had been members of an oath-bound secret society advocating violent rebellion was carefully passed over by both church and moderate nationalists.

The tone was set by the *Weekly Herald* of 23 November 1888, in which the front page was dominated by a flattering sketch of the three men and a lengthy piece of hagiography focusing on their manliness, fortitude and faith under duress (Figure 17). In a description of Allen's address from the dock it was reported, 'his eyes lit up with the fire of enthusiasm and determination', whilst in Larkin's case 'no want of resolution was expressed in his frim face', and as for O'Brien, 'His stalwart form seemed to dilate with proud defiance and scorn as he faced the ermine clad dignitaries.' Overall, 'As true Irishmen and as true patriots they had borne themselves. No trace of flinching did they give… They died as true Catholics and Irishmen should, professing their faith, and with a prayer for their country on their lips.' These safe and convenient themes were taken up at the homilies delivered during Requiem Mass and occasionally at the public meetings. In his 1896 homily Canon Mussely of St Patrick's referred to 'The unfortunate severity which cut short the promising careers of these young men' but was also careful to express relief that 'the bitterness of the strife was slowly departing'. The main speaker at the public meeting was Fr Cusack, president of the local branch of the United Irish League. After a reference to 'the misrule that murdered innocent men' he went on to eulogise each of them in turn. In Allen's case he stressed promise unfulfilled, 'a mere

17 The martyrs respectably and safely groomed and repackaged in 1888

youth …sent to a felon's grave long before his time'. In O'Brien's case he lamented the grief of his friends. When he came to Larkin he launched into a maudlin lament for a family man who left a wife and 'three helpless, fatherless children …Who was to care and labour for them … who was to step forth and take them in his arms when they called for father?' Conflating religious faith and patriotism, he compared their deaths to the sufferings of the martyrs of the early church: 'as martyrdom in the church's sense of the word is heaven's richest and rarest blessing, so I say without hesitation, that death in the cause of one's native land is heaven's next gift'. As for their politics, he adopted a tactic which was to become the norm for both clerical and political speakers at the event when he made a nice distinction between aims and methods: 'The means adopted by the men of 1867 I do not approve of. Their ultimate object, viz. the securing of just rights and privileges for Ireland I approve of with all my heart … I only wish that their spirit was the spirit of the men of today …

Their pure love for Ireland might well put to blush some here present.'[88]

On 27 November 1898 came the incident discussed earlier when Fr McCarthy blessed the foundation stone of the memorial to the martyrs in Moston cemetery, which was followed by a fiery public meeting addressed by Maud Gonne and the ageing James Stephens.[89] In the eyes of church authorities McCarthy was already suspect, hence his dismissal by the bishop in February 1899 despite local Irish objections.[90] The public meeting and resolutions which followed revealed the depth of Irish convictions that prejudice rather than fear of Fenianism was at the root of the problem, but the bishop did not yield.[91]

The lauding of the martyrs as devout family men and patriots seemed sufficient to gloss over the embarrassing political realities of 1867 and lingering Fenian sympathies. In 1900 Fr Flinn in his homily went so far as to totally ignore the political dimension and used the event as an opportunity to scold the congregation for neglect of their spiritual duties: 'It was a matter much to be regretted that the noble example of the Manchester Martyrs was not in these days followed by their countrymen as it should be. He spoke with no uncertainty when he said that many of those present on that occasion refrained from going to mass except on the Martyrs anniversary. He trusted that those would take to heart the lesson taught by the Martyrs in their love and devotion for their holy faith.'[92]

Another safe and well-worked trope was the injustice of the executions. In 1913 Fr Mackey argued that the incident had been an example of both injustice and persecution, and was somewhat carried away in his peroration:

> It might be said that these men had died murderers and rebels against lawful authority. They died on the scaffold it was true, but they knew they never murdered any man; they knew that the evidence on which they were convicted had been proved to be false. The character of the witnesses was such a thing that no other civilised judge would have taken it. Their trial was unjust, and a verdict on the evidence would have meant instant acquittal. The then government, animated by diabolical power, determined to sweep out from the land every attribute of faith in Ireland, and patriots rose up and died by the sword on the scaffold, and in the general slaughter. Every arm that was ever uplifted in the cause of Ireland was nerved and strengthened by the nation's faith.[93]

By this time it was also deemed safe and respectable for clergy to venerate the elderly survivors of the episode. In August 1900 the *Catholic Herald* profiled John Carroll, chosen as chief marshall of that year's Manchester procession. It outlined his involvement in the Fenian activities of 1867, including the rescue, his subsequent imprisonment, his release and his eventual return to live in Manchester. A copy of what Carroll described as his 'treasured memento', namely O'Brien's last letter from his prison cell, was reproduced and in reverential tones described him as likely to be 'One of the most interesting figures in the Martyrs' Memorial procession'.[94] When Edward O'Meagher Condon revisited the city in October 1909 he too was treated as an interesting historical curiosity and deemed perfectly safe to meet. Under the headline 'The Fenian's Return' it was reported how he attended Mass at St Mary's church, called at the presbytery and was 'entertained' by Fr. Walsh and Fr. Prendergast. Later that day he called in at St Patrick's, met Dean Hennessey and was introduced to the Bishop of Aberdeen. When he spoke at a public meeting in the Free Trade Hall in the afternoon, five clergy were on the platform.[95] In November 1914, when war had broken out and Redmond had committed the Irish Volunteers to full support of the British war effort, it was notable that during the public meeting after the martyrs' procession and Mass, the choir of St Patrick's sang both traditional Irish airs and the 'Marseillaise', a gesture of solidarity with the Allied cause.[96]

But when the commemoration came round in November 1916 some careful adjustment of clerical attitudes was clearly under way. The Requiem Mass was offered both for the Manchester Martyrs 'and for those who lost their lives in Dublin in Easter week'. Fr Maspero then proceeded to outline traditional church teaching on prayers for the dead and closed by reminding the congregation that it was incumbent upon them to keep the dead always in their minds and prayers, without specifying any particular group. At the subsequent public meeting Alderman Kenny made the customary link between the Manchester Martyrs and the lives of the saints.[97] The following year, in what reads like a carefully crafted address, Fr Wearden gave a lengthy exposition of Catholic doctrine on insurrection. Having described patriotism as 'the greatest natural virtue', he went on to warn that since such human sentiment could be flawed, the church had laid down certain conditions under which insurrection might be justified. Having outlined these, he turned to the Irish case. Here he acknowledged that the importation of arms by unionists in their campaign against the third Home Rule Bill might be construed as valid grounds for revolt since it threatened the lives and property of those who differed from them in politics and religion and had been tolerated by a government which went on to reward some of those concerned with high office. However, he reminded the congregation that as children of the church they should always follow its teaching and bear in mind what he claimed were the last words of St Patrick: 'As ye are Christians, be ye followers of the teachings of Rome.'[98]

There is no trace of a martyrs' commemoration in November 1918, possibly because the first general election since October 1910 was under way. The following year it was clear that a change of ownership was well advanced. In the morning of 23 November Mass was held at St Anne's church in the Fairfield district. That afternoon a procession consisting of members of the Gaelic League and Sinn Féin gathered in Stevenson Square, the first time the latter had been officially represented at the event. Headed by a pipe band, they walked to the martyrs' memorial in Moston cemetery, where the rosary was recited in Irish.[99] Of the moderate nationalists of the United Irish League there was no trace. By November 1920 it was clear that control had totally changed hands, and it was equally obvious that the church was adjusting its approach once again. It was originally intended that the commemoration would be subsumed into the inaugural convention of the ISDL, the organisation designed by Sinn Féin as the replacement for the United Irish League. On the Sunday morning following the convention the plan was for a procession to follow the traditional route and format, assembling at Bexley Square in Salford, walking into Manchester for Mass at St Patrick's followed by a public meeting in the afternoon. The Mass was to be celebrated 'for the repose of the souls of the Manchester Martyrs, 1916 Martyrs, Alderman McCurtain [sic], Alderman Terence MacSwiney and all who have died for Ireland', clearly confirming the apostolic succession of martyrdom.[100] The procession was banned by the authorities and cancelled by the organisers, but the afternoon meeting went ahead in St Patrick's parochial hall, which had been 'placed at the disposal of the organisers by Fr. Cassidy, P.P.'.[101] The following year the commemoration followed the traditional pattern, assembling at Bexley Square and proceeding past the execution site to S. Patrick's, where this time the name of Kevin Barry, the medical student recently executed by the British forces, was added to those remembered, before a public meeting addressed by the Cumberland-born Sinn Féin TD and ISDL organiser Sean Milroy.[102]

### Contesting ownership: moderate and advanced nationalists

Irish nationalists in Manchester were very well aware of the significance of this commemoration event, and they too shifted their attitude with the passage of time. Through most of the period the commemoration ritual was under the control of moderate nationalists, but they were always conscious of the appeal of the exciting events of 1867 and the lingering romantic appeal of the more advanced school of nationalism. Consequently, the public meeting after Mass was habitually used both to rally local Irish behind moderate nationalism and the parliamentary approach and to address current Irish issues. The result can be seen in a number of recurring themes taken up by guest speakers and on occasions some scarcely credible verbal gymnastics. One of the most frequent themes was an appeal for unity amongst all supporters of Irish self-government, regardless of their views on the eventual degree of self-rule. But there were additional reasons for this constant harping on the need for unity. For nine years after the fall of Parnell in 1891 Irish nationalists were split into two viciously warring factions, and even after reunification in 1900 bitter memories lingered and the prospect of old wounds reopening haunted nationalist leaders. In fact, total unity was never completely restored, with persistent small breakaway factions being led by William O'Brien and Tim Healy.

On occasion even the most impeccably moderate speakers made a pitch to militant sentiment in order to preserve solidarity in nationalist ranks. In 1896 Councillor Dan McCabe made a point of demanding the release of all remaining Irish political prisoners, doubtless with the intention of ensuring that the issue would not be captured by more extreme elements. He stressed how 'he hoped that although they might hold differing ideas, still all had the good of Irish nationalism at heart, and if they all worked unitedly for the cause of Ireland, her salvation could not be far distant'.[103] By 1899 it was clear that the parliamentary factions were moving towards reunification in the form of the new United Irish League, stimulated in part by the experience of joint involvement in the 1798 centenary celebrations. At the 1899 martyrs' commemoration event McCabe spiced appeals for unity with some notably militant language. There was a motion before the meeting calling for the support of all the Irish in Britain and Ireland on the grounds that 'by promoting unity among the people, [it] is preparing the way for the creation of a united, independent and honest Irish parliamentary party'. McCabe urged the need to forget 'the follies of recent years … Work together as in the good old days under Parnell'. The Boer War had broken out in early October and it was already clear that British forces, including many Irish regiments, were struggling against a surprisingly skilful enemy. McCabe declared that

> The only thing the English people understood was force, united force. They should never be respected until they could unite as the Boers were united (loud and prolonged cheers). They were a race and a people much smaller than the Irish, but still they had been able to give an account of themselves, because they were a united people, and a liberty loving people, and were desirous of protecting their own rights (cheers). They should take courage and heart from the example set by the united Boers (cheers).[104]

Following the reunification of the parliamentary party under Redmond in January 1900, Manchester's commemoration seems to have been even more firmly in the hands of moderate nationalists, who spoke with increasing confidence and assurance at the public meetings. Nevertheless, there were still appeals for unity in the face of any latent threat to group solidarity, and at times the rhetoric stretched credibility. In 1902 the meeting was chaired by F.J. Farley, a leading local nationalist, who set the tone when he said, to applause, that 'He had no hesitation in saying there were men in the hall that day who, if necessary, would gladly follow the steps of Allen, Larkin and O'Brien, in the interests and love of their country.' He was followed by John Murphy MP (Kerry East), who made an audacious effort to argue for continuity between Feniansim and the Irish party with some notable redefinitions. He argued that 'What the Fenian movement was in the past, the United Irish League movement was now, for it was animated by the same principles and had the same object in view. Fenianism meant love of Ireland, hatred of her enemies and a desire to set the country free. Parliamentarian though he was, he did not hesitate in saying, that they and he … should take pride now and always in being Fenian (applause).'[105] He also appealed for unity, acknowledging that there might be some who thought current efforts were not enough in terms of energy and aims, but went on: 'To these he would appeal … that when they could not do the best thing, to do the next best thing and join the national organisation in all their strength and in all their numbers and when the blow should be struck for Ireland … it would prove a united blow.' He ended with both a flourish and a qualification that 'They were ready to do as thousands had done before and die for Ireland', but then added that 'No such price was demanded of them listening to him in that hall. Unity and organisation were all that were necessary.'[106]

Since the mid-1880s Irish hopes for home rule had been pinned on the alliance with the Liberal Party, despite indications that some Liberals were less than enthusiastic over home rule. The 1906 election returned a Liberal government with a large overall majority, and as time went on some Irish nationalists became restless with the lack of movement on the issue. Others were uneasy at the Liberal policy of withholding finance for faith schools. Speakers at the commemoration were clearly aware of this impatience and took the opportunity to call for continued unity, reminding the audience that whatever their impatience over the issue of self-government, the alliance with the Liberals had yielded definite benefits to Ireland. In 1908 J.C.R. Lardner MP (Monaghan North) and John Muldoon MP (Wicklow East) reassured their hearers that home rule remained the priority for the party but that in the meantime it had made real gains, particularly in local government reform and, at long last, the provision of Irish university education acceptable to Catholics.[107]

This was the year in which the route of the procession was altered to begin in Bexley Square, Salford, proceed to the site of the execution, pause for silence and the playing of the 'Dead march' and then continue to St Patrick's. One can only speculate that perhaps the change of route to pass the execution site was designed to placate militant sentiment.

In early 1909 Manchester's moderate nationalists and indeed, the movement as a whole, played something of a trump card when an elderly Edward O'Meagher Condon, the great survivor of the 1867 events, returned from the USA and toured Ireland and Britain. In Manchester he visited the sites of that year, met local Catholic clergy as already noted and addressed a public meeting in the Free Trade Hall in the presence of clerics and representatives of nationalist organisations from all parts of the north-west. As if to seal his new-found respectability, he met Chief Constable Peacock, who was in the audience. Introducing Condon, councillor Dan Boyle adroitly linked him with the cause of moderate nationalism by stating that so long as Ireland was denied the right of self-government, 'so long would they stand by the principles of Captain Condon, by the principles of the Irish parliamentary party of today – knowing no other political masters – and responding to the call of no other political leader'. When Condon spoke he made it clear that, looking back, 'I have nothing to regret, nothing to retract, nothing to take back.' Having thus reminded everyone of his patriot credentials, he went on, 'Conditions have changed considerably, however, and instead of waiting for something to happen sometime ... you have resolved to work for Ireland and to use the best means available. The success which has been achieved exceeds anything I had thought possible from these means. We can congratulate heartily the members of the Irish party under their great leader Mar. Redmond.' He went on to list specific gains such as land and housing reform, old-age pensions and a Catholic university, noted how in the USA the Irish party was widely regarded as the vehicle of Irish aspirations and ended by stating that justice for Ireland 'could only be achieved by loyal support of the Party they had elected to represent them in the British parliament'.[108]

There was recognition that the emerging labour movement had the potential to make a significant impact on the political landscape. In 1901 there was an effort to reach out to this novel development when the main speaker at the rally was Edward McHugh of the National Union of Dock Labourers in Britain and Ireland. He declared that 'Whilst it was a good thing ... to die for a cause, it was better to live for it... living for it meant the glorification of the movement.' He claimed the Manchester Martyrs as pioneers of the rights of working men 'because, after all, the Irish question in its various forms was but an effort to secure for the producer the result of his toil'.[109] But it is also clear that for some the burgeoning labour movement was seen as a potential source of division and diversion of Irish political efforts. By late 1913 labour troubles in Dublin had escalated into a large-scale strike led by James Larkin's Transport and General Workers' Union. The conflict escalated, involving clashes with police, fatalities and a 'lockout' by employers orchestrated by the powerful businessman William Martin Murphy. There was extreme distress amongst strikers' families, and Larkin toured Britain to rouse support for the workers' cause. He visited Manchester twice in September 1913, but his most successful event was on 16 November, when he was accompanied by James Connolly, organiser of the union in Ulster, Ben Gillett of the National Union of Dock Labourers in Britain and Ireland and Bill Heywood of the American Industrial Workers of the World. They addressed what was described as 'a huge gathering … an extraordinary meeting' in the Free Trade Hall, where an estimated 10,000 people tried to gain entry, and received 'a tremendous reception'.[110] It is hardly surprising that when the usual martyrs' commemoration was held in the city a bare two weeks later, the main speaker, J.T. Donovan, the UIL Secretary, made a point of stressing that home rule was imminent and 'With reference to the Dublin trouble … asked the people not to allow any subsidiary interest to jeopardise their ideal – national self-government. (applause).' When a collection was taken for relief of distress in Dublin, the chairman made it clear that the money was being sent to the relief fund organised by the Catholic Archbishop Walsh of Dublin.[111]

By November 1911 two successive general elections had made the Liberal government dependent on Irish support and the House of Lords' veto on legislation had been abolished, thereby clearing the ground for a home rule bill. The main speaker at the Manchester commemoration that year was Thomas Scanlon MP (Sligo North), who attempted to claim continuity with the Fenians whilst simultaneously reassuring unionists and Liberals that home rule did not mean separation:

> it would be impossible to overstate what Ireland owes to Manchester and to the sacrifice of those men who gave up their lives in an unavailing effort for their country.… The people of Ireland did not want separation; they wanted the right of Irishmen on their own soil to manage purely Irish affairs – the same right as now enjoyed by the colonies. They wanted a measure that would be safe for the Imperial parliament and safe for the Empire … They wanted an Ireland in which the whole of the people would

be tied together and strengthen the union of this country with Ireland. They were not separatists.[112]

The actual tabling of the Home Rule Bill in April 1912 stimulated excited confidence in nationalist ranks, and this was reflected in that year's commemoration. In addition to the UIL, every significant Irish organisation in the city was represented, including the Foresters, Gaelic League, the Ancient Order of Hibernians and the Gaelic Athletic Association, though members of a hurling club struck a notably militant note with a wreath inscribed 'A Free and Independent Ireland: actions, not words, shall set free our native land'. Both Alderman Boyle, now MP for North Mayo, and William Redmond MP, the party leader's son, were clearly carried away by what Boyle described as 'the greatest of their meetings'. Possibly with an eye to the sentiments expressed on the Gaelic Athletic Association's wreath, he went on to declare that 'There was nothing of the old Fenian movement of which he was not proud'. Redmond proclaimed himself convinced: 'They were winning all along the line ... He offered no apology for the aims and ambitions of the Irish Fenians, he solemnly declared that had he been alive at the time he would not have hesitated to have fought for his native country.' He then went on to try and square the circle: 'They were endeavouring today by constitutional means to bring about precisely the same object.'[113]

One year later the home rule question had become highly inflamed in both Britain and Ireland. By mid-July 1913 the bill had twice passed the Commons and been rejected in the Lords, which meant one more circuit in the Commons before it would become law. In September 1912 more than 250,000 unionists had signed a Solemn League and Covenant to resist home rule 'using all means which may be found necessary', which had been followed in January by the formation of the Ulster Volunteer Force. But the main speaker at the November gathering, J.T. Donovan, was full of confidence, assuring an applauding audience that 'they would be celebrating next year the principle of the Irish people ... to manage and control the internal affairs of their country ... their principles had not changed and made no apology for Allen, Larkin and O'Brien, or their principles ... home rule was now only a matter of weeks'. The unionists and their recent activities he dismissed because 'they were not in earnest, and what they were trying to do was to bluff the British electorate.'[114] By November 1914 the commemoration took place against a very different background. World war had broken out, the Home Rule Act had been passed in September, though suspended for the course of the conflict, John Redmond had pledged the Irish Volunteers to fight for the Allied cause, and a split in their ranks had appeared. Of the 160,000 Volunteers it was estimated that 5,000 had broken away.[115] For Redmond the war was an opportunity to prove that Irish home rule and membership of the United Kingdom and British Empire were perfectly compatible. He also hoped that unionists and nationalists would be bonded by fighting for a common cause, that nationalist participation in the conflict would place a moral obligation on British politicians to confirm home rule when the war ended and that the war experience would help establish the basis of a modern Irish army.[116] All these undercurrents were on show in the Manchester commemoration. Councillor Charles Egan first expressed satisfaction that home rule was law and went on to argue that 'England was fighting rightly for the cause and recognition of the rights of small nations … He absolutely agreed with the Irish leaders being in the forefront to secure that the Irish people should take their full and fair share in the war. (Applause).' Councillor Loughrey of Liverpool paid tribute to the martyrs and was applauded when he made a point of expressing regret at the death of Sergeant Brett. He went on to stress a theme which constantly recurred in nationalist speeches at this time, namely Germany's treatment of Catholic Belgium: 'Belgium had much in common with Ireland, and the Irish with all their hearts extended their sympathy and unsheathed their swords in her defence (Cheers). The great struggle in Europe would end in the triumph of small nations, and in it Ireland had given the lead.'[117] Both speakers 'denounced what was described as the mischievous policy of the small anti-Redmond faction'. It was noted that the music at the meeting included not only the usual airs, but the anthems of the Allied powers, and one headline read 'Irish loyalty at the Annual Celebration'.[118]

The transformation of the political scene by the 1916 rising and subsequent events impacted strongly on these commemoration rituals. The Manchester speeches of that year were a blend of apology, defiance and desperation. One speaker noted that there had been no gathering the previous year but the organisers had decided it was right not to let the sacrifice of 1867 be forgotten. But he went on to say that 'They were not holding that commemoration in any sense of menace or defiance, nor did they want to obstruct in the slightest those who were prosecuting the war to a successful conclusion.' Both speakers went on to reassert their confidence in the parliamentary party and its stance: 'Mr. Redmond had declared the Irish position in regard to the war and with him were the Irish people still … Mr. Redmond had given life-long service to the Irish cause and the Irish party were men to be reckoned with. They would do credit to any country … The policy of Mr. Redmond was the only one by which they could get back freedom for Ireland.'[119] The sense of the political initiative slipping away was even more marked in 1917. For the first time since 1914 the procession was restored, possibly because it was the fiftieth anniversary of the executions. One speaker, J.P. Byrne, managed to be both apologetic and defiant about the event: 'They made no apology to anyone for holding it. But at the same time they did not want to hold it in any spirit of bombast or to aggravate the feelings of those amongst whom they lived.' Councillor Egan presented the traditional arguments for justice and self-government and linked them to an opaque exhortation to united resistance against unspecified opponents: '[He] pleaded for a more cordial understanding amongst Irishmen to let the common enemy see that God had given them intelligence and brains and that they intended to use them in the proper channel.'[120] This was the last Manchester commemoration to be under moderate control.

In 1919 the format of the event was notably different. Sinn Féin and the Gaelic League were the most notable participants, the Irish language was used, the UIL was entirely absent, and the focal point was the martyrs' memorial in Moston cemetery. By 1920 it was clear that ownership of the event had definitely passed to Sinn Féin. The intention had been to fold it into the launch of the ISDL, but the planned procession fell foul of the city authorities, who banned the proceedings, though the public meeting did take place. Moderate nationalists were invisible, save for a rather sad letter to a local newspaper in which the local UIL president dissociated them from a rumoured plan to sabotage Manchester's electricity supply: 'perhaps you will allow me to state that ... the United Irish League, the older organisation of Irishmen in the district, now as always stands for constitutional measures of reform, and dissociated itself entirely from any connection with the so called plot'.[121] The day's proceedings closed with 'A soldier's song', another indication of how Irish opinion had moved.

The following year the *Manchester Guardian* nicely summed up the shift of opinion with the headline 'An Old Martyrdom And A Modern Cause'. The traditional ritual was restored in all its detail – the procession assembled in Bexley Square, walked to the site of the executions where there was a reverential pause, went on to Mass at St Patrick's and then proceeded to a public meeting in the parochial hall. However, it was noted that in addition to the names of the Manchester Martyrs 'have now been added the names of Kevin Barry, Thomas McCurtain, Terence MacSwiney, as well as the Irishmen who fell in Easter week 1916 – and since'. In addition to his role as a TD and in the ISDL, Sean Milroy, the main speaker, was now an adviser to the Irish delegation then engaged in negotiations with the British government in London and shortly to sign the Anglo-Irish Treaty on 6 December. Exactly like so many of his predecessors in this event, he used the occasion to rally support behind the party leaders, indicating a readiness to negotiate on the Ulster question, but assuring the audience that 'Ireland's cause was in the hands of capable and trustworthy men, and when their talk had been concluded he believed that Ireland would have great cause for gratification that it was to these men she had entrusted her cause'.[122]

## Conclusion

In many ways the execution of the Manchester Martyrs and the tradition of commemoration which accumulated so rapidly was one of the most formative events in the development of Irish nationalism in the nineteenth century. It was significant at a variety of levels, not only for what actually happened, but for what contemporary and later generations made of it. One of its most significant features was the fact that it occurred in the diaspora. For Irish migrants around the world their Irish nationalism was usually compounded of personal memories and secondhand accounts of events in Ireland, but this was a clash between nationalists and British authorities in a migrant setting and, moreover, in one of the great cities of Britain itself. This enabled migrants to identify readily with the excitement of the rescue and the tragedy of the executions, and may explain why commemorative events sprang up so fast and persisted so long throughout the diaspora, thereby helping to bind the migrant Irish into the developing narrative of Irish nationalism.

The incidents and their commemoration helped keep alive awareness of the tradition of violent resistance to British rule. Since 1798 the efforts at physical resistance in Ireland in 1803, 1848 and 1867 had proved total military failures, but provided priceless material for a narrative of enduring struggle. The rescue of Kelly and Deasy from under the nose of the police was a notable coup which shocked and deeply embarrassed the authorities in a major British city. Moreover, the hangings added a further powerful emotional dimension to the impact and appeal of the episode and the wider cause, since they were the first executions of Irishmen for a political offence since the hanging of Robert Emmet in 1803. The sense of shock and outrage quickly transformed three rather ordinary young men into the newest members of the pantheon of Irish political martyrs, ideal material for the songs, ballads and political rhetoric which have echoed down the decades.

The regular commemorations of the events were an opportunity that no political group within the Irish nationalist movement could afford to neglect. The gatherings brought together the most politically conscious of the Irish migrant community and could be used to validate ideas on what constituted the nature, aims and methods of Irish nationalism. Hence the keen interest of the Catholic Church and its sustained efforts to both accommodate and steer the commemorations and the care taken by both moderate and advanced nationalists always to incorporate Requiem Mass into the ceremony. In the first processions of 1867 the presence and organising abilities of local Fenians is clear, but from the late 1880s down to 1919 moderate nationalists were clearly in charge. Nonetheless, the speeches at the public meeting which traditionally followed Mass reveal a nervous awareness of both the fissiparous tendencies of the nationalist movement and the ongoing appeal of an alternative outlook. The result could be some notable verbal contortions as speakers sought to justify peaceful means and contemporary policies with reference to a notably violent episode, and tried to keep the faithful in line during the long years when home rule seemed a distant dream and to paper over the occasional signs of strain thrown up by class, the Irish cultural renaissance of the early twentieth century and the lingering appeal of Fenianism. But the political transformation wrought by 1916 and its aftermath illustrated the inherent malleability of such commemorative events in that Sinn Féin was able to take over the occasion and adapt its every detail. In so doing it was able to insert a more confident and assertive form of Irish nationalism into the traditions and public spaces of the city. But by the early years of the new century there were also indications in Manchester that the new dimension of Irish nationalism was making its presence felt in the city.

## Notes

1 Marta Ramon, *A provisional dictator: James Stephens and the Fenian movement* (Dublin: UCD Press, 2007), pp. 57–62.
2 Desmond Ryan, 'John O'Mahony', in T.W. Moody (ed.), *The Fenian movement* (Dublin: Mercier Press, 1968), pp. 63–76.
3 Ramon, *Provisional dictator*, pp. 80–2; John Newsinger, *Fenianism in mid-Victorian Britain* (London: Pluto Press, 1994), pp. 23–4.
4 James Quinn, 'The I.R.B. and Young Ireland: varieties of tension', in F. McGarry and J. McConnell (eds), *The black hand of republicanism: Fenianism in modern Ireland* (Dublin: Irish Academic Press, 2009), pp. 3–4; Richard Davis, 'The I.R.B., a "natural outcome of young Irelandism"?', *History Ireland*, 16:6 (2008), pp. 21–3.
5 Desmond Ryan, 'James Stephens and Thomas Clarke Luby', in Moody (ed.), *The Fenian movement*, pp. 49–62.
6 Vincent Comerford, *The Fenians in context: Irish politics and society 1848–82*

(Dublin: Wolfhound Press, 1998), pp. 65-8, argues strongly for the significance of the social dimension in the movement, but somewhat overstates the case and downplays the ongoing romantic appeal of a diffuse but powerful sense of nationalism.

7  Gerard Moran, 'The National Brotherhood of St. Patrick in Britain in the 1860s', *Irish Studies Review*, 7:3 (December 1999), pp. 325-36; Gerard Moran, 'Nationalists in exile: the National Brotherhood of St. Patrick in Lancashire, 1861-5', in S. Gilley and R. Swift (eds), *The Irish in Victorian Britain: the local dimension* (Dublin: Four Courts Press, 1999), pp. 212-35.
8  Ramon, *Provisional dictator*, pp. 112-13.
9  Gerard Moran, *A radical priest in Mayo: Fr. Patrick Flavelle. The rise and fall of an Irish nationalist, 1825-86* (Dublin: Four Courts Press, 1994).
10  Oliver Rafferty, *The church, the state and the Fenian threat 1861-75* (London: Macmillan, 1999); Oliver Rafferty, 'The Catholic Church and Fenianism', *History Ireland*, 16:6 (2008), pp. 30-4.
11  William J. Lowe, 'Lancashire Fenianism, 1864-71', *Transactions of the Historic Society of Lancashire and Cheshire*, 126 (1976), pp. 156-85; William J. Lowe, *The Irish in mid-Victorian Lancashire: the making of a working class community* (New York: Peter Lang, 1989), pp. 189-201.
12  Matthew Kelly, '"The Irish People" and the disciplining of dissent', in McGarry and McConnell (eds), *The black hand*, pp. 34-52; Ramon, *Provisional dictator*, chap. 5: 'The Irish people'.
13  David M. Wilson, 'Swapping Canada for Ireland: the Fenian invasion of 1866', *History Ireland*, 16:6 (2008), pp. 24-7; later efforts in 1870 were even more ineffective.
14  *Manchester Guardian*, 19 September 1867.
15  The most generally accepted account has Edward O'Meagher Condon as chief organiser, though John Devoy, deeply antagonistic to Condon as a result of the byzantine feuding which came to characterise Irish-American Fenianism, credited Ricard O'Sullivan Burke with the role. See John Devoy, *Recollections of an Irish rebel* introduction by Sean O'Luing (Dublin, 1929; reprinted Shannon: Irish Academic Press, 1969), pp. 240-3.
16  These events unfolded in such a dramatic fashion and have been retold and elaborated to the point where the details in the many accounts vary, but the above has been compiled from John Denvir, *The life of an Irish rebel*, introduction by Leon O'Broin (Dublin, 1910; reprinted Dublin: Irish Academic Press, 1972) and Andrew Glynn *High upon the gallows tree* (Tralee: Anvil Press, 1967); for full details of the events and subsequent trials see *Manchester Guardian* and *Manchester Courier*, 19 September – 15 November 1867.
17  *Manchester City News*, 2 November 1867.
18  *Manchester City News*, 20 November 1867.
19  *Manchester Guardian*, 20 September 1867
20  *Manchester Courier*, 20 September 1867.
21  *Manchester Courier*, 21 October 1867.
22  Acta Primi Episcopi 1852-72, 3 October 1867, Salford Diocese Archives.

23 Borough Gaol Letter Books, March–September 1868, p. 61, MCLAD, M9/69/1/2.
24 *Manchester Courier*, 26 September 1867.
25 *Manchester Guardian*, 9 October 1867. Allen was one of those arrested in the police raids following the rescue.
26 *Manchester Guardian*, 25 September 1867.
27 *Manchester Guardian*, 28 and 29 October 1867.
28 *Manchester Guardian*, 28 October 1867.
29 *Manchester Guardian*, 29 October 1867.
30 *Manchester Guardian*, 2 November 1867.
31 *Manchester Courier*, 25 November 1867.
32 *Manchester Courier*, 25 November 1867.
33 *Manchester Guardian*, 23 November 1867.
34 *Manchester Courier*, 25 November 1867.
35 *Manchester City News*, 25 May 1918; *Manchester Evening Chronicle*, 19 September 1922; *Daily Express*, 2 November 1933; *Manchester Evening News*, 22 November 1935; *Manchester Evening News*, 27 June 1928; Harold Furness, *Famous crimes past and present* (no publication details), Greater Manchester Police Museum, file A6B, 'Fenians'; *Manchester Evening News*, 17 March 2008 – this last a much more sober account. See also Mervyn Busteed, 'Resistance and respectability: dilemmas of Irish migrant politics in Victorian Britain', *Immigrants and Minorities*, 27:2–3 (2009), p. 182.
36 Devoy, *Recollections*, pp. 240–1.
37 Mervyn Busteed, 'The Manchester Martyrs: a Victorian melodrama', *History Ireland*, 16:6 (2008), pp. 35–7.
38 Gary Owens, 'Transforming the martyrs: the Manchester executions and the nationalist imagination', in L. McBride (ed.), *Images, icons and the Irish nationalist imagination* (Dublin: Four Courts Press, 1999), pp. 18–36.
39 *Freeman's Journal*, 25 November 1867.
40 *The Irishman*, 30 November 1867.
41 *The Nation*, 30 November 1867.
42 Jack Doughty, *The Manchester Martyrs: a Fenian tragedy* (Oldham: Jade, 2001), pp. 267–8.
43 Mervyn Busteed, 'Songs in a strange land: ambiguities of identity amongst Irish migrants in mid-Victorian Manchester', *Political Geography*, 17:6 (1998), pp. 627–65.
44 Ian McBride, 'Memory and national identity in modern Ireland', in I. McBride (ed.), *History and memory in modern Ireland* (Cambridge: Cambridge University Press, 2001), pp. 8–9.
45 Yvonne Whelan, 'Monuments, power and contested space: the iconography of Sackville St. (Connell Street) before independence (1922)', *Irish Geography*, 34:1 (2001), pp. 11–33; Yvonne Whelan, 'The construction and destruction of a colonial landscape: monuments to British monarchs in Dublin before and after independence', *Journal of Historical Geography*, 28:4 (2002), pp. 508–33; Yvonne Whelan, *Reinventing modern Dublin: streetscape, iconography and the politics of identity* (Dublin: University College Dublin Press, 2003).

46 Owens, 'Transforming the martyrs', p. 32.
47 *Manchester Examiner and Times*, 2 December 1867.
48 *Freeman's Journal*, 4 December 1867.
49 Mervyn Busteed, 'Nationalism, historical geography of', in R. Kitchin and N. Thrift (eds), *International encyclopaedia of human geography*, vol. 7 (Oxford: Elsevier, 2009), pp. 255–60.
50 Neil Jarman, *Material conflicts: parades and displays in Northern Ireland* (London: Berg, 1997), pp. 5–8.
51 Dominic Bryan, *Orange parades: the politics of ritual, tradition and control* (London: Pluto Press, 2000), pp. 1–28.
52 Roy Foster, *The Irish story: telling tales and making it up in Ireland* (London: Penguin, 2001), p. 212.
53 Laurence M. Geary, 'Introduction', in L.M. Geary (ed.). *Rebellion and remembrance in modern Ireland* (Dublin: Four Courts Press, 2001), p. 14; Jasper J. Tjaden, 'The (re-)construction of "national identity" through selective memory and ritual discourse: the Chilean centenary, 1910', *Studies in Ethnicity and Nationalism*, 12:1 (2012), pp. 46–63.
54 Eric Hobsbawm, 'Introduction: inventing traditions', in E. Hobsbawm and T. Tanger (eds), *The invention of tradition*, Canto edn (Cambridge: Cambridge University Press, 1992), pp. 1–14.
55 Ian McBride, *The siege of Derry in Ulster Protestant mythology* (Dublin: Four Courts Press, 1997), p. 80.
56 Ian McBride, 'Introduction: memory and national identity', in Ian McBride (ed.), *History and memory in modern Ireland* (Cambridge: Cambridge University Press: 2001), p. 35.
57 Peter Goheen, 'Parading: a lively tradition in Victorian Toronto', in A.R.H. Baker and G. Bigger (eds), *Ideology and landscape in historical perspective: essays on the meaning of some places in the past* (Cambridge: Cambridge University Press, 1992), pp. 330–51; Peter Goheen, 'The ritual of the streets in mid-nineteenth century Toronto', *Environment and Planning D: Society and Space*, 11 (1993), pp. 127–45; Lily Kwong and B.S.A. Yeoh, 'The construction of national through the production of ritual and spectacle: an analysis of National Day parades in Singapore', *Political Geography*, 23:1 (2004), pp. 1–16; Joshua Hagen, 'Parades, public space and propaganda: the Nazi culture parades in Munich', *Geografiska Annaler Series B: Human Geography*, 90:4 (2008), pp. 349–67; Erika Kuever, 'Performance, spectacle and visual poetry in the sixtieth anniversary National Day parade in the People's Republic of China', *Studies in Ethnicity and Nationalism*, 12:1 (2012), pp. 6–18.
58 Jarman, *Material conflicts*, p. 34; Yvonne Whelan, 'Performance, spectacle and power', in J. Morrissey, D. Nally, U. Strohmayer and Y. Whelan (eds), *Key concepts in historical geography* (Los Angeles: Sage, 2014), pp. 182–90.
59 Peter Burke, *Popular culture in early modern Europe* (Aldershot: Wildwood House, 1978); D.A. Reid, 'Interpreting the festival calendar: wakes and fairs as carnivals', in D.A. Storch (ed.), *Popular custom and culture in nineteenth century England* (London: Croom Helm, 1982), pp. 125–53.

60 Hagen, 'Parades, public space and propaganda'; this makes the point that in some places the historic spatial layout of an urban settlement can actually impose limits on the effectiveness of public performances.
61 Neil Jarman and Dominic Bryan, *From rights to riots: nationalist parades in the north of Ireland* (Coleraine: Centre for the Study of Conflict, University of Ulster, 1998).
62 Thomas Fraser, 'Introduction', in T.G. Fraser (ed.), *The Irish parading tradition: following the drum* (London: Macmillan, 2000).
63 John Stevenson, *Popular disturbances in England, 1700–1870* (London: Longman, 1979); Mark Harrison, *Crowds and history: mass phenomena in English towns, 1790–1835* (Cambridge: Cambridge University Press, 1988).
64 Miles Ogborn, 'Ordering the city: surveillance, public space and the reform of urban policing in England, 1835–56', *Political Geography*, 12:6 (1993), pp. 505–22.
65 Toby Barnard, 'The uses of 23 October 1641 and Irish Protestant celebrations', *English Historical Review*, 116 (1991), pp. 889–920; James Kelly, 'The emergence of political parading, 1660–1800', in Fraser (ed.), *The Irish parading tradition*, pp. 9–26. Until well into the nineteenth century much of Irish public life at national and local level was dominated by an exclusively Anglican Anglo-Irish elite who numbered about 12%.
66 Jacqueline Hill, 'National festivals, the state and "Protestant ascendancy" in Ireland, 1790–1829', *Irish Historical Studies*, 24 (1984), pp. 30–51.
67 Kevin Haddick-Flynn, *Orangeism: the making of a tradition* (Dublin: Wolfhound Press, 1999).
68 Seamus Dunn, 'Preface', in Jarman and Bryan, *From rights to riots*; P. Goheen, 'Negotiating access to the streets in nineteenth century Toronto', *Journal of Historical Geography*, 20:4 (1994), pp. 430–49.
69 Tom Garvin, 'Defenders, Ribbonmen and others: underground political networks in pre-famine Ireland', in C.H.E. Philbin (ed.), *Nationalism and popular protest in Ireland* (Cambridge: Cambridge University Press, 1987), pp. 219–44.
70 Jarman and Bryan, *From rights to riots*; Sean Farrell, *Ritual and riots: sectarian violence and political culture in Ulster, 1784–1886* (Lexington: University Press of Kentucky, 2000); Clare Murphy, 'Varieties of crowd activity from Fenianism to the Land War, 1867–79', in P. Jupp and E. Magennis (eds), *Crowds in Ireland c. 1720–1920* (London: Macmillan, 2000), pp. 180–1.
71 Gary Owens, 'Nationalism without words: symbolism and ritual behaviour in the repeal "monster meetings" of 1843–5', in S.J. Donnelly and K.A. Miller (eds), *Irish popular culture 1650–1850* (Dublin: Irish Academic Press, 1992); Patrick Geoghegan, *King Dan: the rise of Daniel O'Connell 1775–1829* (Dublin: Gill & Macmillan, 2010).
72 Rafferty, *The church, the state and the Fenian threat*; Rafferty, 'The Catholic Church and Fenianism', pp. 30–4.
73 Bishop William Turner, Pastoral Letter, 3 October 1867, Acti Primi Episcopi, 1852–77, Salford Diocese Archives.

74 *Manchester Courier*, 25 November 1867.
75 *Manchester Examiner and Times*, 25 November 1867; *Manchester Guardian*, 25 November 1867.
76 *Freeman's Journal*, 25 November 1867.
77 *Freeman's Journal*, 4 December 1867.
78 *Manchester Guardian*, 2 December 1867.
79 *Manchester Examiner and Times*, 2 December 1867; *Manchester Guardian*, 2 December 1867; *Manchester Courier*, 2 December 1867.
80 *Freeman's Journal*, 4 December 1867; *Manchester Examiner and Times*, 2 December 1867.
81 *Manchester Examiner and Times*, 2 December 1867.
82 Mervyn Busteed, 'Parading the green: procession as subaltern resistance in Manchester in 1867', *Political Geography*, 24:8 (2005), pp. 903–33.
83 Dan Horner, 'Solemn processions and terrifying violence: spectacle and authority and citizenship during the Lachine Canal strike of 1834', *Urban History Review*, 38:2 (2010), pp. 36–47.
84 *Manchester Evening News*, 23 November 1891.
85 Mervyn Busteed, '"Fostered to trouble the next generation": contesting the ownership of the martyrs' commemoration ritual in Manchester 1888–1921', in N. Moore and Y. Whelan (eds), *Heritage, memory and the politics of identity: new perspectives on the cultural landscape* (Aldershot: Ashgate, 2007), pp. 69–82.
86 A republican equivalent of the Boy Scouts, founded c.1903.
87 *Universal News*, 5 December 1868. I am indebted to Dr John Dunleavy for this reference.
88 *Catholic Herald*, 27 November 1896.
89 *Manchester Courier*, 28 November 1898; *Manchester Evening Chronicle*, 28 November 1898.
90 *Salford Reporter*, 15 February 1899; R.L. Greenall, *The making of Victorian Salford* (Lancaster: Carnegie Publishing, 2000), chap. 10: 'Catholics, Fr. Saffenreuter and the Pendleton Irish'.
91 *Manchester Courier*, 13 February 1899.
92 *Catholic Herald*, 30 November 1900.
93 *Catholic Herald*, 6 December 1913.
94 *Catholic Herald*, 10 August 1900.
95 *Catholic Herald*, 2 October 1909.
96 *Catholic Herald*, 28 November 1914.
97 *Catholic Herald*, 2 December 1916.
98 *Catholic Herald*, 1 December 1917.
99 *Manchester Guardian*, 24 November 1919; *Manchester Evening News*, 24 November 1919.
100 *Manchester Guardian*, 27 November 1920. Thomas MacCurtain, the first Sinn Féin Lord Mayor of Cork city, had been shot by British forces in March; MacSwiney, his successor, died in Brixton prison after a lengthy hunger strike in October.

101 *Catholic Herald*, 4 December 1920.
102 *Manchester Guardian*, 21 November 1921. 'TD' indicates a member of Dáil Éireann – Milroy sat for Cavan-Monaghan.
103 *Catholic Herald*, 27 November 1896.
104 *Catholic Herald*, 1 December 1899.
105 *Manchester Courier*, 24 November 1902.
106 *Catholic Herald*, 28 November 1902.
107 *Manchester Guardian*, 23 November 1908.
108 *Catholic Herald*, 2 October 1909.
109 *Manchester Courier*, 18 November 1901.
110 *Manchester Courier*, 17 November 1913; *Manchester Guardian*, 17 November 1913; *Catholic Herald*, 22 November 1913; M. Herbert, *The wearing of the green: a political history of the Irish in Manchester* (London: Irish in Britain Representation Group, 2001), pp. 88–90.
111 *Catholic Herald*, 6 December 1913. This may have been a reaction to the fact that church authorities had vehemently condemned a scheme to send the children of Dublin families hard hit by the strike to sympathetic families in Britain on the grounds that they were not necessarily going to Catholic homes. The scheme was abandoned, having generated bitter controversy.
112 *Manchester Guardian*, 27 November 1911.
113 *Catholic Herald*, 30 November 1912. Redmond proved true to his word when he enlisted in the British army and served in France during the First World War, earning the DSO. When John Redmond died in March he succeeded his father as MP for Waterford; he subsequently represented the constituency in Dáil Éireann until his death in 1932.
114 *Catholic Herald*, 6 December 1913.
115 Roy Foster, *Modern Ireland 1600–1972* (London: Penguin, 1989), pp. 472–3.
116 Alvin Jackson, *Home rule: an Irish history 1800–2000* (London: Phoenix Press, 2004), pp. 166–71.
117 *Catholic Herald*, 28 November 1914.
118 *Manchester Guardian*, 23 November 1914.
119 *Catholic Herald*, 2 December 1916.
120 *Catholic Herald*, 1 December 1917.
121 *Manchester Evening News*, 26 November 1920.
122 *Manchester Guardian*, 21 November 1921.

# 8

## Decline, revival and rising

Following the events surrounding the rescue of Kelly and Deasy, the execution of the Manchester Martyrs and the subsequent panic, it is difficult to estimate the strength of the Fenian movement in Manchester and elsewhere in Britain. To some extent this is the inevitable result of their clandestine nature, but it also reflects the interaction between developments within the movement and changes in the wider Irish political landscape. The persistent edginess displayed by the moderate nationalists, who for most of the period discussed above were in control of the martyrs' commemoration events and able to exploit them for their political purposes, strongly suggests that there was a lingering Fenian appeal. In fact, there were occasional glimpses of this alternative narrative, especially in the 1870s and 1880s, and the events of the early twentieth century were to see its revival and the emergence of a much more assertive and militant form of Irish nationalism. This was to culminate in the Dublin rising of 1916 and the subsequent War of Independence, which was vividly reflected in Manchester.

### Revisionism and dissent

In August 1868 the IRB adopted its first constitutional document and set about rebuilding its organisation under the influence of a younger, more pragmatic element. The return of a Liberal government under Gladstone in November 1868 encouraged the hope that constitutional methods could bring progress at least on the issues of Irish church disestablishment and land reform. These hopes were to some extent fulfilled when the Church of Ireland was disestablished in 1869 and the first Land Act was passed in 1870. The foundation of the Amnesty Association in June 1869 to campaign for improved prison conditions for Fenian prisoners and their eventual release also raised hopes. These were further reinforced by the formation of Butt's Home Government Association in 1870 and the Home Rule Association of Great Britain formed at the meeting in Manchester in early 1873.

In March 1873 these developments briefly led the IRB to adopt a more permissive attitude towards parliamentary politics. It was decided that members could be allowed to participate in conventional political activity provided this did not compromise the core principles of the movement. Under this dispensation some Fenian activists entered parliament as supporters of home rule, determined to push the issue to the top of the British political agenda, and went on to become stalwarts of the Irish Parliamentary Party. But some of the more traditional elements in the IRB such as John O'Leary and Charles Kickham, popular novelist of Irish rural life and President of the Supreme Council until his death in 1882, were unhappy, and there were indications that their outlook retained some support in Manchester.[1]

The Catholic Church certainly suspected that there was lingering Fenian strength. In January 1870 the Vatican, responding to a request from the Irish hierarchy and pressure from the British government, issued a decree explicitly condemning the Fenian movement. The following month, in the absence of Bishop Turner in Rome, Provost Croskell felt it necessary to drive home the point by means of a supplementary statement sent to the clergy on the subject of the sacrament of Confession:

> I have been informed, on very good authority, that there prevails in this diocese, a widely different mode of directing a certain class of penitents to the sacred tribunal of Confession ... I refer to the case of individuals who are connected to the Fenian Association, which is a Secret Society, forbidden by the church ... no person ... sworn into a society can be permitted to partake of the Sacraments, until he shall have renounced all connection with it ... let us remember that a divided house cannot stand ... Let us discard all partial consideration of person or country ... I trust that all clergy, without a single exception, will in future consider it an imperative duty to refuse the Sacrament to every penitent whom they know to be connected, directly or indirectly, with any secret society, under any pretext whatsoever.[2]

A pastoral letter to the Catholic laity drove home the point, informing them that

> Henceforth ... the members of the Fenian Association, and likewise all who aid or abet the association, are to be excluded from the benefit of sacraments

until they have withdrawn from all association with it, and have sincerely promised never to return to it ... Our most Holy Father has a sincere love and most tender regard for his children the Irish nation ... but he wishes his children to promote the good of their country, not by a spirit of anger and revenge, not by sworn conspiracy, but by all open, lawful, and honourable means.[3]

It was clearly found necessary to repeat the bishop's warning issued in the aftermath of the events of 1867 and to reinforce it with this pastoral letter.

Just occasionally there were indications that clerical fears were not entirely unfounded and that hard-line Fenian sentiment, or at least sympathy, lingered on. In 1874 J.G. Biggar had been elected one of the home rule MPs for Co. Cavan, and in late 1875 he was sworn into the IRB, intending to argue for full participation in parliamentary politics. In parliament he was an early practitioner of the policy of obstructing business until Irish matters were given higher priority. But within the IRB there was still a faction deeply unhappy with the new permissiveness, and on 10 August 1876 the Supreme Council gave members six months to choose between the traditional IRB stance and parliamentary politics. The tensions surfaced in spectacular fashion at a meeting in the Manchester Free Trade Hall on 10 September later that year, when Biggar presided over a lecture on the totally innocuous title of 'Irish wit and humour'. The main speaker was J. O'Connor Power, home rule MP for Mayo. He had been an IRB member since 1866, but he too was convinced of the need to participate in conventional politics and had been expelled from the IRB the previous month.

When the meeting assembled it was estimated that about three thousand people were present, including 'about 200 or 300 Irishmen of the lower class who soon in various ways pronounced themselves to be the advocates of the repeal of the union'. When it was proposed that Biggar take the chair, disorder broke out, and there were loud persistent demands that O'Connor Power answer certain questions before proceedings got under way. When some order had been restored the protesters were allowed to ask him if he adhered to what were described as 'the principles of Wolfe Tone, Emmet and Lord Edward Fitzgerald, and the men of '67 or ... as representative of home rule as laid down by Mr. Butt'.[4] When O'Connor Power, against a background of constant heckling and interruptions, tried to respond and move on to the lecture, the meeting erupted. Fights broke out, bottles and broken chairs were used as weapons, Biggar was slightly hurt, and the glass front and some of the ornamental decoration of the organ in the hall were damaged before the audience were shepherded into the street and dispersed. The incident was described as 'One of the most disorderly meetings ever held in Manchester', an uncomprehending reporter referring to the anti-home-rulers, who were clearly Fenian supporters, as 'repealers' or 'nationalists'.[5] The next year Biggar, by then a member of the Supreme Council, refused to abandon parliamentary politics and was expelled from the IRB.

In the USA the divisions within the movement had become deeper and ever more byzantine. In 1867 Clan na Gael had been founded in the hope of bringing the factions together, and by 1870 they were evolving an uneasy, mutually suspicious working relationship. By the mid-1870s the increasingly dominant personality was John Devoy, a Kildare-born IRB member who had served a term of imprisonment and emigrated under amnesty. In October 1878 he devised an understanding with Charles Stewart Parnell known as 'the New Departure', whereby the Clan would support the Irish Parliamentary Party provided the land issue was central to its programme. From the early months of 1879 the land issue did indeed rise dramatically up the political agenda, climaxing in October in the setting up of the Land League with Parnell as president. But there was an element within the movement in the USA which remained deeply unhappy with this development. In 1880 its leading personality, Jeremiah O'Donovan Rossa, was expelled from the Clan. He set up a rival group, the United Irishmen of America, and launched a newspaper which began a vitriolic campaign against his former associates. He and his supporters went on to launch a series of bomb attacks in Britain using the new explosive, dynamite.[6] These opened with an attack on the armoury of the infantry barracks in Salford on 14 January 1881, which did little damage but killed a child. There followed a series of attacks in Liverpool, Glasgow and, most frequently, London, in which the Mansion House, underground railway stations, Scotland Yard, London Bridge, the House of Commons and the Tower of London suffered. Not to be outdone in militancy, the Clan launched a dynamite campaign of their own. These combined efforts came to an end in early 1885, under the combined pressure of increasingly intensive policing and infiltration of the groups concerned by informers, double agents and *agents provocateurs*.[7]

In early February 1885 John O'Leary, who had been active in the 1848 rising and IRB circles and had been sentenced to twenty years but released under the amnesty of 1871, also came to Manchester to deliver a lecture in the Free Trade Hall. From the outset he denounced what he described as 'the hideous folly and awful criminality of the dynamitards'. O'Donovan Rossa was described as having started out as an honest enthusiast but degenerated into 'a somewhat unscrupulous half madman, so far from assisting Ireland to freedom dynamite would still further enslave it'. But it was clear that a considerable element in the audience were of different persuasion, cheering any mention of Rossa and heckling O'Leary's condemnation of the campaign. The division within Manchester Irish opinion had been further underlined by a meeting at St Wilfrid's church in Hulme, when over 250 people had signed a declaration condemning the dynamiters as neither true Irishmen nor Catholics.[8]

The schism within the nationalist movement over the leadership of Parnell in December 1890 may also have revealed some lingering Fenian sympathy. In the last months of his life, as he strove to retain his position, Parnell increasingly pitched his appeal to what were termed 'the hillside men' of the more advanced nationalist and neo-Fenian tradition.[9] In Manchester the majority of the Irish came out against him, but there were enough supporters to form the Parnell Leadership Committee of Manchester, Salford and District, though it was denigrated by Councillor Dan McCabe in the St Patrick's Day celebrations of March 1891 as consisting of 'a few Parnellites ... drinking his health in a little place in Ancoats ... and it would well hold them all'.[10]

Further indications of some enduring Fenian or neo-Fenian sympathy came with the centenary of the 1798 rebellion. In October 1897 the '98 Centennial Committee, whose president was W.B. Yeats, conducted a series of public meetings in northern cities to publicise plans for the forthcoming commemoration.[11] On 3 October it held a convention in Manchester to discuss ways to commemorate the rising and a memorial to Wolfe Tone, the revolutionary leader.[12] This was followed by a public meeting in the evening, which passed a series of resolutions pledging support and finance for the commemorations. Both the chairman and a local newspaper remarked on the sparse attendance, but that did not deter the speakers, including the main fundraiser, the redoubtable Maud Gonne, who, recalling the French expeditionary force to Ireland led by General Lazare Hoche which had been beaten back by storms in late December 1796, declared that 'If the great French force under Hoche had succeeded in landing at Bantry Bay, their country would now be free.'[13] She went on to claim that the events of 1798 had initiated 'a great and holy struggle for liberty, during which life might be lost, though it would regenerate their country'. When a member of the audience called out that, if attending events in Dublin the following year, 'Every man bring his rifle' it was noted that this was 'a sentiment which was received with some applause'.[14]

It was decided that the best form of commemoration would be a monument to the Manchester Martyrs, thereby expressing the sense of continuity between the ideas, personalities and events of 1798 in Ireland and 1867 in Manchester. The foundation stone of the memorial was laid in St Joseph's cemetery, Moston, on 27 November 1898 'in the presence of some thousands of Irishmen and women'. A procession formed at New Cross in the city and proceeded to the cemetery along streets 'lined with people the whole way'. Once it reached the cemetery, crowd control broke down as people 'forced their way in, climbing the walls and breaking through the shrub fences, despite the efforts of the policemen stationed there'. Both Maud Gonne and an elderly James Stephens spoke briefly, and Fr McCarthy blessed the stone, with the personal consequences already described.[15]

Later that evening there was a public meeting at which some notably militant language was used. Clearly assuming that the large numbers who had turned for the earlier ceremony indicated support for the Fenian outlook, the chairman suggested that their presence 'in the sight of the enemy, must make England understand that that the national pride and spirit of Irishmen had not been quenched … Irishmen had a perfect right, so long as England denied them the rights of citizenship and treated them as an enemy, to fight and injure her at every opportunity.' It was noted that 'The speaker's words were received with cheers and some opposition.'[16] Another speaker expressed confidence that 'The spirit of 1798 and 1867 would rise again before long. They had not had an opportunity of avenging the murder of Allen, Larkin and O'Brien, but please God they would get it before long.'[17] Stephens then spoke briefly in support of Irish political prisoners. Maud Gonne, referring to a current highly inflamed diplomatic stand-off between Britain and France in southern Sudan, appealed for 'a round of cheers for France', which the meeting readily gave.[18] Her reminder of how in the past the French and Irish had fought side by side against the English 'was received with prolonged cheering, and this was repeated when she added that she hoped they would do so again'. Another speaker took up the theme when he 'warned England that until the rights of Ireland were granted, in any situation that might arise with a foreign power, especially France, Ireland might raise an even stronger battalion than fought at Fontenoy'.[19] The chairman was cheered when he concluded proceedings by declaring that so long as England treated Irishmen as enemies, 'so long had they the right to fight and injure her in every particular part'.[20]

The year 1900 saw the unveiling of the completed monument in a much more disciplined ceremony which was a notable mix of both moderate and militant nationalist sentiments. It was part of a series of events spread over the Bank Holiday weekend. The unveiling took place on the afternoon of Sunday 5 August. Headed by the elderly 1867 veteran John Carroll, a procession estimated at ten thousand people gathered at the customary

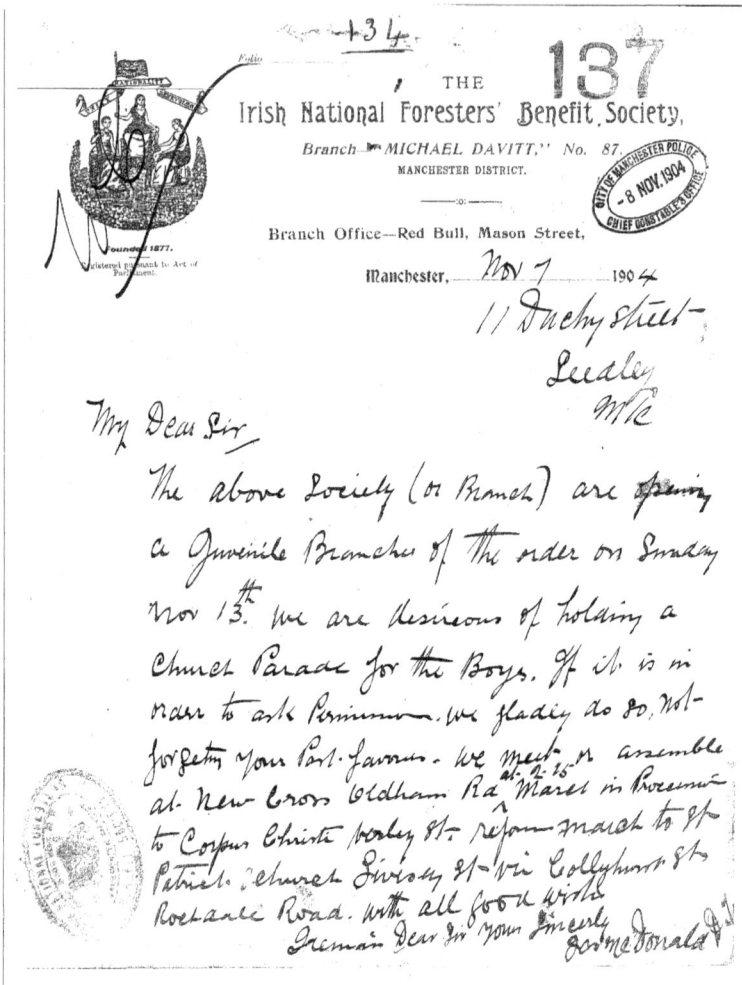

18 The Irish National Foresters organise a procession in 1902

starting place of New Cross and walked to the cemetery along a three-mile route lined by spectators, many of whom wore Irish emblems and applauded. Local branches of the Gaelic Athletic Association (carrying hurleys) and the Gaelic League, together with representatives of organisations from Barrow-in-Furness, Cleator Moor, Liverpool, Scotland, Dublin, Kingstown, Blackrock, Dundalk, Belfast and Cookstown, were present, along with six bands and private carriages escorted by police. Members of the Irish National Foresters, whose annual convention was due to take place in the city the following Tuesday, paraded in green and white costume with ceremonial pikes (Figure 18). To avoid the undignified crush of 1898, entrance to the cemetery was by ticket, though spectators gathered in nearby fields. The unveiling was conducted by John Daly, briefly MP. and now Mayor of Limerick and a long term IRB activist. There were no speeches; 'God save Ireland' was sung, and the procession reformed and returned to the city centre.[21]

A public meeting that evening more than made up for the earlier lack of speeches. Seamus Barrett, IRB member, local Gaelic Athletic Association president and Gaelic League member, declared that the spirit of the martyrs was alive and well and went on to say that 'They could not at present practice those principles, but they could preach them. Their one aim was the absolute independence of Ireland.'[22] As for methods, he was cheered when he continued to argue that 'If Irishmen could not get what they wanted by asking, there was only one other way and they knew what that was.'[23] But all this was exceeded by John Daly, who vigorously castigated the Irish Parliamentary Party, suggesting that, along with the majority of Irish nationalists, they had abandoned the principles for which the Manchester Martyrs had been executed. He went on, 'Would to God they were back again to the year before the men of Manchester died, to the day when the national manhood of Ireland stood ready for a chance of striking at England's power.' Noting the widely admired bravery of the Irish regiments of the British army currently engaged in the Boer War, he argued that if nationalists had remained true to the ideas which had inspired the martyrs of 1867, then 'thousands of Irishmen who had gone forth to crush the Boers in the Transvaal might have found work to do at home … Sentiment alone would never uproot England's supremacy in Ireland.'[24] Manchester's moderate nationalist leaders were conspicuous by their absence. On Bank Holiday Monday Gaelic football and hurling matches were played and there was an evening banquet.[25] At the Foresters' annual convention the following day care was taken to point out that they had played a key role in the monument project.[26]

## Revival and rising

By no means all those who turned out for such events were IRB members or sympathisers, but it is clear that there was at the very least a latent well of admiration for the separatist tradition and perhaps a grudging respect for the fundamentalist purity of its exponents. It is also clear that by the 1890s the actual organisation in Britain had shrunk to small groups of dedicated but isolated people. However, the efforts put into the commem-

19 Conradh na Gaeilge (Gaelic League) organises a language collection in 1908

oration events of the period 1897–1900 had revived interest in the movement and inspired some to become members, leading to something of a revival.[27] One new member recalled that in the 1890s, after the Parnell split, the IRB in Britain had been reduced to very small groups who, whilst they remained true to the movement's principles, were isolated and few in number, and he cited Manchester as an example. Following the renaissance, he reported, there were three cells in Manchester in the years shortly before the First World War.[28] The presence in the city of those highly significant markers of the Irish cultural revival, the Gaelic Athletic Association and the Gaelic League, has already been noted (Figure 19). In 1908 a Manchester branch of the newly formed Sinn Féin party was set up, which grew to a membership of about forty. The members organised fundraising events and passed the proceeds on to Dublin.[29] In accordance with traditional tactics, IRB members secretly infiltrated themselves into the leadership of all three organisations. When the writer P.S. O'Hegarty served on the IRB Supreme Council for 1906–7 he noted that the co-opted member for the north of England was Seamus Barrett, owner of a second-hand clothes shop in Manchester's Deansgate, president of Sinn Féin in the city and, as already noted, active in several other Irish cultural organisations.[30]

On 25 November 1913 the Irish Volunteers had been formed in Dublin with the intention of stiffening the resolve of the British government in support of the third Irish Home Rule Bill, then making its torturous way through parliament, and also partly in response to the Ulster Volunteer Force, launched the previous February in opposition to the bill. By late 1914 the Irish Volunteers were estimated to number between 160,000 and 180,000, and as usual several IRB members had been quietly inserted into leadership roles.[31] The Volunteers' popularity alarmed John Redmond to the point where, in June 1914, he demanded and obtained a majority of places for his nominees on the executive council.[32] In fact, local elements of the UIL had already been linking up with the Volunteers. The first Manchester unit had been launched on 27 March, and in late April it was reported that the UIL branch in the Hulme district had been helping with recruitment. Redmond's move had merely endorsed a trend already under way.[33] Following instruction from former British army members, the first drilling of members was held in early May, with the support of the local branches of the National Foresters and Gaelic League.[34] By the end of July there were 1,700 Volunteers in Manchester alone, with another 800 in surrounding towns, and a county board had been set up. Drill took place twice weekly, and each unit had a fund for the purchase of equipment, including rifles; there were public meetings and talks in support of the movement, and plans were afoot to lay out three rifle ranges and hold a route march through the city on 9 August.[35]

Like so much in British and Irish life, this event was overtaken by the outbreak of the First World War on 4 August 1914. Alderman Dan McCabe, by then an immensely popular Lord Mayor, followed the great majority of nationalists by endorsing Redmond's support of the Allied cause and spoke frequently at recruitment rallies, laying particular emphasis on the devastation and atrocities visited on women and children by German soldiers, especially in small Catholic Belgium.[36] Following the split in the Volunteers in Ireland, the great majority who followed Redmond had renamed themselves the National Volunteers whilst the dissident group retained the title Irish Volunteers.

By September 1914 the IRB had decided that British involvement in the war provided the ideal opportunity to stage a rising; by early 1916 the IRB element within the Irish Volunteers' leadership had secretly set preparations in motion and key members were informed that insurrection was imminent.[37] As Manchester members became aware of the plan, some fourteen made their way quietly to Ireland in the first weeks of 1916. They became part of the 'Kimmage Garrison' based in an old mill on the property of the Plunkett family at Larkfield in south Dublin, where, alongside seventy-seven other Irish expatriates from Britain, they trained in the manufacture of ammunition, grenades and pikes.[38] On the morning of Monday 24 April they were mustered by their commanding officer George Plunkett, boarded a tram to the city centre, marched to insurgent headquarters and were allocated to various strongpoints. Some of the Manchester contingent were based at the main garrison at the General Post Office in O'Connell Street, and others were in a shop at the bottom of the street overlooking the River Liffey. Like all the insurgent garrisons, they surrendered on 29 April and were court-martialled and imprisoned.[39]

## The Manchester campaign

Initially the Manchester Irish, like most of the population of Ireland itself, were shocked at and disapproving of the rising. On 1 May the Manchester county board of the Ancient Order of Hibernians strongly condemned the insurgency and reiterated its support for John Redmond and the Irish Parliamentary Party, and the largest branch of the UIL followed suit.[40] But, as in Ireland, there was a gradual shift in opinion in reaction to the British army's execution of the rebel leaders and subsequent policies such as the threat to extend conscription to Ireland, which seemed imminent in early 1918. The process of alienation was accelerated when, during the War of Independence, the British authorities recruited vigorously aggressive units such as the Black and Tans and the Auxiliaries from ex-servicemen and launched a policy of official reprisals and community punishment for IRA operations.

The role of the Irish in Britain during this period has received relatively little attention, and what little research has been done has led to conflicting conclusions. One authority and some Irish leaders during the conflict regarded their contribution as disappointing, whilst another has argued that overall they performed as well as the average IRA unit in an Irish county.[41] One contribution by the Manchester Irish was focused on the welfare of Irish prisoners in local jails. In the immediate aftermath of the rising the authorities in Ireland detained about 3,500 people and transferred about 2,500 to Britain. For a few weeks in May and June 1916, fifty were held in Knutsford prison in nearby north Cheshire. Fr O'Hanrahan, a Manchester parish priest, set up a prisoners' aid group, largely staffed by members of Cumann na mBan, the republican women's organisation. On Sundays the women brought food, clothes, cigarettes and letters for the prisoners.[42] In the last week of June the prisoners were transferred to Frongoch camp in north Wales. By June 1917 all those detained in the immediate aftermath of the rising had been released.

But some of the Manchester Irish were to prove even more helpful towards Irish prisoners. By early 1918 a British government campaign against the reorganised Sinn Féin and Irish Volunteers, the latter increasingly referred to as the Irish Republican Army, was under way. In May Eamon de Valera, senior surviving officer from the 1916 rising and President of Sinn Féin and the Volunteers, was in Lincoln jail with Sean Milroy and Sean McGarry and plans were made for a rescue. Michael Collins, one of the key personalities of the Irish revolution, and Harry Boland, who hailed from a Manchester Irish family, finalised the plans whilst hiding in the city.[43] The three escapees were taken to Manchester, Milroy and McGarry were lodged with a sympathetic Irish family, and de Valera with a Fr McMahon on the northern side of the city. A few days later a friendly Kerry-born local police officer warned that the presbytery was under surveillance. De Valera was disguised in the uniform of a British colonial soldier and walked across the city in the company of Kathleen Talty, leader of the local Cumann na mBan, to the home of another member, Mary Healy, in Fallowfield. Two weeks later he returned to Ireland via Liverpool. Sympathetic homes in Manchester were clearly part of the network of safe houses for those involved in Irish revolutionary activity in Britain – a local man, Liam McMahon, recalled visits by at least seventeen notable personalities to his Manchester house alone, several staying more than once.[44] Further support for prisoners came with the escape of Austin Stack and five others from Strangeways prison on 26 October 1919. In May 1918, Stack, soon to become Sinn Féin MP for Kerry and prominent in the party leadership cadre, was arrested and imprisoned in Belfast's Crumlin Road jail. There he led a series of disturbances and hunger strikes for political status. On 2 April 1919 he was transferred to Strangeways. An escape plan was devised by a group led by Paddy O'Donoghue, the Manchester IRA leader, and details were smuggled into the prison by Cumann na mBan. Rory O'Connor, the IRA's director of engineering, came over from Dublin to finalise arrangements, and on the appointed day Stack and five others went over the wall and rode off to safe houses using taxis and bicycles provided by local IRA and sympathisers.[45]

That same year a series of events demonstrated how the centre of gravity of Irish opinion in Manchester was shifting in favour of Sinn Féin. On 19 October a crowd variously estimated at anything from seven to twelve thousand filled the Free Trade Hall, the nearby Palladium cinema and the surrounding streets to hear Arthur Griffith, founder of Sinn Féin and acting president of the shadow Irish government in the absence of de Valera in the USA, launch the ISDL. Speakers were greeted with 'an ovation of remarkable warmth ... certainly never in the history of the Irish in Manchester was such a meeting held'.[46] It was a fortnight later that an estimated 15,000 heard Countess Markievicz, Ida Connolly and Hanna Sheehy-Skeffington appeal for funds and direct action in support of Irish and labour causes.[47] The shift of opinion was signalled the following year with the two official events celebrating St Patrick's Day. One was attended by the Lord Mayor, but an alternative gathering was organised by the ISDL and presided over by the Irish-born Liberal councillor Hugh Lee, eventually to become Lord Mayor. Amongst the guests who toasted the recently banned Dáil Éireann was H.F. O'Brien, second-generation Irish, founder of a thriving oil and lubricant firm and mayor of leafy suburban Altrincham.[48] Both were members of the Catenians, a Catholic fellowship for members of the professions. The presence of such prosperous, middle-class businessmen was a significant indicator of the state of Irish opinion in the region. The point was driven home a few days later with the result of the parliamentary by-election in nearby Stockport noted earlier when the Dublin alderman William O'Brien, Secretary of the Irish Transport and General Workers' Union, gained 2,336 votes, a useful indicator of the actual size of the Irish vote.[49]

A much more public and dramatic demonstration was provided when Terence MacSwiney, Sinn Féin Lord Mayor of Cork, died on 25 October 1920 on the seventy-fourth day of a hunger strike in Brixton prison. His body was returned to Cork for the funeral on 31 October, and in Manchester the ISDL organised a mock funeral which turned into a massive public demonstration of Irish feeling. The procession assembled in the traditional gathering place of Stevenson Square and went via Livesey Street, pausing for prayers outside St Patrick's. It then proceeded northwards to Moston cemetery, which was filled to overflowing. Forty branches of the

ISDL took part, along with three dozen clergy. Companies of the Irish National Foresters paraded wearing green sashes. Men, women and children took part: 'The assembly represented all ranks and classes. Men in tall hats and frock coats marched side by side with men in ordinary working clothes, and there were equal contrasts in the women's sections.' Sixty cabs and taxis headed the procession, which, with people walking four abreast, took two hours to pass. The entire route was lined with spectators, many of whom wore Irish colours. At the cemetery a short religious service was held and the many wreaths were laid at the foot of the martyrs' memorial in what was clearly an explicit claim to continuity and legitimacy.[50] These themes were amongst those taken up by the ISDL, which, following its clandestine founding convention in the city over the weekend of 26–28 November, went on to number twenty thousand members at its peak in 400 branches and published a short lived newspaper, *The Irish Exile*. Most of its leaders in the city were arrested in December 1920. By this time the War of Independence in Ireland was steadily becoming more intense. The IRA were attacking police barracks and coastguard stations and ambushing Royal Irish Constabulary and army patrols; the Black and Tans and Auxiliaries were deployed, and eight counties were under martial law by January 1921.[51]

The first Manchester IRA unit had been formally organised in late 1919, partly inspired by the experience of assisting with the escapes from Lincoln. By September three companies with a total strength of about a hundred formally affiliated men and additional units had been set up in surrounding towns.[52] Their purpose was partly to divert British military resources from the campaign in Ireland but above all to acquire arms and ammunition and forward them to Ireland via Liverpool. Manchester became a crucial transhipment point because of particularly keen police surveillance in Glasgow.[53] Seamus Barrett played a key role, purchasing guns and ammunition from British soldiers, storing them in his Deansgate shop and selling them to IRA agents from Ireland. A garage near the city centre was also used for storage. Various means were used to ship the goods to Ireland. One Irish-born musician who frequently visited Ireland over this period carried some in her fiddle case.[54] Paddy O'Donoghue exploited personal connections with a police inspector responsible for security on the Manchester Ship Canal and the captain of a ship regularly trading between Manchester and Dublin to ensure safe passage with no questions asked.[55]

The upsurge of popular support following the death of MacSwiney in October 1920 moved the IRA's high command to further intensify its campaign, and there was a meeting in Manchester in November to plan possible attacks on targets in Britain. The ship canal, local power stations and water pumping plants were surreptitiously inspected and plans made for sabotage, but these had to be abandoned when the British army in Dublin raided the office of Richard Mulcahy, Chief of Staff of the IRA, seized all the documentation and details were published in the newspapers.[56] In February 1921 ten industrial premises in the city were attacked, in March fires were started in farm buildings in surrounding areas, and on 1 April four hotels, a café and two warehouses in the city centre were attacked.[57] The Manchester police, always quite energetic in combating the campaign, responded strongly. Late on 2 April they raided the Irish Club in Erskine Street, meeting place of two of the city's IRA units. Shooting broke out, and one person was killed and two policemen wounded.[58] This was followed by a series of further police operations in which nineteen people were arrested, including the leading officers of the IRA. Seventeen were found guilty and sentenced in July to between five and seventeen years' imprisonment, effectively destroying the organisation in the city.[59]

On 9 July 1921 a truce was agreed between British and Irish forces, and following protracted negotiations, the Anglo-Irish Treaty was signed on 6 December and endorsed by Dáil Éireann in January 1922. As in Ireland, the Manchester Irish community was divided in its reactions. The local branch of the ISDL came out in favour, but when in July 1922 a reception was held in Holy Name church for those who had been imprisoned the previous year and released under a recent amnesty, clear signs of disagreement emerged. Fr Butler, who presided over the event, made a speech in which he welcomed the released prisoners and applauded the Treaty, but whilst some applauded, there were audible murmurs of dissent.[60] Following the outbreak of civil war in Ireland over the issue in June 1922, there was some talk of local dissidents restarting the Manchester campaign, but after a few scattered efforts to attack infrastructure in the north-west, it was clear that large-scale support and resources were lacking and the effort quickly petered out. However, the new Irish Free State government was sufficiently alarmed by the activities of anti-Treaty elements in Britain to request the extradition of their leaders. The British government agreed and 110 people were arrested and deported in March 1923, including eight from Manchester. They were lodged in Mountjoy prison, Dublin, but the deportations were later declared illegal and they were returned to the city in May 1923.[61]

Overall the Manchester campaign resulted in the death of one person and another six were shot and wounded, including five policemen. In all, there were 68 operations carried out, 16% of the total in Britain and 64 installations were destroyed or damaged, mostly by arson.[62] The

Manchester IRA were clearly restricted in what it could do since it was operating in a major British city where the great majority of inhabitants were indifferent or unsympathetic to their cause and probably angry at the violence, damage and disruption to daily life. Moreover, the police, many of whom were ex-servicemen with wartime experience, were alert and energetic. However, to varying degrees the IRA did have the support of some elements in the local Irish population. There is good evidence of a shift of the centre of gravity of Irish opinion within the city towards Sinn Féin. Whilst the great majority were probably passively sympathetic, there were clearly some who were prepared to provide quiet assistance, intelligence, storage space for munitions and safe houses for those on the run or passing through on revolutionary business. Beyond that a very small number of younger men and women were active in gun-running and military activities. In purely military terms the campaign may have diverted some British resources from the campaign in Ireland, and clearly a fair amount of arms and ammunition was shipped to the IRA. However, it is likely that the main impact of the campaign in the city, as in the rest of Britain, was political, in that it literally brought the Irish issue to the doorsteps of Britain and may have underlined the urgent need for a settlement.

## Conclusion

What has been termed the physical force tradition in Irish nationalism experienced drastically fluctuating fortunes in the period under discussion. From the early 1870s to the late 1890s it waned under the combined impact of the revival of a parliamentary alternative, internal dissent and vigorous government counter measures. From the early 1870s the home rule movement became steadily more coherent, organised and assertive, especially under the leadership of Parnell and in its emphasis on the land issue. Indeed, these developments attracted many able Fenians and underlay the enervating schisms within the movement. Other members and sympathisers were alienated by such extreme measures as the dynamite campaigns of the Irish-Americans in the early to mid-1880s. The result was that by the early 1890s the Fenian movement had dwindled to numerical insignificance. Nevertheless, Fenianism did retain a diffuse, lingering, romantic appeal, and there was an envious wistful respect for the ideological purity and consistency of the cast of mind it represented. In addition, the many ballads and songs which the events of 1867 inspired preserved a niche for the Fenians and their deeds within popular nationalism, and this could occasionally surface in the public disputes with more pragmatic Irish politicians and in the support for such projects as the erection of the martyrs' monument in Moston cemetery. As with much else in Irish cultural life, there was a revival discernible in the Fenian movement in the late 1890s and the early years of the twentieth century. Each of the subsequent events down to 1922 was keenly followed by elements within the Manchester Irish population, who were subject to the strains and schisms within the broader nationalist movement after 1916. It is clear that the shift of sympathy from the historic Irish Parliamentary Party to Sinn Féin and a more assertive and militant outlook was closely reflected in the city's Irish community. Some harboured passive sympathy, others provided various forms of assistance to the military campaign, and a few were to become actively involved. Given that the activists were a tiny minority operating in a major British city where the great majority of the population were at least unsympathetic and there was a well-trained and alert police force, the strictures from some of the leaders of the nationalist movement in Ireland seem misplaced. It is also clear that when the conflict between British and Irish forces ceased and the Treaty was signed in December 1921 the great majority of the Manchester Irish accepted the settlement.

## Notes

1 Vincent Comerford, *Charles J. Kickham: a study in Irish nationalism and literature* (Portmarnock: Wolfhound Press, 1979).
2 'To the Clergy of the Diocese of Salford', Acta Primi Episcopi 1852–72, 17 February 1870, Salford Diocese Archives.
3 Acta Primi Episcopi 1852–72, Pastoral Letter, Lent 1870, Salford Diocese Archives.
4 *Manchester Courier*, 11 September 1876. Lord Edward Fitzgerald, a leader of the United Irishmen who planned to stage a rising with French help, died in June 1798 of wounds sustained during his arrest.
5 *Manchester Guardian*, 11 September 1876.
6 Niall Whelehan, 'Scientific warfare or the quickest way to liberate Ireland', *History Ireland*, 16:6 (2008), pp. 42–5.
7 *Manchester Courier*, 17 and 18 January 1881; *Manchester Guardian*, 15 and 18 January 1881; Kenneth Short, *The dynamite war: Irish-American bombers in Victorian Britain* (Atlantic Highlands, NJ: Humanities Press, 1979); Shane Kenna, *War in the shadows: the Irish-Americans who bombed Victorian Britain* (Dublin: Merrion, 2014).
8 *Manchester City News*, 7 February 1885. O'Leary was later active in Irish literary and political circles, though he was always his own man and never gave uncritical support to any movement or outlook. He became something of a paternal hero figure to W.B. Yeats. He died in 1907. See Roy Foster, *W.B.*

*Yeats: a life*, vol. 1: *The apprentice mage* (Oxford: Oxford University Press, 1998), especially pp. 42–5.
9 Robert Key, *The laurel and the ivy: the story of Charles Stewart Parnell and Irish nationalism* (London: Hamish Hamilton, 1993), p. 589.
10 *Manchester Courier*, 23 December 1890; *Manchester Examiner and Times*, 23 December 1890; *Catholic Herald*, 20 March 1891.
11 Foster, *W.B. Yeats*, p. 189.
12 Roy Foster, 'Remembering 1798', in R.F. Foster (ed.), *The Irish story: telling tales and making it up in Ireland* (London: Penguin, 2002), pp. 211–34.
13 *Manchester Examiner and Times*, 4 October 1897.
14 *Manchester Courier*, 4 October 1897.
15 *Catholic Herald*, 25 November 1898.
16 *Manchester Courier*, 28 November 1898. Opposition was not motivated by alarm at the anti-English sentiment but by the mistaken assumption that the speaker was expressing support for the late leader Parnell.
17 *Manchester Guardian*, 28 November 1898.
18 *Manchester Evening Chronicle*, 28 November 1898.
19 *Manchester Courier*, 28 November 1898. At the battle of Fontenoy on 17 April 1745, during the War of Austrian Succession, the cavalry regiments of the French army's Irish Brigade, made up of expatriate Irish, played a decisive role in the defeat of the British and Dutch forces. The notion that 'England's difficulty is Ireland's opportunity' was a basic article of Fenian belief.
20 *Manchester Guardian*, 28 November 1898.
21 *Manchester Courier*, 6 August 1900; *Manchester Guardian*, 6 August 1900; *Catholic Herald*, 10 August 1900.
22 *Catholic Herald*, 10 August 1900.
23 *Manchester Guardian*, 6 August 1900.
24 *Manchester Courier*, 6 August 1900; *Manchester Guardian*, 6 August 1900.
25 *Catholic Herald*, 10 August 1900.
26 *Manchester Evening News*, 10 August 1900.
27 Owen McGee, *The Irish Republican Brotherhood from the Land League to Sinn Fein* (Dublin: Four Courts Press, 2005); Matthew Kelly, *The Fenian ideal and Irish nationalism* (Woodbridge: Boydell Press, 2008).
28 P.S. O'Hegarty, Witness Statement 26, pp. 7 and 12, Dublin, Bureau of Military History, Online Collections, www.bureauofmilitaryhistory/ie/bmsearch/search.jsp (accessed 15 September 2013). Henceforth Witness Statements in this collection are designated WS.
29 Patrick O'Donoghue, WS 26, p. 6; O'Donoghue later commanded the IRA in Manchester.
30 P.S. O'Hegarty, WS 26, p. 6.
31 Ronan Fanning, *Fatal path: British government and Irish revolution* (London: Faber & Faber, 2013), p. 136; Kelly, *The Fenian ideal*, pp. 232–3.
32 Dermot Meleady, *John Redmond: the national leader* (Dublin: Merrion, 2014), pp. 274–8.
33 *Manchester Guardian*, 30 April 1914.

34 *Catholic Herald*, 9 and 16 May 1914.
35 *Catholic Herald*, 20 June and 11 July 1914; *Manchester Guardian*, 29 June and 27 July 1914.
36 *Manchester Guardian*, 21 November 1914.
37 Fearghal McGarry, *The rising: Ireland 1916* (Oxford: Oxford University Press, 2010), p. 111.
38 Patrick O'Donoghue, WS 847, p. 2; Seamus Robinson, WS 156, pp. 10–13; Ann Matthews, *The Kimmage garrison: making billy-can bombs at Larkfield* (Dublin: Four Courts Press, 2010). A pike was a long wooden staff headed by a spike and a backward-curving blade used to unseat a horseman. It was an iconic weapon widely used by the insurgent Irish peasantry in the 1798 rising.
39 Charles Townshend, *Easter 1916: the Irish rebellion* (London: Penguin, 2006).
40 *Manchester Guardian*, 1 May 1916.
41 Michael Hopkinson, *The Irish war of independence* (Dublin: Gill & Macmillan, 2002), p. 147, suggests that the Irish in Britain failed to realise their potential, and a similar view was expressed by some of the leading personalities of the revolutionary period. See Keiko Inoue, 'Dáil propaganda and the Irish Self-Determination League of Great Britain during the Anglo-Irish war', *Irish Studies Review*, 6:1 (April 1998), pp. 50–2. For a contrary view see Peter Hart, 'Operations abroad: the I.R.A. in Britain', *English Historical Review*, 115 (2000), p. 99, and Peter Hart, *The I.R.A. at war: 1916–23* (Oxford: Oxford University Press, 2003), p. 175. David Shaw, 'The I.R.A. in Liverpool and Manchester 1919–1923' (MA dissertation, Institute of Irish Studies, University of Liverpool, 2009), provides a good balanced overview of the conflict at a local level. Gerard Noonan, *The I.R.A. in Britain 1919–1923* (Liverpool: Liverpool University Press, 2014) is a general survey of the campaign.
42 Eamon Morkan, WS 411, p. 13.
43 Mrs Sean O'Donovan, born Kathleen Boland, sister of Harry, claimed that her father and grandfather had both been involved in the Manchester Martyrs incident. Mrs S. O'Donovan, WS 586, p. 1.
44 Liam McMahon, WS 274, pp. 12, 25.
45 Eugene Loughran, WS 526, pp. 3–4; Liam McMahon, WS 526, pp. 3–4; Patrick O'Donoghue, WS 847, pp. 7–10; Mrs Austin Stack, WS 418, pp. 20–1.
46 *Manchester Guardian*, 20 October 1919; *Catholic Herald*, 25 October 1919.
47 *Manchester Guardian*, 20 October 1919; *Catholic Herald*, 6 December 1919.
48 *Catholic Herald*, 20 March 1920; *The Illustrated Dairy*, 1:2 (August 1903), p. 1. Lee, Vice President of the ISDL, was to become Lord Mayor of Manchester in 1945–46; his son followed in his footsteps and became Lord Mayor in 1981. For the Catenians, see James Hagerty, *The Catenian Association: a centenary history 1908–2008* (London: Catenian Association, 2008).
49 *Manchester Guardian*, 12 April 1920.
50 *Manchester Guardian*, 1 November 1920.
51 Charles Townshend, *The republic: the fight for Irish independence* (London: Allen Lane, 2013).
52 Hart, 'Operations abroad', p. 72; Patrick O'Donoghue, WS 847, p. 5.

53  John Gallogly, WS 244, p. 20
54  Thomas Young, WS 531, p. 6.
55  Patrick O'Donoghue, WS 847, p. 6.
56  John Plunkett, WS 865, p. 41; Gearoid Ua h-Ullachain, WS 336, pp. 14–19.
57  M. Herbert, *The wearing of the green: a political history of the Irish in Manchester* (London: Irish in Britain Representation Group, 2001), pp. 108–12; David Shaw, *The I.R.A.*, pp. 16–18; Patrick O'Donoghue, 'Manchester Battalion', pp. 2–3, Dublin, Bureau of Military History, Military Service Pensions Collection, MA/MSPC/RO/608.
58  *Manchester Guardian*, 5 and 6 April 1921, 6 May 1921; *Manchester Evening Chronicle*, 9 September 1933.
59  *Manchester Guardian*, 16 July 1921.
60  *Manchester Guardian*, 21 February 1922.
61  *Manchester Guardian*, 13 March, 20 March and 13 May 1923.
62  Hart, 'Operations abroad', pp. 91–3.

# Conclusion

From early modern times there was constant interaction between the Manchester region and Ireland, and these linkages fluctuated in nature and intensity. It is clear that there was constant movement of people, with Irish merchants travelling to the city to oversee the sale of goods, originally linen yarn, then livestock and later food, especially dairy produce and meat. There was also an ongoing military dimension. Personnel and supplies were bought or requisitioned in Manchester for campaigns in Ireland, and there was a sporadic flow of refugees and wounded soldiers through the city in troubled times. From early days there was also an ebb and flow of people, including vagrants, some of them from Ireland seeking better prospects in Britain, others Irish men and women who were expedited on their way home by both national legislation and local by-laws and charities. But by the late eighteenth century one type of temporary Irish migrant, the seasonal harvester, was becoming an integral part of the agricultural labour force in Britain, welcomed by local farmers, if not by native labourers. It is also clear that by the end of the eighteenth century better economic opportunities in Britain were attracting increasing numbers of Irish, who settled as permanent residents in Manchester. This inflow grew steadily, especially in the 1840s, reaching a peak in the early 1860s.

Whilst there were some Irish in every part of the city, their general lack of resources meant that they tended to concentrate in the poorer working-class districts of the city in distinct residential neighbourhoods. The result was that a significant portion of the Irish population lived a good deal of their family and social life in Irish-dominated, though not totally homogeneous, neighbourhoods. There they conducted a lively communal life, often centred on the local public house and Catholic parish. To some extent this social geography reflected the traditions of a rural people who at key times of the agricultural year had worked their land on a cooperative basis. However, it also reflected a defensive reaction to a stressful alien and sometimes actively hostile urban and cultural environment. But the migrant Irish also provided easy targets for a newly organised police force anxious to justify its existence and cost as it applied newly evolving ideas on acceptable behaviour in public space. All too often it did so in an unsympathetic and overly forceful manner which provoked a violent reaction from the Irish, thereby reinforcing a sense of communal identity.

The growing Irish presence in Britain in the early years of the nineteenth century also provoked a revival of those anti-Irish and anti-Catholic sentiments which were key dimensions of historic English, and later British, popular nationalism. The strongly working-class nature of the influx, especially from 1815 onwards, unhappily coincided with widespread anxieties over the challenges to the traditional ordering of society provoked by the fast-accelerating processes of urban industrial development in several regions of Britain. Manchester played a key role in the analysis and publicising of these problems, and in James Phillips Kay it found an observer who dissected and publicised them by skilful deployment of personal experience, statistics and sincere Christian concern for both the individuals concerned and the fate of society in general. Embedded within his widely read book, his argument that the Irish had played a key role in lowering the standards and values of the entire working class was absorbed by many other anxious analysts of the 'condition of England' question, and for a time historic anti-Irish sentiment was revived in the novel context of urban industrial Britain, with the Irish as scapegoats. Running in parallel and interacting with this was a revival of anti-Catholicism, partly in reaction to the fact that the great majority of the Irish migrants were Catholic, and partly in reaction to changes in the broader religious landscape of Britain. Whilst such feelings gradually ebbed during the century, in some places they were forcefully articulated by local preachers and itinerant lecturers and at times could provoke outbreaks of violence.

But for several reasons sectarian conflict in Manchester was never as widespread or as enduring as in Merseyside or Clydeside. The Irish influx into the city never reached the volume or intensity experienced in Liverpool or Glasgow. Consequently, the institutions of the city, whilst certainly under strain in the late 1840s, were never in danger of being overwhelmed. It is also true that the Irish influx into Manchester, drawn from the intensely Catholic counties of north-west Ireland, was overwhelmingly Catholic, whereas the inflow to Liverpool and Glasgow drew heavily from Ulster and included a larger Protestant element. One element making up the sectarian conflict in Ireland was therefore not present in great numbers. There were outbreaks in the first half of the century, but they were sporadic and small-scale and had largely died away by the 1860s. It is also true that the civic ethos of Manchester was quite liberal and inclusive, more preoccupied with modern commercial development than historic debates and sentiments. The economic structure of the city may also have played a part, in that it was much more broadly based and stable than Liverpool, where working-class employment came to be dominated by demanding and irregular dock work.

The result was that the Irish in Manchester, as in much of Britain in this period, were in an ambivalent position, in that they were engaged with the city but also simultaneously to some extent lived a life apart. From the outset they were a distinctive people – indeed until the arrival of large numbers of Jews from the imperial Russian pogroms of the second half of the century, they were the most exotic element in the Manchester population. They were distinctive in religion and accent, and often in language, history and politics. In the late 1840s the large influx was also notable for its poverty and high rate of infectious disease. Their mix of limited economic resources, traditional social solidarity and reaction to the alien environment in which they found themselves meant that they concentrated in districts such as Little Ireland and the much longer-lived Angel Meadow. In these areas much community life was concentrated around the local Catholic church. This provided not only spiritual ministrations but clergy who were also community leaders and brokers between their parishioners and wider society. The parish was also the base for a dense network of religious, cultural, social and mutual aid groups, the Catholic version of the 'associational culture' which was such a notable feature of life in mid-Victorian British cities. For the Protection and Rescue Society the prime concern was to patrol the boundaries of the faith community by ensuring the safety of children deemed vulnerable to the dangers of Protestant proselytism and moral and physical harm.

Residential clustering and church-based community life were therefore factors which helped keep the Irish apart and preserve a distinctive presence. The same can be said for the St Patrick's Day celebrations and the commemorations for the Manchester Martyrs. Each 17 March was an occasion for relaxed, convivial fraternisation amongst fellow Irish, when in almost liminal moments the combination of atmosphere, company, nostalgia and music transported participants back to Ireland. The martyrs' commemoration events were rather more serious given their origin. They had about them an air of respectable defiance which sent a message about the serious nature of Irish political aspirations.

These same political aspirations served to mark out the Irish. Given the small number of native Catholics in Great Britain, Catholic emancipation was an issue of the greatest direct concern to the Irish, and it was O'Connell's campaigns in Ireland which eventually brought success. The impact in Britain as a whole was if anything to rouse traditional Protestant fears. The issue of religious education certainly marked out the Irish through their tenacious defence of church schools and the energetic measures taken to mobilise the Catholic vote for local and parliamentary elections. Home rule also served to differentiate the Catholic Irish in Britain, since it was an issue outside the mainstream of British political concerns until it was adopted by the Liberals in 1886 and even then was seen by significant sections of the political class as a threat to the constitution and national and imperial unity. The home rule campaign was a reflection of another development which differentiated the Irish in Britain, namely the growing confidence and assertiveness of Irish nationalism and its representatives in both Britain and Ireland. The Irish in Britain shared to the full in this new sense of national awareness, which was articulated through a succession of organisations. Some of these were Irish adaptations of the Victorian mania for fraternal and mutual aid organisations, others were political, and from the turn of the century, still others were cultural.

Alongside such groups was the tradition of violent separatism, which, whilst it waxed and waned during the period, never died and, even in its weakest phases, retained a lingering, romantic appeal, not least through music, song and ballad. Its sporadic manifestations in Manchester, in 1848, 1867, 1881 and 1920–21, served to remind the general population of the Irish presence, their distinctive political demands and their occasional deployment of violence.

But there were also factors which drew the Irish into the city mainstream. Whilst a significant number lived in distinct neighbourhoods, these were never uniformly Irish. Only a very few small streets were exclusively Irish; non-Irish districts were nearby, and the Irish had to move out of their particular neighbourhoods for work. Moreover, there were issues in which the Irish made common cause with the native population. Amongst these were trade union rights, parliamentary reform, Corn Law repeal and, at times, Chartism. In periods of economic distress the Irish suffered as much as and possibly more than many, and some clergy were prominent in agitation for improved living and working conditions. By the end of the period the rise of the labour movement and its concern with material issues was beginning to attract Irish attention and support, thereby drawing them close to those of similar class background in the local population, and causing some anxiety in the Catholic Church in the process.

As for the distinctive issues which concerned the Irish and the occasions they celebrated, though their nature may have made them stand out, the ways in which they expressed them drew them closer to mainstream British societal norms. From at least the 1860s onwards the Irish took part in electoral politics in Manchester. Their concentration in Angel Meadow and parts of Ancoats meant they could have a notable impact on both School Board and municipal elections and possibly some limited effect on parliamentary contests, whilst the links with the local Liberals drew them in the same direction. The Liberals and the city as a whole thereby benefited from the services of a number of notably skilled first- and second-generation Irish councillors, who, whilst certainly taking up the issues arising in areas notable for poor living conditions, also used their opportunities to argue for distinctive Irish and Catholic concerns. Thus the Irish were drawn into the civic life of one of the most dynamic and prosperous cities of the nineteenth-century British state, accepting its norms and traditions whilst simultaneously arguing for some distinctively Irish preoccupations.

Even the St Patrick's Day celebrations and the martyrs' commemoration conformed to what were regarded as the respectable norms of the time. Here the Catholic Church played a role, since it was anxious to ensure that its flock behaved as responsible and sober citizens, and it was partly its influence which saw the 17 March celebrations become increasingly structured and respectable. As for the martyrs' commemorations, from the outset care was taken to ensure that Manchester's traditional public spaces for assembly and procession were used and that demeanour in the processions was serious and orderly. Until the very end of the period the event was under moderate control, and when Sinn Féin and the ISDL took over, they adopted the traditional format and route. Even the divisive issue of Catholic schools served to some extent to encourage a pragmatic alliance with the largely Anglican Church party on the School Boards and was a point at which Catholic demands and Conservative policy converged.

The situation of the Irish in the city can be best appreciated if it is realised that they were in a sense performing and presenting Irishness before a variety of audiences with sometimes conflicting expectations. Before an Irish audience the stress was on a historic Irish identity and a distinctive set of demands in terms of religion, education and politics. But even within the Irish population there were sometimes divergent expectations. Due respect had to be shown to the agenda of the Catholic Church, especially in terms of a significant role in public events, respectable behaviour and advocacy of church causes. Militant political spirits had to be accommodated and reassured that Irish issues, above all self-government, were being pursued with appropriate fervour and not allowed to slip out of focus. After 1900 care had to be taken to avoid reopening the recent split over the Parnell leadership, and the burgeoning organisations arising from the cultural revival had to be reckoned with. But all this had to be done before a critical local British audience who always had to be reassured that Irish concerns and the methods used to pursue them did not seriously threaten British norms of constitutional propriety, a process which was periodically rendered more difficult by a revival of the physical force tradition. Irish leaders had therefore to ensure that whilst they argued the cause for Irish concerns, especially self-government, they had to reassure their supporters amongst the Manchester population that self-government did not mean separation and would be perfectly compatible with local loyalty and membership of the United Kingdom and the British Empire. The result could sometimes be quite difficult political balancing acts and verbal gymnastics on public occasions.

In the end the extraordinary feature of the Manchester Irish is that they remained so Irish. Doubtless there were many who through choice or perhaps because of a peripatetic life style broke their links with the Irish community or the Catholic Church on arrival in the city. Still others may have quietly conformed to the social and cultural norms of an increasingly prosperous and self-confident city and abandoned any effort to preserve or express a sense of Irishness. This would not be surprising considering the dynamic nature of the city they lived in. Like all the major urban centres of Britain in the second half of the nineteenth century, Manchester developed a distinct, confident civic identity and an increasingly activist city council. Meanwhile, at the national level the British state assumed a growing interventionist role whilst simultaneously evolving into the centre of a world empire. Yet, despite the various forces bearing down upon them, the Irish in British cities remained an element which to some extent managed to participate whilst remaining somewhat apart. Subject to these varying influences, they devised a hybrid sense of identity, composed of elements of their traditional loyalties and concerns, but expressed through the evolving institutions and mores of the city in which they had settled.

# Index

'98 Centennial Committee 252

Act of Disestablishment 88
Act of Emancipation 91
Act of Union 15, 87, 120
agrarian agitation 190–1
agriculture 7–8, 15, 16
alcohol 32–3, 62, 98–9
alienation 258
Allen, W. 215, 228–9
alliance, Chartists and repealers 161–8
Allison, W.P. 23, 25
ambivalence 270
America, Fenian movement 209–11, 251
American Civil War 209
Amnesty Association 249
'*An address of the Irish and English Repealers of Manchester to the Sovereign People of France*' 162
Ancient Order of Hibernians 258
Ancoats 49, 50, 102
Angel Meadow 4, 46–56
   Catholic Lads' Club 105
   census 1851 58–9, 62
   clearance and restoration 70–1 n60
   context and overview 41
   description 46–7
   development 47–8
   geology 48
   housing 49
   Irish people 57–9
   living conditions 48–53
   lodging houses 52–3
   map 13, 47
   moral improvement 63–6
   percentage of Irish 57
   personal safety 54
   public health 51
   reports on 49–51
   societal threats 53–6
   street life 56
   summary and conclusion 66–7
Anglo-French War 146
Anglo-Irish Treaty 138, 262, 263
Anglo-Irish union, campaign for repeal 152–9
anti-Catholic riots 62–3, 88–9, 94
anti-Catholic sentiment 3, 14, 85–95, 186, 269
Anti-Corn Law League 154–5, 156, 158, 271
anti-emancipation petition 151–2
anti-Irish sentiment 3, 31–3, 44, 269
Arkwright, R. 15, 48
Armitt, T. 9
arrests 163, 165, 167, 211–12, 262
Ashton-under-Lyne 166–7
Ashworth, J. 179
associationalism 96–104, 110, 121
authority, attitudes to 45
Auxiliaries 258, 261

## INDEX 275

ballads 8, 11, 263
Ballingarry insurrection 166
Bamford, S. 18
banal nationalism 219
baptisms, Catholic Church 78
Barrett, S. 255, 257, 261
Barry, K. 232
Belgium, Germany's treatment of 238
Bellevue Gardens demonstration 195
Biggar, J.G. 250–1
Bilsborrow, Bishop J. 65, 103, 105, 187
bishops, British right of veto 150
'Black '47' 42
Black and Tans 258, 261
Black Joe 153
blanketeers 148
Blennerhassett, R.P. 190
blight 42
Bodkin, M. 133, 180, 192
Boland, H. 259
bombings 251
book
  focus 3
  structure and overview 4–6
  summary and conclusion 268–73
*Book of Martyrs* (Foxe) 85
Boyle, D. 100, 131, 134, 135, 180–1, 182, 189, 193, 195, 196–7, 199, 235, 237
Brett, Police Sergeant 212–13, 215, 216
Bright, J. 190, 191
British Army, raid on IRA office 262
British authorities 258–9, 261
British–Irish relationship 31, 193
British party politics 134
Broomhead, Fr 80, 96–7
Brotherhood of St Peter 98
Brown, W. 178
Burns, L. 30, 31
Burns, M. 30–1
Butler, Fr 262
Butt, I. 176, 189–90, 249
Byrne, J.P. 239

campaign for parliamentary reform 147, 148–9, 154–9
Canada 210
Carlyle, T. 30–1
carnival 222
Carroll, J. 230–1, 253

Casartelli, Bishop L.C. 95, 106, 194, 196, 198
Casey Charity 80
Cassidy, Fr 232
Catholic Association 87, 150–1
Catholic associationism 96–104
Catholic Church 4
  to 1845 75–84
  allocation of parishes 105–6
  anti-Catholic sentiment 85–95
  associationism 96–104, 110, 121
  attendance 96–7
  attitude to commemoration 223–4
  attitude to Fenian movement 208, 214, 228–32, 249–50
  attitude to oath-bound organisations 149
  baptisms 78
  care of children 100–4
  centrality 270
  clergy 80–3
  context and overview 75
  Corpus Christi processions 222
  development 86
  dioceses 75
  effect of immigration 77–9
  electoral politics 194
  famine refugees 97
  first Bishop 173
  Irish influx 109
  and Irish population 104–9
  leakage 100–3
  local politics 174–5
  moral improvement 64
  organisation 88
  parliamentary politics 196–8
  politics 161–2
  reforms 96
  St Patrick's Day, 1848 161–2
  St Patrick's Day celebrations 129–30
  sectarian violence 91–2
  summary and conclusion 109–10
  tensions 104–6, 110
  as threat 85, 93
  visibility 86
Catholic Committee 150
Catholic emancipation 28, 32, 79, 87, 90–1, 150–2, 271
Catholic Federation 195–6, 197
*Catholic Herald* 230–1

Catholic hierarchy 88
Catholicism 1–2, 84–5, 97
Catholic Lads' Club 105
Catholic Needlework Guild 98
Catholic population 12–15, 75, 76
Catholic Registration Societies 187–9
Catholic Relief Act 87
Catholics
  material and social success 79–80
  political participation 187–9
  suspicion of 75–6
  urbanisation 76
Catholic schools 64–5
Catholic Total Abstinence Society 98–9
Catholic Working Lads' Club, The 65
Cato Street conspiracy 148
cattle trade 8
cellars 51, 52, 53, 62
censuses 10, 14, 57–9, 62
ceremonies, commemorative 219
chain migration 60–1
charities, aid for injured activists 150
Chartism 124, 154–9, 271
  alliance with repealers 161–8
  conventions 158
  decline 164, 167
  and Irish Confederates 160–8
  loss of momentum 158
  mass meeting, 1848 164
  meeting, March 1842 156–7
  meeting, October 1841 156
  militancy 164–5
  revival 161
Chester Castle 211
children 100–4, 107, 110
cholera 20–2, 28, 50
Christian Doctrine Confraternity 97
Christianity, Ireland 118–19
Churchill, W. 196–7
Church of England 75–6, 173
Church of Ireland 94, 120, 248
church schools 79, 98, 109, 130–1, 194–5, 197, 271
cities 28–9
city status 173
civic ethos 270
civil unrest 147
civil war 262
Clan na Gael 251

class-based alliance 145
clergy
  additional roles 82
  community roles 82–3
  respect for 80, 82
Clerkenwell prison bombing 94
clubs 63–4, 65–6, 159–60
Clynes, J.R. 194, 198, 199
Cobden, R. 156
Coercion Bill for Ireland 153
Coigley, Fr J. 146–7
Collins, M. 259
Combination Acts 147
commemoration
  attitude of Church 223–4, 225
  change of march route 235
  changing context of 237–8
  control of 232, 239–40, 241
  creation of tradition 224–8
  death of MacSwiney 260–1
  extension of 239
  flexibility 220–1
  as instruction 221
  Manchester Martyrs 219–24, 270–1, 272
  national past 219
  ownership of 223, 232–40
  as political activity 223
  political utility of 240–1
  redefining 241
  rituals 5
  significance 240
  Sinn Féin control 239
  Wolfe Tone 252
  *see also* parades and processions
communal identity 269
community solidarity 62–3
compassion fatigue 44
condition of England question 28, 34
*condition of the working class in England, The* (Engels) 30
Confederate Clubs 124, 207
Confederates 159–68
confraternities 97–8
Connolly, I. 198, 260
Connolly, J. 198, 236
Conradh na Gaeilge (Gaelic League) 133, 256, 257
Conservative Party 178–9, 182

# INDEX

Constables' Accounts 9
contagion theory 20–1
contingent contagionism 25
continuity, nationalist claims to 261
Cornwell Lewis, G. 11–12
Corpus Christi processions 222
Corrupt Practices Act 1884 177
Corydon, J.J. 211
cotton working 7, 15
Court Leet records 9
crime 33–4, 56
criminal justice, against industrial action 147
Croskell, Provost 249–50
Crumlin Road jail 259–60
Cullen, P. (Archbishop and Cardinal) 208, 223
cultural revival 256–7
culture, impact 2
Cumann na mBan 259, 260
Curran, E. 156
Cusack, Fr 107, 228–30

Daly, J. 255
D'Arcy McGee, T. 159, 160
data sources 2
Davis, T. 158, 159
Davitt, M. 190
Deasy, T. 211–13
demonstrations 106, 148, 157, 195
detentions 259
de Trafford family 76
de Valera, E. 259
Devlin, J. 135, 140
devotional revolution 96
Devoy, J. 251
diaspora 139–40
Dillon, J. 139–40, 192, 198
Dillon, J.B. 158
Diocesan Temperance Crusade 104
disease 42–3, 44–5, 49, 80, 270
distillation 32–3, 62
Dixon, J. 146
doggerel 15, 77
Doherty, J. 149, 153
Donovan, D. 155–6
Donovan, J.T. 236, 237
Doyle, C. 156
drunkenness 123

dual loyalty 139
Dublin rising 5
Duffy, C.G. 158, 159
Dunn, Mr 52–3, 54
Dyson, Councillor 175

Easter Rising 137, 238, 258
economic depression, 1842 157
economic growth 34
economic resources 59
Education Acts 182, 183, 193
education bills 192–3, 194–5, 196
education, dual system 182–3
Egan, C. 238, 239
electoral politics 5, 272
  Catholic Church 194
  Catholic participation 187–9
  context and overview 172–3
  general election 1885 191
  municipal elections 173–82
  parliamentary politics 189–99
  participation 186–7, 199–200
  School Board elections 182–9
  summary and conclusion 199–200
  voter illiteracy 184–5
  voting strength 172–3
  women's enfranchisement 198
  *see also* religious education
Emancipation Bill 91, 151
emigration 15–17, 43, 104, 107
Emmet Brigade, The 164
employment 1
Engels, F. 30–1, 48–9.50
Esmonde, J. 135
Europe 161, 219
evangelicalism 64, 86, 121
Ewart, P. 15, 60

famine 41–3, 160–1
famine fever 44–5
famine refugees 43, 97
Farley, F.J. 180, 181–2, 234
*Federationist, The* 196
Fenian Brotherhood 206–7
Fenian convention, 1865 210
Fenian movement
  America 209–11, 251
  attitude of Church 208, 214, 228–32, 249–50

commemoration poster 227
context and overview 206
decline 263
division 210–11
failed rising 211
Ireland and Britain 206–12
loss of political initiative 237–8
ownership of commemoration 232–40
parliamentary politics 249
propaganda 208–9, 218
public meetings 211
rumours 214
strength of 248
summary and conclusion 240–1
tradition of commemoration 224–8
*see also* commemoration; Irish nationalists; Irish Republican Brotherhood (IRB); Manchester Martyrs
Fenian raids 210
Fenian scare 94
Finnigan, J. 163
First World War 136–7
Flinn, Fr 230
food prices 157
food shortages 16, 41, 147
Fox, T. 95
Foy, J. 126
*Freeman's Journal* 11
free trade 15

Gaelic League 133, 256, 257
Gavazzi, 'Father' 94
general elections 153, 190–1, 194, 197, 198, 199
geographic change 93
geology 18, 48
George III 119
Germany, treatment of Belgium 238
Gillett, B. 236
Gladstone, W.E. 190, 191–2, 248
'God save Ireland' (Sullivan) 218
Gonne, M. 105, 230, 252, 253
Gould, W. 215
Griffith, A. 198, 260
growth, Manchester 18
Guild of St Agnes 65
guilds 97

Habeas Corpus 146, 148, 165
Hampden Clubs 148
Harrington, T. 139
Harrop, J. 45–6
*Harvest, The* 100, 102, 104, 107–9
Hayden, J. 133, 134
Hazleton, R. 136
Healy, T.M. 132, 133, 233
Hearne, Fr D. 82–3, 93, 122, 155
Heinrick. H. 172
Henry, M. 129–30, 131
Heywood, A. 214
Heywood, B. 236
hillside men 252
Home Government Association 249
home rule 131–6, 176, 178, 191–2, 234–7, 271
*see also* Irish nationalists
Home Rule Act 136, 237
Home Rule Association 176, 190
Home Rule Association of Great Britain 249
Home Rule Bill 135–6, 182, 237, 257
Home Rule Confederation 189
House of Lords' veto on legislation 236
housing 49, 52, 61–2, 63, 66–7
*see also* living conditions
Howard, R.B. 49–50
hunger strikes 259, 260
Hunt, H. 148

identity
 communal 269
 hybrid 6
 maintenance 3
 Manchester 273
 as social construction 3
ideologies, national 219
illiteracy, of voters 184–5
imports 8
Independent Labour Party 133–4, 180
industrial action 147, 157, 236
industrial development, Angel Meadow 47–8
industrial revolution 28
information linkages 60–1
integration 2
interaction 3, 268
invention of tradition 221

INDEX 279

Ireland
  civil war 262
  early Christianity 118–19
  interest in 108–9
  political opinion 137
Irish-Americans 206, 209–10
Irish Anglican Church 87–8
Irish Catholic Association 90, 91
Irish Church Temporalities Act 1833 88
Irish Confederates 159–68
Irish Council Bill 134
Irish cultural revival 5
*Irish Exile, The* 261
Irish Free State government 262
Irish immigrants, image of 31
Irish in Britain, role of 259–60
Irish Lambs 156
Irish Land Act 1881 190
Irish National Foresters 100, 105, 179, 254–5
Irish nationalism 6, 158–9
Irish nationalists 190–2
  arrests and deportations 262
  British campaign against 259
  calls for unity 233–4
  context and overview 248
  criticism of 255
  decline 255–6
  division 233, 250–1, 263
  gains 235
  and Liberal Party 190–4, 197, 198–9
  Manchester campaign 258–63
  municipal elections 178, 179–80
  ownership of commemoration 232–40
  parliamentary politics 189–93, 197–8
  physical force tradition 263
  revisionism and dissent 248–55
  revival 255–8
  role of Irish in Britain 259–60
  School Board elections 189
  violence 251–2
  *see also* Fenian movement; home rule
Irish National Land League 190
Irish National League 179
Irishness
  performance of 2, 272–3
  preservation of 273

Irish Parliamentary Party 131–3, 135, 237–8, 249, 255, 263
Irish people
  Angel Meadow 57–9
  attitude to authority 45
  as burden 46
  community solidarity 62–3
  hospitality 60
  image of 32–4, 44, 57
  political organisation 179
*Irish People, The* 209
Irish poor
  attitudes to 27, 29, 30–1
  commission into 27, 82
  as undeserving 44
Irish Poor Report 62, 77
Irish population 77, 172
Irish prisoners 259
Irish Republican Army (IRA) 6, 259, 261–3
Irish Republican Brotherhood (IRB) 6, 105, 206–7
  constitution 248
  decline 256
  infiltration of groups 257
  meeting, September 1876 250–1
  opportunism 258
  organisation 211
  parliamentary politics 248–9, 250–1
  *see also* Easter Rising; Fenian movement
Irish Republic, provisional government 211
Irish Self-Determination League of Great Britain (ISDL) 128, 198, 260, 261
Irish Volunteers 136, 257
Irish voters 174–8

Jacobite rising 13–14
John Mitchel Club 165
joint action 157
joint Liberal and Irish nationalist ticket 179–80
jokes 31–2
Jones, E. 165

Kay, Fr 152
Kay, J.P. 23–6, 34, 38 n76, 51, 269

photo 24
publications 26, 27–8, 29–30, 31
on River Irk 48
role of religion 55
societal threats 53–4
world view 26
Kelly, T.F. 139
Kelly, T.J. 210, 211–13
Kenny, Alderman 231
Kershaw, Canon 99, 131
Kickham, C. 249
Kiernan, T.B. 190
Kilmainham Treaty 190
Kimmage Garrison 258
Knights of the Blessed Sacrament 98
Kohl, J.G. 61

labour movement 235–6, 272
Labour Party 180–2, 199
Lalor, J.F. 161
Lamartine, A. de 163
Land Act 1870 248–9
land cultivation 16
Land League 251
land reform 161, 190, 251
lapse rate 2
Larkin, J. 236
Larkin, M. 215, 228–9
Lavelle, Fr 208
Lavery, P. 80
League Police 156
leakage 100–3
Lee, D. 79, 80, 121–2
legislation, housing and living
    conditions 52, 63
legitimacy, nationalist claims to 261
leisure pursuits 98
Leyland, J. 7
Liberal governments, need for Irish
    support 236
Liberal– Labour-Irish alliance 197
Liberal Party 130–1, 178–9, 190–4, 197–9,
    234–5
Lichfield House Compact 153, 155
links 34
    businesses 108–9
    commercial 7–12
    context and overview 7
    development of 4

early connections 7–12
emphasis on 108–9
fluctuations 268
military 9–10
see also emigration; migration
Little Ireland 4, 18–20
    cholera 22–3
    Engels on 31
    land use map 19
    notoriety 22–3
    reports on 22, 27
    riots 157
Liverpool Scotland Road constituency 173
living conditions 26–7, 30–1, 48–53, 63,
    271
    see also housing
local electoral alliance 179–80
local politics
    religious education 175
    scandals 178–9
    see also municipal elections
local studies 2
lodging houses 52–3, 67
Loughrey, Cllr 238
loyalism 145–6
loyalties 173
Luby, T.C. 207
Lynch, Fr 132–3, 193

McCabe, D. 95, 98, 103, 104, 107, 132,
    133, 134, 137, 139, 179, 180, 181 189,
    192–3, 196, 233, 252, 257–8
McCarthy, Fr 105–6, 230, 253
McGarry, S. 259
McHugh, E. 235–6
Mackey, Fr 230
McMahon, Fr 259
McManus, T.B. 208
McNeil, Canon H. 93
MacSwiney, T. 260–1
Maguire, T. 215, 216
mainstream, Irish in 271–2
Manchester
    growth of city 174
    identity 273
    Irish population 46
    as locus of research 2–3
    overview of 17–18
    reports on 29–30

INDEX 281

Manchester and Salford Catholic Association 90, 149
Manchester and Salford Sanitary Association 50, 52, 55–6
Manchester Catholic Literary Society 98
Manchester Catholic Registration Society 79
Manchester Constitutional Society 145
Manchester Corresponding Society 146
Manchester Council
  discussion of Fenian movement 214
  membership 179
*Manchester Courier* 32, 43, 90–1, 95, 129, 131, 134, 151–2, 197, 213–14, 217
Manchester Diocesan Church Association 94
*Manchester Examiner and Times* 219–20
Manchester Geographical Society 106
*Manchester Guardian* 32, 53, 151, 152, 179, 212, 213, 217, 239
*Manchester Herald* 145
Manchester IRA campaign 258–63
Manchester jail 214
Manchester Martyrs 5, 94, 106–7, 212–19, 270–1, 272
  adoption by labour movement 235–6
  attitude of Church 228–32
  campaign for mercy 216
  change of march route 235
  commemoration 105–6, 219–24, 227, 232–41
  hangings 216, 218
  illustration 229
  memorabilia 218
  Moston memorial 105, 230, 231, 239, 252–4
  press coverage 213–14, 217, 218–20, 228
  propaganda 218
  reactions to sentences 215–16, 217–18
  representation 228–32
  sentences 215
  significance 240
  songs and ballads 218
  tradition of commemoration 224–8
  trial 215
*Manchester Observer* 148–9
Manchester Police Act 1839 173
Manchester prison escapes 259–60
Manchester Protestant Operatives' Association 94
Manchester Regiment 13–14
Markievicz, Countess 198, 260
marriage 59, 64
martial law 166
Masonic Order 149
Maspero, Fr 231
Mass 96–7
Mass for the Manchester Martyrs 106–7
Mathew, Fr T. 83, 98–9, 123
Maynooth Seminary 88
Meagher, T.F. 159, 162, 163, 164, 165, 167
Mercer, Rev. 53, 54, 63
miasmatic theory 21
middle class 2
migrants 10–12, 59, 146, 268
migration 14, 60–1, 77–9
militancy 251
military links 268
Milroy, S. 239, 259
Mitchel, J. 159, 160–1, 163, 164, 165
mixed marriages 64
monuments 219
moral improvement, Angel Meadow 63–6
morality 26–7, 54
*Morning Post* 50
Moston memorial 105, 230, 231, 239, 252–4, 261
multi-family occupation 49, 61
municipal elections 173–82, 272
  conduct of 177
  home rule as issue 176
  Irish nationalists 178, 179–80
  Irish voters 174–6, 177
  issues 180
  Labour Party 180
  local electoral alliance 179–80
  New Cross 175, 176, 177, 178, 179, 180–1
  organisation and administration 176–7
  party politics 174
  polling stations 177
  St Michael's 175, 176, 177–8, 179
  women voters 177
Murphy, J. 234

Murphy, W. 94–5
Murphy, W. M. 236
Murray, J. 156
music 98, 127–8
Mussely, Dean (Canon) 106–7, 228
mutual-aid groups 100
mutual benefit societies 99–100

*Nation, The* 158–9, 161, 172
National Brotherhood of St Patrick 125, 207–9
national guard 164
national ideologies 219
nationalism 118, 131–6, 173
nationalist–Liberal alliance 178
National University of Ireland 134
nation states reorganisation 219
native reactions 2
New Cross 175, 176, 177, 178, 179, 180–1, 184–5
New Departure 251
newspapers, attitudes to Irish 31–2
Nolan, J. 128
Nonconformity 85–6
norms, conforming to 272
*Northern Star* 154

oath-bound organisations, attitude of Church 149
O'Brien, B. 155
O'Brien, M. 215, 228–9
O'Brien, W. 133, 199, 233
occupation density 61, 149
O'Connell, D. 5, 82–3, 87, 124, 150–1, 152, 153–5, 156, 158, 159, 160, 161
O'Connor, F. 154–5, 157, 162, 163, 164, 167
O'Connor Power, J. 250
O'Connor, R. 260
O'Connor, T.P. 179, 195, 196
O'Donoghue, P. 261
O'Donovan Rossa, J. 251–2
O'Hanrahan, Fr 259
O'Hegarty, P.S. 257
O'Leary, J. 249, 251–2
O'Mahony, J. 206, 210
O'Malley, W. 133
O'Meagher Condon, E. 215, 216, 231, 235
O'Neill, C. 178, 189
Orange Order 89–90, 91–2, 120, 223

Order of St Patrick 119
O'Sullivan Burke, R. 217
othering 34, 85
outflow, causes 1
Oxford Movement 86–7

Palladius 119
papal aggression 88
parades and processions 63, 89, 91, 92, 105, 120, 123, 127, 157, 165–6
 change of Manchester Martyrs march route 235
 commemoration 221–2
 death of MacSwiney 260–1
 Irish National Foresters 254–5
 Irish tradition 222–3
 Moston memorial 253–5
 political 223
 routes 222
 tradition of commemoration 224–8
 traditions 222
parliamentary alliances 153
parliamentary constituencies 174
parliamentary politics 189–99
 attitude of IRB 248–9, 250
 Catholic Church 196–8
 conflicting interests 193
 by-election, Manchester North West 196–7
 home rule 191–2
 Irish nationalists 189–93
 meetings 1918, 1919 198
 religious education 192–3, 194–5
 transformation 198
 women's enfranchisement 198
parliamentary reform 147, 148–9, 154–9, 271
Parnell, C.S. 132, 179, 190, 191, 192, 251, 252
Parnell Leadership Committee of Manchester, Salford and District 252
participation, and separation 273
party politics, municipal elections 174
Party Processions Act 92
passenger steam service 8
Patriotic Society 145
payments to distressed people 9
Peel, R. 88

people, flow of 268
People's Budget 197
People's Charter 154
performance of Irishness 138–40, 272–3
permanent settlement 12–18
personal safety, Angel Meadow 54
Peterloo 29, 148
philanthropy 98
*phythophthora infestans* 42
Pietism 30
Pitt, W. (Younger) 87
place 2
Playfair, L. 82
Plug Strikes 157
Plunkett, G. 258
Police Act 1844 52
policing 28–9
political activity 2, 82–3, 105
　alliance of Chartists and repealers 161–8
　arrests 163
　campaign for parliamentary reform 147, 148–9, 154–9
　Catholic emancipation 150–2
　charities' aid 150
　Chartism 154–9
　context and overview 145
　Irish leadership 149
　loyalties 149
　militancy 164–5
　motion for repeal of union 153
　public meetings 163–5
　public meetings, repeal of union 152–3
　radicalism 145–6
　repeal associations 153
　repeal of union 152–4
　repression 146–7, 164, 165–6, 167
　summary and conclusion 168
　support for 149–50
　trade unions 147, 149
　violence 166–7
political aspirations 271
political campaigning 3
political consciousness 152
political dependence 134–5
political initiative, loss of 237–8
political involvement 5, 79, 145
political organisation 179

political processions 223
political scandals 178–9
politics
　Catholic Church 161–2
　division 137–8
　polarity 120
　St Patrick's Day celebrations 130–8
polling stations 177
Poor Law Guardians 43, 103
poor relief 43–6, 69 n29
population decline, Ireland 42–3
population growth 16, 41, 145
poverty 1, 9, 11–12, 43, 270
prejudice 31–3, 84
Presbyterians 120–1
press coverage, Manchester Martyrs 213–14, 217, 218–20, 228
priests, itinerant 12–13
Primrose, A. (Earl of Rosebery) 192
Prince Charles Edward Stuart 13–14
prisoners' aid group 259
privies 52
Progressive Municipal Programme 180
propaganda 208–9, 218
prosperity 59, 79–80
prostitution 54
Protestant element 2
Protestantism 28, 89–90
Protestant Orange Order processions 63
Protestants, threat of Catholicism 86–7
protests 106, 148, 157, 165
provisions trade 8
public commemoration 220–1
public health 23, 25–7, 51
　*see also* Kay, J.P.
public houses, dangers of 103
public institutions, risks for Catholic children 103
public meetings 192, 194, 232–3, 253, 255, 260
Puritanism 76

radicalism 29–30, 145–6, 148–50
Ragged School movement 64
rail services, effect on provisions trade 8
Reach, A. 50, 61–2
'Real Irish Night' concerts 126
recreation 63–4, 65–6
recusants 75–6

Redmond, J. 133–7, 193–8, 234, 237–8, 257
Redmond, W.A. 136, 237
Redmond, W.H.K. 135–6
Reform Act 1868 173–4
Reformation 75–6
Reformation Society 145
reform movement, militancy 146
regiments 10
regional studies 2
Relief Act 1780 85
religion
   and moral improvement 64
   social role 55–6
religious education 79, 98, 109, 130–1, 194–5, 271
   local politics 175, 178
   parliamentary politics 192–3, 197
   School Board elections 183, 185–6
Repeal Association 124, 153–4, 159
repeal of union 152–4, 160–8
reprisals policy 258–9
research, themes and scope 1–2
residential segregation 59–62, 67, 270–1
responsibility, for living conditions 51–2
Returns of Papists, 1767 14
revolutions 124, 161
Ribbonmen 121, 123
Ribbon societies 223
riots 62–3, 88–9, 94, 157
ritualism 94
River Irk 48–9
River Medlock 18–20
Roberts, W.R. 210, 211
Rochdale Road Visiting Committee of the Sanitary Association 48, 50, 51–2
Rosebery, Earl of (Archibald Primrose) 192
Rossall, Fr 104, 107
Russell, Lord J. 88

Sacred Congregation of Propaganda 88
safe houses 259
Saffenreuter, Fr 106
St Augustine's church 80
St Bridget's orphanage 80
St Chad's church 76
St George's church 91–2
St James' church 106
St Mary's Catholic church 15, 77, 97–8
St Michael's 175–9, 184–5
St Patrick 77, 118–21
St Patrick's boys' school 80
St Patrick's church 105, 106–7
St Patrick's church, cemetery, orphanage and school 81
St Patrick's Day 4–5, 99, 118–20, 128, 140–1, 161–2
St Patrick's Day celebrations 101–2, 104–5, 106, 107–8, 270–1, 272
   America 119
   associationism 121
   Catholic Church 129–30
   changes in practice 140–1
   convivial and inclusive 121–6, 140–1
   decline 125, 126
   disturbances 122–4
   fear of 124
   Irish nationalism 260
   multidimensional 140
   music 127–8
   parliamentary politics 193–4
   participation 127, 130
   performance of Irishness 138–40
   police and military presence 125–6
   politics 130–8, 141, 223
   re-emergence 125, 126
   respectability 126–30
   shifts of emphasis 121, 130, 138
   structure and emphasis 126–7
   symbolism 128–9
St Patrick's Old Boys' Association 98
St Peter's Fields 18, 148
St William's church and school 65–6
Salford Diocese Catholic Protection and Rescue Society 100–1, 103–4, 105, 110, 270
Salford Diocese Temperance Crusade 99
Sanitary Reform proposal 52–3
sanitation 49, 50–1, 63
scandals, political 178–9
Scanlon, T. 236
scapegoating 2, 3
School Board elections 182–9, 272
   participation 199–200
School Boards 183, 189

# INDEX

schools 64–5
   church schools 79, 98, 109, 130–1, 194–5, 197, 271
   dual system 182–3
   St Patrick's boys' school 80
   seasonal harvesters 268
Secret Ballot Act 1872 176–7
sectarian conflict, comparative evaluation 269–70
sectarianism 63, 91–2, 93–4, 120
selective remembering 220, 221
self-government 131–3, 134, 135–6
senate wing 210
separateness 270–1, 273
separatism 271
settlement patterns 1, 12–18, 46, 268–9, 270–1
sewers 52
sex trade 54
Shackleton, E. 106
shamrock 119
Sheehy-Skeffington, H. 198, 260
Shore, E. 215
Sinn Féin 137, 198, 257, 260, 263
Six Acts 148
Slagg, J. 190
slums 53
Smith O'Brien, W. 161, 163, 164, 165, 167
social change 93
social class 79
social control 28–9
social geography 268–9
social memory 220
social unrest, fear of 29
societal threats, Angel Meadow 53–6
Society of United Englishmen 146
Society of United Irishmen 146
sodalities 98
Solemn League and Covenant against Home Rule 135, 237
songs and ballads 218, 263
soup kitchens 43, 61
spaces, for commemorative events 222
Special Boards of Health 21, 26
Special Commission 215
sports 98
Stack, A. 259–60
Stephens, J. 105, 206–7, 208–9, 210, 230, 253

Stevenson Square 165, 225
Stockport, anti-Catholic riots 62–3
Stowell, Rev. H. 92–3, 94
Strangeways *see* Manchester prison escapes
street hawker 55illus
street life, Angel Meadow 56
strikes 147, 236
success, Catholic Irish population 79–80

Taylor, J. 60
tea party 162–3
temperance campaigns 83, 98–9, 104, 105, 123, 199
textile industry 15–16
theatre 98
themes 1–2, 3
Theobold, Mrs 165
Thomas, J.S. 62
Thompson, Fr 66
Tithe Rent Charge Act 1838 88
tithes 88, 153
toilets 49, 50–1
Tone, W. 252
Toole, Canon 184, 224
Touchstone, W. 175
trade unions 147, 149–50, 271
traditions
   creation of 224–8
   of violent resistance 240
transport 16, 18, 20, 29
Transport and General Workers' Union 236
Treason Felony Act 1848 165, 215
'Trooping the Castle Guard' 120
troops, supply of 9–10
truce, British and Irish forces 262
Turner, Bishop 214, 223–4, 225
Turner, J.A. 60
typhus 44

Ulster Volunteer Force 135, 237, 257
Union Clubs 148
unionists 237
Union of Gasworkers and General Labourers 180
United Irish League 194–5, 197, 198, 199, 200, 233, 234, 257

*United Irishman, The* 160–1
United Irishmen of America 251
University Settlement 63–4
Unlawful Oaths Act 1797 147
unrest 147
urbanisation 28, 76

vagrancy 9
Vatican, condemnation of Fenian movement 249
Vaughan, Bishop 99, 100–2, 103, 104–5, 129–30
veterans, charity 10
Veto Controversy 150
violence 33–4, 91–2, 190, 223, 240, 251–2, 262
violent separatism 271
voter illiteracy 184–5
voting strength 172–3, 174

Walker, T. 146
War of Independence 137, 138, 258, 261
waste disposal 48
water supply 49
Watkin, E. 156
Wearden, Fr 231
weavers, industrial action 147
*Weekly Herald* 228
West of Ireland Association 108
Wiseman, Cardinal N. 88
women 177, 198, 259, 260
workhouses, risks for Catholic children 103
working conditions 30
Working Lads' Clubs 65–6
World War I 237–8, 257–8

Yeats, W.B. 252
Young Ireland 158–9
young people, dangers to 101–3

EU authorised representative for GPSR:
Easy Access System Europe, Mustamäe tee 50,
10621 Tallinn, Estonia
gpsr.requests@easproject.com

www.ingramcontent.com/pod-product-compliance
Lightning Source LLC
Chambersburg PA
CBHW082105250426
43673CB00067B/1799